SCHAUM'S OUTLINE OF

THEORY AND PROBLEMS

OF

LAPLACE
TRANSFORMS

•

MURRAY R. SPIEGEL, Ph.D.

Former Professor and Chairman,

Mathematics Department

Rensselaer Polytechnic Institute

Hartford Graduate Center

•

SCHAUM'S OUTLINE SERIES

McGRAW-HILL

*New York   San Francisco   Washington, D.C. Auckland   Bogotá   Caracas   Lisbon
London   Madrid   Mexico City   Milan   Montreal   New Delhi
San Juan   Singapore   Sydney   Tokyo   Toronto*

60231

33   CUS CUS   06 05

McGraw-Hill

A Division of The McGraw·Hill Companies

Preface

The theory of Laplace transforms or Laplace transformation, also referred to as operational calculus, has in recent years become an essential part of the mathematical background required of engineers, physicists, mathematicians and other scientists. This is because, in addition to being of great theoretical interest in itself, Laplace transform methods provide easy and effective means for the solution of many problems arising in various fields of science and engineering.

The subject originated in attempts to justify rigorously certain "operational rules" used by Heaviside in the latter part of the 19th century for solving equations in electromagnetic theory. These attempts finally proved successful in the early part of the 20th century through the efforts of Bromwich, Carson, van der Pol and other mathematicians who employed complex variable theory.

This book is designed for use as a supplement to all current standard texts or as a textbook for a formal course in Laplace transform theory and applications. It should also be of considerable value to those taking courses in mathematics, physics, electrical engineering, mechanics, heat flow or any of the numerous other fields in which Laplace transform methods are employed.

Each chapter begins with a clear statement of pertinent definitions, principles and theorems together with illustrative and other descriptive material. This is followed by graded sets of solved and supplementary problems. The solved problems serve to illustrate and amplify the theory, bring into sharp focus those fine points without which the student continually feels himself on unsafe ground, and provide the repetition of basic principles so vital to effective learning. Numerous proofs of theorems and derivations of formulas are included among the solved problems. The large number of supplementary problems with answers serve as a complete review of the material in each chapter.

Topics covered include the properties of Laplace transforms and inverse Laplace transforms together with applications to ordinary and partial differential equations, integral equations, difference equations and boundary-value problems. The theory using complex variables is not treated until the last half of the book. This is done, first, so that the student may comprehend and appreciate more fully the theory, and the power, of the complex inversion formula and, second, to meet the needs of those who wish only an introduction to the subject. Chapters on complex variable theory and Fourier series and integrals, which are important in a discussion of the complex inversion formula, have been included for the benefit of those unfamiliar with these topics.

Considerably more material has been included here than can be covered in most first courses. This has been done to make the book more flexible, to provide a more useful book of reference and to stimulate further interest in the topics.

I wish to take this opportunity to thank the staff of the Schaum Publishing Company for their splendid cooperation.

M. R. Spiegel

CONTENTS

CONTENTS

Chapter 1

The Laplace Transform

DEFINITION OF THE LAPLACE TRANSFORM

Let $F(t)$ be a function of t specified for $t > 0$. Then the *Laplace transform* of $F(t)$, denoted by $\mathcal{L}\{F(t)\}$, is defined by

$$\mathcal{L}\{F(t)\} = f(s) = \int_0^\infty e^{-st} F(t)\, dt \tag{1}$$

where we assume at present that the parameter s is real. Later it will be found useful to consider s complex.

The Laplace transform of $F(t)$ is said to *exist* if the integral (1) *converges* for some value of s; otherwise it does not exist. For sufficient conditions under which the Laplace transform does exist, see Page 2.

NOTATION

If a function of t is indicated in terms of a capital letter, such as $F(t)$, $G(t)$, $Y(t)$, etc., the Laplace transform of the function is denoted by the corresponding lower case letter, i.e. $f(s)$, $g(s)$, $y(s)$, etc. In other cases, a tilde ($\sim$) can be used to denote the Laplace transform. Thus, for example, the Laplace transform of $u(t)$ is $\tilde{u}(s)$.

LAPLACE TRANSFORMS OF SOME ELEMENTARY FUNCTIONS

The adjacent table shows Laplace transforms of various elementary functions. For details of evaluation using definition (1), see Problems 1 and 2. For a more extensive table see Appendix B, Pages 245 to 254.

	$F(t)$	$\mathcal{L}\{F(t)\} = f(s)$
1.	1	$\dfrac{1}{s}$ $s > 0$
2.	t	$\dfrac{1}{s^2}$ $s > 0$
3.	t^n $n = 0, 1, 2, \ldots$	$\dfrac{n!}{s^{n+1}}$ $s > 0$ *Note.* Factorial $n = n! = 1 \cdot 2 \cdots n$ Also, by definition $0! = 1$.
4.	e^{at}	$\dfrac{1}{s-a}$ $s > a$
5.	$\sin at$	$\dfrac{a}{s^2+a^2}$ $s > 0$
6.	$\cos at$	$\dfrac{s}{s^2+a^2}$ $s > 0$
7.	$\sinh at$	$\dfrac{a}{s^2-a^2}$ $s > |a|$
8.	$\cosh at$	$\dfrac{s}{s^2-a^2}$ $s > |a|$

SECTIONAL OR PIECEWISE CONTINUITY

A function is called *sectionally continuous* or *piecewise continuous* in an interval $\alpha \le t \le \beta$ if the interval can be subdivided into a finite number of intervals in each of which the function is continuous and has finite right and left hand limits.

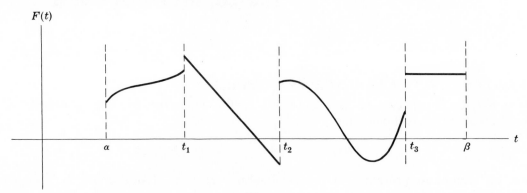

Fig. 1-1

An example of a function which is sectionally continuous is shown graphically in Fig. 1-1 above. This function has discontinuities at t_1, t_2 and t_3. Note that the right and left hand limits at t_2, for example, are represented by $\lim_{\epsilon \to 0} F(t_2 + \epsilon) = F(t_2 + 0) = F(t_2+)$ and $\lim_{\epsilon \to 0} F(t_2 - \epsilon) = F(t_2 - 0) = F(t_2-)$ respectively, where ϵ is positive.

FUNCTIONS OF EXPONENTIAL ORDER

If real constants $M > 0$ and γ exist such that for all $t > N$

$$|e^{-\gamma t} F(t)| < M \qquad \text{or} \qquad |F(t)| < Me^{\gamma t}$$

we say that $F(t)$ is a *function of exponential order* γ *as* $t \to \infty$ or, briefly, is of *exponential order*.

> **Example 1.** $F(t) = t^2$ is of exponential order 3 (for example), since $|t^2| = t^2 < e^{3t}$ for all $t > 0$.

> **Example 2.** $F(t) = e^{t^3}$ is not of exponential order since $|e^{-\gamma t} e^{t^3}| = e^{t^3 - \gamma t}$ can be made larger than any given constant by increasing t.

Intuitively, functions of exponential order cannot "grow" in absolute value more rapidly than $Me^{\gamma t}$ as t increases. In practice, however, this is no restriction since M and γ can be as large as desired.

Bounded functions, such as $\sin at$ or $\cos at$, are of exponential order.

SUFFICIENT CONDITIONS FOR EXISTENCE OF LAPLACE TRANSFORMS

Theorem 1-1.   If $F(t)$ is sectionally continuous in every finite interval $0 \le t \le N$ and of exponential order γ for $t > N$, then its Laplace transform $f(s)$ exists for all $s > \gamma$.

For a proof of this see Problem 47. It must be emphasized that the stated conditions are *sufficient* to guarantee the existence of the Laplace transform. If the conditions are not satisfied, however, the Laplace transform may or may not exist [see Problem 32]. Thus the conditions are not *necessary* for the existence of the Laplace transform.

For other sufficient conditions, see Problem 145.

SOME IMPORTANT PROPERTIES OF LAPLACE TRANSFORMS

In the following list of theorems we assume, unless otherwise stated, that all functions satisfy the conditions of *Theorem 1-1* so that their Laplace transforms exist.

1.   **Linearity property.**

   Theorem 1-2.   If c_1 and c_2 are any constants while $F_1(t)$ and $F_2(t)$ are functions with Laplace transforms $f_1(s)$ and $f_2(s)$ respectively, then

$$\mathcal{L}\{c_1 F_1(t) + c_2 F_2(t)\} \;=\; c_1\mathcal{L}\{F_1(t)\} + c_2\mathcal{L}\{F_2(t)\} \;=\; c_1 f_1(s) + c_2 f_2(s) \qquad (2)$$

The result is easily extended to more than two functions.

   Example. $\mathcal{L}\{4t^2 - 3\cos 2t + 5e^{-t}\} \;=\; 4\mathcal{L}\{t^2\} - 3\mathcal{L}\{\cos 2t\} + 5\mathcal{L}\{e^{-t}\}$

$$= \; 4\left(\frac{2!}{s^3}\right) - 3\left(\frac{s}{s^2+4}\right) + 5\left(\frac{1}{s+1}\right)$$

$$= \; \frac{8}{s^3} - \frac{3s}{s^2+4} + \frac{5}{s+1}$$

The symbol $\mathcal{L}$, which transforms $F(t)$ into $f(s)$, is often called the *Laplace transformation operator*.   Because of the property of $\mathcal{L}$ expressed in this theorem, we say that $\mathcal{L}$ is a *linear operator* or that it has the *linearity property*.

2.   **First translation or shifting property.**

   Theorem 1-3.   If $\mathcal{L}\{F(t)\} = f(s)$ then

$$\mathcal{L}\{e^{at}F(t)\} \;=\; f(s-a) \qquad (3)$$

   Example.   Since $\mathcal{L}\{\cos 2t\} = \dfrac{s}{s^2+4},$ we have

$$\mathcal{L}\{e^{-t}\cos 2t\} \;=\; \frac{s+1}{(s+1)^2+4} \;=\; \frac{s+1}{s^2+2s+5}$$

3.   **Second translation or shifting property.**

   Theorem 1-4.   If $\mathcal{L}\{F(t)\} = f(s)$ and $G(t) = \begin{cases} F(t-a) & t > a \\ 0 & t < a \end{cases},$ then

$$\mathcal{L}\{G(t)\} \;=\; e^{-as}f(s) \qquad (4)$$

   Example.   Since $\mathcal{L}\{t^3\} = \dfrac{3!}{s^4} = \dfrac{6}{s^4},$ the Laplace transform of the function

$$G(t) \;=\; \begin{cases} (t-2)^3 & t > 2 \\ 0 & t < 2 \end{cases}$$

is $6e^{-2s}/s^4$.

4.   **Change of scale property.**

   Theorem 1-5.   If $\mathcal{L}\{F(t)\} = f(s),$ then

$$\mathcal{L}\{F(at)\} \;=\; \frac{1}{a}f\left(\frac{s}{a}\right) \qquad (5)$$

   Example.   Since $\mathcal{L}\{\sin t\} = \dfrac{1}{s^2+1},$ we have

$$\mathcal{L}\{\sin 3t\} \;=\; \frac{1}{3}\frac{1}{(s/3)^2+1} \;=\; \frac{3}{s^2+9}$$

5. Laplace transform of derivatives.

Theorem 1-6. If $\mathcal{L}\{F(t)\} = f(s)$, then

$$\mathcal{L}\{F'(t)\} = s\,f(s) - F(0) \tag{6}$$

if $F(t)$ is continuous for $0 \leqq t \leqq N$ and of exponential order for $t > N$ while $F'(t)$ is sectionally continuous for $0 \leqq t \leqq N$.

Example. If $F(t) = \cos 3t$, then $\mathcal{L}\{F(t)\} = \dfrac{s}{s^2+9}$ and we have

$$\mathcal{L}\{F'(t)\} = \mathcal{L}\{-3\sin 3t\} = s\left(\frac{s}{s^2+9}\right) - 1 = \frac{-9}{s^2+9}$$

The method is useful in finding Laplace transforms without integration [see Problem 15].

Theorem 1-7. If in *Theorem 1-6*, $F(t)$ fails to be continuous at $t = 0$ but $\lim\limits_{t \to 0} F(t) = F(0+)$ exists [but is not equal to $F(0)$, which may or may not exist], then

$$\mathcal{L}\{F'(t)\} = s\,f(s) - F(0+) \tag{7}$$

Theorem 1-8. If in *Theorem 1-6*, $F(t)$ fails to be continuous at $t = a$, then

$$\mathcal{L}\{F'(t)\} = s\,f(s) - F(0) - e^{-as}\{F(a+) - F(a-)\} \tag{8}$$

where $F(a+) - F(a-)$ is sometimes called the *jump* at the discontinuity $t = a$. For more than one discontinuity, appropriate modifications can be made.

Theorem 1-9. If $\mathcal{L}\{F(t)\} = f(s)$, then

$$\mathcal{L}\{F''(t)\} = s^2 f(s) - s\,F(0) - F'(0) \tag{9}$$

if $F(t)$ and $F'(t)$ are continuous for $0 \leqq t \leqq N$ and of exponential order for $t > N$ while $F''(t)$ is sectionally continuous for $0 \leqq t \leqq N$.

If $F(t)$ and $F'(t)$ have discontinuities, appropriate modification of (9) can be made as in *Theorems 1-7* and *1-8*.

Theorem 1-10. If $\mathcal{L}\{F(t)\} = f(s)$, then

$$\mathcal{L}\{F^{(n)}(t)\} = s^n f(s) - s^{n-1} F(0) - s^{n-2} F'(0) - \cdots - s\,F^{(n-2)}(0) - F^{(n-1)}(0) \tag{10}$$

if $F(t), F'(t), \ldots, F^{(n-1)}(t)$ are continuous for $0 \leqq t \leqq N$ and of exponential order for $t > N$ while $F^{(n)}(t)$ is sectionally continuous for $0 \leqq t \leqq N$.

6. Laplace transform of integrals.

Theorem 1-11. If $\mathcal{L}\{F(t)\} = f(s)$, then

$$\mathcal{L}\left\{\int_0^t F(u)\,du\right\} = \frac{f(s)}{s} \tag{11}$$

Example. Since $\mathcal{L}\{\sin 2t\} = \dfrac{2}{s^2+4}$, we have

$$\mathcal{L}\left\{\int_0^t \sin 2u\,du\right\} = \frac{2}{s(s^2+4)}$$

as can be verified directly.

7. Multiplication by t^n.

Theorem 1-12.   If $\mathcal{L}\{F(t)\} = f(s)$,   then

$$\mathcal{L}\{t^n F(t)\} = (-1)^n \frac{d^n}{ds^n} f(s) = (-1)^n f^{(n)}(s) \tag{12}$$

Example. Since $\mathcal{L}\{e^{2t}\} = \dfrac{1}{s-2}$,   we have

$$\mathcal{L}\{te^{2t}\} = -\frac{d}{ds}\left(\frac{1}{s-2}\right) = \frac{1}{(s-2)^2}$$

$$\mathcal{L}\{t^2 e^{2t}\} = \frac{d^2}{ds^2}\left(\frac{1}{s-2}\right) = \frac{2}{(s-2)^3}$$

8. Division by t.

Theorem 1-13.   If $\mathcal{L}\{F(t)\} = f(s)$,   then

$$\mathcal{L}\left\{\frac{F(t)}{t}\right\} = \int_s^\infty f(u)\,du \tag{13}$$

provided $\lim\limits_{t \to 0} F(t)/t$ exists.

Example. Since $\mathcal{L}\{\sin t\} = \dfrac{1}{s^2+1}$ and $\lim\limits_{t \to 0} \dfrac{\sin t}{t} = 1$,   we have

$$\mathcal{L}\left\{\frac{\sin t}{t}\right\} = \int_s^\infty \frac{du}{u^2+1} = \tan^{-1}(1/s)$$

9. Periodic functions.

Theorem 1-14.   Let $F(t)$ have period $T > 0$ so that $F(t+T) = F(t)$ [see Fig. 1-2].

Then
$$\mathcal{L}\{F(t)\} = \frac{\displaystyle\int_0^T e^{-st} F(t)\,dt}{1 - e^{-sT}} \tag{14}$$

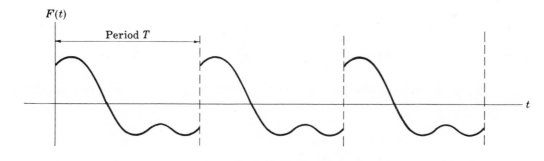

Fig. 1-2

10. Behavior of $f(s)$ as $s \to \infty$.

Theorem 1-15.   If $\mathcal{L}\{F(t)\} = f(s)$,   then

$$\lim_{s \to \infty} f(s) = 0 \tag{15}$$

11. Initial-value theorem.

Theorem 1-16.   If the indicated limits exist, then

$$\lim_{t \to 0} F(t) = \lim_{s \to \infty} s f(s) \tag{16}$$

12. Final-value theorem.

      Theorem 1-17.   If the indicated limits exist, then

$$\lim_{t \to \infty} F(t) \;=\; \lim_{s \to 0} s\,f(s) \tag{17}$$

13. Generalization of initial-value theorem.

      If $\;\lim_{t \to 0} F(t)/G(t) = 1,\;$ then we say that for values of t near $t = 0$ [small t], $F(t)$ is *close to* $G(t)$ and we write $F(t) \sim G(t)$ as $t \to 0$.

      Similarly if $\;\lim_{s \to \infty} f(s)/g(s) = 1,\;$ then we say that for large values of s, $f(s)$ is *close to* $g(s)$ and we write $f(s) \sim g(s)$ as $s \to \infty$.

      With this notation we have the following generalization of *Theorem 1-16*.

      Theorem 1-18.   If $\;F(t) \sim G(t)\;$ as $\;t \to 0,\;$ then $f(s) \sim g(s)$ as $s \to \infty$ where $f(s) = \mathcal{L}\{F(t)\}$ and $g(s) = \mathcal{L}\{G(t)\}$.

14. Generalization of final-value theorem.

      If $\;\lim_{t \to \infty} F(t)/G(t) = 1,\;$ we write $F(t) \sim G(t)$ as $t \to \infty$. Similarly if $\;\lim_{s \to 0} f(s)/g(s) = 1$, we write $f(s) \sim g(s)$ as $s \to 0$. Then we have the following generalization of *Theorem 1-17*.

      Theorem 1-19.   If $\;F(t) \sim G(t)\;$ as $\;t \to \infty,\;$ then $f(s) \sim g(s)$ as $s \to 0$ where $f(s) = \mathcal{L}\{F(t)\}$ and $g(s) = \mathcal{L}\{G(t)\}$.

METHODS OF FINDING LAPLACE TRANSFORMS

    Various means are available for determining Laplace transforms as indicated in the following list.

1.   Direct method.   This involves direct use of definition *(1)*.

2.   Series method.   If $F(t)$ has a power series expansion given by

$$F(t) \;=\; a_0 + a_1 t + a_2 t^2 + \cdots \;=\; \sum_{n=0}^{\infty} a_n t^n \tag{18}$$

its Laplace transform can be obtained by taking the sum of the Laplace transforms of each term in the series.   Thus

$$\mathcal{L}\{F(t)\} \;=\; \frac{a_0}{s} + \frac{a_1}{s^2} + \frac{2!\,a_2}{s^3} + \cdots \;=\; \sum_{n=0}^{\infty} \frac{n!\,a_n}{s^{n+1}} \tag{19}$$

    A condition under which the result is valid is that the series *(19)* be convergent for $s > \gamma$. See Problems 34, 36, 39 and 48.

3.   Method of differential equations.   This involves finding a differential equation satisfied by $F(t)$ and then using the above theorems.   See Problems 34 and 48.

4.   Differentiation with respect to a parameter.   See Problem 20.

5.   Miscellaneous methods involving special devices such as indicated in the above theorems, for example *Theorem 1-13*.

6.   Use of Tables (see Appendix).

EVALUATION OF INTEGRALS

If $f(s) = \mathcal{L}\{F(t)\}$, then

$$\int_0^\infty e^{-st} F(t)\, dt = f(s) \tag{20}$$

Taking the limit as $s \to 0$, we have

$$\int_0^\infty F(t)\, dt = f(0) \tag{21}$$

assuming the integral to be convergent.

The results (20) and (21) are often useful in evaluating various integrals. See Problems 45 and 46.

SOME SPECIAL FUNCTIONS

I. The Gamma function.

If $n > 0$, we define the *gamma function* by

$$\Gamma(n) = \int_0^\infty u^{n-1} e^{-u}\, du \tag{22}$$

The following are some important properties of the gamma function.

1. $$\Gamma(n+1) = n\,\Gamma(n), \quad n > 0$$

Thus since $\Gamma(1) = 1$, we have $\Gamma(2) = 1$, $\Gamma(3) = 2! = 2$, $\Gamma(4) = 3!$ and in general $\Gamma(n+1) = n!$, if n is a positive integer. For this reason the function is sometimes called the *factorial function*.

2. $$\Gamma(\tfrac{1}{2}) = \sqrt{\pi}$$

3. $$\Gamma(p)\,\Gamma(1-p) = \frac{\pi}{\sin p\pi}, \quad 0 < p < 1$$

4. For large n,
$$\Gamma(n+1) \sim \sqrt{2\pi n}\; n^n\, e^{-n}$$

[Here $\sim$ means "approximately equal to for large n". More exactly, we write $F(n) \sim G(n)$ if $\lim_{n \to \infty} F(n)/G(n) = 1$.] This is called *Stirling's formula*.

5. For $n < 0$ we can define $\Gamma(n)$ by
$$\Gamma(n) = \frac{\Gamma(n+1)}{n}$$

II. Bessel functions.

We define a *Bessel function of order n* by

$$J_n(t) = \frac{t^n}{2^n\,\Gamma(n+1)}\left\{1 - \frac{t^2}{2(2n+2)} + \frac{t^4}{2\cdot 4(2n+2)(2n+4)} - \cdots\right\} \tag{23}$$

Some important properties are

1. $J_{-n}(t) = (-1)^n J_n(t)$ if n is a positive integer

2. $J_{n+1}(t) = \dfrac{2n}{t} J_n(t) - J_{n-1}(t)$

3. $\dfrac{d}{dt}\{t^n J_n(t)\} = t^n J_{n-1}(t)$. If $n = 0$, we have $J_0'(t) = -J_1(t)$.

4. $e^{\frac{1}{2}t(u - 1/u)} = \displaystyle\sum_{n=-\infty}^{\infty} J_n(t)u^n$

This is called the *generating function* for the Bessel functions.

5. $J_n(t)$ satisfies *Bessel's differential equation*.

$$t^2 Y''(t) + t Y'(t) + (t^2 - n^2) Y(t) = 0$$

It is convenient to define $J_n(it) = i^{-n} I_n(t)$ where $I_n(t)$ is called the *modified Bessel function of order n*.

III. The Error function is defined as

$$\text{erf}(t) = \frac{2}{\sqrt{\pi}} \int_0^t e^{-u^2}\, du \tag{24}$$

IV. The Complementary Error function is defined as

$$\text{erfc}(t) = 1 - \text{erf}(t) = 1 - \frac{2}{\sqrt{\pi}} \int_0^t e^{-u^2} du = \frac{2}{\sqrt{\pi}} \int_t^\infty e^{-u^2} du \tag{25}$$

V. The Sine and Cosine integrals are defined by

$$\text{Si}(t) = \int_0^t \frac{\sin u}{u}\, du \tag{26}$$

$$\text{Ci}(t) = \int_t^\infty \frac{\cos u}{u}\, du \tag{27}$$

VI. The Exponential integral is defined as

$$\text{Ei}(t) = \int_t^\infty \frac{e^{-u}}{u}\, du \tag{28}$$

VII. The Unit Step function, also called *Heaviside's unit function,* is defined as

$$u(t-a) = \begin{cases} 0 & t < a \\ 1 & t > a \end{cases} \tag{29}$$

See Fig. 1-3.

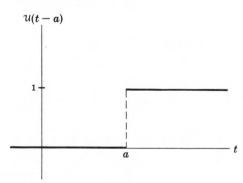

Fig. 1-3

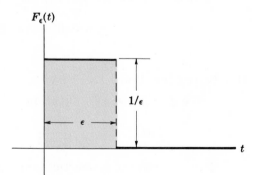

Fig. 1-4

VIII. The Unit Impulse function or Dirac delta function.

Consider the function

$$F_\epsilon(t) = \begin{cases} 1/\epsilon & 0 \leqq t \leqq \epsilon \\ 0 & t > \epsilon \end{cases} \tag{30}$$

where $\epsilon > 0$, whose graph appears in Fig. 1-4.

It is geometrically evident that as $\epsilon \to 0$ the height of the rectangular shaded region increases indefinitely and the width decreases in such a way that the area is always equal to 1, i.e. $\int_0^\infty F_\epsilon(t)\, dt = 1$.

This idea has led some engineers and physicists to think of a limiting function, denoted by $\delta(t)$, approached by $F_\epsilon(t)$ as $\epsilon \to 0$. This limiting function they have called the *unit impulse function* or *Dirac delta function*. Some of its properties are

1. $\qquad \int_0^\infty \delta(t)\, dt = 1$

2. $\qquad \int_0^\infty \delta(t)\, G(t)\, dt = G(0)$ $\qquad$ for any continuous function $G(t)$.

3. $\qquad \int_0^\infty \delta(t-a)\, G(t)\, dt = G(a)$ $\qquad$ for any continuous function $G(t)$.

Although mathematically speaking such a function does not exist, manipulations or operations using it can be made rigorous.

IX. Null functions. If $\mathcal{N}(t)$ is a function of t such that for all $t > 0$

$$\int_0^t \mathcal{N}(u)\, du = 0 \tag{31}$$

we call $\mathcal{N}(t)$ a *null function*.

$\qquad$ **Example.** The function $F(t) = \begin{cases} 1 & t = 1/2 \\ -1 & t = 1 \\ 0 & \text{otherwise} \end{cases}$ $\quad$ is a null function.

In general, any function which is zero at all but a countable set of points [i.e. a set of points which can be put into one-to-one correspondence with the natural numbers $1, 2, 3, \ldots$] is a null function.

LAPLACE TRANSFORMS OF SPECIAL FUNCTIONS

$\qquad$ In the following table we have listed Laplace transforms of various special functions. For a more extensive list see Appendix B, Page 245.

Table of Laplace transforms of special functions

	$F(t)$	$f(s) = \mathcal{L}\{F(t)\}$
1.	t^n	$\dfrac{\Gamma(n+1)}{s^{n+1}}$ Note that if $n = 0, 1, 2, \ldots$ this reduces to entry 3, Page 1.
2.	$J_0(at)$	$\dfrac{1}{\sqrt{s^2 + a^2}}$
3.	$J_n(at)$	$\dfrac{(\sqrt{s^2 + a^2} - s)^n}{a^n \sqrt{s^2 + a^2}}$
4.	$\sin \sqrt{t}$	$\dfrac{\sqrt{\pi}}{2s^{3/2}}\, e^{-1/4s}$
5.	$\dfrac{\cos \sqrt{t}}{\sqrt{t}}$	$\sqrt{\dfrac{\pi}{s}}\, e^{-1/4s}$

Table of Laplace transforms of special functions (cont.)

	$F(t)$	$f(s) = \mathcal{L}\{F(t)\}$
6.	erf (t)	$\dfrac{e^{s^2/4}}{s}$ erfc $(s/2)$
7.	erf $(\sqrt{t}\,)$	$\dfrac{1}{s\sqrt{s+1}}$
8.	Si (t)	$\dfrac{1}{s} \tan^{-1} \dfrac{1}{s}$
9.	Ci (t)	$\dfrac{\ln(s^2+1)}{2s}$
10.	Ei (t)	$\dfrac{\ln(s+1)}{s}$
11.	$\mathcal{U}(t-a)$	$\dfrac{e^{-as}}{s}$
12.	$\delta(t)$	1
13.	$\delta(t-a)$	e^{-as}
14.	$\mathcal{N}(t)$	0

Solved Problems

LAPLACE TRANSFORMS OF SOME ELEMENTARY FUNCTIONS

1. Prove that: (a) $\mathcal{L}\{1\} = \dfrac{1}{s},\ s > 0$;   (b) $\mathcal{L}\{t\} = \dfrac{1}{s^2},\ s > 0$;   (c) $\mathcal{L}\{e^{at}\} = \dfrac{1}{s-a},\ s > a$.

(a)
$$\mathcal{L}\{1\} = \int_0^\infty e^{-st}(1)\,dt = \lim_{P\to\infty} \int_0^P e^{-st}\,dt$$
$$= \lim_{P\to\infty} \frac{e^{-st}}{-s}\bigg|_0^P = \lim_{P\to\infty} \frac{1-e^{-sP}}{s} = \frac{1}{s} \quad \text{if } s > 0$$

(b)
$$\mathcal{L}\{t\} = \int_0^\infty e^{-st}(t)\,dt = \lim_{P\to\infty} \int_0^P t\,e^{-st}\,dt$$
$$= \lim_{P\to\infty} (t)\left(\frac{e^{-st}}{-s}\right) - (1)\left(\frac{e^{-st}}{s^2}\right)\bigg|_0^P = \lim_{P\to\infty}\left(\frac{1}{s^2} - \frac{e^{-sP}}{s^2} - \frac{Pe^{-sP}}{s}\right)$$
$$= \frac{1}{s^2} \quad \text{if } s > 0$$

where we have used integration by parts.

(c) $\mathcal{L}\{e^{at}\} = \int_0^\infty e^{-st}(e^{at})\,dt = \lim_{P \to \infty} \int_0^P e^{-(s-a)t}\,dt$

$= \lim_{P \to \infty} \frac{e^{-(s-a)t}}{-(s-a)}\Big|_0^P = \lim_{P \to \infty} \frac{1 - e^{-(s-a)P}}{s-a} = \frac{1}{s-a}$ if $s > a$

For methods not employing direct integration, see Problem 15.

2. Prove that   (a) $\mathcal{L}\{\sin at\} = \dfrac{a}{s^2 + a^2}$,   (b) $\mathcal{L}\{\cos at\} = \dfrac{s}{s^2 + a^2}$ if $s > 0$.

(a) $\mathcal{L}\{\sin at\} = \int_0^\infty e^{-st} \sin at\,dt = \lim_{P \to \infty} \int_0^P e^{-st} \sin at\,dt$

$= \lim_{P \to \infty} \frac{e^{-st}(-s \sin at - a \cos at)}{s^2 + a^2}\Big|_0^P$

$= \lim_{P \to \infty} \left\{ \frac{a}{s^2 + a^2} - \frac{e^{-sP}(s \sin aP + a \cos aP)}{s^2 + a^2} \right\}$

$= \frac{a}{s^2 + a^2}$ if $s > 0$

(b) $\mathcal{L}\{\cos at\} = \int_0^\infty e^{-st} \cos at\,dt = \lim_{P \to \infty} \int_0^P e^{-st} \cos at\,dt$

$= \lim_{P \to \infty} \frac{e^{-st}(-s \cos at + a \sin at)}{s^2 + a^2}\Big|_0^P$

$= \lim_{P \to \infty} \left\{ \frac{s}{s^2 + a^2} - \frac{e^{-sP}(s \cos aP - a \sin aP)}{s^2 + a^2} \right\}$

$= \frac{s}{s^2 + a^2}$ if $s > 0$

We have used here the results

$$\int e^{\alpha t} \sin \beta t\,dt = \frac{e^{\alpha t}(\alpha \sin \beta t - \beta \cos \beta t)}{\alpha^2 + \beta^2} \tag{1}$$

$$\int e^{\alpha t} \cos \beta t\,dt = \frac{e^{\alpha t}(\alpha \cos \beta t + \beta \sin \beta t)}{\alpha^2 + \beta^2} \tag{2}$$

Another method.   Assuming that the result of Problem 1(c) holds for complex numbers (which can be proved), we have

$$\mathcal{L}\{e^{iat}\} = \frac{1}{s - ia} = \frac{s + ia}{s^2 + a^2} \tag{3}$$

But $e^{iat} = \cos at + i \sin at$.   Hence

$$\mathcal{L}\{e^{iat}\} = \int_0^\infty e^{-st}(\cos at + i \sin at) \tag{4}$$

$= \int_0^\infty e^{-st} \cos at\,dt + i \int_0^\infty e^{-st} \sin at\,dt = \mathcal{L}\{\cos at\} + i\mathcal{L}\{\sin at\}$

From (3) and (4) we have on equating real and imaginary parts,

$$\mathcal{L}\{\cos at\} = \frac{s}{s^2 + a^2}, \qquad \mathcal{L}\{\sin at\} = \frac{a}{s^2 + a^2}$$

3. Prove that   (a) $\mathcal{L}\{\sinh at\} = \dfrac{a}{s^2 - a^2}$,   (b) $\mathcal{L}\{\cosh at\} = \dfrac{s}{s^2 - a^2}$ if $s > |a|$.

(a)
$$\mathcal{L}\{\sinh at\} = \mathcal{L}\left\{\frac{e^{at} - e^{-at}}{2}\right\} = \int_0^\infty e^{-st}\left(\frac{e^{at} - e^{-at}}{2}\right) dt$$

$$= \frac{1}{2}\int_0^\infty e^{-st} e^{at} \, dt - \frac{1}{2}\int_0^\infty e^{-st} e^{-at} \, dt$$

$$= \frac{1}{2}\mathcal{L}\{e^{at}\} - \frac{1}{2}\mathcal{L}\{e^{-at}\}$$

$$= \frac{1}{2}\left\{\frac{1}{s-a} - \frac{1}{s+a}\right\} = \frac{a}{s^2 - a^2} \quad \text{for } s > |a|$$

Another method.   Using the linearity property of the Laplace transformation, we have at once

$$\mathcal{L}\{\sinh at\} = \mathcal{L}\left\{\frac{e^{at} - e^{-at}}{2}\right\} = \frac{1}{2}\mathcal{L}\{e^{at}\} - \frac{1}{2}\mathcal{L}\{e^{-at}\}$$

$$= \frac{1}{2}\left\{\frac{1}{s-a} - \frac{1}{s+a}\right\} = \frac{a}{s^2 - a^2} \quad \text{for } s > |a|$$

(b) As in part (a),

$$\mathcal{L}\{\cosh at\} = \mathcal{L}\left\{\frac{e^{at} + e^{-at}}{2}\right\} = \frac{1}{2}\mathcal{L}\{e^{at}\} + \frac{1}{2}\mathcal{L}\{e^{-at}\}$$

$$= \frac{1}{2}\left\{\frac{1}{s-a} + \frac{1}{s+a}\right\} = \frac{s}{s^2 - a^2} \quad \text{for } s > |a|$$

4. Find $\mathcal{L}\{F(t)\}$ if $F(t) = \begin{cases} 5 & 0 < t < 3 \\ 0 & t > 3 \end{cases}$

By definition,

$$\mathcal{L}\{F(t)\} = \int_0^\infty e^{-st} F(t) \, dt = \int_0^3 e^{-st}\,(5)\, dt + \int_3^\infty e^{-st}\,(0)\, dt$$

$$= 5\int_0^3 e^{-st} \, dt = 5\frac{e^{-st}}{-s}\Big|_0^3 = \frac{5(1 - e^{-3s})}{s}$$

THE LINEARITY PROPERTY

5. Prove the *linearity property* [*Theorem 1-2, Page 3*].

Let $\mathcal{L}\{F_1(t)\} = f_1(s) = \displaystyle\int_0^\infty e^{-st} F_1(t) \, dt$ and $\mathcal{L}\{F_2(t)\} = f_2(s) = \displaystyle\int_0^\infty e^{-st} F_2(t) \, dt$.   Then if c_1 and c_2 are any constants,

$$\mathcal{L}\{c_1 F_1(t) + c_2 F_2(t)\} = \int_0^\infty e^{-st} \{c_1 F_1(t) + c_2 F_2(t)\} \, dt$$

$$= c_1 \int_0^\infty e^{-st} F_1(t) \, dt + c_2 \int_0^\infty e^{-st} F_2(t) \, dt$$

$$= c_1 \mathcal{L}\{F_1(t)\} + c_2 \mathcal{L}\{F_2(t)\}$$

$$= c_1 f_1(s) + c_2 f_2(s)$$

The result is easily generalized [see Problem 61].

6. Find $\quad \mathcal{L} \{4e^{5t} + 6t^3 - 3 \sin 4t + 2 \cos 2t\}$.

By the linearity property [Problem 5] we have

$$\mathcal{L} \{4e^{5t} + 6t^3 - 3 \sin 4t + 2 \cos 2t\} \;=\; 4 \,\mathcal{L} \{e^{5t}\} \,+\, 6 \,\mathcal{L} \{t^3\} \,-\, 3 \,\mathcal{L} \{\sin 4t\} \,+\, 2 \,\mathcal{L} \{\cos 2t\}$$

$$=\; 4 \left(\frac{1}{s-5} \right) \,+\, 6 \left(\frac{3!}{s^4} \right) \,-\, 3 \left(\frac{4}{s^2 + 16} \right) \,+\, 2 \left(\frac{s}{s^2 + 4} \right)$$

$$=\; \frac{4}{s-5} \,+\, \frac{36}{s^4} \,-\, \frac{12}{s^2 + 16} \,+\, \frac{2s}{s^2 + 4}$$

where $s > 5$.

TRANSLATION AND CHANGE OF SCALE PROPERTIES

7. Prove the *first translation or shifting property*: If $\mathcal{L} \{F(t)\} = f(s)$, then $\mathcal{L} \{e^{at} F(t)\} = f(s-a)$.

We have $\qquad\qquad \mathcal{L} \{F(t)\} \;=\; \int_0^\infty e^{-st} F(t) \, dt \;=\; f(s)$

Then $\qquad\qquad \mathcal{L} \{e^{at} F(t)\} \;=\; \int_0^\infty e^{-st} \{e^{at} F(t)\} \, dt$

$$=\; \int_0^\infty e^{-(s-a)t} F(t) \, dt \;=\; f(s-a)$$

8. Find $\quad$ (a) $\mathcal{L} \{t^2 e^{3t}\}$, (b) $\mathcal{L} \{e^{-2t} \sin 4t\}$, (c) $\mathcal{L} \{e^{4t} \cosh 5t\}$, (d) $\mathcal{L} \{e^{-2t} (3 \cos 6t - 5 \sin 6t)\}$.

(a) $\mathcal{L} \{t^2\} = \dfrac{2!}{s^3} = \dfrac{2}{s^3}$. $\quad$ Then $\quad \mathcal{L} \{t^2 e^{3t}\} = \dfrac{2}{(s-3)^3}$.

(b) $\mathcal{L} \{\sin 4t\} = \dfrac{4}{s^2 + 16}$. $\quad$ Then $\quad \mathcal{L} \{e^{-2t} \sin 4t\} = \dfrac{4}{(s+2)^2 + 16} = \dfrac{4}{s^2 + 4s + 20}$.

(c) $\mathcal{L} \{\cosh 5t\} = \dfrac{s}{s^2 - 25}$. $\quad$ Then $\quad \mathcal{L} \{e^{4t} \cosh 5t\} = \dfrac{s-4}{(s-4)^2 - 25} = \dfrac{s-4}{s^2 - 8s - 9}$.

Another method.

$$\mathcal{L} \{e^{4t} \cosh 5t\} \;=\; \mathcal{L} \left\{ e^{4t} \left(\frac{e^{5t} + e^{-5t}}{2} \right) \right\} \;=\; \frac{1}{2} \mathcal{L} \{e^{9t} + e^{-t}\}$$

$$=\; \frac{1}{2} \left\{ \frac{1}{s-9} + \frac{1}{s+1} \right\} \;=\; \frac{s-4}{s^2 - 8s - 9}$$

(d) $\mathcal{L} \{3 \cos 6t - 5 \sin 6t\} = 3 \,\mathcal{L} \{\cos 6t\} - 5 \,\mathcal{L} \{\sin 6t\}$

$$=\; 3 \left(\frac{s}{s^2 + 36} \right) - 5 \left(\frac{6}{s^2 + 36} \right) = \frac{3s - 30}{s^2 + 36}$$

Then $\qquad \mathcal{L} \{e^{-2t} (3 \cos 6t - 5 \sin 6t)\} \;=\; \dfrac{3(s+2) - 30}{(s+2)^2 + 36} \;=\; \dfrac{3s - 24}{s^2 + 4s + 40}$

9. Prove the *second translation or shifting property*:

If $\mathcal{L}\{F(t)\} = f(s)$ and $G(t) = \begin{cases} F(t-a) & t > a \\ 0 & t < a \end{cases}$, then $\mathcal{L}\{G(t)\} = e^{-as} f(s)$.

$$\mathcal{L}\{G(t)\} = \int_0^\infty e^{-st} G(t)\, dt = \int_0^a e^{-st} G(t)\, dt + \int_a^\infty e^{-st} G(t)\, dt$$

$$= \int_0^a e^{-st} (0)\, dt + \int_a^\infty e^{-st} F(t-a)\, dt$$

$$= \int_a^\infty e^{-st} F(t-a)\, dt$$

$$= \int_0^\infty e^{-s(u+a)} F(u)\, du$$

$$= e^{-as} \int_0^\infty e^{-su} F(u)\, du$$

$$= e^{-as} f(s)$$

where we have used the substitution $t = u + a$.

10. Find $\mathcal{L}\{F(t)\}$ if $F(t) = \begin{cases} \cos(t - 2\pi/3) & t > 2\pi/3 \\ 0 & t < 2\pi/3 \end{cases}$.

Method 1.

$$\mathcal{L}\{F(t)\} = \int_0^{2\pi/3} e^{-st} (0)\, dt + \int_{2\pi/3}^\infty e^{-st} \cos(t - 2\pi/3)\, dt$$

$$= \int_0^\infty e^{-s(u+2\pi/3)} \cos u\, du$$

$$= e^{-2\pi s/3} \int_0^\infty e^{-su} \cos u\, du = \frac{s e^{-2\pi s/3}}{s^2 + 1}$$

Method 2. Since $\mathcal{L}\{\cos t\} = \dfrac{s}{s^2 + 1}$, it follows from Problem 9, with $a = 2\pi/3$, that

$$\mathcal{L}\{F(t)\} = \frac{s e^{-2\pi s/3}}{s^2 + 1}$$

11. Prove the *change of scale property*: If $\mathcal{L}\{F(t)\} = f(s)$, then $\mathcal{L}\{F(at)\} = \dfrac{1}{a} f\left(\dfrac{s}{a}\right)$.

$$\mathcal{L}\{F(at)\} = \int_0^\infty e^{-st} F(at)\, dt$$

$$= \int_0^\infty e^{-s(u/a)} F(u)\, d(u/a)$$

$$= \frac{1}{a} \int_0^\infty e^{-su/a} F(u)\, du$$

$$= \frac{1}{a} f\left(\frac{s}{a}\right)$$

using the transformation $t = u/a$.

12. Given that $\mathcal{L}\left\{\dfrac{\sin t}{t}\right\} = \tan^{-1}(1/s)$, find $\mathcal{L}\left\{\dfrac{\sin at}{t}\right\}$.

By Problem 11,

$$\mathcal{L}\left\{\frac{\sin at}{at}\right\} \;=\; \frac{1}{a}\,\mathcal{L}\left\{\frac{\sin at}{t}\right\} \;=\; \frac{1}{a}\tan^{-1}\{1/(s/a)\} \;=\; \frac{1}{a}\tan^{-1}(a/s)$$

Then $\mathcal{L}\left\{\dfrac{\sin at}{t}\right\} = \tan^{-1}(a/s)$.

LAPLACE TRANSFORM OF DERIVATIVES

13. Prove *Theorem 1-6*: If $\mathcal{L}\{F(t)\} = f(s)$, then $\mathcal{L}\{F'(t)\} = s\,f(s) - F(0)$.

Using integration by parts, we have

$$\mathcal{L}\{F'(t)\} \;=\; \int_0^\infty e^{-st}\,F'(t)\,dt \;=\; \lim_{P\to\infty}\int_0^P e^{-st}\,F'(t)\,dt$$

$$=\; \lim_{P\to\infty}\left\{ e^{-st}\,F(t)\,\Big|_0^P \;+\; s\int_0^P e^{-st}\,F(t)\,dt\right\}$$

$$=\; \lim_{P\to\infty}\left\{ e^{-sP}\,F(P) \;-\; F(0) \;+\; s\int_0^P e^{-st}\,F(t)\,dt\right\}$$

$$=\; s\int_0^\infty e^{-st}\,F(t)\,dt \;-\; F(0)$$

$$=\; s\,f(s) \;-\; F(0)$$

using the fact that $F(t)$ is of exponential order γ as $t\to\infty$, so that $\lim_{P\to\infty} e^{-sP}\,F(P) = 0$ for $s > \gamma$.

For cases where $F(t)$ is not continuous at $t=0$, see Problem 68.

14. Prove *Theorem 1-9*, Page 4: If $\mathcal{L}\{F(t)\} = f(s)$ then $\mathcal{L}\{F''(t)\} = s^2 f(s) - s\,F(0) - F'(0)$.

By Problem 13,
$$\mathcal{L}\{G'(t)\} \;=\; s\,\mathcal{L}\{G(t)\} \;-\; G(0) \;=\; s\,g(s) \;-\; G(0)$$

Let $G(t) = F'(t)$. Then
$$\mathcal{L}\{F''(t)\} \;=\; s\,\mathcal{L}\{F'(t)\} \;-\; F'(0)$$

$$=\; s\,[s\,\mathcal{L}\{F(t)\} - F(0)] \;-\; F'(0)$$

$$=\; s^2\,\mathcal{L}\{F(t)\} \;-\; s\,F(0) \;-\; F'(0)$$

$$=\; s^2 f(s) \;-\; s\,F(0) \;-\; F'(0)$$

The generalization to higher order derivatives can be proved by using mathematical induction [see Problem 65].

15. Use *Theorem 1-6*, Page 4, to derive each of the following Laplace transforms:

(a) $\mathcal{L}\{1\} = \dfrac{1}{s}$, (b) $\mathcal{L}\{t\} = \dfrac{1}{s^2}$, (c) $\mathcal{L}\{e^{at}\} = \dfrac{1}{s-a}$.

Theorem 1-6 states, under suitable conditions given on Page 4, that

$$\mathcal{L}\{F'(t)\} \;=\; s\,\mathcal{L}\{F(t)\} \;-\; F(0) \tag{1}$$

(a) Let $F(t) = 1$. Then $F'(t) = 0$, $F(0) = 1$, and (1) becomes

$$\mathcal{L}\{0\} = 0 = s\,\mathcal{L}\{1\} - 1 \qquad \text{or} \qquad \mathcal{L}\{1\} = 1/s \tag{2}$$

(b) Let $F(t) = t$. Then $F'(t) = 1$, $F(0) = 0$, and (1) becomes using part (a)

$$\mathcal{L}\{1\} = 1/s = s\,\mathcal{L}\{t\} - 0 \qquad \text{or} \qquad \mathcal{L}\{t\} = 1/s^2 \tag{3}$$

By using mathematical induction we can similarly show that $\mathcal{L}\{t^n\} = n!/s^{n+1}$ for any positive integer n.

(c) Let $F(t) = e^{at}$. Then $F'(t) = ae^{at}$, $F(0) = 1$, and (1) becomes

$$\mathcal{L}\{ae^{at}\} = s\,\mathcal{L}\{e^{at}\} - 1, \quad \text{i.e.} \quad a\,\mathcal{L}\{e^{at}\} = s\,\mathcal{L}\{e^{at}\} - 1 \quad \text{or} \quad \mathcal{L}\{e^{at}\} = 1/(s-a)$$

16. Use *Theorem 1-9* to show that $\mathcal{L}\{\sin at\} = \dfrac{a}{s^2 + a^2}$.

Let $F(t) = \sin at$. Then $F'(t) = a\cos at$, $F''(t) = -a^2 \sin at$, $F(0) = 0$, $F'(0) = a$. Hence from the result

$$\mathcal{L}\{F''(t)\} = s^2\,\mathcal{L}\{F(t)\} - s\,F(0) - F'(0)$$

we have

$$\mathcal{L}\{-a^2 \sin at\} = s^2\,\mathcal{L}\{\sin at\} - s\,(0) - a$$

i.e.

$$-a^2\,\mathcal{L}\{\sin at\} = s^2\,\mathcal{L}\{\sin at\} - a$$

or

$$\mathcal{L}\{\sin at\} = \frac{a}{s^2 + a^2}$$

LAPLACE TRANSFORM OF INTEGRALS

17. Prove *Theorem 1-11*: If $\mathcal{L}\{F(t)\} = f(s)$, then $\mathcal{L}\left\{\displaystyle\int_0^t F(u)\,du\right\} = f(s)/s$.

Let $G(t) = \displaystyle\int_0^t F(u)\,du$. Then $G'(t) = F(t)$ and $G(0) = 0$. Taking the Laplace transform of both sides, we have

$$\mathcal{L}\{G'(t)\} = s\,\mathcal{L}\{G(t)\} - G(0) = s\,\mathcal{L}\{G(t)\} = f(s)$$

Thus

$$\mathcal{L}\{G(t)\} = \frac{f(s)}{s} \qquad \text{or} \qquad \mathcal{L}\left\{\int_0^t F(u)\,du\right\} = \frac{f(s)}{s}$$

18. Find $\mathcal{L}\left\{\displaystyle\int_0^t \frac{\sin u}{u}\,du\right\}$.

We have by the Example following *Theorem 1-13* on Page 5,

$$\mathcal{L}\left\{\frac{\sin t}{t}\right\} = \tan^{-1}\frac{1}{s}$$

Thus by Problem 17,

$$\mathcal{L}\left\{\int_0^t \frac{\sin u}{u}\,du\right\} = \frac{1}{s}\tan^{-1}\frac{1}{s}$$

MULTIPLICATION BY POWERS OF t

19. Prove *Theorem 1-12*, Page 5:

If $\mathcal{L}\{F(t)\} = f(s)$, then $\mathcal{L}\{t^n F(t)\} = (-1)^n \dfrac{d^n}{ds^n} f(s) = (-1)^n f^{(n)}(s)$ where $n = 1, 2, 3, \ldots$.

We have
$$f(s) = \int_0^\infty e^{-st} F(t)\, dt$$

Then by Leibnitz's rule for differentiating under the integral sign,

$$\frac{df}{ds} = f'(s) = \frac{d}{ds} \int_0^\infty e^{-st} F(t)\, dt = \int_0^\infty \frac{\partial}{\partial s} e^{-st} F(t)\, dt$$

$$= \int_0^\infty -t e^{-st} F(t)\, dt$$

$$= -\int_0^\infty e^{-st} \{t\, F(t)\}\, dt$$

$$= -\mathcal{L}\{t\, F(t)\}$$

Thus
$$\mathcal{L}\{t\, F(t)\} = -\frac{df}{ds} = -f'(s) \tag{1}$$

which proves the theorem for $n = 1$.

To establish the theorem in general, we use *mathematical induction*. Assume the theorem true for $n = k$, i.e. assume

$$\int_0^\infty e^{-st} \{t^k F(t)\}\, dt = (-1)^k f^{(k)}(s) \tag{2}$$

Then

$$\frac{d}{ds} \int_0^\infty e^{-st} \{t^k F(t)\}\, dt = (-1)^k f^{(k+1)}(s)$$

or by Leibnitz's rule,

$$-\int_0^\infty e^{-st} \{t^{k+1} F(t)\}\, dt = (-1)^k f^{(k+1)}(s)$$

i.e.

$$\int_0^\infty e^{-st} \{t^{k+1} F(t)\}\, dt = (-1)^{k+1} f^{(k+1)}(s) \tag{3}$$

It follows that *if* (2) is true, i.e. if the theorem holds for $n = k$, then (3) is true, i.e. the theorem holds for $n = k + 1$. But by (1) the theorem is true for $n = 1$. Hence it is true for $n = 1 + 1 = 2$ and $n = 2 + 1 = 3$, etc., and thus for all positive integer values of n.

To be completely rigorous, it is necessary to prove that Leibnitz's rule can be applied. For this, see Problem 166.

20. Find   (a) $\mathcal{L}\{t \sin at\}$,   (b) $\mathcal{L}\{t^2 \cos at\}$.

(a) Since $\mathcal{L}\{\sin at\} = \dfrac{a}{s^2 + a^2}$,   we have by Problem 19

$$\mathcal{L}\{t \sin at\} = -\frac{d}{ds}\left(\frac{a}{s^2 + a^2}\right) = \frac{2as}{(s^2 + a^2)^2}$$

Another method.

Since
$$\mathcal{L}\{\cos at\} = \int_0^\infty e^{-st} \cos at \, dt = \frac{s}{s^2 + a^2}$$

we have by differentiating with respect to the parameter a [using Leibnitz's rule],

$$\frac{d}{da} \int_0^\infty e^{-st} \cos at \, dt = \int_0^\infty e^{-st} \{-t \sin at\} \, dt = -\mathcal{L}\{t \sin at\}$$

$$= \frac{d}{da}\left(\frac{s}{s^2 + a^2}\right) = -\frac{2as}{(s^2 + a^2)^2}$$

from which

$$\mathcal{L}\{t \sin at\} = \frac{2as}{(s^2 + a^2)^2}$$

Note that the result is equivalent to $\dfrac{d}{da}\mathcal{L}\{\cos at\} = \mathcal{L}\left\{\dfrac{d}{da}\cos at\right\}$.

(b) Since $\mathcal{L}\{\cos at\} = \dfrac{s}{s^2 + a^2}$, we have by Problem 19

$$\mathcal{L}\{t^2 \cos at\} = \frac{d^2}{ds^2}\left(\frac{s}{s^2 + a^2}\right) = \frac{2s^3 - 6a^2 s}{(s^2 + a^2)^3}$$

We can also use the second method of part (a) by writing

$$\mathcal{L}\{t^2 \cos at\} = \mathcal{L}\left\{-\frac{d^2}{da^2}(\cos at)\right\} = -\frac{d^2}{da^2}\mathcal{L}\{\cos at\}$$

which gives the same result.

DIVISION BY t

21. Prove *Theorem 1-13*, Page 5: If $\mathcal{L}\{F(t)\} = f(s)$, then $\mathcal{L}\left\{\dfrac{F(t)}{t}\right\} = \displaystyle\int_s^\infty f(u)\,du$.

Let $G(t) = \dfrac{F(t)}{t}$. Then $F(t) = t\,G(t)$. Taking the Laplace transform of both sides and using Problem 19, we have

$$\mathcal{L}\{F(t)\} = -\frac{d}{ds}\mathcal{L}\{G(t)\} \qquad \text{or} \qquad f(s) = -\frac{dg}{ds}$$

Then integrating, we have

$$g(s) = -\int_\infty^s f(u)\,du = \int_s^\infty f(u)\,du \qquad\qquad (1)$$

i.e.

$$\mathcal{L}\left\{\frac{F(t)}{t}\right\} = \int_s^\infty f(u)\,du$$

Note that in (1) we have chosen the "constant of integration" so that $\lim\limits_{s \to \infty} g(s) = 0$ [see *Theorem 1-15*, Page 5].

22. (a) Prove that $\displaystyle\int_0^\infty \frac{F(t)}{t}\,dt = \int_0^\infty f(u)\,du$ provided that the integrals converge.

(b) Show that $\displaystyle\int_0^\infty \frac{\sin t}{t}\,dt = \frac{\pi}{2}$.

(a) From Problem 21,

$$\int_0^\infty e^{-st}\frac{F(t)}{t}\,dt = \int_s^\infty f(u)\,du$$

Then taking the limit as $s \to 0+$, assuming the integrals converge, the required result is obtained.

(b) Let $F(t) = \sin t$ so that $f(s) = 1/(s^2 + 1)$ in part (a).   Then

$$\int_0^\infty \frac{\sin t}{t}\, dt \;=\; \int_0^\infty \frac{du}{u^2 + 1} \;=\; \tan^{-1} u \Big|_0^\infty \;=\; \frac{\pi}{2}$$

PERIODIC FUNCTIONS

23. Prove *Theorem 1-14*, Page 5:   If $F(t)$ has period $T > 0$ then

$$\mathcal{L}\{F(t)\} \;=\; \frac{\displaystyle\int_0^T e^{-st}\, F(t)\, dt}{1 - e^{-sT}}$$

We have

$$\mathcal{L}\{F(t)\} \;=\; \int_0^\infty e^{-st}\, F(t)\, dt$$

$$=\; \int_0^T e^{-st}\, F(t)\, dt \;+\; \int_T^{2T} e^{-st}\, F(t)\, dt \;+\; \int_{2T}^{3T} e^{-st}\, F(t)\, dt \;+\; \cdots$$

In the second integral let $t = u + T$, in the third integral let $t = u + 2T$, etc.   Then

$$\mathcal{L}\{F(t)\} \;=\; \int_0^T e^{-su}\, F(u)\, du \;+\; \int_0^T e^{-s(u+T)}\, F(u+T)\, du \;+\; \int_0^T e^{-s(u+2T)}\, F(u+2T)\, du \;+\; \cdots$$

$$=\; \int_0^T e^{-su}\, F(u)\, du \;+\; e^{-sT}\int_0^T e^{-su}\, F(u)\, du \;+\; e^{-2sT}\int_0^T e^{-su}\, F(u)\, du \;+\; \cdots$$

$$=\; (1 + e^{-sT} + e^{-2sT} + \cdots)\int_0^T e^{-su}\, F(u)\, du$$

$$=\; \frac{\displaystyle\int_0^T e^{-su}\, F(u)\, du}{1 - e^{-sT}}$$

where we have used the periodicity to write $F(u + T) = F(u)$, $F(u + 2T) = F(u)$, ..., and the fact that

$$1 + r + r^2 + r^3 + \cdots \;=\; \frac{1}{1-r}, \qquad |r| < 1$$

24. (a) Graph the function

$$F(t) \;=\; \begin{cases} \sin t & 0 < t < \pi \\ 0 & \pi < t < 2\pi \end{cases}$$

extended periodically with period 2π.

(b) Find $\mathcal{L}\{F(t)\}$.

(a) The graph appears in Fig. 1-5.

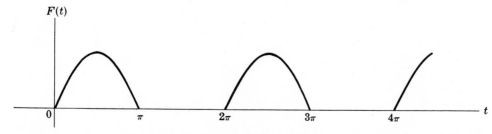

Fig. 1-5

(b) By Problem 23, since $T = 2\pi$, we have

$$\mathcal{L}\{F(t)\} \;=\; \frac{1}{1 - e^{-2\pi s}} \int_0^{2\pi} e^{-st} F(t)\, dt$$

$$=\; \frac{1}{1 - e^{-2\pi s}} \int_0^{\pi} e^{-st} \sin t\, dt$$

$$=\; \frac{1}{1 - e^{-2\pi s}} \left\{ \frac{e^{-st}(-s \sin t - \cos t)}{s^2 + 1} \right\} \Big|_0^{\pi}$$

$$=\; \frac{1}{1 - e^{-2\pi s}} \left\{ \frac{1 + e^{-\pi s}}{s^2 + 1} \right\} \;=\; \frac{1}{(1 - e^{-\pi s})(s^2 + 1)}$$

using the integral (1) of Problem 2, Page 11.

The graph of the function $F(t)$ is often called a *half wave rectified sine curve*.

INITIAL AND FINAL VALUE THEOREMS

25. Prove the *initial-value theorem*: $\lim\limits_{t \to 0} F(t) \;=\; \lim\limits_{s \to \infty} s\, f(s)$.

By Problem 13,

$$\mathcal{L}\{F'(t)\} \;=\; \int_0^{\infty} e^{-st} F'(t)\, dt \;=\; s\, f(s) \,-\, F(0) \qquad\qquad (1)$$

But if $F'(t)$ is sectionally continuous and of exponential order, we have

$$\lim_{s \to \infty} \int_0^{\infty} e^{-st} F'(t)\, dt \;=\; 0 \qquad\qquad (2)$$

Then taking the limit as $s \to \infty$ in (1), assuming $F(t)$ continuous at $t = 0$, we find that

$$0 \;=\; \lim_{s \to \infty} s\, f(s) \,-\, F(0) \qquad \text{or} \qquad \lim_{s \to \infty} s\, f(s) \;=\; F(0) \;=\; \lim_{t \to 0} F(t)$$

If $F(t)$ is not continuous at $t = 0$, the required result still holds but we must use *Theorem 1-7*, Page 4.

26. Prove the *final-value theorem*: $\lim\limits_{t \to \infty} F(t) \;=\; \lim\limits_{s \to 0} s\, f(s)$.

By Problem 13,

$$\mathcal{L}\{F'(t)\} \;=\; \int_0^{\infty} e^{-st} F'(t)\, dt \;=\; s\, f(s) \,-\, F(0)$$

The limit of the left hand side as $s \to 0$ is

$$\lim_{s \to 0} \int_0^{\infty} e^{-st} F'(t)\, dt \;=\; \int_0^{\infty} F'(t)\, dt \;=\; \lim_{P \to \infty} \int_0^{P} F'(t)\, dt$$

$$=\; \lim_{P \to \infty} \{F(P) - F(0)\} \;=\; \lim_{t \to \infty} F(t) \,-\, F(0)$$

The limit of the right hand side as $s \to 0$ is

$$\lim_{s \to 0} s\, f(s) \,-\, F(0)$$

Thus

$$\lim_{t \to \infty} F(t) \,-\, F(0) \;=\; \lim_{s \to 0} s\, f(s) \,-\, F(0)$$

or, as required,

$$\lim_{t \to \infty} F(t) \;=\; \lim_{s \to 0} s\, f(s)$$

If $F(t)$ is not continuous, the result still holds but we must use *Theorem 1-7*, Page 4.

27. Illustrate Problems 25 and 26 for the function $F(t) = 3e^{-2t}$.

We have $F(t) = 3e^{-2t}$, $f(s) = \mathcal{L}\{F(t)\} = \dfrac{3}{s+2}$.

By the initial-value theorem (Problem 25),

$$\lim_{t \to 0} 3e^{-2t} = \lim_{s \to \infty} \frac{3s}{s+2}$$

or $3 = 3$, which illustrates the theorem.

By the final-value theorem (Problem 26),

$$\lim_{t \to \infty} 3e^{-2t} = \lim_{s \to 0} \frac{3s}{s+2}$$

or $0 = 0$, which illustrates the theorem.

THE GAMMA FUNCTION

28. Prove: (a) $\Gamma(n+1) = n\,\Gamma(n)$, $n > 0$; (b) $\Gamma(n+1) = n!$, $n = 1, 2, 3, \ldots$.

(a) $\Gamma(n+1) = \displaystyle\int_0^\infty u^n e^{-u}\, du = \lim_{P \to \infty} \int_0^P u^n e^{-u}\, du$

$$= \lim_{P \to \infty} \left\{ (u^n)(-e^{-u}) \Big|_0^P - \int_0^P (-e^{-u})(nu^{n-1})\, du \right\}$$

$$= \lim_{P \to \infty} \left\{ -P^n e^{-P} + n \int_0^P u^{n-1} e^{-u}\, du \right\}$$

$$= n \int_0^\infty u^{n-1} e^{-u}\, du = n\,\Gamma(n) \quad \text{if } n > 0$$

(b) $\Gamma(1) = \displaystyle\int_0^\infty e^{-u}\, du = \lim_{P \to \infty} \int_0^P e^{-u}\, du = \lim_{P \to \infty} (1 - e^{-P}) = 1.$

Put $n = 1, 2, 3, \ldots$ in $\Gamma(n+1) = n\,\Gamma(n)$. Then

$$\Gamma(2) = 1\,\Gamma(1) = 1, \quad \Gamma(3) = 2\,\Gamma(2) = 2 \cdot 1 = 2!, \quad \Gamma(4) = 3\,\Gamma(3) = 3 \cdot 2! = 3!$$

In general, $\Gamma(n+1) = n!$ if n is a positive integer.

29. Prove: $\displaystyle\int_0^\infty e^{-u^2}\, du = \frac{\sqrt{\pi}}{2}.$

Let $I_P = \displaystyle\int_0^P e^{-x^2}\, dx = \int_0^P e^{-y^2}\, dy$ and let $\lim_{P \to \infty} I_P = I$, the required value of the integral. Then

$$I_P^2 = \left(\int_0^P e^{-x^2}\, dx \right) \left(\int_0^P e^{-y^2}\, dy \right)$$

$$= \int_0^P \int_0^P e^{-(x^2+y^2)}\, dx\, dy$$

$$= \iint_{\mathcal{R}_P} e^{-(x^2+y^2)}\, dx\, dy$$

where $\mathcal{R}_P$ is the square $OACE$ of side P [see Fig. 1-6].

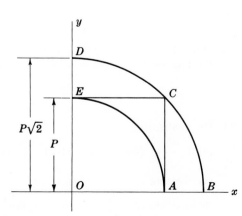

Fig. 1-6

Since the integrand is positive, we have

$$\iint\limits_{\mathcal{R}_1} e^{-(x^2+y^2)}\, dx\, dy \;\leqq\; I_P^2 \;\leqq\; \iint\limits_{\mathcal{R}_2} e^{-(x^2+y^2)}\, dx\, dy \tag{1}$$

where $\mathcal{R}_1$ and $\mathcal{R}_2$ are the regions in the first quadrant bounded by the circles having radii P and $P\sqrt{2}$ respectively.

Using polar coordinates (r, θ) we have from (1),

$$\int_{\theta=0}^{\pi/2}\int_{r=0}^{P} e^{-r^2} r\, dr\, d\theta \;\leqq\; I_P^2 \;\leqq\; \int_{\theta=0}^{\pi/2}\int_{r=0}^{P\sqrt{2}} e^{-r^2} r\, dr\, d\theta \tag{2}$$

or

$$\frac{\pi}{4}(1 - e^{-P^2}) \;\leqq\; I_P^2 \;\leqq\; \frac{\pi}{4}(1 - e^{-2P^2}) \tag{3}$$

Then taking the limit as $P \to \infty$ in (3), we find $\displaystyle\lim_{P\to\infty} I_P^2 = I^2 = \pi/4$ and $I = \sqrt{\pi}/2$.

30. Prove: $\Gamma(\tfrac{1}{2}) = \sqrt{\pi}$.

$\Gamma(\tfrac{1}{2}) = \displaystyle\int_0^\infty u^{-1/2} e^{-u}\, du$. Letting $u = v^2$, this integral becomes on using Problem 29

$$2\int_0^\infty e^{-v^2}\, dv \;=\; 2\left(\frac{\sqrt{\pi}}{2}\right) \;=\; \sqrt{\pi}$$

31. Prove: $\mathcal{L}\{t^n\} = \dfrac{\Gamma(n+1)}{s^{n+1}}$ if $n > -1,\ s > 0$.

$\mathcal{L}\{t^n\} = \displaystyle\int_0^\infty e^{-st} t^n\, dt$. Letting $st = u$, assuming $s > 0$, this becomes

$$\mathcal{L}\{t^n\} \;=\; \int_0^\infty e^{-u}\left(\frac{u}{s}\right)^n d\left(\frac{u}{s}\right) \;=\; \frac{1}{s^{n+1}}\int_0^\infty u^n e^{-u}\, du \;=\; \frac{\Gamma(n+1)}{s^{n+1}}$$

32. Prove: $\mathcal{L}\{t^{-1/2}\} = \sqrt{\pi/s},\quad s > 0$.

Let $n = -1/2$ in Problem 31. Then

$$\mathcal{L}\{t^{-1/2}\} \;=\; \frac{\Gamma(\tfrac{1}{2})}{s^{1/2}} \;=\; \frac{\sqrt{\pi}}{s^{1/2}} \;=\; \sqrt{\frac{\pi}{s}}$$

Note that although $F(t) = t^{-1/2}$ does not satisfy the sufficient conditions of *Theorem 1-1*, Page 2, the Laplace transform does exist. The function does satisfy the conditions of the theorem in Prob. 145.

33. By assuming $\Gamma(n+1) = n\Gamma(n)$ holds for all n, find:

(a) $\Gamma(-\tfrac{1}{2})$, (b) $\Gamma(-\tfrac{3}{2})$, (c) $\Gamma(-\tfrac{5}{2})$, (d) $\Gamma(0)$, (e) $\Gamma(-1)$, (f) $\Gamma(-2)$.

(a) Letting $n = -\tfrac{1}{2}$, $\Gamma(\tfrac{1}{2}) = -\tfrac{1}{2}\Gamma(-\tfrac{1}{2})$. Then $\Gamma(-\tfrac{1}{2}) = -2\Gamma(\tfrac{1}{2}) = -2\sqrt{\pi}$.

(b) Letting $n = -\tfrac{3}{2}$, $\Gamma(-\tfrac{1}{2}) = -\tfrac{3}{2}\Gamma(-\tfrac{3}{2})$. Then $\Gamma(-\tfrac{3}{2}) = -\tfrac{2}{3}\Gamma(-\tfrac{1}{2}) = (2)(\tfrac{2}{3})\sqrt{\pi} = \tfrac{4}{3}\sqrt{\pi}$ by part (a).

(c) Letting $n = -\tfrac{5}{2}$, $\Gamma(-\tfrac{3}{2}) = -\tfrac{5}{2}\Gamma(-\tfrac{5}{2})$. Then $\Gamma(-\tfrac{5}{2}) = -\tfrac{2}{5}\Gamma(-\tfrac{3}{2}) = -(2)(\tfrac{2}{3})(\tfrac{2}{5})\sqrt{\pi} = -\tfrac{8}{15}\sqrt{\pi}$ by part (b).

(*d*) Letting $n = 0$, $\Gamma(1) = 0 \cdot \Gamma(0)$ and it follows that $\Gamma(0)$ must be infinite, since $\Gamma(1) = 1$.

(*e*) Letting $n = -1$, $\Gamma(0) = -1\,\Gamma(-1)$ and it follows that $\Gamma(-1)$ must be infinite.

(*f*) Letting $n = -2$, $\Gamma(-1) = -2\,\Gamma(-2)$ and it follows that $\Gamma(-2)$ must be infinite.

In general if p is any positive integer or zero, $\Gamma(-p)$ is infinite and [see Problem 170],

$$\Gamma(-p - \tfrac{1}{2}) \;=\; (-1)^{p+1} \left(\frac{2}{1}\right)\left(\frac{2}{3}\right)\left(\frac{2}{5}\right) \cdots \left(\frac{2}{2p+1}\right) \sqrt{\pi}$$

BESSEL FUNCTIONS

34. (*a*) Find $\mathcal{L}\{J_0(t)\}$ where $J_0(t)$ is the Bessel function of order zero.

(*b*) Use the result of (*a*) to find $\mathcal{L}\{J_0(at)\}$.

(*a*) *Method 1, using series.* Letting $n = 0$ in equation (*23*), Page 7, we find

$$J_0(t) \;=\; 1 \;-\; \frac{t^2}{2^2} \;+\; \frac{t^4}{2^2\,4^2} \;-\; \frac{t^6}{2^2\,4^2\,6^2} \;+\; \cdots$$

Then $\mathcal{L}\{J_0(t)\}$

$$= \;\; \frac{1}{s} \;-\; \frac{1}{2^2}\frac{2!}{s^3} \;+\; \frac{1}{2^2\,4^2}\frac{4!}{s^5} \;-\; \frac{1}{2^2\,4^2\,6^2}\frac{6!}{s^7} \;+\; \cdots$$

$$= \;\; \frac{1}{s}\left\{ 1 \;-\; \frac{1}{2}\left(\frac{1}{s^2}\right) \;+\; \frac{1\cdot 3}{2\cdot 4}\left(\frac{1}{s^4}\right) \;-\; \frac{1\cdot 3\cdot 5}{2\cdot 4\cdot 6}\left(\frac{1}{s^6}\right) \;+\; \cdots \right\}$$

$$= \;\; \frac{1}{s}\left\{ \left(1 + \frac{1}{s^2}\right)^{-1/2} \right\} \;\;=\;\; \frac{1}{\sqrt{s^2 + 1}}$$

using the binomial theorem [see Problem 172].

Method 2, using differential equations. The function $J_0(t)$ satisfies the differential equation

$$t\,J_0''(t) \;+\; J_0'(t) \;+\; t\,J_0(t) \;=\; 0 \tag{1}$$

[see Property 5, Page 8, with $n = 0$]. Taking the Laplace transform of both sides of (*1*) and using *Theorems 1-6* and *1-9*, Page 4, and *Theorem 1-12*, Page 5, together with $J_0(0) = 1$, $J_0'(0) = 0$, $y = \mathcal{L}\{J_0(t)\}$, we have

$$-\frac{d}{ds}\{s^2 y - s(1) - 0\} \;+\; \{sy - 1\} \;-\; \frac{dy}{ds} \;=\; 0$$

from which
$$\frac{dy}{ds} \;=\; -\frac{sy}{s^2 + 1}$$

Thus
$$\frac{dy}{y} \;=\; -\frac{s\,ds}{s^2 + 1}$$

and by integration
$$y \;=\; \frac{c}{\sqrt{s^2 + 1}}$$

Now $\displaystyle\lim_{s \to \infty} s\,y(s) = \frac{cs}{\sqrt{s^2 + 1}} = c$ and $\displaystyle\lim_{t \to 0} J_0(t) = 1$. Thus by the initial-value theorem [Page 5], we have $c = 1$ and so $\mathcal{L}\{J_0(t)\} = 1/\sqrt{s^2 + 1}$.

For another method, see Problem 165.

(*b*) By Problem 11,

$$\mathcal{L}\{J_0(at)\} \;\;=\;\; \frac{1}{a}\,\frac{1}{\sqrt{(s/a)^2 + 1}} \;\;=\;\; \frac{1}{\sqrt{s^2 + a^2}}$$

35. Find $\mathcal{L}\{J_1(t)\}$, where $J_1(t)$ is Bessel's function of order one.

From Property 3 for Bessel functions, Page 7, we have $J_0'(t) = -J_1(t)$. Hence

$$\mathcal{L}\{J_1(t)\} \;=\; -\mathcal{L}\{J_0'(t)\} \;=\; -[s\,\mathcal{L}\{J_0(t)\} - 1]$$

$$=\; 1 - \frac{s}{\sqrt{s^2+1}} \;=\; \frac{\sqrt{s^2+1} - s}{\sqrt{s^2+1}}$$

The methods of infinite series and differential equations can also be used [see Problem 178, Page 41].

THE SINE, COSINE AND EXPONENTIAL INTEGRALS

36. Prove: $\mathcal{L}\{\mathrm{Si}\,(t)\} = \mathcal{L}\left\{\displaystyle\int_0^t \frac{\sin u}{u}\,du\right\} = \dfrac{1}{s}\tan^{-1}\dfrac{1}{s}$.

Method 1. Let $F(t) = \displaystyle\int_0^t \frac{\sin u}{u}\,du$. Then $F(0) = 0$ and $F'(t) = \dfrac{\sin t}{t}$ or $t\,F'(t) = \sin t$.

Taking the Laplace transform,

$$\mathcal{L}\{t\,F'(t)\} \;=\; \mathcal{L}\{\sin t\} \qquad \text{or} \qquad -\frac{d}{ds}\{s\,f(s) - F(0)\} \;=\; \frac{1}{s^2+1}$$

i.e.
$$\frac{d}{ds}\{s\,f(s)\} \;=\; \frac{-1}{s^2+1}$$

Integrating,
$$s\,f(s) \;=\; -\tan^{-1}s \;+\; c$$

By the initial value theorem, $\displaystyle\lim_{s\to\infty} s\,f(s) = \lim_{t\to 0} F(t) = F(0) = 0$ so that $c = \pi/2$. Thus

$$s\,f(s) \;=\; \frac{\pi}{2} - \tan^{-1}s \;=\; \tan^{-1}\frac{1}{s} \qquad \text{or} \qquad f(s) \;=\; \frac{1}{s}\tan^{-1}\frac{1}{s}$$

Method 2. See Problem 18.

Method 3. Using infinite series, we have

$$\int_0^t \frac{\sin u}{u}\,du \;=\; \int_0^t \frac{1}{u}\left(u - \frac{u^3}{3!} + \frac{u^5}{5!} - \frac{u^7}{7!} + \cdots\right) du$$

$$=\; t - \frac{t^3}{3\cdot 3!} + \frac{t^5}{5\cdot 5!} - \frac{t^7}{7\cdot 7!} + \cdots$$

Then
$$\mathcal{L}\left\{\int_0^t \frac{\sin u}{u}\right\} \;=\; \mathcal{L}\left\{t - \frac{t^3}{3\cdot 3!} + \frac{t^5}{5\cdot 5!} - \frac{t^7}{7\cdot 7!} + \cdots\right\}$$

$$=\; \frac{1}{s^2} - \frac{1}{3\cdot 3!}\cdot\frac{3!}{s^4} + \frac{1}{5\cdot 5!}\cdot\frac{5!}{s^6} - \frac{1}{7\cdot 7!}\cdot\frac{7!}{s^8} + \cdots$$

$$=\; \frac{1}{s^2} - \frac{1}{3s^4} + \frac{1}{5s^6} - \frac{1}{7s^8} + \cdots$$

$$=\; \frac{1}{s}\left\{\frac{(1/s)}{1} - \frac{(1/s)^3}{3} + \frac{(1/s)^5}{5} - \frac{(1/s)^7}{7} + \cdots\right\}$$

$$=\; \frac{1}{s}\tan^{-1}\frac{1}{s}$$

using the series $\tan^{-1}x = x - x^3/3 + x^5/5 - x^7/7 + \cdots,\ \ |x| < 1$.

Method 4.   Letting $u = tv$,

$$\int_0^t \frac{\sin u}{u} \, du = \int_0^1 \frac{\sin tv}{v} \, dv$$

Then

$$\mathcal{L}\left\{ \int_0^t \frac{\sin u}{u} \, du \right\} = \mathcal{L}\left\{ \int_0^1 \frac{\sin tv}{v} \, dv \right\}$$

$$= \int_0^\infty e^{-st} \left\{ \int_0^1 \frac{\sin tv}{v} \, dv \right\} dt$$

$$= \int_0^1 \frac{1}{v} \left\{ \int_0^\infty e^{-st} \sin tv \, dt \right\} dv$$

$$= \int_0^1 \frac{\mathcal{L}\{\sin tv\}}{v} \, dv = \int_0^1 \frac{dv}{s^2 + v^2}$$

$$= \frac{1}{s} \tan^{-1} \frac{v}{s} \Big|_0^1 = \frac{1}{s} \tan^{-1} \frac{1}{s}$$

where we have assumed permissibility of change of order of integration.

37. Prove: $\mathcal{L}\{\mathrm{Ci}\,(t)\} = \mathcal{L}\left\{ \int_t^\infty \frac{\cos u}{u} \, du \right\} = \dfrac{\ln(s^2 + 1)}{2s}$.

We use the principle of Method 1 in Problem 36. Let $F(t) = \displaystyle\int_t^\infty \frac{\cos u}{u} \, du$ so that $F'(t) = -\dfrac{\cos t}{t}$ and $t\,F'(t) = -\cos t$.   Taking the Laplace transform, we have

$$-\frac{d}{ds}\{s\,f(s) - F(0)\} = \frac{-s}{s^2 + 1} \qquad \text{or} \qquad \frac{d}{ds}\{s\,f(s)\} = \frac{s}{s^2 + 1}$$

Then by integration, $s\,f(s) = \tfrac{1}{2} \ln(s^2 + 1) + c$

By the final-value theorem, $\displaystyle\lim_{s \to 0} s\,f(s) = \lim_{t \to \infty} F(t) = 0$ so that $c = 0$.   Thus

$$s\,f(s) = \tfrac{1}{2} \ln(s^2 + 1) \qquad \text{or} \qquad f(s) = \frac{\ln(s^2 + 1)}{2s}$$

We can also use Method 4 of Problem 36 [see Problem 153].

38. Prove: $\mathcal{L}\{\mathrm{Ei}\,(t)\} = \mathcal{L}\left\{ \int_t^\infty \frac{e^{-u}}{u} \, du \right\} = \dfrac{\ln(s + 1)}{s}$.

Let $F(t) = \displaystyle\int_t^\infty \frac{e^{-u}}{u} \, du$.   Then $t\,F'(t) = -e^{-t}$.   Taking the Laplace transform, we find

$$-\frac{d}{ds}\{s\,f(s) - F(0)\} = \frac{-1}{s + 1} \qquad \text{or} \qquad \frac{d}{ds}\{s\,f(s)\} = \frac{1}{s + 1}$$

Integrating, $s\,f(s) = \ln(s + 1) + c$

Applying the final-value theorem as in **Problem 37**, we find $c = 0$ and so

$$f(s) = \frac{\ln(s + 1)}{s}$$

For another method similar to that of Method 4, Problem 36, see Problem 153.

THE ERROR FUNCTION

39. Prove: $\mathcal{L}\left\{\text{erf}\sqrt{t}\right\} \;=\; \mathcal{L}\left\{\dfrac{2}{\sqrt{\pi}}\displaystyle\int_0^{\sqrt{t}} e^{-u^2}\,du\right\} \;=\; \dfrac{1}{s\sqrt{s+1}}.$

Using infinite series, we have

$$\mathcal{L}\left\{\frac{2}{\sqrt{\pi}}\int_0^{\sqrt{t}} e^{-u^2}\,du\right\} \;=\; \mathcal{L}\left\{\frac{2}{\sqrt{\pi}}\int_0^{\sqrt{t}}\left(1 - u^2 + \frac{u^4}{2!} - \frac{u^6}{3!} + \cdots\right)du\right\}$$

$$= \; \mathcal{L}\left\{\frac{2}{\sqrt{\pi}}\left(t^{1/2} - \frac{t^{3/2}}{3} + \frac{t^{5/2}}{5\cdot 2!} - \frac{t^{7/2}}{7\cdot 3!} + \cdots\right)\right\}$$

$$= \; \frac{2}{\sqrt{\pi}}\left\{\frac{\Gamma(3/2)}{s^{3/2}} - \frac{\Gamma(5/2)}{3s^{5/2}} + \frac{\Gamma(7/2)}{5\cdot 2!\; s^{7/2}} - \frac{\Gamma(9/2)}{7\cdot 3!\; s^{9/2}} + \cdots\right\}$$

$$= \; \frac{1}{s^{3/2}} - \frac{1}{2}\frac{1}{s^{5/2}} + \frac{1\cdot 3}{2\cdot 4}\frac{1}{s^{7/2}} - \frac{1\cdot 3\cdot 5}{2\cdot 4\cdot 6}\frac{1}{s^{9/2}} + \cdots$$

$$= \; \frac{1}{s^{3/2}}\left\{1 - \frac{1}{2}\frac{1}{s} + \frac{1\cdot 3}{2\cdot 4}\frac{1}{s^2} - \frac{1\cdot 3\cdot 5}{2\cdot 4\cdot 6}\frac{1}{s^3} + \cdots\right\}$$

$$= \; \frac{1}{s^{3/2}}\left(1 + \frac{1}{s}\right)^{-1/2} \;=\; \frac{1}{s\sqrt{s+1}}$$

using the binomial theorem [see Problem 172].

For another method, see Problem 175(a).

IMPULSE FUNCTIONS.   THE DIRAC DELTA FUNCTION.

40. Prove that $\mathcal{L}\left\{\mathcal{U}(t-a)\right\} = \dfrac{e^{-as}}{s}$ where $\mathcal{U}(t-a)$ is Heaviside's unit step function.

We have $\mathcal{U}(t-a) \;=\; \begin{cases} 1 & t > a \\ 0 & t < a \end{cases}.$ Then

$$\mathcal{L}\left\{\mathcal{U}(t-a)\right\} \;=\; \int_0^a e^{-st}\,(0)\,dt \;+\; \int_a^\infty e^{-st}\,(1)\,dt$$

$$= \; \lim_{P\to\infty}\int_a^P e^{-st}\,dt \;=\; \lim_{P\to\infty}\frac{e^{-st}}{-s}\Big|_a^P$$

$$= \; \lim_{P\to\infty}\frac{e^{-as} - e^{-sP}}{s} \;=\; \frac{e^{-as}}{s}$$

Another method.

Since $\mathcal{L}\{1\} = 1/s$, we have by Problem 9, $\mathcal{L}\{\mathcal{U}(t-a)\} = e^{-as}/s$.

41. Find $\mathcal{L}\left\{F_\epsilon(t)\right\}$ where $F_\epsilon(t)$ is defined by (30), Page 8.

We have $F_\epsilon(t) \;=\; \begin{cases} 1/\epsilon & 0 \le t \le \epsilon \\ 0 & t > \epsilon \end{cases}.$ Then

$$\mathcal{L}\left\{F_\epsilon(t)\right\} \;=\; \int_0^\infty e^{-st} F_\epsilon(t)\,dt$$

$$= \; \int_0^\epsilon e^{-st}\,(1/\epsilon)\,dt \;+\; \int_\epsilon^\infty e^{-st}\,(0)\,dt$$

$$= \; \frac{1}{\epsilon}\int_0^\epsilon e^{-st}\,dt \;=\; \frac{1 - e^{-s\epsilon}}{\epsilon s}$$

42. (*a*) Show that $\lim\limits_{\epsilon \to 0} \mathcal{L}\{F_\epsilon(t)\} = 1$ in Problem 41.

(*b*) Is the result in (*a*) the same as $\mathcal{L}\left\{\lim\limits_{\epsilon \to 0} F_\epsilon(t)\right\}$? Explain.

(*a*) This follows at once since

$$\lim_{\epsilon \to 0} \frac{1 - e^{-s\epsilon}}{s\epsilon} \;=\; \lim_{\epsilon \to 0} \frac{1 - (1 - s\epsilon + s^2\epsilon^2/2! - \cdots)}{s\epsilon} \;=\; \lim_{\epsilon \to 0}\left(1 - \frac{s\epsilon}{2!} + \cdots\right) \;=\; 1$$

It also follows by use of L'Hospital's rule.

(*b*) Mathematically speaking, $\lim\limits_{\epsilon \to 0} F_\epsilon(t)$ does not exist, so that $\mathcal{L}\left\{\lim\limits_{\epsilon \to 0} F_\epsilon(t)\right\}$ is not defined. Nevertheless it proves useful to consider $\delta(t) = \lim\limits_{\epsilon \to 0} F_\epsilon(t)$ to be such that $\mathcal{L}\{\delta(t)\} = 1$. We call $\delta(t)$ the *Dirac delta function* or *impulse function*.

43. Show that $\mathcal{L}\{\delta(t - a)\} = e^{-as}$, where $\delta(t)$ is the Dirac delta function.

This follows from Problem 9 and the fact that $\mathcal{L}\{\delta(t)\} = 1$.

44. Indicate which of the following are null functions.

(*a*) $F(t) = \begin{cases} 1 & t = 1 \\ 0 & \text{otherwise} \end{cases}$, (*b*) $F(t) = \begin{cases} 1 & 1 \leq t \leq 2 \\ 0 & \text{otherwise} \end{cases}$, (*c*) $F(t) = \delta(t)$.

(*a*) $F(t)$ is a null function, since $\displaystyle\int_0^t F(u)\,du = 0$ for all $t > 0$.

(*b*) If $t < 1$, we have $\displaystyle\int_0^t F(u)\,du = 0$.

If $1 \leq t \leq 2$, we have $\displaystyle\int_0^t F(u)\,du = \int_1^t (1)\,du = t - 1$.

If $t > 2$, we have $\displaystyle\int_0^t F(u)\,du = \int_1^2 (1)\,du = 1$.

Since $\displaystyle\int_0^t F(u)\,du \neq 0$ for all $t > 0$, $F(t)$ is not a null function.

(*c*) Since $\displaystyle\int_0^t \delta(u)\,du = 1$ for all $t > 0$, $\delta(t)$ is not a null function.

EVALUATION OF INTEGRALS

45. Evaluate   (*a*) $\displaystyle\int_0^\infty t\,e^{-2t}\cos t\,dt$,   (*b*) $\displaystyle\int_0^\infty \frac{e^{-t} - e^{-3t}}{t}\,dt$.

(*a*) By Problem 19,

$$\mathcal{L}\{t\cos t\} \;=\; \int_0^\infty t\,e^{-st}\cos t\,dt$$

$$=\; -\frac{d}{ds}\,\mathcal{L}\{\cos t\} \;=\; -\frac{d}{ds}\left(\frac{s}{s^2 + 1}\right) \;=\; \frac{s^2 - 1}{(s^2 + 1)^2}$$

Then letting $s = 2$, we find $\displaystyle\int_0^\infty t e^{-2t} \cos t \, dt = \frac{3}{25}$.

(b) If $F(t) = e^{-t} - e^{-3t}$, then $f(s) = \mathcal{L}\{F(t)\} = \dfrac{1}{s+1} - \dfrac{1}{s+3}$. Thus by Problem 21,

$$\mathcal{L}\left\{\frac{e^{-t} - e^{-3t}}{t}\right\} = \int_s^\infty \left\{\frac{1}{u+1} - \frac{1}{u+3}\right\} du$$

or

$$\int_0^\infty e^{-st}\left(\frac{e^{-t} - e^{-3t}}{t}\right) dt = \ln\left(\frac{s+3}{s+1}\right)$$

Taking the limit as $s \to 0+$, we find $\displaystyle\int_0^\infty \frac{e^{-t} - e^{-3t}}{t} \, dt = \ln 3$.

46. Show that (a) $\displaystyle\int_0^\infty J_0(t) \, dt = 1$, (b) $\displaystyle\int_0^\infty e^{-t} \operatorname{erf}\sqrt{t} \, dt = \sqrt{2}/2$.

(a) By Problem 34, $\displaystyle\int_0^\infty e^{-st} J_0(t) \, dt = \frac{1}{\sqrt{s^2 + 1}}$

Then letting $s \to 0+$ we find $\displaystyle\int_0^\infty J_0(t) \, dt = 1$.

(b) By Problem 39, $\displaystyle\int_0^\infty e^{-st} \operatorname{erf}\sqrt{t} \, dt = \frac{1}{s\sqrt{s+1}}$

Then letting $s \to 1$, we find $\displaystyle\int_0^\infty e^{-t} \operatorname{erf}\sqrt{t} \, dt = \sqrt{2}/2$.

MISCELLANEOUS PROBLEMS

47. Prove *Theorem 1-1*, Page 2.

We have for any positive number N,

$$\int_0^\infty e^{-st} F(t) \, dt = \int_0^N e^{-st} F(t) \, dt + \int_N^\infty e^{-st} F(t) \, dt$$

Since $F(t)$ is sectionally continuous in every finite interval $0 \leqq t \leqq N$, the first integral on the right exists. Also the second integral on the right exists, since $F(t)$ is of exponential order γ for $t > N$. To see this we have only to observe that in such case

$$\left|\int_N^\infty e^{-st} F(t) \, dt\right| \leqq \int_N^\infty |e^{-st} F(t)| \, dt$$

$$\leqq \int_0^\infty e^{-st} |F(t)| \, dt$$

$$\leqq \int_0^\infty e^{-st} M e^{\gamma t} \, dt = \frac{M}{s - \gamma}$$

Thus the Laplace transform exists for $s > \gamma$.

48. Find $\mathcal{L}\{\sin\sqrt{t}\}$.

Method 1, using series.

$$\sin\sqrt{t} = \sqrt{t} - \frac{(\sqrt{t})^3}{3!} + \frac{(\sqrt{t})^5}{5!} - \frac{(\sqrt{t})^7}{7!} + \cdots = t^{1/2} - \frac{t^{3/2}}{3!} + \frac{t^{5/2}}{5!} - \frac{t^{7/2}}{7!} + \cdots$$

Then the Laplace transform is

$$\mathcal{L}\{\sin\sqrt{t}\} = \frac{\Gamma(3/2)}{s^{3/2}} - \frac{\Gamma(5/2)}{3!\,s^{5/2}} + \frac{\Gamma(7/2)}{5!\,s^{7/2}} - \frac{\Gamma(9/2)}{7!\,s^{9/2}} + \cdots$$

$$= \frac{\sqrt{\pi}}{2s^{3/2}}\left\{1 - \left(\frac{1}{2^2\,s}\right) + \frac{(1/2^2\,s)^2}{2!} - \frac{(1/2^2\,s)^3}{3!} + \cdots\right\}$$

$$= \frac{\sqrt{\pi}}{2\,s^{3/2}}\,e^{-1/2^2 s} = \frac{\sqrt{\pi}}{2\,s^{3/2}}\,e^{-1/4s}$$

Method 2, using differential equations.

Let $Y(t) = \sin\sqrt{t}$. Then by differentiating twice we find

$$4tY'' + 2Y' + Y = 0$$

Taking the Laplace transform, we have if $y = \mathcal{L}\{Y(t)\}$

$$-4\frac{d}{ds}\{s^2 y - s\,Y(0) - Y'(0)\} + 2\{s\,y - Y(0)\} + y = 0$$

or

$$4\,s^2\,y' + (6\,s - 1)y = 0$$

Solving,

$$y = \frac{c}{s^{3/2}}\,e^{-1/4s}$$

For small values of t, we have $\sin\sqrt{t} \sim \sqrt{t}$ and $\mathcal{L}\{\sqrt{t}\} = \sqrt{\pi}/2s^{3/2}$. For large s, $y \sim c/s^{3/2}$. It follows by comparison that $c = \sqrt{\pi}/2$. Thus

$$\mathcal{L}\{\sin\sqrt{t}\} = \frac{\sqrt{\pi}}{2\,s^{3/2}}\,e^{-1/4s}$$

49. Find $\mathcal{L}\left\{\dfrac{\cos\sqrt{t}}{\sqrt{t}}\right\}$.

Let $F(t) = \sin\sqrt{t}$. Then $F'(t) = \dfrac{\cos\sqrt{t}}{2\sqrt{t}}$, $F(0) = 0$. Hence by Problem 48,

$$\mathcal{L}\{F'(t)\} = \frac{1}{2}\mathcal{L}\left\{\frac{\cos\sqrt{t}}{\sqrt{t}}\right\} = s\,f(s) - F(0) = \frac{\sqrt{\pi}}{2\,s^{1/2}}\,e^{-1/4s}$$

from which

$$\mathcal{L}\left\{\frac{\cos\sqrt{t}}{\sqrt{t}}\right\} = \frac{\sqrt{\pi}}{s^{1/2}}\,e^{-1/4s}$$

The method of series can also be used [see Problem 175(b)].

50. Show that

$$\mathcal{L}\{\ln t\} = \frac{\Gamma'(1) - \ln s}{s} = -\frac{\gamma + \ln s}{s}$$

where $\gamma = .5772156\ldots$ is *Euler's constant*.

We have

$$\Gamma(r) = \int_0^\infty u^{r-1}\,e^{-u}\,du$$

Then differentiating with respect to r, we find

$$\Gamma'(r) \;=\; \int_0^\infty u^{r-1}\, e^{-u} \ln u \; du$$

from which

$$\Gamma'(1) \;=\; \int_0^\infty e^{-u} \ln u \; du$$

Letting $u = st$, $s > 0$, this becomes

$$\Gamma'(1) \;=\; s \int_0^\infty e^{-st} (\ln s + \ln t)\, dt$$

Hence

$$\mathcal{L}\{\ln t\} \;=\; \int_0^\infty e^{-st} \ln t \; dt \;=\; \frac{\Gamma'(1)}{s} - \ln s \int_0^\infty e^{-st}\, dt$$

$$=\; \frac{\Gamma'(1)}{s} - \frac{\ln s}{s} \;=\; -\frac{\gamma + \ln s}{s}$$

Another method.   We have for $k > -1$,

$$\int_0^\infty e^{-st}\, t^k \; dt \;=\; \frac{\Gamma(k+1)}{s^{k+1}}$$

Then differentiating with respect to k,

$$\int_0^\infty e^{-st}\, t^k \ln t \; dt \;=\; \frac{\Gamma'(k+1) - \Gamma(k+1) \ln s}{s^{k+1}}$$

Letting $k = 0$ we have, as required,

$$\int_0^\infty e^{-st} \ln t \; dt \;=\; \mathcal{L}\{\ln t\} \;=\; \frac{\Gamma'(1) - \ln s}{s} \;=\; -\frac{\gamma + \ln s}{s}$$

Supplementary Problems

LAPLACE TRANSFORMS OF ELEMENTARY FUNCTIONS

51.   Find the Laplace transforms of each of the following functions. In each case specify the values of s for which the Laplace transform exists.

(a) $2e^{4t}$	*Ans.* (a) $2/(s-4)$,	$s > 4$
(b) $3e^{-2t}$	(b) $3/(s+2)$,	$s > -2$
(c) $5t - 3$	(c) $(5-3s)/s^2$,	$s > 0$
(d) $2t^2 - e^{-t}$	(d) $(4+4s-s^3)/s^3(s+1)$,	$s > 0$
(e) $3 \cos 5t$	(e) $3s/(s^2+25)$,	$s > 0$
(f) $10 \sin 6t$	(f) $60/(s^2+36)$,	$s > 0$
(g) $6 \sin 2t - 5 \cos 2t$	(g) $(12-5s)/(s^2+4)$,	$s > 0$
(h) $(t^2+1)^2$	(h) $(s^4+4s^2+24)/s^5$,	$s > 0$
(i) $(\sin t - \cos t)^2$	(i) $(s^2-2s+4)/s(s^2+4)$,	$s > 0$
(j) $3 \cosh 5t - 4 \sinh 5t$	(j) $(3s-20)/(s^2-25)$,	$s > 5$

52. Evaluate   (a) $\mathcal{L}\{(5e^{2t}-3)^2\}$,   (b) $\mathcal{L}\{4\cos^2 2t\}$.

   Ans. (a) $\dfrac{25}{s-4}-\dfrac{30}{s-2}+\dfrac{9}{s}$, $s>4$ (b) $\dfrac{2}{s}+\dfrac{2s}{s^2+16}$, $s>0$

53. Find $\mathcal{L}\{\cosh^2 4t\}$.   *Ans.* $\dfrac{s^2-32}{s(s^2-64)}$

54. Find $\mathcal{L}\{F(t)\}$ if   (a) $F(t) = \begin{cases} 0 & 0<t<2 \\ 4 & t>2 \end{cases}$,   (b) $F(t) = \begin{cases} 2t & 0\leqq t\leqq 5 \\ 1 & t>5 \end{cases}$

   Ans. (a) $4e^{-2s}/s$ (b) $\dfrac{2}{s^2}(1-e^{-5s})-\dfrac{9}{s}e^{-5s}$

55. Prove that $\mathcal{L}\{t^n\} = \dfrac{n!}{s^{n+1}}$, $n=1,2,3,\ldots$.

56. Investigate the existence of the Laplace transform of each of the following functions.

   (a) $1/(t+1)$, (b) e^{t^2-t}, (c) $\cos t^2$ *Ans.* (a) exists, (b) does not exist, (c) exists

LINEARITY, TRANSLATION AND CHANGE OF SCALE PROPERTIES

57. Find $\mathcal{L}\{3t^4 - 2t^3 + 4e^{-3t} - 2\sin 5t + 3\cos 2t\}$.

   Ans. $\dfrac{72}{s^5}-\dfrac{12}{s^4}+\dfrac{4}{s+3}-\dfrac{10}{s^2+25}+\dfrac{3s}{s^2+4}$

58. Evaluate each of the following.

   (a) $\mathcal{L}\{t^3 e^{-3t}\}$ *Ans.* (a) $6/(s+3)^4$

   (b) $\mathcal{L}\{e^{-t}\cos 2t\}$ (b) $(s+1)/(s^2+2s+5)$

   (c) $\mathcal{L}\{2e^{3t}\sin 4t\}$ (c) $8/(s^2-6s+25)$

   (d) $\mathcal{L}\{(t+2)^2 e^t\}$ (d) $(4s^2-4s+2)/(s-1)^3$

   (e) $\mathcal{L}\{e^{2t}(3\sin 4t - 4\cos 4t)\}$ (e) $(20-4s)/(s^2-4s+20)$

   (f) $\mathcal{L}\{e^{-4t}\cosh 2t\}$ (f) $(s+4)/(s^2+8s+12)$

   (g) $\mathcal{L}\{e^{-t}(3\sinh 2t - 5\cosh 2t)\}$ (g) $(1-5s)/(s^2+2s-3)$

59. Find   (a) $\mathcal{L}\{e^{-t}\sin^2 t\}$,   (b) $\mathcal{L}\{(1+te^{-t})^3\}$.

   Ans. (a) $\dfrac{2}{(s+1)(s^2+2s+5)}$ (b) $\dfrac{1}{s}+\dfrac{3}{(s+1)^2}+\dfrac{6}{(s+2)^3}+\dfrac{6}{(s+3)^4}$

60. Find $\mathcal{L}\{F(t)\}$ if $F(t) = \begin{cases} (t-1)^2 & t>1 \\ 0 & 0<t<1 \end{cases}$.   *Ans.* $2e^{-s}/s^3$

61. If $F_1(t)$, $F_2(t)$, $\ldots$, $F_n(t)$ have Laplace transforms $f_1(s)$, $f_2(s)$, $\ldots$, $f_n(s)$ respectively and $c_1, c_2, \ldots, c_n$ are any constants, prove that

$$\mathcal{L}\{c_1 F_1(t) + c_2 F_2(t) + \cdots + c_n F_n(t)\} = c_1 f_1(s) + c_2 f_2(s) + \cdots + c_n f_n(s)$$

62. If $\mathcal{L}\{F(t)\} = \dfrac{s^2 - s + 1}{(2s + 1)^2(s - 1)}$, find $\mathcal{L}\{F(2t)\}$.   *Ans.* $(s^2 - 2s + 4)/4(s + 1)^2(s - 2)$

63. If $\mathcal{L}\{F(t)\} = \dfrac{e^{-1/s}}{s}$, find $\mathcal{L}\{e^{-t}F(3t)\}$.   *Ans.* $\dfrac{e^{-3/(s+1)}}{s + 1}$

64. If $f(s) = \mathcal{L}\{F(t)\}$, prove that for $r > 0$,

$$\mathcal{L}\{r^t F(at)\} = \frac{1}{a} f\left(\frac{s - \ln r}{a}\right)$$

LAPLACE TRANSFORMS OF DERIVATIVES

65. (a) If $\mathcal{L}\{F(t)\} = f(s)$, prove that

$$\mathcal{L}\{F'''(t)\} = s^3 f(s) - s^2 F(0) - s F'(0) - F''(0)$$

stating appropriate conditions on $F(t)$.

(b) Generalize the result of (a) and prove by use of mathematical induction.

66. Given $F(t) = \begin{cases} 2t & 0 \leqq t \leqq 1 \\ t & t > 1 \end{cases}$.   (a) Find $\mathcal{L}\{F(t)\}$.   (b) Find $\mathcal{L}\{F'(t)\}$.   (c) Does the result $\mathcal{L}\{F'(t)\} = s\mathcal{L}\{F(t)\} - F(0)$ hold for this case?   Explain.

Ans. (a) $\dfrac{2}{s^2} - \dfrac{e^{-s}}{s} - \dfrac{e^{-s}}{s^2}$, (b) $\dfrac{2}{s} - \dfrac{e^{-s}}{s}$

67. (a) If $F(t) = \begin{cases} t^2 & 0 < t \leqq 1 \\ 0 & t > 1 \end{cases}$, find $\mathcal{L}\{F''(t)\}$.

(b) Does the result $\mathcal{L}\{F''(t)\} = s^2\mathcal{L}\{F(t)\} - s F(0) - F'(0)$ hold in this case?   Explain.
Ans. (a) $2(1 - e^{-s})/s$

68. Prove: (a) *Theorem 1-7*, Page 4; (b) *Theorem 1-8*, Page 4.

LAPLACE TRANSFORMS OF INTEGRALS

69. Verify directly that $\mathcal{L}\left\{\displaystyle\int_0^t (u^2 - u + e^{-u})\,du\right\} = \dfrac{1}{s}\mathcal{L}\{t^2 - t + e^{-t}\}$.

70. If $f(s) = \mathcal{L}\{F(t)\}$, show that $\mathcal{L}\left\{\displaystyle\int_0^t dt_1 \int_0^{t_1} F(u)\,du\right\} = \dfrac{f(s)}{s^2}$.

$\left[\text{The double integral is sometimes briefly written as } \displaystyle\int_0^t \int_0^t F(t)\,dt^2.\right]$

71. Generalize the result of Problem 70.

72. Show that $\mathcal{L}\left\{\displaystyle\int_0^t \frac{1 - e^{-u}}{u}\,du\right\} = \dfrac{1}{s}\ln\left(1 + \dfrac{1}{s}\right)$.

73. Show that $\displaystyle\int_{t=0}^{\infty} \int_{u=0}^{t} \frac{e^{-t}\sin u}{u}\,du\,dt = \dfrac{\pi}{4}$.

MULTIPLICATION BY POWERS OF t

74. Prove that   (a) $\mathcal{L}\{t\cos at\} = \dfrac{s^2 - a^2}{(s^2 + a^2)^2}$

            (b) $\mathcal{L}\{t\sin at\} = \dfrac{2as}{(s^2 + a^2)^2}$

75. Find $\mathcal{L}\{t(3\sin 2t - 2\cos 2t)\}$.   *Ans.* $\dfrac{8 + 12s - 2s^2}{(s^2 + 4)^2}$

76. Show that $\mathcal{L}\{t^2\sin t\} = \dfrac{6s^2 - 2}{(s^2 + 1)^3}$.

77. Evaluate   (a) $\mathcal{L}\{t\cosh 3t\}$,   (b) $\mathcal{L}\{t\sinh 2t\}$.   *Ans.* (a) $(s^2 + 9)/(s^2 - 9)^2$,   (b) $4s/(s^2 - 4)^2$

78. Find   (a) $\mathcal{L}\{t^2\cos t\}$,   (b) $\mathcal{L}\{(t^2 - 3t + 2)\sin 3t\}$.

    Ans. (a) $(2s^3 - 6s)/(s^2 + 1)^3$,   (b) $\dfrac{6s^4 - 18s^3 + 126s^2 - 162s + 432}{(s^2 + 9)^3}$

79. Find $\mathcal{L}\{t^3\cos t\}$.   *Ans.* $\dfrac{6s^4 - 36s^2 + 6}{(s^2 + 1)^4}$

80. Show that $\displaystyle\int_0^\infty t\,e^{-3t}\sin t\,dt = \dfrac{3}{50}$.

DIVISION BY t

81. Show that $\mathcal{L}\left\{\dfrac{e^{-at} - e^{-bt}}{t}\right\} = \ln\left(\dfrac{s + b}{s + a}\right)$.

82. Show that $\mathcal{L}\left\{\dfrac{\cos at - \cos bt}{t}\right\} = \dfrac{1}{2}\ln\left(\dfrac{s^2 + b^2}{s^2 + a^2}\right)$.

83. Find $\mathcal{L}\left\{\dfrac{\sinh t}{t}\right\}$.   *Ans.* $\dfrac{1}{2}\ln\left(\dfrac{s + 1}{s - 1}\right)$

84. Show that $\displaystyle\int_0^\infty \dfrac{e^{-3t} - e^{-6t}}{t}\,dt = \ln 2$.

    [*Hint.* Use Problem 81.]

85. Evaluate $\displaystyle\int_0^\infty \dfrac{\cos 6t - \cos 4t}{t}\,dt$.   *Ans.* $\ln(2/3)$

86. Show that $\displaystyle\int_0^\infty \dfrac{\sin^2 t}{t^2}\,dt = \dfrac{\pi}{2}$.

PERIODIC FUNCTIONS

87. Find $\mathcal{L}\{F(t)\}$ where $F(t)$ is the periodic function shown graphically in Fig. 1-7 below.

    Ans. $\dfrac{1}{s}\tanh\dfrac{s}{2}$

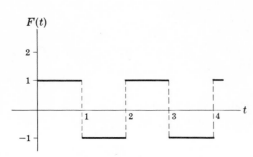

Fig. 1-7

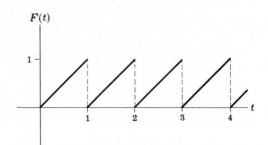

Fig. 1-8

88. Find $\mathcal{L}\{F(t)\}$ where $F(t)$ is the periodic function shown graphically in Fig. 1-8 above.

Ans. $\dfrac{1}{s^2} - \dfrac{e^{-s}}{s(1-e^{-s})}$

89. Let $F(t) = \begin{cases} 3t & 0 < t < 2 \\ 6 & 2 < t < 4 \end{cases}$ where $F(t)$ has period 4. (*a*) Graph $F(t)$. (*b*) Find $\mathcal{L}\{F(t)\}$.

Ans. (*b*) $\dfrac{3 - 3e^{-2s} - 6se^{-4s}}{s^2(1-e^{-4s})}$

90. If $F(t) = t^2$, $0 < t < 2$ and $F(t+2) = F(t)$, find $\mathcal{L}\{F(t)\}$.

Ans. $\dfrac{2 - 2e^{-2s} - 4se^{-2s} - 4s^2e^{-2s}}{s^3(1-e^{-2s})}$

91. Find $\mathcal{L}\{F(t)\}$ where $F(t) = \begin{cases} t & 0 < t < 1 \\ 0 & 1 < t < 2 \end{cases}$ and $F(t+2) = F(t)$ for $t > 0$.

Ans. $\dfrac{1 - e^{-s}(s+1)}{s^2(1-e^{-2s})}$

92. (*a*) Show that the function $F(t)$ whose graph is the triangular wave shown in Fig. 1-9 has the Laplace transform $\dfrac{1}{s^2} \tanh \dfrac{s}{2}$.

(*b*) How can the result in (*a*) be obtained from Problem 87? Explain.

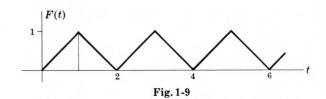

Fig. 1-9

INITIAL AND FINAL-VALUE THEOREMS

93. Verify the initial-value theorem for the functions (*a*) $3 - 2\cos t$, (*b*) $(2t+3)^2$, (*c*) $t + \sin 3t$.

94. Verify the final-value theorem for the functions (*a*) $1 + e^{-t}(\sin t + \cos t)$, (*b*) $t^3 e^{-2t}$.

95. Discuss the applicability of the final-value theorem for the function $\cos t$.

96. If $F(t) \sim ct^p$ as $t \to 0$ where $p > -1$, prove that $f(s) \sim c\,\Gamma(p+1)/s^{p+1}$ as $s \to \infty$.

97. If $F(t) \sim ct^p$ as $t \to \infty$ where $p > -1$, prove that $f(s) \sim c\,\Gamma(p+1)/s^{p+1}$ as $s \to \infty$.

THE GAMMA FUNCTION

98. Evaluate   (a) $\Gamma(5)$, (b) $\dfrac{\Gamma(3)\,\Gamma(4)}{\Gamma(7)}$, (c) $\Gamma(5/2)$, (d) $\dfrac{\Gamma(3/2)\,\Gamma(4)}{\Gamma(11/2)}$.

   Ans. (a) 24, (b) 1/60, (c) $3\sqrt{\pi}/4$, (d) 32/315

99. Find   (a) $\mathcal{L}\{t^{1/2} + t^{-1/2}\}$, (b) $\mathcal{L}\{t^{-1/3}\}$, (c) $\mathcal{L}\{(1 + \sqrt{t}\,)^4\}$.
   Ans. (a) $(2s+1)\sqrt{\pi}/2s^{3/2}$, (b) $\Gamma(2/3)/s^{2/3}$, (c) $(s^2 + 2\sqrt{\pi}\,s^{3/2} + 6s + 3\sqrt{\pi}\,s^{1/2} + 2)/s^3$

100. Find   (a) $\mathcal{L}\left\{\dfrac{e^{-2t}}{\sqrt{t}}\right\}$,   (b) $\mathcal{L}\{t^{7/2}\,e^{3t}\}$.

   Ans. (a) $\sqrt{\pi/(s+2)}$, (b) $105\sqrt{\pi}/16(s-3)^{9/2}$

BESSEL FUNCTIONS

101. Show that $\mathcal{L}\{e^{-at}\,J_0(bt)\} = \dfrac{1}{\sqrt{s^2 - 2as + a^2 + b^2}}$.

102. Show that $\mathcal{L}\{t\,J_0(at)\} = \dfrac{s}{(s^2 + a^2)^{3/2}}$.

103. Find   (a) $\mathcal{L}\{e^{-3t}\,J_0(4t)\}$, (b) $\mathcal{L}\{t\,J_0(2t)\}$.   *Ans.* (a) $\dfrac{1}{\sqrt{s^2 + 6s + 25}}$, (b) $\dfrac{s}{(s^2 + 4)^{3/2}}$

104. Prove that   (a) $J_0'(t) = -J_1(t)$, (b) $\dfrac{d}{dt}\{t^n\,J_n(t)\} = t^n\,J_{n-1}(t)$.

105. If $I_0(t) = J_0(it)$, show that $\mathcal{L}\{I_0(at)\} = \dfrac{1}{\sqrt{s^2 - a^2}}$, $a > 0$.

106. Find $\mathcal{L}\{t\,J_0(t)\,e^{-t}\}$.   *Ans.* $(s-1)/(s^2 - 2s + 2)^{3/2}$

107. Show that   (a) $\displaystyle\int_0^\infty J_0(t)\,dt = 1$, (b) $\displaystyle\int_0^\infty e^{-t}\,J_0(t)\,dt = \dfrac{\sqrt{2}}{2}$.

108. Find the Laplace transform of $\dfrac{d^2}{dt^2}\{e^{2t}\,J_0(2t)\}$.   *Ans.* $\dfrac{s^2}{\sqrt{s^2 - 4s + 8}} - s - 2$

109. Show that $\mathcal{L}\{t\,J_1(t)\} = \dfrac{1}{(s^2 + 1)^{3/2}}$.

110. Prove that $\mathcal{L}\{J_0(a\sqrt{t}\,)\} = \dfrac{e^{-a^2/4s}}{s}$.

111. Evaluate $\displaystyle\int_0^\infty t\,e^{-3t}\,J_0(4t)\,dt$.   *Ans.* 3/125

112. Prove that $\mathcal{L}\{J_n(t)\} = \dfrac{(\sqrt{s^2 + 1} - s)^n}{\sqrt{s^2 + 1}}$ and thus obtain $\mathcal{L}\{J_n(at)\}$.

THE SINE, COSINE AND EXPONENTIAL INTEGRALS

113. Evaluate   (a) $\mathcal{L}\{e^{2t}\,\mathrm{Si}\,(t)\}$, (b) $\mathcal{L}\{t\,\mathrm{Si}\,(t)\}$.

   Ans. (a) $\tan^{-1}(s-2)/(s-2)$, (b) $\dfrac{\tan^{-1}s}{s^2} - \dfrac{1}{s(s^2 + 1)}$

114. Show that $\mathcal{L}\{t^2 \operatorname{Ci}(t)\} = \dfrac{\ln(s^2+1)}{s^3} - \dfrac{3s^2+1}{s(s^2+1)^2}$.

115. Find (a) $\mathcal{L}\{e^{-3t}\operatorname{Ei}(t)\}$, (b) $\mathcal{L}\{t\operatorname{Ei}(t)\}$.

   Ans. (a) $\dfrac{\ln(s+4)}{s+3}$, (b) $\dfrac{\ln(s+1)}{s^2} - \dfrac{1}{s(s+1)}$

116. Find (a) $\mathcal{L}\{e^{-t}\operatorname{Si}(2t)\}$, (b) $\mathcal{L}\{te^{-2t}\operatorname{Ei}(3t)\}$.

   Ans. (a) $\dfrac{\tan^{-1}(s+1)/2}{s+1}$, (b) $\dfrac{1}{(s+2)^2}\ln\left(\dfrac{s+5}{3}\right) - \dfrac{1}{(s+2)(s+5)}$

THE ERROR FUNCTION

117. Evaluate (a) $\mathcal{L}\{e^{3t}\operatorname{erf}\sqrt{t}\}$, (b) $\mathcal{L}\{t\operatorname{erf}(2\sqrt{t})\}$.

   Ans. (a) $\dfrac{1}{(s-3)\sqrt{s-2}}$, (b) $\dfrac{3s+8}{s^2(s+4)^{3/2}}$

118. Show that $\mathcal{L}\{\operatorname{erfc}\sqrt{t}\} = \dfrac{1}{\sqrt{s+1}\,\{\sqrt{s+1}+1\}}$.

119. Find $\mathcal{L}\left\{\displaystyle\int_0^t \operatorname{erf}\sqrt{u}\,du\right\}$.   Ans. $1/s^2\sqrt{s+1}$

THE UNIT STEP FUNCTION, IMPULSE FUNCTIONS, AND THE DIRAC DELTA FUNCTION

120. (a) Show that in terms of Heaviside's unit step function, the function $F(t) = \begin{cases} e^{-t} & 0 < t < 3 \\ 0 & t > 3 \end{cases}$ can be written as $e^{-t}\{1 - \mathcal{U}(t-3)\}$. (b) Use $\mathcal{L}\{\mathcal{U}(t-a)\} = e^{-as}/s$ to find $\mathcal{L}\{F(t)\}$.

   Ans. (b) $\dfrac{1 - e^{-3(s+1)}}{s+1}$

121. Show that $F(t) = \begin{cases} F_1(t) & 0 < t < a \\ F_2(t) & t > a \end{cases}$ can be written as

$$F(t) = F_1(t) + \{F_2(t) - F_1(t)\}\,\mathcal{U}(t-a)$$

122. If $F(t) = F_1(t)$ for $0 < t < a_1$, $F_2(t)$ for $a_1 < t < a_2$, ..., $F_{n-1}(t)$ for $a_{n-2} < t < a_{n-1}$, and $F_n(t)$ for $t > a_{n-1}$, show that

$$F(t) = F_1(t) + \{F_2(t) - F_1(t)\}\,\mathcal{U}(t-a_1) + \cdots + \{F_n(t) - F_{n-1}(t)\,\mathcal{U}(t-a_{n-1})$$

123. Express in terms of Heaviside's unit step functions.

   (a) $F(t) = \begin{cases} t^2 & 0 < t < 2 \\ 4t & t > 2 \end{cases}$ (b) $F(t) = \begin{cases} \sin t & 0 < t < \pi \\ \sin 2t & \pi < t < 2\pi \\ \sin 3t & t > 2\pi \end{cases}$

   Ans. (a) $t^2 + (4t - t^2)\,\mathcal{U}(t-2)$, (b) $\sin t + (\sin 2t - \sin t)\,\mathcal{U}(t-\pi) + (\sin 3t - \sin 2t)\,\mathcal{U}(t-2\pi)$

124. Show that $\mathcal{L}\{t^2\,\mathcal{U}(t-2)\} = \dfrac{2e^{-2s}}{s^3}(1 + 2s + 2s^2)$, $s > 0$.

125. Evaluate   (a) $\int_{-\infty}^{\infty} \cos 2t \; \delta(t - \pi/3) \; dt$,   (b) $\int_{-\infty}^{\infty} e^{-t} \, \mathcal{U}(t - 2) \; dt$.   Ans. (a) $-1/2$, (b) e^{-2}

126. (a) If $\delta'(t - a)$ denotes the formal derivative of the delta function, show that

$$\int_{0}^{\infty} F(t) \; \delta'(t - a) \; dt \;\; = \;\; -F'(a)$$

(b) Evaluate $\int_{0}^{\infty} e^{-4t} \, \delta'(t - 2) \; dt$.
Ans. (b) $4e^{-8}$

127. Let $G_\epsilon(t) = 1/\epsilon$ for $0 \leqq t < \epsilon$, 0 for $\epsilon \leqq t < 2\epsilon$, $-1/\epsilon$ for $2\epsilon \leqq t < 3\epsilon$, and 0 for $t \geqq 3\epsilon$.

(a) Find $\mathcal{L}\{G_\epsilon(t)\}$.   (b) Find $\lim\limits_{\epsilon \to 0} \mathcal{L}\{G_\epsilon(t)\}$.   (c) Is $\lim\limits_{\epsilon \to 0} \mathcal{L}\{G_\epsilon(t)\} = \mathcal{L}\left\{ \lim\limits_{\epsilon \to 0} G_\epsilon(t) \right\}$?   (d) Discuss geometrically the results of (a) and (b).

128. Generalize Problem 127 by defining a function $G_\epsilon(t)$ in terms of ϵ and n so that $\lim\limits_{\epsilon \to 0} G_\epsilon(t) = s^n$ where $n = 2, 3, 4, \ldots$.

EVALUATION OF INTEGRALS

129. Evaluate $\int_{0}^{\infty} t^3 \, e^{-t} \sin t \; dt$.   Ans. 0

130. Show that $\int_{0}^{\infty} \frac{e^{-t} \sin t}{t} \; dt \;\; = \;\; \frac{\pi}{4}$.

131. Prove that   (a) $\int_{0}^{\infty} J_n(t) \; dt \;\; = \;\; 1$,   (b) $\int_{0}^{\infty} t \, J_n(t) \; dt \;\; = \;\; n$

132. Prove that $\int_{0}^{\infty} u \, e^{-u^2} \, J_0(au) \; du \;\; = \;\; \tfrac{1}{2} e^{-a^2/4}$.

133. Show that $\int_{0}^{\infty} t \, e^{-t} \, \mathrm{Ei}\,(t) \; dt \;\; = \;\; \ln 2 \, - \, \tfrac{1}{2}$.

134. Show that $\int_{0}^{\infty} u \, e^{-u^2} \, \mathrm{erf}\, u \; du \;\; = \;\; \frac{\sqrt{2}}{4}$.

MISCELLANEOUS PROBLEMS

135. If $F(t) \;=\; \begin{cases} \sin t & 0 < t < \pi \\ 0 & t > \pi \end{cases}$,   show that $\mathcal{L}\{F(t)\} = \dfrac{1 + e^{-\pi s}}{s^2 + 1}$.

136. If $F(t) \;=\; \begin{cases} \cos t & 0 < t < \pi \\ \sin t & t > \pi \end{cases}$,   find $\mathcal{L}\{F(t)\}$.   Ans. $\dfrac{s + (s - 1)e^{-\pi s}}{s^2 + 1}$

137. Show that $\mathcal{L}\{\sin^3 t\} \;\; = \;\; \dfrac{6}{(s^2 + 1)(s^2 + 9)}$.

138. Establish entries (a) 16, (b) 17, (c) 20, (d) 28 in the Table of Page 246.

139. Find   (a) $\mathcal{L}\{\sinh^3 2t\}$, (b) $\mathcal{L}\{t^3 \cos 4t\}$.

   Ans. (a) $\dfrac{48}{(s^2 - 36)(s^2 - 4)}$, (b) $\dfrac{6s^4 - 576s^2 + 1536}{(s^2 + 16)^4}$

140. If $F(t) = 5 \sin 3 (t - \pi/4)$ for $t > \pi/4$ and 0 for $t < \pi/4$, find $\mathcal{L}\{F(t)\}$.   *Ans.* $e^{-\pi s/4}/(s^2 + 9)$

141. If $\mathcal{L}\{t F(t)\} = \dfrac{1}{s(s^2 + 1)}$,   find $\mathcal{L}\{e^{-t} F(2t)\}$.

142. Find   (a) $\mathcal{L}\{\sinh 2t \cos 2t\}$, (b) $\mathcal{L}\{\cosh 2t \cos 2t\}$.
   Ans. (a) $2(s^2 - 8)/(s^4 + 64)$, (b) $s^3/(s^4 + 64)$

143. Let $F(t) = \begin{cases} t + n & 2n \leqq t < 2n + 1 \\ n - t & 2n + 1 \leqq t < 2n + 2 \end{cases}$, $n = 0, 1, 2, \ldots$. Show that

$$\mathcal{L}\{F(t)\} = \frac{1}{s^2} \sum_{n=0}^{\infty} \{(3ns + 1) e^{-2ns} - 2[(2n + 1)s + 1] e^{-(2n+1)s} + [(n + 2)s + 1] e^{-(2n+2)s}\}$$

144. (a) Show that $\mathcal{L}\{\sin^5 t\} = \dfrac{120}{(s^2 + 1)(s^2 + 9)(s^2 + 25)}$.

   (b) Using the results of part (a) and Problem 137, can you arrive at a corresponding result for $\mathcal{L}\{\sin^{2n-1} t\}$ where n is any positive integer? Justify your conjectures.

145. Suppose that $F(t)$ is unbounded as $t \to 0$. Prove that $\mathcal{L}\{F(t)\}$ exists if the following conditions are satisfied:

   (a) $F(t)$ is sectionally continuous in any interval $N_1 \leqq t \leqq N$ where $N_1 > 0$,

   (b) $\lim\limits_{t \to 0} t^n F(t) = 0$ for some constant n such that $0 < n < 1$,

   (c) $F(t)$ is of exponential order γ for $t > N$.

146. Show that   (a) $\mathcal{L}\{J_0(t) \sin t\} = \dfrac{1}{\sqrt{s} \sqrt[4]{s^2 + 4}} \sin \{\tfrac{1}{2} \tan^{-1} (2/s)\}$

   (b) $\mathcal{L}\{J_0(t) \cos t\} = \dfrac{1}{\sqrt{s} \sqrt[4]{s^2 + 4}} \cos \{\tfrac{1}{2} \tan^{-1} (2/s)\}$

147. Let $F(t) = \begin{cases} t G(t) & t > 1 \\ 0 & 0 < t < 1 \end{cases}$.   Prove that $\mathcal{L}\{F(t)\} = -\dfrac{d}{ds} [e^{-s} \mathcal{L}\{G(t + 1)\}]$.

148. If $\mathcal{L}\{F''(t)\} = \tan^{-1} (1/s)$, $F(0) = 2$ and $F'(0) = -1$, find $\mathcal{L}\{F(t)\}$.

   Ans. $\dfrac{2s - 1 + \tan^{-1} 1/s}{s^2}$

149. Prove that $\mathcal{L}\{e^{\alpha t} F(\beta t)\} = \dfrac{1}{\beta} f\left(\dfrac{s - \alpha}{\beta}\right)$ where α and β are constants and $\mathcal{L}\{F(t)\} = f(s)$.

150. Show that the Laplace transform of e^{e^t} does not exist, while the Laplace transform of e^{-e^t} does exist.

151. (a) Show that $\mathcal{L}\left\{\dfrac{\sin^2 t}{t}\right\} = \dfrac{1}{4}\ln\left(\dfrac{s^2+4}{s^2}\right).$

(b) Evaluate $\displaystyle\int_0^\infty \dfrac{e^{-t}\sin^2 t}{t}\,dt.$

Ans. (b) $\frac{1}{4}\ln 5$

152. (a) Find $\mathcal{L}\left\{\dfrac{1-J_0(t)}{t}\right\}.$ (b) Show that $\displaystyle\int_0^\infty \dfrac{e^{-t}\{1-J_0(t)\}}{t}\,dt = \ln\left(\dfrac{\sqrt{2}+1}{2}\right).$

153. Work Problems 37 and 38 by using Method 4 of Problem 36.

154. Suppose that $\mathcal{L}\{F(t)\}$ exists for $s = a$ where a is real. Prove that it also exists for all $s > a$.

155. Find the Laplace transform of the periodic function $F(t)$ shown graphically in Fig. 1-10.

Ans. $\dfrac{1 - e^{-as} - as\,e^{-as}}{s^2(1 - e^{-as})}\tan\theta_0$

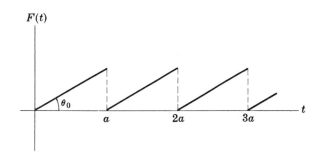

Fig. 1-10

156. Prove that

$$\mathcal{L}\{\sin t^2\} = \sum_{n=1}^\infty \dfrac{(-1)^{n-1}(4n-2)!}{(2n-1)!\,s^{2n+1}}$$

157. Show that $\mathcal{L}\{\sin^6 t\} = \dfrac{6!}{s(s^2+4)(s^2+16)(s^2+36)}$ and generalize [see Prob. 144].

158. Find $\mathcal{L}\{t\,e^{-2t}J_0(t\sqrt{2}\,)\}.$ Ans. $\dfrac{s+2}{(s^2+4s+6)^{3/2}}$

159. Find $\mathcal{L}\{t\,\mathcal{U}(t-1) + t^2\,\delta(t-1)\}.$ Ans. $e^{-s}(s^2+s+1)/s^2$

160. Find $\mathcal{L}\{\cos t\,\ln t\,\delta(t-\pi)\}.$ Ans. $-e^{-\pi s}\ln\pi$

161. Let $F(t)$ and $G(t)$ be sectionally continuous in every finite interval and of exponential order as $t \to \infty$. Prove that $\mathcal{L}\{F(t)\,G(t)\}$ exists.

162. The *Laguerre polynomials* $L_n(t)$ are defined by

$$L_n(t) = \dfrac{e^t}{n!}\dfrac{d^n}{dt^n}\{t^n\,e^{-t}\}\qquad n = 0, 1, 2, \ldots$$

(a) Find $L_0(t), L_1(t), \ldots, L_4(t).$ (b) Find $\mathcal{L}\{L_n(t)\}.$

163. (a) Let a, b, α, β and Λ be constants. Prove that

$$\mathcal{L}\{at^{-\alpha} + bt^{-\beta}\} = \Lambda\{as^{-\alpha} + bs^{-\beta}\}$$

if and only if $\alpha + \beta = 1$ and $\Lambda = \pm\sqrt{\pi}\csc\alpha\pi.$

(b) A function $F(t)$ is said to be its own Laplace transform if $\mathcal{L}\{F(t)\} = F(s)$. Can the function $F(t) = at^{-\alpha} + bt^{-\beta}$ be its own Laplace transform? Explain.

164. If $F(t)$ and $G(t)$ have Laplace transforms, is it true that $F(t)\,G(t)$ also has a Laplace transform? Justify your conclusion.

165. Use the result $\quad J_0(t) = \dfrac{1}{\pi} \displaystyle\int_0^\pi \cos(t\sin\theta)\,d\theta \quad$ to show that $\quad \mathcal{L}\{J_0(t)\} = \dfrac{1}{\sqrt{s^2+1}}.$

166. Prove that Leibnitz's rule can be applied in Problem 19, stating suitable restrictions on $F(t)$.

167. (a) Prove that $\quad \displaystyle\int_0^\infty e^{-st}\left(\dfrac{1-\cos t}{t^2}\right) dt \;=\; \dfrac{\pi}{2} - s\ln\left(\dfrac{s^2}{s^2+1}\right) + 2\tan^{-1} s.$

    (b) Prove that $\quad \displaystyle\int_0^\infty \dfrac{1-\cos t}{t^2}\,dt \;=\; \dfrac{\pi}{2}.$

168. Let $F(t) = 0$ if t is irrational and 1 if t is rational. (a) Prove that $\mathcal{L}\{F(t)\}$ exists and is equal to zero. (b) Is the function a null function? Explain.

169. Show that $\quad \displaystyle\int_0^\infty t^2\,J_0(t)\,dt \;=\; -1.$

170. Prove that if p is any positive integer,

$$\Gamma\left(-p-\tfrac{1}{2}\right) \;=\; (-1)^{p+1}\left(\dfrac{2}{1}\right)\left(\dfrac{2}{3}\right)\left(\dfrac{2}{5}\right)\cdots\left(\dfrac{2}{2p+1}\right)\sqrt{\pi}$$

171. Verify the entries (a) 55, (b) 61, (c) 64, (d) 65, (e) 81 in the Table of Appendix B, Pages 248 and 250.

172. Using the binomial theorem show that for $|x| < 1$,

$$(1+x)^{-1/2} \;=\; 1 - \dfrac{1}{2}x + \dfrac{1\cdot 3}{2\cdot 4}x^2 - \dfrac{1\cdot 3\cdot 5}{2\cdot 4\cdot 6}x^3 + \cdots$$

and thus verify the summation of the infinite series in Problems 34 and 39.

173. Use infinite series to find the Laplace transforms of (a) $\sin t$, (b) $\cos t$, (c) e^{at}, (d) $\cos\sqrt{t}$.

174. Prove that $\quad \mathcal{L}\{\text{erf}(t)\} \;=\; \dfrac{e^{s^2/4}}{s}\,\text{erfc}(s/2) \quad$ and thus find $\mathcal{L}\{\text{erf}(at)\}$.

175. (a) Find $\mathcal{L}\{\text{erf}\sqrt{t}\}$ by using the method of differential equations.
    (b) Find $\mathcal{L}\{\cos\sqrt{t}/\sqrt{t}\}$ using infinite series.

176. Show that (a) $\quad \displaystyle\int_0^\infty J_0(2\sqrt{tu})\cos u\,du \;=\; \sin t,$

    (b) $\quad \displaystyle\int_0^\infty J_0(2\sqrt{tu})\sin u\,du \;=\; \cos t.$

177. Show that $\displaystyle\int_0^\infty J_0(2\sqrt{tu})\, J_0(u)\, du \;=\; J_0(t).$

178. Use (a) infinite series, (b) differential equations to find $\mathcal{L}\{J_1(t)\}$. See Problem 35.

179. If $s > 0$ and $n > 1$, prove that

$$\mathcal{L}\left\{\frac{t^{n-1}}{1-e^{-t}}\right\} \;=\; \Gamma(n)\left\{\frac{1}{s^n} + \frac{1}{(s+1)^n} + \frac{1}{(s+2)^n} + \cdots\right\}$$

180. Prove that if $n > 1$,

$$\zeta(n) \;=\; \frac{1}{\Gamma(n)}\int_0^\infty \frac{t^{n-1}}{e^t - 1}\, dt \;=\; \frac{1}{1^n} + \frac{1}{2^n} + \frac{1}{3^n} + \cdots$$

The function $\zeta(n)$ is called the *Riemann zeta function*.

181. If $f(s) = \mathcal{L}\{F(t)\}$, show that

$$\mathcal{L}\left\{\int_0^\infty \frac{t^u\, F(u)}{\Gamma(u+1)}\, du\right\} \;=\; \frac{f(\ln s)}{s\,\ln s}$$

182. If $L_n(t)$, $n = 0, 1, 2, \ldots$, are the Laguerre polynomials [see Problem 162], prove that

$$\sum_{n=0}^\infty \frac{L_n(t)}{n!} \;=\; e\, J_0(2\sqrt{t})$$

183. Let $J(a, t) = \displaystyle\int_0^\infty e^{-u^2 t}\cos au\, du.$ (a) Show that $\dfrac{\partial J}{\partial a} = -\dfrac{a}{2t} J$ where $J(0, t) = \sqrt{\pi}\,/2\sqrt{t}.$ (b) By solving the differential equation in (a) show that

$$J(a, t) \;=\; \int_0^\infty e^{-u^2 t}\cos au\, du \;=\; \frac{\sqrt{\pi}}{2\sqrt{t}}\, e^{-a^2/4t}$$

184. Use Problem 183 to find $\mathcal{L}\left\{\dfrac{\cos\sqrt{t}}{\sqrt{t}}\right\}$ [see Problem 49, Page 29].

185. Prove that $\displaystyle\int_0^\infty \frac{e^{-\sqrt{2}\,t}\sinh t \sin t}{t}\, dt \;=\; \frac{\pi}{8}.$

Chapter 2

The Inverse Laplace Transform

DEFINITION OF INVERSE LAPLACE TRANSFORM

If the Laplace transform of a function $F(t)$ is $f(s)$, i.e. if $\mathcal{L}\{F(t)\} = f(s)$, then $F(t)$ is called an *inverse Laplace transform* of $f(s)$ and we write symbolically $F(t) = \mathcal{L}^{-1}\{f(s)\}$ where $\mathcal{L}^{-1}$ is called the *inverse Laplace transformation operator*.

Example. Since $\mathcal{L}\{e^{-3t}\} = \dfrac{1}{s+3}$ we can write

$$\mathcal{L}^{-1}\left\{\frac{1}{s+3}\right\} = e^{-3t}$$

UNIQUENESS OF INVERSE LAPLACE TRANSFORMS. LERCH'S THEOREM

Since the Laplace transform of a null function $\mathcal{N}(t)$ is zero [see Chapter 1, Page 9], it is clear that if $\mathcal{L}\{F(t)\} = f(s)$ then also $\mathcal{L}\{F(t) + \mathcal{N}(t)\} = f(s)$. From this it follows that we can have two different functions with the same Laplace transform.

Example. The two different functions $F_1(t) = e^{-3t}$ and $F_2(t) = \begin{cases} 0 & t = 1 \\ e^{-3t} & \text{otherwise} \end{cases}$ have the same Laplace transform, i.e. $1/(s+3)$.

If we allow null functions, we see that the inverse Laplace transform is not unique. It is unique, however, if we disallow null functions [which do not in general arise in cases of physical interest]. This result is indicated in

Theorem 2-1. *Lerch's theorem.* If we restrict ourselves to functions $F(t)$ which are sectionally continuous in every finite interval $0 \leqq t \leqq N$ and of exponential order for $t > N$, then the inverse Laplace transform of $f(s)$, i.e. $\mathcal{L}^{-1}\{f(s)\} = F(t)$, is unique. We shall always assume such uniqueness unless otherwise stated.

SOME INVERSE LAPLACE TRANSFORMS

The following results follow at once from corresponding entries on **Page 1.**

Table of Inverse Laplace Transforms

	$f(s)$	$\mathcal{L}^{-1}\{f(s)\} = F(t)$
1.	$\dfrac{1}{s}$	1
2.	$\dfrac{1}{s^2}$	t
3.	$\dfrac{1}{s^{n+1}}$ $n = 0, 1, 2, \ldots$	$\dfrac{t^n}{n!}$
4.	$\dfrac{1}{s-a}$	e^{at}
5.	$\dfrac{1}{s^2+a^2}$	$\dfrac{\sin at}{a}$
6.	$\dfrac{s}{s^2+a^2}$	$\cos at$
7.	$\dfrac{1}{s^2-a^2}$	$\dfrac{\sinh at}{a}$
8.	$\dfrac{s}{s^2-a^2}$	$\cosh at$

SOME IMPORTANT PROPERTIES OF INVERSE LAPLACE TRANSFORMS

In the following list we have indicated various important properties of inverse Laplace transforms. Note the analogy of Properties 1-8 with the corresponding properties on Pages 3-5.

1. **Linearity property.**

   Theorem 2-2.   If c_1 and c_2 are any constants while $f_1(s)$ and $f_2(s)$ are the Laplace transforms of $F_1(t)$ and $F_2(t)$ respectively, then

$$\mathcal{L}^{-1}\{c_1 f_1(s) + c_2 f_2(s)\} = c_1 \mathcal{L}^{-1}\{f_1(s)\} + c_2 \mathcal{L}^{-1}\{f_2(s)\} \qquad (1)$$
$$= c_1 F_1(t) + c_2 F_2(t)$$

The result is easily extended to more than two functions.

   Example.

$$\mathcal{L}^{-1}\left\{\frac{4}{s-2} - \frac{3s}{s^2+16} + \frac{5}{s^2+4}\right\} = 4\,\mathcal{L}^{-1}\left\{\frac{1}{s-2}\right\} - 3\,\mathcal{L}^{-1}\left\{\frac{s}{s^2+16}\right\}$$
$$+ 5\,\mathcal{L}^{-1}\left\{\frac{1}{s^2+4}\right\}$$
$$= 4e^{2t} - 3\cos 4t + \frac{5}{2}\sin 2t$$

Because of this property we can say that $\mathcal{L}^{-1}$ is a *linear operator* or that it has the *linearity property*.

2. **First translation or shifting property.**

   Theorem 2-3.   If $\mathcal{L}^{-1}\{f(s)\} = F(t)$,   then

$$\mathcal{L}^{-1}\{f(s-a)\} = e^{at} F(t) \qquad (2)$$

Example. Since $\mathcal{L}^{-1}\left\{\dfrac{1}{s^2+4}\right\} = \dfrac{1}{2}\sin 2t$, we have

$$\mathcal{L}^{-1}\left\{\frac{1}{s^2-2s+5}\right\} = \mathcal{L}^{-1}\left\{\frac{1}{(s-1)^2+4}\right\} = \frac{1}{2}e^t\sin 2t$$

3. Second translation or shifting property.

     Theorem 2-4.   If $\mathcal{L}^{-1}\{f(s)\} = F(t)$,   then

$$\mathcal{L}^{-1}\{e^{-as}f(s)\} = \begin{cases} F(t-a) & t > a \\ 0 & t < a \end{cases} \tag{3}$$

     Example. Since $\mathcal{L}^{-1}\left\{\dfrac{1}{s^2+1}\right\} = \sin t$,   we have

$$\mathcal{L}^{-1}\left\{\frac{e^{-\pi s/3}}{s^2+1}\right\} = \begin{cases} \sin(t-\pi/3) & \text{if } t > \pi/3 \\ 0 & \text{if } t < \pi/3 \end{cases}$$

4. Change of scale property.

     Theorem 2-5.   If $\mathcal{L}^{-1}\{f(s)\} = F(t)$,   then

$$\mathcal{L}^{-1}\{f(ks)\} = \frac{1}{k}F\left(\frac{t}{k}\right) \tag{4}$$

     Example. Since $\mathcal{L}^{-1}\left\{\dfrac{s}{s^2+16}\right\} = \cos 4t$,   we have

$$\mathcal{L}^{-1}\left\{\frac{2s}{(2s)^2+16}\right\} = \frac{1}{2}\cos\frac{4t}{2} = \frac{1}{2}\cos 2t$$

as is verified directly.

5. Inverse Laplace transform of derivatives.

     Theorem 2-6.   If $\mathcal{L}^{-1}\{f(s)\} = F(t)$,   then

$$\mathcal{L}^{-1}\{f^{(n)}(s)\} = \mathcal{L}^{-1}\left\{\frac{d^n}{ds^n}f(s)\right\} = (-1)^n\, t^n\, F(t) \tag{5}$$

     Example. Since $\mathcal{L}^{-1}\left\{\dfrac{1}{s^2+1}\right\} = \sin t$ and $\dfrac{d}{ds}\left(\dfrac{1}{s^2+1}\right) = \dfrac{-2s}{(s^2+1)^2}$,   we have

$$\mathcal{L}^{-1}\left\{\frac{-2s}{(s^2+1)^2}\right\} = -t\sin t \qquad \text{or} \qquad \mathcal{L}^{-1}\left\{\frac{s}{(s^2+1)^2}\right\} = \frac{1}{2}t\sin t$$

6. Inverse Laplace transform of integrals.

     Theorem 2-7.   If $\mathcal{L}^{-1}\{f(s)\} = F(t)$,   then

$$\mathcal{L}^{-1}\left\{\int_s^\infty f(u)\, du\right\} = \frac{F(t)}{t} \tag{6}$$

     Example. Since $\mathcal{L}^{-1}\left\{\dfrac{1}{s(s+1)}\right\} = \mathcal{L}^{-1}\left\{\dfrac{1}{s} - \dfrac{1}{s+1}\right\} = 1 - e^{-t}$,   we have

$$\mathcal{L}^{-1}\left\{\int_s^\infty \left(\frac{1}{u} - \frac{1}{u+1}\right) du\right\} = \mathcal{L}^{-1}\left\{\ln\left(1+\frac{1}{s}\right)\right\} = \frac{1-e^{-t}}{t}$$

7. Multiplication by s^n.

Theorem 2-8. If $\mathcal{L}^{-1}\{f(s)\} = F(t)$ and $F(0) = 0$, then

$$\mathcal{L}^{-1}\{s\,f(s)\} = F'(t) \tag{7}$$

Thus multiplication by s has the effect of *differentiating* $F(t)$.

If $F(0) \neq 0$, then

$$\mathcal{L}^{-1}\{s\,f(s) - F(0)\} = F'(t) \tag{8}$$

or
$$\mathcal{L}^{-1}\{s\,f(s)\} = F'(t) + F(0)\,\delta(t) \tag{9}$$

where $\delta(t)$ is the Dirac delta function or unit impulse function [see Page 9].

Example. Since $\mathcal{L}^{-1}\left\{\dfrac{1}{s^2+1}\right\} = \sin t$ and $\sin 0 = 0$, then

$$\mathcal{L}^{-1}\left\{\frac{s}{s^2+1}\right\} = \frac{d}{dt}(\sin t) = \cos t$$

Generalizations to $\mathcal{L}^{-1}\{s^n f(s)\}$, $n = 2, 3, \ldots$, are possible.

8. Division by s.

Theorem 2-9. If $\mathcal{L}^{-1}\{f(s)\} = F(t)$, then

$$\mathcal{L}^{-1}\left\{\frac{f(s)}{s}\right\} = \int_0^t F(u)\,du \tag{10}$$

Thus division by s (or multiplication by $1/s$) has the effect of *integrating* $F(t)$ from 0 to t.

Example. Since $\mathcal{L}^{-1}\left\{\dfrac{1}{s^2+4}\right\} = \dfrac{1}{2}\sin 2t$, we have

$$\mathcal{L}^{-1}\left\{\frac{1}{s(s^2+4)}\right\} = \int_0^t \frac{1}{2}\sin 2u\,du = \frac{1}{4}(1 - \cos 2t)$$

Generalizations to $\mathcal{L}^{-1}\{f(s)/s^n\}$, $n = 2, 3, \ldots$, are possible [see Problem 70].

9. The Convolution property.

Theorem 2-10. If $\mathcal{L}^{-1}\{f(s)\} = F(t)$ and $\mathcal{L}^{-1}\{g(s)\} = G(t)$, then

$$\mathcal{L}^{-1}\{f(s)\,g(s)\} = \int_0^t F(u)\,G(t-u)\,du = F * G \tag{11}$$

We call $F * G$ the *convolution* or *faltung* of F and G, and the theorem is called the *convolution theorem* or *property*.

From Problem 21, we see that $F * G = G * F$.

Example. Since $\mathcal{L}^{-1}\left\{\dfrac{1}{s-1}\right\} = e^t$ and $\mathcal{L}^{-1}\left\{\dfrac{1}{s-2}\right\} = e^{2t}$, we have

$$\mathcal{L}^{-1}\left\{\frac{1}{(s-1)(s-2)}\right\} = \int_0^t e^u e^{2(t-u)}\,du = e^{2t} - e^t$$

METHODS OF FINDING INVERSE LAPLACE TRANSFORMS

Various means are available for determining inverse Laplace transforms, as indicated in the following list. Compare with Page 6.

1. **Partial fractions method.** Any rational function $P(s)/Q(s)$ where $P(s)$ and $Q(s)$ are polynomials, with the degree of $P(s)$ less than that of $Q(s)$, can be written as the sum of rational functions [called *partial fractions*] having the form $\dfrac{A}{(as+b)^r}$, $\dfrac{As+B}{(as^2+bs+c)^r}$ where $r = 1, 2, 3, \ldots$. By finding the inverse Laplace transform of each of the partial fractions, we can find $\mathcal{L}^{-1}\{P(s)/Q(s)\}$.

> **Example 1.** $\dfrac{2s-5}{(3s-4)(2s+1)^3} = \dfrac{A}{3s-4} + \dfrac{B}{(2s+1)^3} + \dfrac{C}{(2s+1)^2} + \dfrac{D}{2s+1}$

> **Example 2.** $\dfrac{3s^2-4s+2}{(s^2+2s+4)^2(s-5)} = \dfrac{As+B}{(s^2+2s+4)^2} + \dfrac{Cs+D}{s^2+2s+4} + \dfrac{E}{s-5}$

The constants A, B, C, etc., can be found by clearing of fractions and equating of like powers of s on both sides of the resulting equation or by using special methods [see Problems 24-28]. A method related to this uses the *Heaviside expansion formula* [see below].

2. **Series methods.** If $f(s)$ has a series expansion in inverse powers of s given by

$$f(s) = \frac{a_0}{s} + \frac{a_1}{s^2} + \frac{a_2}{s^3} + \frac{a_3}{s^4} + \cdots \tag{12}$$

then under suitable conditions we can invert term by term to obtain

$$F(t) = a_0 + a_1 t + \frac{a_2 t^2}{2!} + \frac{a_3 t^3}{3!} + \cdots \tag{13}$$

See Problem 40. Series expansions other than those of the form (*12*) can sometimes be used. See Problem 41.

3. **Method of differential equations.** See Problem 41.

4. **Differentiation with respect to a parameter.** See Problems 13 and 38.

5. **Miscellaneous methods using the above theorems.**

6. **Use of Tables** (see Appendix B).

7. **The Complex Inversion formula.** This formula, which supplies a powerful direct method for finding inverse Laplace transforms, uses complex variable theory and is considered in Chapter 6.

THE HEAVISIDE EXPANSION FORMULA

Let $P(s)$ and $Q(s)$ be polynomials where $P(s)$ has degree less than that of $Q(s)$. Suppose that $Q(s)$ has n distinct zeros α_k, $k = 1, 2, 3, \ldots, n$. Then

$$\mathcal{L}^{-1}\left\{\frac{P(s)}{Q(s)}\right\} = \sum_{k=1}^{n} \frac{P(\alpha_k)}{Q'(\alpha_k)} e^{\alpha_k t} \tag{14}$$

This is often called *Heaviside's expansion theorem* or *formula*. See Problems 29-31.

The formula can be extended to other cases [see Problems 105 and 111].

THE BETA FUNCTION

If $m > 0$, $n > 0$, we define the *beta function* as

$$B(m, n) = \int_0^1 u^{m-1} (1-u)^{n-1} \, du \qquad (15)$$

We can show the following properties [see Problems 32 and 33]:

1. $B(m, n) = \dfrac{\Gamma(m) \, \Gamma(n)}{\Gamma(m+n)}$

2. $\displaystyle\int_0^{\pi/2} \sin^{2m-1} \theta \, \cos^{2n-1} \theta \, d\theta = \dfrac{1}{2} B(m, n) = \dfrac{\Gamma(m) \, \Gamma(n)}{2 \, \Gamma(m+n)}$

EVALUATION OF INTEGRALS

The Laplace transformation is often useful in evaluating definite integrals. See, for example, Problems 35-37.

Solved Problems

INVERSE LAPLACE TRANSFORMS

1. **Prove that** (a) $\mathcal{L}^{-1}\left\{\dfrac{1}{s-a}\right\} = e^{at}$, (b) $\mathcal{L}^{-1}\left\{\dfrac{1}{s^{n+1}}\right\} = \dfrac{t^n}{n!}$, $n = 0, 1, 2, 3, \ldots$, where $0! = 1$,

(c) $\mathcal{L}^{-1}\left\{\dfrac{1}{s^2+a^2}\right\} = \dfrac{\sin at}{a}$, (d) $\mathcal{L}^{-1}\left\{\dfrac{s}{s^2+a^2}\right\} = \cos at$, (e) $\mathcal{L}^{-1}\left\{\dfrac{1}{s^2-a^2}\right\} = \dfrac{\sinh at}{a}$,

(f) $\mathcal{L}^{-1}\left\{\dfrac{s}{s^2-a^2}\right\} = \cosh at$.

(a) $\mathcal{L}\{e^{at}\} = \dfrac{1}{s-a}$. Then $\mathcal{L}^{-1}\left\{\dfrac{1}{s-a}\right\} = e^{at}$.

(b) $\mathcal{L}\left\{\dfrac{t^n}{n!}\right\} = \dfrac{1}{n!}\mathcal{L}\{t^n\} = \dfrac{1}{n!}\left(\dfrac{n!}{s^{n+1}}\right) = \dfrac{1}{s^{n+1}}$. Then $\mathcal{L}^{-1}\left\{\dfrac{1}{s^{n+1}}\right\} = \dfrac{t^n}{n!}$ for $n = 0, 1, 2, 3, \ldots$.

(c) $\mathcal{L}\left\{\dfrac{\sin at}{a}\right\} = \dfrac{1}{a}\mathcal{L}\{\sin at\} = \dfrac{1}{a} \cdot \dfrac{a}{s^2+a^2} = \dfrac{1}{s^2+a^2}$. Then $\mathcal{L}^{-1}\left\{\dfrac{1}{s^2+a^2}\right\} = \dfrac{\sin at}{a}$.

(d) $\mathcal{L}\{\cos at\} = \dfrac{s}{s^2+a^2}$. Then $\mathcal{L}^{-1}\left\{\dfrac{s}{s^2+a^2}\right\} = \cos at$.

(e) $\mathcal{L}\left\{\dfrac{\sinh at}{a}\right\} = \dfrac{1}{a}\mathcal{L}\left\{\sinh at\right\} = \dfrac{1}{a}\cdot\dfrac{a}{s^2-a^2} = \dfrac{1}{s^2-a^2}.$ Then $\mathcal{L}^{-1}\left\{\dfrac{1}{s^2-a^2}\right\} = \dfrac{\sinh at}{a}.$

(f) $\mathcal{L}\left\{\cosh at\right\} = \dfrac{s}{s^2-a^2}.$ Then $\mathcal{L}^{-1}\left\{\dfrac{s}{s^2-a^2}\right\} = \cosh at.$

2. Prove that $\mathcal{L}^{-1}\left\{\dfrac{1}{s^{n+1}}\right\} = \dfrac{t^n}{\Gamma(n+1)}$ for $n > -1.$

$$\mathcal{L}\left\{\dfrac{t^n}{\Gamma(n+1)}\right\} = \dfrac{1}{\Gamma(n+1)}\cdot\mathcal{L}\left\{t^n\right\} = \dfrac{1}{\Gamma(n+1)}\cdot\dfrac{\Gamma(n+1)}{s^{n+1}} = \dfrac{1}{s^{n+1}}, \qquad n > -1$$

by Problem 31, Page 22.

Then $\mathcal{L}^{-1}\left\{\dfrac{1}{s^{n+1}}\right\} = \dfrac{t^n}{\Gamma(n+1)},$ $n > -1.$ Note that if $n = 0, 1, 2, 3, \ldots,$ then $\Gamma(n+1) = n!$ and the result is equivalent to that of Problem 1(b).

3. Find each of the following inverse Laplace transforms.

(a) $\mathcal{L}^{-1}\left\{\dfrac{1}{s^2+9}\right\}$ (c) $\mathcal{L}^{-1}\left\{\dfrac{1}{s^4}\right\}$ (e) $\mathcal{L}^{-1}\left\{\dfrac{s}{s^2-16}\right\}$

(b) $\mathcal{L}^{-1}\left\{\dfrac{4}{s-2}\right\}$ (d) $\mathcal{L}^{-1}\left\{\dfrac{s}{s^2+2}\right\}$ (f) $\mathcal{L}^{-1}\left\{\dfrac{1}{s^2-3}\right\}$ (g) $\mathcal{L}^{-1}\left\{\dfrac{1}{s^{3/2}}\right\}$

(a) $\mathcal{L}^{-1}\left\{\dfrac{1}{s^2+9}\right\} = \dfrac{\sin 3t}{3}$ [Problem 1(c)]

(b) $\mathcal{L}^{-1}\left\{\dfrac{4}{s-2}\right\} = 4e^{2t}$ [Problem 1(a)]

(c) $\mathcal{L}^{-1}\left\{\dfrac{1}{s^4}\right\} = \dfrac{t^3}{3!} = \dfrac{t^3}{6}$ [Problems 1(b) or 2]

(d) $\mathcal{L}^{-1}\left\{\dfrac{s}{s^2+2}\right\} = \cos\sqrt{2}\,t$ [Problem 1(d)]

(e) $\mathcal{L}^{-1}\left\{\dfrac{6s}{s^2-16}\right\} = 6\cosh 4t$ [Problem 1(f)]

(f) $\mathcal{L}^{-1}\left\{\dfrac{1}{s^2-3}\right\} = \dfrac{\sinh\sqrt{3}\,t}{\sqrt{3}}$ [Problem 1(e)]

(g) $\mathcal{L}^{-1}\left\{\dfrac{1}{s^{3/2}}\right\} = \dfrac{t^{1/2}}{\Gamma(3/2)} = \dfrac{t^{1/2}}{\frac{1}{2}\Gamma(\frac{1}{2})} = \dfrac{2t^{1/2}}{\sqrt{\pi}} = 2\sqrt{\dfrac{t}{\pi}}$ [Problem 2]

LINEARITY, TRANSLATION AND CHANGE OF SCALE PROPERTIES

4. Prove the *linearity property* for the inverse Laplace transformation [*Theorem 2-2, Page 43*].

By Problem 5, Page 12, we have

$$\mathcal{L}\left\{c_1 F_1(t) + c_2 F_2(t)\right\} = c_1\mathcal{L}\left\{F_1(t)\right\} + c_2\mathcal{L}\left\{F_2(t)\right\} = c_1 f_1(s) + c_2 f_2(s)$$

Then
$$\mathcal{L}^{-1}\{c_1 f_1(s) + c_2 f_2(s)\} = c_1 F_1(t) + c_2 F_2(t)$$
$$= c_1 \mathcal{L}^{-1}\{f_1(s)\} + c_2 \mathcal{L}^{-1}\{f_2(s)\}$$

The result is easily generalized [see Problem 52].

5. Find (a) $\mathcal{L}^{-1}\left\{\dfrac{5s+4}{s^3} - \dfrac{2s-18}{s^2+9} + \dfrac{24-30\sqrt{s}}{s^4}\right\}$

   (b) $\mathcal{L}^{-1}\left\{\dfrac{6}{2s-3} - \dfrac{3+4s}{9s^2-16} + \dfrac{8-6s}{16s^2+9}\right\}.$

(a) $\mathcal{L}^{-1}\left\{\dfrac{5s+4}{s^3} - \dfrac{2s-18}{s^2+9} + \dfrac{24-30\sqrt{s}}{s^4}\right\}$

$\quad = \mathcal{L}^{-1}\left\{\dfrac{5}{s^2} + \dfrac{4}{s^3} - \dfrac{2s}{s^2+9} + \dfrac{18}{s^2+9} + \dfrac{24}{s^4} - \dfrac{30}{s^{7/2}}\right\}$

$\quad = 5t + 4(t^2/2!) - 2\cos 3t + 18(\tfrac{1}{3}\sin 3t) + 24(t^3/3!) - 30\{t^{5/2}/\Gamma(7/2)\}$

$\quad = 5t + 2t^2 - 2\cos 3t + 6\sin 3t + 4t^3 - 16t^{5/2}/\sqrt{\pi}$

since $\Gamma(7/2) = \tfrac{5}{2} \cdot \tfrac{3}{2} \cdot \tfrac{1}{2} \Gamma(\tfrac{1}{2}) = \tfrac{15}{8}\sqrt{\pi}.$

(b) $\mathcal{L}^{-1}\left\{\dfrac{6}{2s-3} - \dfrac{3+4s}{9s^2-16} + \dfrac{8-6s}{16s^2+9}\right\}$

$\quad = \mathcal{L}^{-1}\left\{\dfrac{3}{s-3/2} - \dfrac{1}{3}\left(\dfrac{1}{s^2-16/9}\right) - \dfrac{4}{9}\left(\dfrac{s}{s^2-16/9}\right) + \dfrac{1}{2}\left(\dfrac{1}{s^2+9/16}\right) - \dfrac{3}{8}\left(\dfrac{s}{s^2+9/16}\right)\right\}$

$\quad = 3e^{3t/2} - \tfrac{1}{4}\sinh 4t/3 - \tfrac{4}{9}\cosh 4t/3 + \tfrac{2}{3}\sin 3t/4 - \tfrac{3}{8}\cos 3t/4$

6. Prove the *first translation or shifting property*: If $\mathcal{L}^{-1}\{f(s)\} = F(t)$, then
$$\mathcal{L}^{-1}\{f(s-a)\} = e^{at} F(t)$$

By Problem 7, Page 13, we have $\mathcal{L}\{e^{at} F(t)\} = f(s-a)$.   Then
$$\mathcal{L}^{-1}\{f(s-a)\} = e^{at} F(t)$$

Another method.   Since $f(s) = \displaystyle\int_0^\infty e^{-st} F(t)\, dt$, we have

$$f(s-a) = \int_0^\infty e^{-(s-a)t} F(t)\, dt = \int_0^\infty e^{-st}\{e^{at} F(t)\}\, dt = \mathcal{L}\{e^{at} F(t)\}$$

Then
$$\mathcal{L}^{-1}\{f(s-a)\} = e^{at} F(t)$$

7. Find each of the following:

(a) $\mathcal{L}^{-1}\left\{\dfrac{6s-4}{s^2-4s+20}\right\}$ (c) $\mathcal{L}^{-1}\left\{\dfrac{3s+7}{s^2-2s-3}\right\}$

(b) $\mathcal{L}^{-1}\left\{\dfrac{4s+12}{s^2+8s+16}\right\}$ (d) $\mathcal{L}^{-1}\left\{\dfrac{1}{\sqrt{2s+3}}\right\}$

(a) $\mathcal{L}^{-1}\left\{\dfrac{6s-4}{s^2-4s+20}\right\} = \mathcal{L}^{-1}\left\{\dfrac{6s-4}{(s-2)^2+16}\right\} = \mathcal{L}^{-1}\left\{\dfrac{6(s-2)+8}{(s-2)^2+16}\right\}$

$\quad = 6\mathcal{L}^{-1}\left\{\dfrac{s-2}{(s-2)^2+16}\right\} + 2\mathcal{L}^{-1}\left\{\dfrac{4}{(s-2)^2+16}\right\}$

$\quad = 6e^{2t}\cos 4t + 2e^{2t}\sin 4t = 2e^{2t}(3\cos 4t + \sin 4t)$

(b)

$$\mathcal{L}^{-1}\left\{\frac{4s+12}{s^2+8s+16}\right\} = \mathcal{L}^{-1}\left\{\frac{4s+12}{(s+4)^2}\right\} = \mathcal{L}^{-1}\left\{\frac{4(s+4)-4}{(s+4)^2}\right\}$$

$$= 4\,\mathcal{L}^{-1}\left\{\frac{1}{s+4}\right\} - 4\,\mathcal{L}^{-1}\left\{\frac{1}{(s+4)^2}\right\}$$

$$= 4\,e^{-4t} - 4t\,e^{-4t} = 4\,e^{-4t}(1-t)$$

(c)

$$\mathcal{L}^{-1}\left\{\frac{3s+7}{s^2-2s-3}\right\} = \mathcal{L}^{-1}\left\{\frac{3s+7}{(s-1)^2-4}\right\} = \mathcal{L}^{-1}\left\{\frac{3(s-1)+10}{(s-1)^2-4}\right\}$$

$$= 3\,\mathcal{L}^{-1}\left\{\frac{s-1}{(s-1)^2-4}\right\} + 5\,\mathcal{L}^{-1}\left\{\frac{2}{(s-1)^2-4}\right\}$$

$$= 3\,e^t\cosh 2t + 5\,e^t\sinh 2t = e^t(3\cosh 2t + 5\sinh 2t)$$

$$= 4\,e^{3t} - e^{-t}$$

For another method, see Problem 24.

(d)

$$\mathcal{L}^{-1}\left\{\frac{1}{\sqrt{2s+3}}\right\} = \frac{1}{\sqrt{2}}\,\mathcal{L}^{-1}\left\{\frac{1}{(s+3/2)^{1/2}}\right\}$$

$$= \frac{1}{\sqrt{2}}\,e^{-3t/2}\,\frac{t^{-1/2}}{\Gamma(1/2)} = \frac{1}{\sqrt{2\pi}}\,t^{-1/2}\,e^{-3t/2}$$

8. Prove the *second translation or shifting property*:

If $\mathcal{L}^{-1}\{f(s)\} = F(t)$,   then $\mathcal{L}^{-1}\{e^{-as}f(s)\} = G(t)$ where

$$G(t) = \begin{cases} F(t-a) & t > a \\ 0 & t < a \end{cases}$$

Method 1.   By Problem 9, Page 14, we have $\mathcal{L}\{G(t)\} = e^{-as}f(s)$.   Then

$$\mathcal{L}^{-1}\{e^{-as}f(s)\} = G(t)$$

Method 2.   Since $f(s) = \displaystyle\int_0^\infty e^{-st}F(t)\,dt$,   we have

$$e^{-as}f(s) = \int_0^\infty e^{-as}e^{-st}F(t)\,dt = \int_0^\infty e^{-s(t+a)}F(t)\,dt$$

$$= \int_a^\infty e^{-su}F(u-a)\,du \qquad [\text{letting } t+a=u]$$

$$= \int_0^a e^{-st}(0)\,dt + \int_a^\infty e^{-st}F(t-a)\,dt$$

$$= \int_0^\infty e^{-st}G(t)\,dt$$

from which the required result follows.

It should be noted that we can write $G(t)$ in terms of the Heaviside unit step function as $F(t-a)\,\mathcal{U}(t-a)$.

9. Find each of the following:

$$(a)\ \mathcal{L}^{-1}\left\{\frac{e^{-5s}}{(s-2)^4}\right\},\quad (b)\ \mathcal{L}^{-1}\left\{\frac{se^{-4\pi s/5}}{s^2+25}\right\},\quad (c)\ \mathcal{L}^{-1}\left\{\frac{(s+1)e^{-\pi s}}{s^2+s+1}\right\},\quad (d)\ \mathcal{L}^{-1}\left\{\frac{e^{4-3s}}{(s+4)^{5/2}}\right\}.$$

(a) Since $\mathcal{L}^{-1}\left\{\dfrac{1}{(s-2)^4}\right\} = e^{2t}\mathcal{L}^{-1}\left\{\dfrac{1}{s^4}\right\} = \dfrac{t^3 e^{2t}}{3!} = \dfrac{1}{6}t^3 e^{2t}$, we have by Problem 8,

$$\mathcal{L}^{-1}\left\{\frac{e^{-5s}}{(s-2)^4}\right\} = \begin{cases} \frac{1}{6}(t-5)^3 e^{2(t-5)} & t > 5 \\ 0 & t < 5 \end{cases}$$

$$= \tfrac{1}{6}(t-5)^3 e^{2(t-5)}\, \mathcal{U}(t-5)$$

(b) Since $\mathcal{L}^{-1}\left\{\dfrac{s}{s^2+25}\right\} = \cos 5t$,

$$\mathcal{L}^{-1}\left\{\frac{se^{-4\pi s/5}}{s^2+25}\right\} = \begin{cases} \cos 5(t - 4\pi/5) & t > 4\pi/5 \\ 0 & t < 4\pi/5 \end{cases}$$

$$= \begin{cases} \cos 5t & t > 4\pi/5 \cdot \\ 0 & t < 4\pi/5 \end{cases}$$

$$= \cos 5t\ \mathcal{U}(t - 4\pi/5)$$

(c) We have

$$\mathcal{L}^{-1}\left\{\frac{s+1}{s^2+s+1}\right\} = \mathcal{L}^{-1}\left\{\frac{s+1}{(s+\frac{1}{2})^2+\frac{3}{4}}\right\}$$

$$= \mathcal{L}^{-1}\left\{\frac{s+\frac{1}{2}+\frac{1}{2}}{(s+\frac{1}{2})^2+\frac{3}{4}}\right\}$$

$$= \mathcal{L}^{-1}\left\{\frac{s+\frac{1}{2}}{(s+\frac{1}{2})^2+\frac{3}{4}}\right\} + \frac{1}{\sqrt{3}}\mathcal{L}^{-1}\left\{\frac{\sqrt{3}/2}{(s+\frac{1}{2})^2+\frac{3}{4}}\right\}$$

$$= e^{-\frac{1}{2}t}\cos\frac{\sqrt{3}\,t}{2} + \frac{1}{\sqrt{3}}e^{-\frac{1}{2}t}\sin\frac{\sqrt{3}\,t}{2}$$

$$= \frac{e^{-\frac{1}{2}t}}{\sqrt{3}}\left(\sqrt{3}\cos\frac{\sqrt{3}\,t}{2} + \sin\frac{\sqrt{3}\,t}{2}\right)$$

Thus

$$\mathcal{L}^{-1}\left\{\frac{(s+1)e^{-\pi s}}{s^2+s+1}\right\}$$

$$= \begin{cases} \dfrac{e^{-\frac{1}{2}(t-\pi)}}{\sqrt{3}}\left\{\sqrt{3}\cos\dfrac{\sqrt{3}}{2}(t-\pi) + \sin\dfrac{\sqrt{3}}{2}(t-\pi)\right\} & t > \pi \\[2mm] 0 & t < \pi \end{cases}$$

$$= \frac{e^{-\frac{1}{2}(t-\pi)}}{\sqrt{3}}\left\{\sqrt{3}\cos\frac{\sqrt{3}}{2}(t-\pi) + \sin\frac{\sqrt{3}}{2}(t-\pi)\right\}\mathcal{U}(t-\pi)$$

(d) We have $\mathcal{L}^{-1}\left\{\dfrac{1}{(s+4)^{5/2}}\right\} = e^{-4t}\mathcal{L}^{-1}\left\{\dfrac{1}{s^{5/2}}\right\}$

$$= e^{-4t}\frac{t^{3/2}}{\Gamma(5/2)} = \frac{4t^{3/2}e^{-4t}}{3\sqrt{\pi}}$$

Thus
$$\mathcal{L}^{-1}\left\{\frac{e^{4-3s}}{(s+4)^{5/2}}\right\} = e^4 \, \mathcal{L}^{-1}\left\{\frac{e^{-3s}}{(s+4)^{5/2}}\right\}$$

$$= \begin{cases} \dfrac{4e^4 \, (t-3)^{3/2} \, e^{-4(t-3)}}{3\sqrt{\pi}} & t > 3 \\ 0 & t < 3 \end{cases}$$

$$= \begin{cases} \dfrac{4 \, (t-3)^{3/2} \, e^{-4(t-4)}}{3\sqrt{\pi}} & t > 3 \\ 0 & t < 3 \end{cases}$$

$$= \frac{4 \, (t-3)^{3/2} \, e^{-4(t-4)}}{3\sqrt{\pi}} \, u(t-3)$$

10. Prove the *change of scale property*: If $\mathcal{L}^{-1}\{f(s)\} = F(t)$, then

$$\mathcal{L}^{-1}\{f(ks)\} = \frac{1}{k} F(t/k)$$

Method 1. By Problem 11, Page 14, we have on replacing a by $1/k$, $\mathcal{L}\{F(t/k)\} = k \, f(ks)$. Then

$$\mathcal{L}^{-1}\{f(ks)\} = \frac{1}{k} F(t/k)$$

Method 2. Since $f(s) = \displaystyle\int_0^\infty e^{-st} F(t) \, dt$, we have

$$f(ks) = \int_0^\infty e^{-kst} F(t) \, dt = \int_0^\infty e^{-su} F(u/k) \, d(u/k) \qquad [\text{letting } u = kt]$$

$$= \frac{1}{k} \int_0^\infty e^{-su} F(u/k) \, du = \frac{1}{k} \mathcal{L}\{F(t/k)\}$$

Then $\mathcal{L}^{-1}\{f(ks)\} = \dfrac{1}{k} F(t/k)$.

11. If $\mathcal{L}^{-1}\left\{\dfrac{e^{-1/s}}{s^{1/2}}\right\} = \dfrac{\cos 2\sqrt{t}}{\sqrt{\pi t}}$, find $\mathcal{L}^{-1}\left\{\dfrac{e^{-a/s}}{s^{1/2}}\right\}$ where $a > 0$.

By Problem 10, replacing s by ks, we have

$$\mathcal{L}^{-1}\left\{\frac{e^{-1/ks}}{(ks)^{1/2}}\right\} = \frac{1}{k} \frac{\cos 2\sqrt{t/k}}{\sqrt{\pi(t/k)}} = \frac{1}{\sqrt{k}} \frac{\cos 2\sqrt{t/k}}{\sqrt{\pi t}}$$

or

$$\mathcal{L}^{-1}\left\{\frac{e^{-1/ks}}{s^{1/2}}\right\} = \frac{\cos 2\sqrt{t/k}}{\sqrt{\pi t}}$$

Then letting $k = 1/a$,

$$\mathcal{L}^{-1}\left\{\frac{e^{-a/s}}{s^{1/2}}\right\} = \frac{\cos 2\sqrt{at}}{\sqrt{\pi t}}$$

INVERSE LAPLACE TRANSFORMS OF DERIVATIVES AND INTEGRALS

12. Prove *Theorem 2-6*, Page 44: $\mathcal{L}^{-1}\{f^{(n)}(s)\} = (-1)^n \, t^n \, F(t), \quad n = 1, 2, 3, \ldots.$

Since $\mathcal{L}\{t^n F(t)\} = (-1)^n \dfrac{d^n}{ds^n} f(s) = (-1)^n f^{(n)}(s)$ [see Problem 19, Page 17], we have

$$\mathcal{L}^{-1}\{f^{(n)}(s)\} = (-1)^n \, t^n \, F(t)$$

13. Find $\mathcal{L}^{-1}\left\{\dfrac{s}{(s^2+a^2)^2}\right\}$.

We have $\dfrac{d}{ds}\left\{\dfrac{1}{s^2+a^2}\right\} = \dfrac{-2s}{(s^2+a^2)^2}$. Thus $\dfrac{s}{(s^2+a^2)^2} = -\dfrac{1}{2}\dfrac{d}{ds}\left(\dfrac{1}{s^2+a^2}\right)$.

Then since $\mathcal{L}^{-1}\left\{\dfrac{1}{s^2+a^2}\right\} = \dfrac{\sin at}{a}$, we have by Problem 12,

$$\mathcal{L}^{-1}\left\{\dfrac{s}{(s^2+a^2)^2}\right\} = -\dfrac{1}{2}\mathcal{L}^{-1}\left\{\dfrac{d}{ds}\left(\dfrac{1}{s^2+a^2}\right)\right\}$$

$$= \dfrac{1}{2}t\left(\dfrac{\sin at}{a}\right) = \dfrac{t\sin at}{2a}$$

Another method. Differentiating with respect to the parameter a, we find,

$$\dfrac{d}{da}\left(\dfrac{s}{s^2+a^2}\right) = \dfrac{-2as}{(s^2+a^2)^2}$$

Hence

$$\mathcal{L}^{-1}\left\{\dfrac{d}{da}\left(\dfrac{s}{s^2+a^2}\right)\right\} = \mathcal{L}^{-1}\left\{\dfrac{-2as}{(s^2+a^2)^2}\right\}$$

or

$$\dfrac{d}{da}\left\{\mathcal{L}^{-1}\left(\dfrac{s}{s^2+a^2}\right)\right\} = -2a\,\mathcal{L}^{-1}\left\{\dfrac{s}{(s^2+a^2)^2}\right\}$$

i.e.

$$\mathcal{L}^{-1}\left\{\dfrac{s}{(s^2+a^2)^2}\right\} = -\dfrac{1}{2a}\dfrac{d}{da}(\cos at) = -\dfrac{1}{2a}(-t\sin at) = \dfrac{t\sin at}{2a}$$

14. Find $\mathcal{L}^{-1}\left\{\ln\left(1+\dfrac{1}{s^2}\right)\right\}$.

Let $f(s) = \ln\left(1+\dfrac{1}{s^2}\right) = \mathcal{L}\{F(t)\}$. Then $f'(s) = \dfrac{-2}{s(s^2+1)} = -2\left\{\dfrac{1}{s}-\dfrac{s}{s^2+1}\right\}$.

Thus since $\mathcal{L}^{-1}\{f'(s)\} = -2(1-\cos t) = -t\,F(t)$, $F(t) = \dfrac{2(1-\cos t)}{t}$.

MULTIPLICATION AND DIVISION BY POWERS OF s

15. Prove *Theorem 2-9*: $\mathcal{L}^{-1}\left\{\dfrac{f(s)}{s}\right\} = \displaystyle\int_0^t F(u)\,du$.

Let $G(t) = \displaystyle\int_0^t F(u)\,du$. Then $G'(t) = F(t)$, $G(0) = 0$. Thus

$$\mathcal{L}\{G'(t)\} = s\,\mathcal{L}\{G(t)\} - G(0) = s\,\mathcal{L}\{G(t)\} = f(s)$$

and so $\mathcal{L}\{G(t)\} = \dfrac{f(s)}{s}$ or $\mathcal{L}^{-1}\left\{\dfrac{f(s)}{s}\right\} = G(t) = \displaystyle\int_0^t F(u)\,du$

Compare Problem 17, Page 16.

16. Prove that $\mathcal{L}^{-1}\left\{\dfrac{f(s)}{s^2}\right\} = \displaystyle\int_0^t\int_0^v F(u)\,du\,dv.$

Let $G(t) = \displaystyle\int_0^t\int_0^v F(u)\,du\,dv.$ Then $G'(t) = \displaystyle\int_0^t F(u)\,du$ and $G''(t) = F(t).$ Since $G(0) = G'(0) = 0,$

$$\mathcal{L}\{G''(t)\} = s^2\,\mathcal{L}\{G(t)\} - s\,G(0) - G'(0) = s^2\,\mathcal{L}\{G(t)\} = f(s)$$

Thus $\qquad \mathcal{L}\{G(t)\} = \dfrac{f(s)}{s^2} \qquad$ or $\qquad \mathcal{L}^{-1}\left\{\dfrac{f(s)}{s^2}\right\} = G(t) = \displaystyle\int_0^t\int_0^v F(u)\,du\,dv$

The result can be written $\qquad \mathcal{L}^{-1}\left\{\dfrac{f(s)}{s^2}\right\} = \displaystyle\int_0^t\int_0^t F(t)\,dt^2.$

In general, $\qquad\qquad \mathcal{L}^{-1}\left\{\dfrac{f(s)}{s^n}\right\} = \displaystyle\int_0^t\int_0^t\cdots\int_0^t F(t)\,dt^n$

17. Evaluate $\mathcal{L}^{-1}\left\{\dfrac{1}{s^3(s^2+1)}\right\}.$

Since $\mathcal{L}^{-1}\left\{\dfrac{1}{s^2+1}\right\} = \sin t,$ we have by repeated application of Problem 15,

$$\mathcal{L}^{-1}\left\{\dfrac{1}{s(s^2+1)}\right\} = \int_0^t \sin u\,du = 1 - \cos t$$

$$\mathcal{L}^{-1}\left\{\dfrac{1}{s^2(s^2+1)}\right\} = \int_0^t (1-\cos u)\,du = t - \sin t$$

$$\mathcal{L}^{-1}\left\{\dfrac{1}{s^3(s^2+1)}\right\} = \int_0^t (u-\sin u)\,du = \dfrac{t^2}{2} + \cos t - 1$$

Check: $\mathcal{L}\left\{\dfrac{t^2}{2} + \cos t - 1\right\} = \dfrac{1}{s^3} + \dfrac{s}{s^2+1} - \dfrac{1}{s} = \dfrac{s^2+1+s^4-s^2(s^2+1)}{s^3(s^2+1)} = \dfrac{1}{s^3(s^2+1)}$

18. Given that $\mathcal{L}^{-1}\left\{\dfrac{s}{(s^2+1)^2}\right\} = \dfrac{1}{2}t\sin t,$ **find** $\mathcal{L}^{-1}\left\{\dfrac{1}{(s^2+1)^2}\right\}.$

Method 1. By *Theorem 2-9* [Problem 15], we have

$$\mathcal{L}^{-1}\left\{\dfrac{1}{(s^2+1)^2}\right\} = \mathcal{L}^{-1}\left\{\dfrac{1}{s}\cdot\dfrac{s}{(s^2+1)^2}\right\} = \int_0^t \tfrac{1}{2}u\sin u\,du$$

$$= (\tfrac{1}{2}u)(-\cos u) - (\tfrac{1}{2})(-\sin u)\Big|_0^t$$

$$= \tfrac{1}{2}(\sin t - t\cos t)$$

Method 2. By *Theorem 2-8*, we have

$$\mathcal{L}^{-1}\left\{s\cdot\dfrac{s}{(s^2+1)^2}\right\} = \mathcal{L}^{-1}\left\{\dfrac{s^2+1-1}{(s^2+1)^2}\right\} = \mathcal{L}^{-1}\left\{\dfrac{1}{s^2+1}\right\} - \mathcal{L}^{-1}\left\{\dfrac{1}{(s^2+1)^2}\right\}$$

$$= \dfrac{d}{dt}\{\tfrac{1}{2}t\sin t\} = \tfrac{1}{2}(t\cos t + \sin t)$$

Then $\mathcal{L}^{-1}\left\{\dfrac{1}{(s^2+1)^2}\right\} = \mathcal{L}^{-1}\left\{\dfrac{1}{s^2+1}\right\} - \tfrac{1}{2}(t\cos t + \sin t) = \tfrac{1}{2}(\sin t - t\cos t)$

19. Find　$\mathcal{L}^{-1}\left\{\dfrac{1}{s}\ln\left(1+\dfrac{1}{s^2}\right)\right\}$.

Using Problem 14, we find

$$\mathcal{L}^{-1}\left\{\frac{1}{s}\ln\left(1+\frac{1}{s^2}\right)\right\} \;=\; \int_0^t \frac{2(1-\cos u)}{u}\,du \;=\; 2\int_0^t \frac{1-\cos u}{u}\,du$$

THE CONVOLUTION THEOREM

20. Prove the *convolution theorem*:　If　$\mathcal{L}^{-1}\{f(s)\}=F(t)$　and　$\mathcal{L}^{-1}\{g(s)\}=G(t)$,　then

$$\mathcal{L}^{-1}\{f(s)\,g(s)\} \;=\; \int_0^t F(u)\,G(t-u)\,du \;=\; F*G$$

Method 1.　The required result follows if we can prove that

$$\mathcal{L}\left\{\int_0^t F(u)\,G(t-u)\,du\right\} \;=\; f(s)\,g(s) \tag{1}$$

where　$f(s)=\mathcal{L}\{F(t)\}$,　$g(s)=\mathcal{L}\{G(t)\}$.　To show this we note that the left side of *(1)* is

$$\int_{t=0}^{\infty} e^{-st}\left\{\int_{u=0}^{t} F(u)\,G(t-u)\,du\right\} dt$$

$$=\; \int_{t=0}^{\infty}\int_{u=0}^{t} e^{-st}\,F(u)\,G(t-u)\,du\,dt \;=\; \lim_{M\to\infty} s_M$$

where
$$s_M \;=\; \int_{t=0}^{M}\int_{u=0}^{t} e^{-st}\,F(u)\,G(t-u)\,du\,dt \tag{2}$$

The region in the tu plane over which the integration *(2)* is performed is shown shaded in Fig. 2-1.

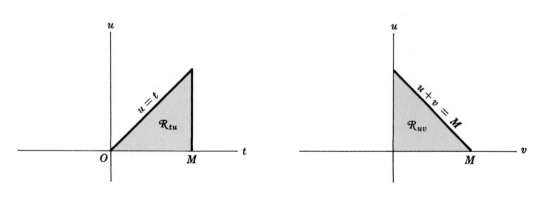

Fig. 2-1　　　　　　　　　　　　　　　　Fig. 2-2

Letting　$t-u=v$　or　$t=u+v$,　the shaded region $\mathcal{R}_{tu}$ of the tu plane is transformed into the shaded region $\mathcal{R}_{uv}$ of the uv plane shown in Fig. 2-2. Then by a theorem on transformation of multiple integrals, we have

$$s_M \;=\; \iint_{\mathcal{R}_{tu}} e^{-st}\,F(u)\,G(t-u)\,du\,dt \;=\; \iint_{\mathcal{R}_{uv}} e^{-s(u+v)}\,F(u)\,G(v)\left|\frac{\partial(u,t)}{\partial(u,v)}\right|\,du\,dv \tag{3}$$

where the *Jacobian of the transformation* is

$$J = \frac{\partial(u, t)}{\partial(u, v)} = \begin{vmatrix} \dfrac{\partial u}{\partial u} & \dfrac{\partial u}{\partial v} \\[2mm] \dfrac{\partial t}{\partial u} & \dfrac{\partial t}{\partial v} \end{vmatrix} = \begin{vmatrix} 1 & 0 \\ 1 & 1 \end{vmatrix} = 1$$

Thus the right side of (*3*) is

$$s_M = \int_{v=0}^{M} \int_{u=0}^{M-v} e^{-s(u+v)} F(u)\, G(v)\, du\, dv \tag{4}$$

Let us define a new function

$$K(u, v) = \begin{cases} e^{-s(u+v)} F(u)\, G(v) & \text{if } u + v \leqq M \\ 0 & \text{if } u + v > M \end{cases} \tag{5}$$

This function is defined over the square of Fig. 2-3 but, as indicated in (*5*), is zero over the unshaded portion of the square. In terms of this new function we can write (*4*) as

$$s_M = \int_{v=0}^{M} \int_{u=0}^{M} K(u, v)\, du\, dv$$

Then

$$\lim_{M \to \infty} s_M = \int_0^\infty \int_0^\infty K(u, v)\, du\, dv$$

$$= \int_0^\infty \int_0^\infty e^{-s(u+v)} F(u)\, G(v)\, du\, dv$$

$$= \left\{ \int_0^\infty e^{-su} F(u)\, du \right\} \left\{ \int_0^\infty e^{-sv} G(v)\, dv \right\}$$

$$= f(s)\, g(s)$$

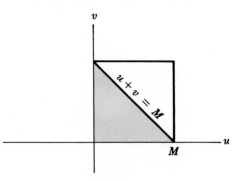

Fig. 2-3

which establishes the theorem.

We call $\displaystyle\int_0^t F(u)\, G(t-u)\, du = F * G$ the *convolution integral* or, briefly, *convolution* of F and G.

For a direct method of establishing the convolution theorem, see Problem 85.

21. Prove that $F * G = G * F$.

Letting $t - u = v$ or $u = t - v$, we have

$$F * G = \int_0^t F(u)\, G(t-u)\, du = \int_0^t F(t-v)\, G(v)\, dv$$

$$= \int_0^t G(v)\, F(t-v)\, dv = G * F$$

This shows that the *convolution* of F and G obeys the *commutative law* of algebra. It also obeys the *associative law* and *distributive law* [see Problems 80 and 81].

22. Evaluate each of the following by use of the convolution theorem.

(a) $\mathcal{L}^{-1}\left\{\dfrac{s}{(s^2+a^2)^2}\right\}$, (b) $\mathcal{L}^{-1}\left\{\dfrac{1}{s^2(s+1)^2}\right\}$.

(a) We can write $\dfrac{s}{(s^2+a^2)^2} = \dfrac{s}{s^2+a^2} \cdot \dfrac{1}{s^2+a^2}$. Then since $\mathcal{L}^{-1}\left\{\dfrac{s}{s^2+a^2}\right\} = \cos at$ and

$\mathcal{L}^{-1}\left\{\dfrac{1}{s^2+a^2}\right\} = \dfrac{\sin at}{a}$, we have by the convolution theorem,

$$\mathcal{L}^{-1}\left\{\frac{s}{(s^2+a^2)^2}\right\} = \int_0^t \cos au \cdot \frac{\sin a\,(t-u)}{a}\,du$$

$$= \frac{1}{a}\int_0^t (\cos au)(\sin at \cos au - \cos at \sin au)\,du$$

$$= \frac{1}{a}\sin at \int_0^t \cos^2 au\,du \;-\; \frac{1}{a}\cos at \int_0^t \sin au \cos au\,du$$

$$= \frac{1}{a}\sin at \int_0^t \left(\frac{1+\cos 2au}{2}\right)du \;-\; \frac{1}{a}\cos at \int_0^t \frac{\sin 2au}{2}\,du$$

$$= \frac{1}{a}\sin at \left(\frac{t}{2}+\frac{\sin 2at}{4a}\right) - \frac{1}{a}\cos at \left(\frac{1-\cos 2at}{4a}\right)$$

$$= \frac{1}{a}\sin at \left(\frac{t}{2}+\frac{\sin at \cos at}{2a}\right) - \frac{1}{a}\cos at \left(\frac{\sin^2 at}{2a}\right)$$

$$= \frac{t \sin at}{2a}$$

Compare Problem 13, Page 53.

(b) We have $\mathcal{L}^{-1}\left\{\dfrac{1}{s^2}\right\} = t$, $\mathcal{L}^{-1}\left\{\dfrac{1}{(s+1)^2}\right\} = t\,e^{-t}$. Then by the convolution theorem,

$$\mathcal{L}^{-1}\left\{\frac{1}{s^2(s+1)^2}\right\} = \int_0^t (ue^{-u})(t-u)\,du$$

$$= \int_0^t (ut - u^2)\,e^{-u}\,du$$

$$= (ut - u^2)(-e^{-u}) - (t-2u)(e^{-u}) + (-2)(-e^{-u})\Big|_0^t$$

$$= te^{-t} + 2e^{-t} + t - 2$$

Check: $\mathcal{L}\{te^{-t}+2e^{-t}+t-2\} = \dfrac{1}{(s+1)^2} + \dfrac{2}{s+1} + \dfrac{1}{s^2} - \dfrac{2}{s}$

$$= \frac{s^2 + 2s^2(s+1) + (s+1)^2 - 2s(s+1)^2}{s^2(s+1)^2} = \frac{1}{s^2(s+1)^2}$$

23. Show that $\displaystyle\int_0^t \int_0^v F(u)\,du\,dv = \int_0^t (t-u)\,F(u)\,du$.

By the convolution theorem, if $f(s) = \mathcal{L}\{F(t)\}$, we have

$$\mathcal{L}\left\{\int_0^t (t-u)\,F(u)\,du\right\} \;=\; \mathcal{L}\{t\}\,\mathcal{L}\{F(t)\} \;=\; \frac{f(s)}{s^2}$$

Then by Problem 16,

$$\int_0^t (t-u)\,F(u)\,du \;=\; \mathcal{L}^{-1}\left\{\frac{f(s)}{s^2}\right\} \;=\; \int_0^t \int_0^v F(u)\,du\,dv$$

The result can be written

$$\int_0^t \int_0^t F(t)\,dt^2 \;=\; \int_0^t (t-u)\,F(u)\,du$$

In general, we can prove that [see Problems 83 and 84],

$$\int_0^t \int_0^t \cdots \int_0^t F(t)\,dt^n \;=\; \int_0^t \frac{(t-u)^{n-1}}{(n-1)!}\,F(u)\,du$$

PARTIAL FRACTIONS

24. Find $\mathcal{L}^{-1}\left\{\dfrac{3s+7}{s^2-2s-3}\right\}$.

Method 1.
$$\frac{3s+7}{s^2-2s-3} \;=\; \frac{3s+7}{(s-3)(s+1)} \;=\; \frac{A}{s-3} + \frac{B}{s+1} \tag{1}$$

Multiplying by $(s-3)(s+1)$, we obtain

$$3s+7 \;=\; A(s+1) + B(s-3) \;=\; (A+B)s + A - 3B$$

Equating coefficients, $A+B=3$ and $A-3B=7$; then $A=4$, $B=-1$,

$$\frac{3s+7}{(s-3)(s+1)} \;=\; \frac{4}{s-3} - \frac{1}{s+1}$$

and
$$\mathcal{L}^{-1}\left\{\frac{3s+7}{(s-3)(s+1)}\right\} \;=\; 4\,\mathcal{L}^{-1}\left\{\frac{1}{s-3}\right\} - \mathcal{L}^{-1}\left\{\frac{1}{s+1}\right\}$$
$$=\; 4e^{3t} - e^{-t}$$

Method 2. Multiply both sides of *(1)* by $s-3$ and let $s \to 3$. Then

$$\lim_{s\to 3}\frac{3s+7}{s+1} \;=\; A + \lim_{s\to 3}\frac{B(s-3)}{s+1} \quad\text{or}\quad A = 4$$

Similarly multiplying both sides of *(1)* by $s+1$ and letting $s \to -1$, we have

$$\lim_{s\to -1}\frac{3s+7}{s-3} \;=\; \lim_{s\to -1}\frac{A(s+1)}{s-3} + B \quad\text{or}\quad B = -1$$

Using these values we obtain the result in Method 1. See also Problem 7(c), Page 50.

25. Find $\mathcal{L}^{-1}\left\{\dfrac{2s^2-4}{(s+1)(s-2)(s-3)}\right\}$.

We have
$$\frac{2s^2-4}{(s+1)(s-2)(s-3)} \;=\; \frac{A}{s+1} + \frac{B}{s-2} + \frac{C}{s-3} \tag{1}$$

Let us use the procedure of Method 2, Problem 24.

Multiply both sides of (1) by $s + 1$ and let $s \to -1$; then

$$A = \lim_{s \to -1} \frac{2s^2 - 4}{(s-2)(s-3)} = -\frac{1}{6}$$

Multiply both sides of (1) by $s - 2$ and let $s \to 2$; then

$$B = \lim_{s \to 2} \frac{2s^2 - 4}{(s+1)(s-3)} = -\frac{4}{3}$$

Multiply both sides of (1) by $s - 3$ and let $s \to 3$; then

$$C = \lim_{s \to 3} \frac{2s^2 - 4}{(s+1)(s-2)} = \frac{7}{2}$$

Thus

$$\mathcal{L}^{-1}\left\{\frac{2s^2 - 4}{(s+1)(s-2)(s-3)}\right\} = \mathcal{L}^{-1}\left\{\frac{-1/6}{s+1} + \frac{-4/3}{s-2} + \frac{7/2}{s-3}\right\}$$

$$= -\frac{1}{6}e^{-t} - \frac{4}{3}e^{2t} + \frac{7}{2}e^{3t}$$

The procedure of Method 1, Problem 24, can also be used. However, it will be noted that the present method is less tedious. It can be used whenever the denominator has *distinct linear factors*.

26. Find $\mathcal{L}^{-1}\left\{\dfrac{5s^2 - 15s - 11}{(s+1)(s-2)^3}\right\}$.

$$\frac{5s^2 - 15s - 11}{(s+1)(s-2)^3} = \frac{A}{s+1} + \frac{B}{(s-2)^3} + \frac{C}{(s-2)^2} + \frac{D}{s-2} \qquad (1)$$

A procedure analogous to that of Problem 25 can be used to find A and B.

Multiply both sides of (1) by $s + 1$ and let $s \to -1$; then

$$A = \lim_{s \to -1} \frac{5s^2 - 15s - 11}{(s-2)^3} = \frac{-1}{3}$$

Multiply both sides of (1) by $(s - 2)^3$ and let $s \to 2$; then

$$B = \lim_{s \to 2} \frac{5s^2 - 15s - 11}{s+1} = -7$$

The method fails to determine C and D. However, since we know A and B, we have from (1),

$$\frac{5s^2 - 15s - 11}{(s+1)(s-2)^3} = \frac{-1/3}{s+1} + \frac{-7}{(s-2)^3} + \frac{C}{(s-2)^2} + \frac{D}{s-2} \qquad (2)$$

To determine C and D we can substitute two values for s, say $s = 0$ and $s = 1$, from which we find respectively,

$$\frac{11}{8} = -\frac{1}{3} + \frac{7}{8} + \frac{C}{4} - \frac{D}{2}, \qquad \frac{21}{2} = -\frac{1}{6} + 7 + C - D$$

i.e. $3C - 6D = 10$ and $3C - 3D = 11$, from which $C = 4$, $D = 1/3$.   Thus

$$\mathcal{L}^{-1}\left\{\frac{5s^2 - 15s - 11}{(s+1)(s-2)^3}\right\} = \mathcal{L}^{-1}\left\{\frac{-1/3}{s+1} + \frac{-7}{(s-2)^3} + \frac{4}{(s-2)^2} + \frac{1/3}{s-2}\right\}$$

$$= -\frac{1}{3}e^{-t} - \frac{7}{2}t^2 e^{2t} + 4t\, e^{2t} + \frac{1}{3}e^{2t}$$

Another method. On multiplying both sides of (2) by s and letting $s \to \infty$, we find $0 = -\frac{1}{3} + D$ which gives $D = \frac{1}{3}$. Then C can be found as above by letting $s = 0$.

This method can be used when we have some *repeated linear factors*.

27. Find $\mathcal{L}^{-1}\left\{\dfrac{3s+1}{(s-1)(s^2+1)}\right\}$.

$$\frac{3s+1}{(s-1)(s^2+1)} = \frac{A}{s-1} + \frac{Bs+C}{s^2+1} \tag{1}$$

Multiply both sides by $s-1$ and let $s \to 1$; then $A = \lim\limits_{s \to 1} \dfrac{3s+1}{s^2+1} = 2$ and

$$\frac{3s+1}{(s-1)(s^2+1)} = \frac{2}{s-1} + \frac{Bs+C}{s^2+1} \tag{2}$$

To determine B and C, let $s = 0$ and 2 (for example); then

$$-1 = -2 + C, \qquad \frac{7}{5} = 2 + \frac{2B+C}{5}$$

from which $C = 1$ and $B = -2$. Thus we have

$$\mathcal{L}^{-1}\left\{\frac{3s+1}{(s-1)(s^2+1)}\right\} = \mathcal{L}^{-1}\left\{\frac{2}{s-1} + \frac{-2s+1}{s^2+1}\right\}$$

$$= 2\mathcal{L}^{-1}\left\{\frac{1}{s-1}\right\} - 2\mathcal{L}^{-1}\left\{\frac{s}{s^2+1}\right\} + \mathcal{L}^{-1}\left\{\frac{1}{s^2+1}\right\}$$

$$= 2e^t - 2\cos t + \sin t$$

Another method. Multiplying both sides of (2) by s and letting $s \to \infty$, we find at once that $B = -2$.

28. Find $\mathcal{L}^{-1}\left\{\dfrac{s^2+2s+3}{(s^2+2s+2)(s^2+2s+5)}\right\}$.

Method 1.

$$\frac{s^2+2s+3}{(s^2+2s+2)(s^2+2s+5)} = \frac{As+B}{s^2+2s+2} + \frac{Cs+D}{s^2+2s+5} \tag{1}$$

Multiplying by $(s^2+2s+2)(s^2+2s+5)$,

$$s^2 + 2s + 3 = (As+B)(s^2+2s+5) + (Cs+D)(s^2+2s+2)$$

$$= (A+C)s^3 + (2A+B+2C+D)s^2 + (5A+2B+2C+2D)s + 5B + 2D$$

Then $A+C = 0$, $2A+B+2C+D = 1$, $5A+2B+2C+2D = 2$, $5B+2D = 3$. Solving, $A = 0$, $B = \frac{1}{3}$, $C = 0$, $D = \frac{2}{3}$. Thus

$$\mathcal{L}^{-1}\left\{\frac{s^2+2s+3}{(s^2+2s+2)(s^2+2s+5)}\right\} = \mathcal{L}^{-1}\left\{\frac{1/3}{s^2+2s+2} + \frac{2/3}{s^2+2s+5}\right\}$$

$$= \frac{1}{3}\mathcal{L}^{-1}\left\{\frac{1}{(s+1)^2+1}\right\} + \frac{2}{3}\mathcal{L}^{-1}\left\{\frac{1}{(s+1)^2+4}\right\}$$

$$= \frac{1}{3}e^{-t}\sin t + \frac{2}{3}\cdot\frac{1}{2}e^{-t}\sin 2t$$

$$= \frac{1}{3}e^{-t}(\sin t + \sin 2t)$$

Method 2.   Let $s = 0$ in (1): $\dfrac{3}{10} = \dfrac{B}{2} + \dfrac{D}{5}$

Multiply (1) by s and let $s \to \infty$: $0 = A + C$

Let $s = 1$: $\dfrac{3}{20} = \dfrac{A+B}{5} + \dfrac{C+D}{8}$

Let $s = -1$: $\dfrac{1}{2} = -A + B + \dfrac{D-C}{4}$

Solving, $A = 0$, $B = \frac{1}{3}$, $C = 0$, $D = \frac{2}{3}$ as in Method 1.

This illustrates the case of *non-repeated quadratic factors*.

Method 3. Since $s^2 + 2s + 2 = 0$ for $s = -1 \pm i$, we can write

$$s^2 + 2s + 2 = (s+1-i)(s+1+i)$$

Similarly $$s^2 + 2s + 5 = (s+1-2i)(s+1+2i)$$

Then

$$\frac{s^2 + 2s + 3}{(s^2+2s+2)(s^2+2s+5)} = \frac{s^2 + 2s + 3}{(s+1-i)(s+1+i)(s+1-2i)(s+1+2i)}$$

$$= \frac{A}{s+1-i} + \frac{B}{s+1+i} + \frac{C}{s+1-2i} + \frac{D}{s+1+2i}$$

Solving for A, B, C, D, we find $A = 1/6i$, $B = -1/6i$, $C = 1/6i$, $D = -1/6i$. Thus the required inverse Laplace transform is

$$\frac{e^{-(1-i)t}}{6i} - \frac{e^{-(1+i)t}}{6i} + \frac{e^{-(1-2i)t}}{6i} - \frac{e^{-(1+2i)t}}{6i} = \tfrac{1}{3}e^{-t}\left(\frac{e^{it} - e^{-it}}{2i}\right) + \tfrac{1}{3}e^{-t}\left(\frac{e^{2it} - e^{-2it}}{2i}\right)$$

$$= \tfrac{1}{3}e^{-t}\sin t + \tfrac{1}{3}e^{-t}\sin 2t$$

$$= \tfrac{1}{3}e^{-t}(\sin t + \sin 2t)$$

This shows that the case of non-repeated quadratic factors can be reduced to non-repeated linear factors using complex numbers.

HEAVISIDE'S EXPANSION FORMULA

29. Prove Heaviside's expansion formula (*14*), Page 46.

Since $Q(s)$ is a polynomial with n distinct zeros $\alpha_1, \alpha_2, \ldots, \alpha_n$, we can write according to the method of partial fractions,

$$\frac{P(s)}{Q(s)} = \frac{A_1}{s-\alpha_1} + \frac{A_2}{s-\alpha_2} + \cdots + \frac{A_k}{s-\alpha_k} + \cdots + \frac{A_n}{s-\alpha_n} \qquad (1)$$

Multiplying both sides by $s - \alpha_k$ and letting $s \to \alpha_k$, we find using L'Hospital's rule,

$$A_k = \lim_{s \to \alpha_k} \frac{P(s)}{Q(s)}(s-\alpha_k) = \lim_{s \to \alpha_k} P(s)\left\{\frac{s-\alpha_k}{Q(s)}\right\}$$

$$= \lim_{s \to \alpha_k} P(s) \lim_{s \to \alpha_k}\left(\frac{s-\alpha_k}{Q(s)}\right) = P(\alpha_k) \lim_{s \to \alpha_k}\frac{1}{Q'(s)} = \frac{P(\alpha_k)}{Q'(\alpha_k)}$$

Thus (1) can be written

$$\frac{P(s)}{Q(s)} = \frac{P(\alpha_1)}{Q'(\alpha_1)}\frac{1}{s-\alpha_1} + \cdots + \frac{P(\alpha_k)}{Q'(\alpha_k)}\frac{1}{s-\alpha_k} + \cdots + \frac{P(\alpha_n)}{Q'(\alpha_n)}\frac{1}{s-\alpha_n}$$

Then taking the inverse Laplace transform, we have as required

$$\mathcal{L}^{-1}\left\{\frac{P(s)}{Q(s)}\right\} = \frac{P(\alpha_1)}{Q'(\alpha_1)}e^{\alpha_1 t} + \cdots + \frac{P(\alpha_k)}{Q'(\alpha_k)}e^{\alpha_k t} + \cdots + \frac{P(\alpha_n)}{Q'(\alpha_n)}e^{\alpha_n t} = \sum_{k=1}^{n}\frac{P(\alpha_k)}{Q'(\alpha_k)}e^{\alpha_k t}$$

30. Find $\mathcal{L}^{-1}\left\{\dfrac{2s^2 - 4}{(s+1)(s-2)(s-3)}\right\}$.

We have $P(s) = 2s^2 - 4$, $Q(s) = (s+1)(s-2)(s-3) = s^3 - 4s^2 + s + 6$, $Q'(s) = 3s^2 - 8s + 1$, $\alpha_1 = -1$, $\alpha_2 = 2$, $\alpha_3 = 3$. Then the required inverse is by Problem 29,

$$\frac{P(-1)}{Q'(-1)}e^{-t} + \frac{P(2)}{Q'(2)}e^{2t} + \frac{P(3)}{Q'(3)}e^{3t} = \frac{-2}{12}e^{-t} + \frac{4}{-3}e^{2t} + \frac{14}{4}e^{3t} = -\frac{1}{6}e^{-t} - \frac{4}{3}e^{2t} + \frac{7}{2}e^{3t}$$

Compare with Problem 25.

31. Find $\mathcal{L}^{-1}\left\{\dfrac{3s+1}{(s-1)(s^2+1)}\right\}$.

We have $P(s) = 3s+1$, $Q(s) = (s-1)(s^2+1) = s^3 - s^2 + s - 1$, $Q'(s) = 3s^2 - 2s + 1$, $\alpha_1 = 1$, $\alpha_2 = i$, $\alpha_3 = -i$ since $s^2 + 1 = (s-i)(s+i)$. Then by the Heaviside expansion formula the required inverse is

$$\frac{P(1)}{Q'(1)}e^t + \frac{P(i)}{Q'(i)}e^{it} + \frac{P(-i)}{Q'(-i)}e^{-it} \qquad (1)$$

$$= \frac{4}{2}e^t + \frac{3i+1}{-2-2i}e^{it} + \frac{-3i+1}{-2+2i}e^{-it}$$

$$= 2e^t + (-1 - \tfrac{1}{2}i)(\cos t + i\sin t) + (-1 + \tfrac{1}{2}i)(\cos t - i\sin t)$$

$$= 2e^t - \cos t + \tfrac{1}{2}\sin t - \cos t + \tfrac{1}{2}\sin t$$

$$= 2e^t - 2\cos t + \sin t$$

Compare with Problem 27.

Note that some labor can be saved by observing that the last two terms in (1) are complex conjugates of each other.

THE BETA FUNCTION

32. Prove that $B(m, n) = \displaystyle\int_0^1 x^{m-1}(1-x)^{n-1}\, dx = \dfrac{\Gamma(m)\,\Gamma(n)}{\Gamma(m+n)}$ where $m > 0$, $n > 0$.

Consider

$$G(t) = \int_0^t x^{m-1}(t-x)^{n-1}\, dx$$

Then by the convolution theorem, we have

$$\mathcal{L}\{G(t)\} = \mathcal{L}\{t^{m-1}\}\,\mathcal{L}\{t^{n-1}\}$$

$$= \frac{\Gamma(m)}{s^m} \cdot \frac{\Gamma(n)}{s^n} = \frac{\Gamma(m)\,\Gamma(n)}{s^{m+n}}$$

Thus $\qquad G(t) = \mathcal{L}^{-1}\left\{\dfrac{\Gamma(m)\,\Gamma(n)}{s^{m+n}}\right\} = \dfrac{\Gamma(m)\,\Gamma(n)}{\Gamma(m+n)}\, t^{m+n-1}$

or $\qquad \displaystyle\int_0^t x^{m-1}(t-x)^{n-1}\, dx = \dfrac{\Gamma(m)\,\Gamma(n)}{\Gamma(m+n)}\, t^{m+n-1}$

Letting $t = 1$, we obtain the required result.

33. Prove that $\displaystyle\int_0^{\pi/2} \sin^{2m-1}\theta\ \cos^{2n-1}\theta\ d\theta\ =\ \frac{1}{2}B(m,n)\ =\ \frac{\Gamma(m)\,\Gamma(n)}{2\,\Gamma(m+n)}.$

From Problem 32, we have

$$B(m,n)\ =\ \int_0^1 x^{m-1}(1-x)^{n-1}\,dx\ =\ \frac{\Gamma(m)\,\Gamma(n)}{\Gamma(m+n)}$$

Letting $x=\sin^2\theta$, this becomes

$$B(m,n)\ =\ 2\int_0^{\pi/2}\sin^{2m-1}\theta\ \cos^{2n-1}\theta\ d\theta\ =\ \frac{\Gamma(m)\,\Gamma(n)}{\Gamma(m+n)}$$

from which the required result follows.

34. Evaluate   (a) $\displaystyle\int_0^{\pi/2}\sin^4\theta\cos^6\theta\ d\theta,$ (b) $\displaystyle\int_0^{\pi}\cos^4\theta\ d\theta,$ (c) $\displaystyle\int_0^{\pi/2}\frac{d\theta}{\sqrt{\tan\theta}}.$

(a) Let $2m-1=4$, $2n-1=6$ in Problem 33. Then $m=5/2$, $n=7/2$, and we have

$$\int_0^{\pi/2}\sin^4\theta\cos^6\theta\ d\theta\ =\ \frac{\Gamma(5/2)\,\Gamma(7/2)}{2\,\Gamma(6)}\ =\ \frac{(3/2)(1/2)\sqrt{\pi}\cdot(5/2)(3/2)(1/2)\sqrt{\pi}}{2\cdot 5\cdot 4\cdot 3\cdot 2\cdot 1}\ =\ \frac{3\pi}{512}$$

(b) Since $\cos\theta$ is symmetric about $\theta=\pi/2$, we have

$$\int_0^{\pi}\cos^4\theta\ d\theta\ =\ 2\int_0^{\pi/2}\cos^4\theta\ d\theta$$

Then letting $2m-1=0$ and $2n-1=4$, i.e. $m=1/2$ and $n=5/2$ in Problem 33, we find

$$2\int_0^{\pi/2}\cos^4\theta\ d\theta\ =\ 2\left[\frac{\Gamma(1/2)\,\Gamma(5/2)}{2\,\Gamma(3)}\right]$$

$$=\ 2\left[\frac{\sqrt{\pi}\cdot(3/2)(1/2)\sqrt{\pi}}{2\cdot 2\cdot 1}\right]\ =\ \frac{3\pi}{8}$$

(c) $\displaystyle\int_0^{\pi/2}\frac{d\theta}{\sqrt{\tan\theta}}\ =\ \int_0^{\pi/2}\sin^{-1/2}\theta\ \cos^{1/2}\theta\ d\theta$

Letting $2m-1=-1/2$ and $2n-1=1/2$, or $m=1/4$ and $n=3/4$ in Problem 33, we find

$$\int_0^{\pi/2}\frac{d\theta}{\sqrt{\tan\theta}}\ =\ \frac{\Gamma(1/4)\,\Gamma(3/4)}{2\,\Gamma(1)}\ =\ \frac{1}{2}\,\frac{\pi}{\sin(\pi/4)}\ =\ \frac{\pi\sqrt{2}}{2}$$

using the result $\Gamma(p)\,\Gamma(1-p)\ =\ \pi/(\sin p\pi),\ \ 0<p<1.$

EVALUATION OF INTEGRALS

35. Evaluate $\displaystyle\int_0^t J_0(u)\,J_0(t-u)\,du.$

Let $G(t)\ =\ \displaystyle\int_0^t J_0(u)\,J_0(t-u)\,du.$ Then by the convolution theorem,

$$\mathcal{L}\{G(t)\}\ =\ \mathcal{L}\{J_0(t)\}\,\mathcal{L}\{J_0(t)\}\ =\ \left(\frac{1}{\sqrt{s^2+1}}\right)\left(\frac{1}{\sqrt{s^2+1}}\right)\ =\ \frac{1}{s^2+1}$$

Hence
$$G(t)\ =\ \mathcal{L}^{-1}\left\{\frac{1}{s^2+1}\right\}\ =\ \sin t$$

and so
$$G(t)\ =\ \int_0^t J_0(u)\,J_0(t-u)\,du\ =\ \sin t$$

36. Show that $\int_0^\infty \cos x^2 \, dx = \frac{1}{2}\sqrt{\pi/2}$.

Let $G(t) = \int_0^\infty \cos tx^2 \, dx$. Then taking the Laplace transform, we find

$$\mathcal{L}\{G(t)\} = \int_0^\infty e^{-st} \, dt \int_0^\infty \cos tx^2 \, dx$$

$$= \int_0^\infty dx \int_0^\infty e^{-st} \cos tx^2 \, dt$$

$$= \int_0^\infty \mathcal{L}\{\cos tx^2\} \, dx = \int_0^\infty \frac{s}{s^2 + x^4} \, dx$$

Letting $x^2 = s\tan\theta$ or $x = \sqrt{s}\sqrt{\tan\theta}$, this integral becomes on using Problem 34(c),

$$\frac{1}{2\sqrt{s}} \int_0^{\pi/2} (\tan\theta)^{-1/2} \, d\theta = \frac{1}{2\sqrt{s}}\left(\frac{\pi\sqrt{2}}{2}\right) = \frac{\pi\sqrt{2}}{4\sqrt{s}}$$

Inverting, we find

$$G(t) = \int_0^\infty \cos tx^2 \, dx = \frac{\pi\sqrt{2}}{4}\mathcal{L}^{-1}\left(\frac{1}{\sqrt{s}}\right) = \left(\frac{\pi\sqrt{2}}{4}\right)\left(\frac{t^{-1/2}}{\sqrt{\pi}}\right) = \frac{\sqrt{2\pi}}{4}t^{-1/2}$$

Letting $t = 1$ we have, as required,

$$\int_0^\infty \cos x^2 \, dx = \frac{\sqrt{2\pi}}{4} = \frac{1}{2}\sqrt{\frac{\pi}{2}}$$

MISCELLANEOUS PROBLEMS

37. Show that $\int_0^\infty e^{-x^2} \, dx = \frac{1}{2}\sqrt{\pi}$.

Consider $G(t) = \int_0^\infty e^{-tx^2} \, dx$. Then taking Laplace transforms,

$$\mathcal{L}\{G(t)\} = \int_0^\infty \frac{dx}{s + x^2} = \frac{1}{\sqrt{s}}\tan^{-1}\frac{x}{\sqrt{s}}\Big|_0^\infty = \frac{\pi}{2\sqrt{s}}$$

Thus by inverting,

$$G(t) = \int_0^\infty e^{-tx^2} \, dx = \frac{\pi}{2}\frac{t^{-1/2}}{\sqrt{\pi}} = \frac{1}{2}\sqrt{\pi}\, t^{-1/2}$$

and the required result follows on letting $t = 1$.

Another method.

Letting $x^2 = u$ or $x = \sqrt{u}$, the required integral becomes

$$\frac{1}{2}\int_0^\infty u^{-1/2}e^{-u} \, du = \frac{1}{2}\Gamma(\tfrac{1}{2})$$

But by Problem 32 with $m = n = \frac{1}{2}$, we have

$$\{\Gamma(\tfrac{1}{2})\}^2 = \int_0^1 x^{-1/2}(1-x)^{-1/2} \, dx = \int_0^1 \frac{dx}{\sqrt{x(1-x)}}$$

$$= \int_0^1 \frac{dx}{\sqrt{\tfrac{1}{4} - (\tfrac{1}{2}-x)^2}} = \sin^{-1}(1-2x)\Big|_0^1 = \pi$$

Thus $\Gamma(\tfrac{1}{2}) = \sqrt{\pi}$ and so the required integral has the value $\frac{1}{2}\sqrt{\pi}$. See also Problem 29, Page 22.

38. Find $\mathcal{L}^{-1}\left\{\dfrac{1}{(s^2+a^2)^{3/2}}\right\}$.

We have [see Problem 34, Page 23], $\mathcal{L}\{J_0(at)\} = \dfrac{1}{\sqrt{s^2+a^2}}$.   Then differentiating with respect to a, we find

$$\frac{d}{da}\,\mathcal{L}\{J_0(at)\} \;=\; \frac{d}{da}\left\{\frac{1}{\sqrt{s^2+a^2}}\right\} \qquad\text{or}\qquad \mathcal{L}\left[\frac{d}{da}\{J_0(at)\}\right] \;=\; \frac{-a}{(s^2+a^2)^{3/2}}$$

i.e.
$$\mathcal{L}\{t\,J_0'(at)\} \;=\; \frac{-a}{(s^2+a^2)^{3/2}}$$

Thus
$$\mathcal{L}^{-1}\left\{\frac{1}{(s^2+a^2)^{3/2}}\right\} \;=\; -\frac{t}{a}\,J_0'(at) \;=\; \frac{t\,J_1(at)}{a}$$

since $J_0'(u) = -J_1(u)$.

39. Find $\mathcal{L}^{-1}\left\{\dfrac{1}{(s^2+2s+5)^{3/2}}\right\}$.

The required inverse can be written as

$$\mathcal{L}^{-1}\left\{\frac{1}{[(s+1)^2+4]^{3/2}}\right\} \;=\; e^{-t}\,\mathcal{L}^{-1}\left\{\frac{1}{(s^2+4)^{3/2}}\right\} \;=\; \frac{te^{-t}}{2}\,J_1(2t)$$

using Problem 38.

40. Find $\mathcal{L}^{-1}\left\{\dfrac{e^{-1/s}}{s}\right\}$.

Using infinite series, we find

$$\frac{1}{s}\,e^{-1/s} \;=\; \frac{1}{s}\left\{1 - \frac{1}{s} + \frac{1}{2!\,s^2} - \frac{1}{3!\,s^3} + \cdots\right\}$$

$$=\; \frac{1}{s} - \frac{1}{s^2} + \frac{1}{2!\,s^3} - \frac{1}{3!\,s^4} + \cdots$$

Inverting term by term,

$$\mathcal{L}\left\{\frac{1}{s}\,e^{-1/s}\right\} \;=\; 1 - t + \frac{t^2}{(2!)^2} - \frac{t^3}{(3!)^2} + \cdots$$

$$=\; 1 - t + \frac{t^2}{1^2\,2^2} - \frac{t^3}{1^2\,2^2\,3^2} + \cdots$$

$$=\; 1 - \frac{(2t^{1/2})^2}{2^2} + \frac{(2t^{1/2})^4}{2^2\,4^2} - \frac{(2t^{1/2})^6}{2^2\,4^2\,6^2} + \cdots$$

$$=\; J_0(2\sqrt{t}\,)$$

41. Find $\mathcal{L}^{-1}\{e^{-\sqrt{s}}\}$.

Let $y = e^{-\sqrt{s}}$; then $y' = -\dfrac{e^{-\sqrt{s}}}{2s^{1/2}}$, $y'' = \dfrac{e^{-\sqrt{s}}}{4s} + \dfrac{e^{-\sqrt{s}}}{4s^{3/2}}$.   Thus

$$4s\,y'' \;+\; 2y' \;-\; y \;=\; 0 \tag{1}$$

Now $y'' = \mathcal{L}\{t^2 Y\}$ so that $sy'' = \mathcal{L}\left\{\dfrac{d}{dt}[t^2 Y]\right\} = \mathcal{L}\{t^2 Y' + 2tY\}$. Also, $y' = \mathcal{L}\{-tY\}$. Thus (1) can be written

$$4\,\mathcal{L}\{t^2 Y' + 2tY\} - 2\,\mathcal{L}\{tY\} - \mathcal{L}\{Y\} = 0 \qquad \text{or} \qquad 4t^2 Y' + (6t-1)Y = 0$$

which can be written

$$\frac{dY}{Y} + \left(\frac{6t-1}{4t^2}\right) dt = 0 \qquad \text{or} \qquad \ln Y + \frac{3}{2}\ln t + \frac{1}{4t} = c_1$$

i.e.

$$Y = \frac{c}{t^{3/2}} e^{-1/4t}$$

Now $tY = \dfrac{c}{t^{1/2}} e^{-1/4t}$. Thus

$$\mathcal{L}\{tY\} = -\frac{d}{ds}\mathcal{L}\{Y\} = -\frac{d}{ds}(e^{-\sqrt{s}}) = \frac{e^{-\sqrt{s}}}{2\sqrt{s}}$$

For large t, $tY \sim \dfrac{c}{t^{1/2}}$ and $\mathcal{L}\{tY\} \sim \dfrac{c\sqrt{\pi}}{s^{1/2}}$. For small s, $\dfrac{e^{-\sqrt{s}}}{2\sqrt{s}} \sim \dfrac{1}{2s^{1/2}}$. Hence by the final value theorem, $c\sqrt{\pi} = 1/2$ or $c = 1/2\sqrt{\pi}$. It follows that

$$\mathcal{L}^{-1}\{e^{-\sqrt{s}}\} = \frac{1}{2\sqrt{\pi}\,t^{3/2}} e^{-1/4t}$$

Another method. Using infinite series, we have formally

$$\mathcal{L}^{-1}\{e^{-\sqrt{s}}\} = \mathcal{L}^{-1}\left\{1 - s^{1/2} + \frac{s}{2!} - \frac{s^{3/2}}{3!} + \frac{s^2}{4!} - \frac{s^{5/2}}{5!} + \cdots\right\}$$

$$= \mathcal{L}^{-1}\{1\} - \mathcal{L}\{s^{1/2}\} + \mathcal{L}^{-1}\left\{\frac{s}{2!}\right\} - \mathcal{L}^{-1}\left\{\frac{s^{3/2}}{3!}\right\} + \cdots \tag{1}$$

Using the results of Problem 170, Page 40 [see also Problem 33, Page 22] we have for p equal to zero or any positive integer,

$$\mathcal{L}^{-1}\{s^{p+1/2}\} = \frac{t^{-p-3/2}}{\Gamma(-p-\frac{1}{2})}$$

$$= \frac{(-1)^{p+1}}{\sqrt{\pi}}\left(\frac{1}{2}\right)\left(\frac{3}{2}\right)\left(\frac{5}{2}\right)\cdots\left(\frac{2p+1}{2}\right) t^{-p-3/2} \tag{2}$$

while $\mathcal{L}^{-1}\{s^p\} = 0$. Then from (1) using (2) we have

$$\mathcal{L}^{-1}\{e^{-\sqrt{s}}\} = \frac{t^{-3/2}}{2\sqrt{\pi}} - \left(\frac{1}{2}\right)\left(\frac{3}{2}\right)\frac{t^{-5/2}}{3!\sqrt{\pi}} + \left(\frac{1}{2}\right)\left(\frac{3}{2}\right)\left(\frac{5}{2}\right)\frac{t^{-7/2}}{5!\sqrt{\pi}} + \cdots$$

$$= \frac{1}{2\sqrt{\pi}\,t^{3/2}}\left\{1 - \left(\frac{1}{2^2 t}\right) + \frac{(1/2^2 t)^2}{2!} - \frac{(1/2^2 t)^3}{3!} + \cdots\right\} = \frac{1}{2\sqrt{\pi}\,t^{3/2}} e^{-1/4t}$$

42. Find $\mathcal{L}^{-1}\left\{\dfrac{e^{-\sqrt{s}}}{s}\right\}$.

From Problems 41 and 15 we have

$$\mathcal{L}^{-1}\left\{\frac{e^{-\sqrt{s}}}{s}\right\} = \int_0^t \left\{\frac{1}{2\sqrt{\pi}\,u^{3/2}} e^{-1/4u}\right\} du = \frac{2}{\sqrt{\pi}}\int_{1/2\sqrt{t}}^{\infty} e^{-v^2}\,dv \qquad (\text{letting } u = 1/4v^2)$$

$$= \operatorname{erfc}\left(\frac{1}{2\sqrt{t}}\right)$$

43. Find $\mathcal{L}^{-1}\left\{\dfrac{e^{-x\sqrt{s}}}{s}\right\}$.

In Problem 42 use the change of scale property (4), Page 44, with $k = x^2$. Then

$$\mathcal{L}^{-1}\left\{\frac{e^{-\sqrt{x^2 s}}}{x^2 s}\right\} \;=\; \frac{1}{x^2}\,\text{erfc}\left(\frac{1}{2\sqrt{t/x^2}}\right)$$

from which

$$\mathcal{L}^{-1}\left\{\frac{e^{-x\sqrt{s}}}{s}\right\} \;=\; \text{erfc}\left(\frac{x}{2\sqrt{t}}\right)$$

Note that this is entry 87 in the Table on Page 250.

44. Find $\mathcal{L}^{-1}\left\{\dfrac{2s^3 + 10s^2 + 8s + 40}{s^2(s^2 + 9)}\right\}$.

Since $\dfrac{1}{s^2(s^2 + 9)} = \dfrac{1}{9}\left(\dfrac{1}{s^2} - \dfrac{1}{s^2 + 9}\right)$, we have

$$\frac{2s^3 + 10s^2 + 8s + 40}{s^2(s^2 + 9)} \;=\; \frac{1}{9}\left\{\frac{2s^3 + 10s^2 + 8s + 40}{s^2} - \frac{2s^3 + 10s^2 + 8s + 40}{s^2 + 9}\right\}$$

$$=\; \frac{1}{9}\left\{\left(2s + 10 + \frac{8}{s} + \frac{40}{s^2}\right) - \left(2s + 10 + \frac{-10s - 50}{s^2 + 9}\right)\right\}$$

$$=\; \frac{1}{9}\left\{\frac{8}{s} + \frac{40}{s^2} + \frac{10s}{s^2 + 9} + \frac{50}{s^2 + 9}\right\}$$

and so

$$\mathcal{L}^{-1}\left\{\frac{2s^3 + 10s^2 + 8s + 40}{s^2(s^2 + 9)}\right\} \;=\; \frac{1}{9}\left(8 + 40t + 10\cos 3t + \frac{50}{3}\sin 3t\right)$$

$$=\; \frac{1}{27}\,(24 + 120t + 30\cos 3t + 50\sin 3t)$$

We can also use the method of partial fractions.

45. Prove that $J_0(t) = \dfrac{1}{\pi}\displaystyle\int_{-1}^{1} e^{itw}(1 - w^2)^{-1/2}\,dw$.

We have [see Problem 34, Page 23],

$$\mathcal{L}\{J_0(t)\} \;=\; \frac{1}{\sqrt{s^2 + 1}}$$

Now

$$\frac{1}{\sqrt{s^2 + 1}} \;=\; \frac{1}{\sqrt{s + i}} \cdot \frac{1}{\sqrt{s - i}}$$

Using the fact that $\mathcal{L}^{-1}\left\{\dfrac{1}{\sqrt{s + a}}\right\} = \dfrac{t^{-1/2}\,e^{-at}}{\sqrt{\pi}}$, we have by the convolution theorem,

$$J_0(t) \;=\; \mathcal{L}^{-1}\left\{\frac{1}{\sqrt{s^2 + 1}}\right\} \;=\; \mathcal{L}^{-1}\left\{\frac{1}{\sqrt{s + i}} \cdot \frac{1}{\sqrt{s - i}}\right\}$$

$$=\; \int_0^t \frac{u^{-1/2}\,e^{-iu}}{\sqrt{\pi}} \cdot \frac{(t - u)^{-1/2}\,e^{i(t - u)}}{\sqrt{\pi}}\,du$$

$$=\; \frac{1}{\pi}\int_0^t e^{i(t - 2u)}\,u^{-1/2}(t - u)^{-1/2}\,du$$

Letting $u = tv$ this becomes

$$J_0(t) = \frac{1}{\pi} \int_0^1 e^{it(1-2v)} v^{-1/2} (1-v)^{-1/2} \, dv$$

or if $1 - 2v = w$,

$$J_0(t) = \frac{1}{\pi} \int_{-1}^1 e^{itw} (1-w^2)^{-1/2} \, dw$$

46. Prove that $J_0(t) = \frac{1}{\pi} \int_0^\pi \cos(t \cos\theta) \, d\theta.$

Let $w = \cos\theta$ in the result of Problem 45.   Then

$$J_0(t) = \frac{1}{\pi} \int_0^\pi e^{it\cos\theta} \, d\theta = \frac{1}{\pi} \int_0^\pi \cos(t\cos\theta) \, d\theta + \frac{i}{\pi} \int_0^\pi \sin(t\cos\theta) \, d\theta$$

Equating real and imaginary parts or by showing directly that the last integral is zero, we have as required

$$J_0(t) = \frac{1}{\pi} \int_0^\pi \cos(t\cos\theta) \, d\theta$$

Another method.

Let $G(t) = \frac{1}{\pi} \int_0^\pi \cos(t\cos\theta) \, d\theta = \frac{2}{\pi} \int_0^{\pi/2} \cos(t\cos\theta) \, d\theta.$ Then taking Laplace transforms,

$$\mathcal{L}\{G(t)\} = \frac{2}{\pi} \int_0^{\pi/2} \frac{s}{s^2 + \cos^2\theta} \, d\theta = \frac{2}{\pi} \int_0^{\pi/2} \frac{s \sec^2\theta}{s^2 \tan^2\theta + s^2 + 1} \, d\theta$$

$$= \frac{2}{\pi} \frac{1}{\sqrt{s^2+1}} \tan^{-1}\left(\frac{s\tan\theta}{\sqrt{s^2+1}}\right)\Bigg|_0^{\pi/2} = \frac{1}{\sqrt{s^2+1}}$$

Thus $G(t) = \mathcal{L}^{-1}\left\{\dfrac{1}{\sqrt{s^2+1}}\right\} = J_0(t),$ as required.

Supplementary Problems

INVERSE LAPLACE TRANSFORMS

47. Determine each of the following:

(a) $\mathcal{L}^{-1}\left\{\dfrac{3}{s+4}\right\}$ (c) $\mathcal{L}^{-1}\left\{\dfrac{8s}{s^2+16}\right\}$ (e) $\mathcal{L}^{-1}\left\{\dfrac{3s-12}{s^2+8}\right\}$ (g) $\mathcal{L}^{-1}\left\{\dfrac{1}{s^5}\right\}$ (i) $\mathcal{L}^{-1}\left\{\dfrac{12}{4-3s}\right\}$

(b) $\mathcal{L}^{-1}\left\{\dfrac{1}{2s-5}\right\}$ (d) $\mathcal{L}^{-1}\left\{\dfrac{6}{s^2+4}\right\}$ (f) $\mathcal{L}^{-1}\left\{\dfrac{2s-5}{s^2-9}\right\}$ (h) $\mathcal{L}^{-1}\left\{\dfrac{1}{s^{7/2}}\right\}$ (j) $\mathcal{L}^{-1}\left\{\dfrac{s+1}{s^{4/3}}\right\}$

Ans. (a) $3e^{-4t}$ (e) $3\cos 2\sqrt{2}\,t - 3\sqrt{2}\sin 2\sqrt{2}\,t$ (i) $-4e^{4t/3}$

(b) $\frac{1}{2}e^{5t/2}$ (f) $2\cosh 3t - \frac{5}{3}\sinh 3t$ (j) $(t^{-2/3} + 3t^{1/3})/\Gamma(\frac{1}{3})$

(c) $8\cos 4t$ (g) $t^4/24$

(d) $3\sin 2t$ (h) $8t^{5/2}/15\sqrt{\pi}$

48. Find   (a) $\mathcal{L}^{-1}\left\{\left(\dfrac{\sqrt{s}-1}{s}\right)^2\right\}$,   (b) $\mathcal{L}^{-1}\left\{\dfrac{2s+1}{s(s+1)}\right\}$.

   Ans. (a) $1+t-4t^{1/2}/\sqrt{\pi}$ (b) $1+e^{-t}$

49. Find   (a) $\mathcal{L}^{-1}\left\{\dfrac{3s-8}{4s^2+25}\right\}$,   (b) $\mathcal{L}^{-1}\left\{\dfrac{5s+10}{9s^2-16}\right\}$.

   Ans. (a) $\tfrac{3}{4}\cos 5t/2 - \tfrac{4}{5}\sin 5t/2$ (b) $\tfrac{5}{9}\cosh 4t/3 + \tfrac{5}{6}\sinh 4t/3$

50. (a) Show that the functions $F(t)=\begin{cases} t & t\neq 3 \\ 5 & t=3 \end{cases}$ and $G(t)=t$ have the same Laplace transforms.

   (b) Discuss the significance of the result in (a) as far as uniqueness of inverse Laplace transforms is concerned.

51. Find   (a) $\mathcal{L}^{-1}\left\{\dfrac{3s-8}{s^2+4}-\dfrac{4s-24}{s^2-16}\right\}$,   (b) $\mathcal{L}^{-1}\left\{\dfrac{3s-2}{s^{5/2}}-\dfrac{7}{3s+2}\right\}$.

   Ans. (a) $3\cos 2t - 4\sin 2t - 4\cosh 4t + 6\sinh 4t$

   (b) $6t^{1/2}/\sqrt{\pi} - 8t^{3/2}/3\sqrt{\pi} - \tfrac{7}{3}e^{-2t/3}$

52. (a) If $F_1(t)=\mathcal{L}^{-1}\{f_1(s)\}$, $F_2(t)=\mathcal{L}^{-1}\{f_2(s)\}$, $F_3(t)=\mathcal{L}^{-1}\{f_3(s)\}$,   and c_1, c_2, c_3 are any constants, prove that
$$\mathcal{L}^{-1}\{c_1 f_1(s) + c_2 f_2(s) + c_3 f_3(s)\} = c_1 F_1(t) + c_2 F_2(t) + c_3 F_3(t)$$
stating any restrictions.   (b) Generalize the result of part (a) to n functions.

53. Find $\mathcal{L}^{-1}\left\{\dfrac{3(s^2-1)^2}{2s^5}+\dfrac{4s-18}{9-s^2}+\dfrac{(s+1)(2-s^{1/2})}{s^{5/2}}\right\}$.

   Ans. $\tfrac{1}{2}-t-\tfrac{3}{2}t^2+\tfrac{1}{16}t^4+4t^{1/2}/\sqrt{\pi}+8t^{3/2}/3\sqrt{\pi}-4\cosh 3t+6\sinh 3t$

54. Find   (a) $\mathcal{L}^{-1}\left\{\dfrac{s}{(s+1)^5}\right\}$,   (b) $\mathcal{L}^{-1}\left\{\dfrac{s}{(s+1)^{5/2}}\right\}$.

   Ans. (a) $\dfrac{e^{-t}}{24}(4t^3-t^4)$,   (b) $\dfrac{2t^{1/2}(3-2t)}{3\sqrt{\pi}}$

55. Find   (a) $\mathcal{L}^{-1}\left\{\dfrac{3s-14}{s^2-4s+8}\right\}$,   (b) $\mathcal{L}^{-1}\left\{\dfrac{8s+20}{s^2-12s+32}\right\}$.

   Ans. (a) $e^{2t}(3\cos 2t - 4\sin 2t)$,   (b) $21e^{8t}-13e^{4t}$

56. Find   (a) $\mathcal{L}^{-1}\left\{\dfrac{3s+2}{4s^2+12s+9}\right\}$,   (b) $\mathcal{L}^{-1}\left\{\dfrac{5s-2}{3s^2+4s+8}\right\}$.

   Ans. (a) $\tfrac{3}{4}e^{-3t/2}-\tfrac{5}{8}t\,e^{-3t/2}$,   (b) $\dfrac{e^{-2t/3}}{15}\{25\cos 2\sqrt{5}\,t/3 - 8\sqrt{5}\sin 2\sqrt{5}\,t/3\}$

57. Find   (a) $\mathcal{L}^{-1}\left\{\dfrac{1}{\sqrt[3]{8s-27}}\right\}$,   (b) $\mathcal{L}^{-1}\left\{\dfrac{1}{\sqrt{s^2-4s+20}}\right\}$.

   Ans. (a) $t^{-2/3}\,e^{27t/8}/2\,\Gamma(\tfrac{1}{3})$,   (b) $e^{2t}J_0(4t)$

58. Find   (a) $\mathcal{L}^{-1}\left\{\dfrac{e^{-2s}}{s^2}\right\}$,   (b) $\mathcal{L}^{-1}\left\{\dfrac{8e^{-3s}}{s^2+4}\right\}$,   (c) $\mathcal{L}^{-1}\left\{\dfrac{e^{-s}}{\sqrt{s+1}}\right\}$.

Ans. (a) $\begin{cases} t-2 & t>2 \\ 0 & t<2 \end{cases}$ or $(t-2)\,\mathcal{U}(t-2)$.   (b) $\begin{cases} 4\sin 2(t-3) & t>3 \\ 0 & t<3 \end{cases}$ or $4\sin 2(t-3)\,\mathcal{U}(t-3)$.

(c) $\begin{cases} (t-1)^{-1/2}/\sqrt{\pi} & t>1 \\ 0 & t<1 \end{cases}$ or $(t-1)^{-1/2}\,\mathcal{U}(t-1)/\sqrt{\pi}$.

59. Find   (a) $\mathcal{L}^{-1}\left\{\dfrac{se^{-2s}}{s^2+3s+2}\right\}$,   (b) $\mathcal{L}^{-1}\left\{\dfrac{e^{-3s}}{s^2-2s+5}\right\}$.

Ans. (a) $\begin{cases} 2e^{-2(t-2)} - e^{-(t-2)} & t>2 \\ 0 & t<2 \end{cases}$ or $\{2e^{-2(t-2)} - e^{-(t-2)}\}\,\mathcal{U}(t-2)$

(b) $\begin{cases} \frac{1}{2}e^{(t-3)}\sin 2(t-3) & t>3 \\ 0 & t<3 \end{cases}$ or $\frac{1}{2}e^{(t-3)}\sin 2(t-3)\,\mathcal{U}(t-3)$

60. If $\displaystyle\int_0^\infty e^{-st}F(t)\,dt = f(s)$ and $\displaystyle\int_0^\infty e^{-st}G(t)\,dt = f(ps+q)$, where p and q are constants, find a relationship between $F(t)$ and $G(t)$.   *Ans.* $G(t) = e^{-qt/p}\,F(t/p)/p$

61. If $\mathcal{L}^{-1}\left\{\dfrac{1}{s\sqrt{s+1}}\right\} = \operatorname{erf}\sqrt{t}$, find $\mathcal{L}^{-1}\left\{\dfrac{1}{s\sqrt{s+a}}\right\}$, $a>0$.   *Ans.* $\operatorname{erf}\sqrt{at}\,/\sqrt{a}$

62. If $\mathcal{L}^{-1}\left\{\dfrac{(\sqrt{s^2+1}-s)^n}{\sqrt{s^2+1}}\right\} = J_n(t)$, find $\mathcal{L}^{-1}\left\{\dfrac{(\sqrt{s^2+a^2}-s)^n}{\sqrt{s^2+a^2}}\right\}$.   *Ans.* $a^n J_n(at)$

63. Find   (a) $\mathcal{L}^{-1}\left\{\dfrac{1}{\sqrt{s}\,(s-1)}\right\}$,   (b) $\mathcal{L}^{-1}\left\{\dfrac{e^{-2s}}{\sqrt{s^2+9}}\right\}$.

Ans. (a) $e^t\operatorname{erf}\sqrt{t}$,   (b) $\begin{cases} J_0(3t-6) & t>2 \\ 0 & t<2 \end{cases}$ or $J_0(3t-6)\,\mathcal{U}(t-2)$

INVERSE LAPLACE TRANSFORMS OF DERIVATIVES AND INTEGRALS

64. Use *Theorem 2-6*, Page 44, to find

(a) $\mathcal{L}^{-1}\{1/(s-a)^3\}$ given that $\mathcal{L}^{-1}\{1/(s-a)\} = e^{at}$,

(b) $\mathcal{L}^{-1}\{s/(s^2-a^2)^2\}$ given that $\mathcal{L}^{-1}\{1/(s^2-a^2)\} = (\sinh at)/a$.

65. Use the fact that $\mathcal{L}^{-1}\{1/s\} = 1$ to find $\mathcal{L}^{-1}\{1/s^n\}$ where $n = 2,3,4,\ldots$. Thus find $\mathcal{L}^{-1}\{1/(s-a)^n\}$.

66. Find $\mathcal{L}^{-1}\left\{\dfrac{s+1}{(s^2+2s+2)^2}\right\}$.   *Ans.* $\frac{1}{2}te^{-t}\sin t$

67. Find   (a) $\mathcal{L}^{-1}\left\{\ln\left(\dfrac{s+2}{s+1}\right)\right\}$,   (b) $\mathcal{L}^{-1}\left\{\dfrac{1}{s}\ln\left(\dfrac{s+2}{s+1}\right)\right\}$.

Ans. (a) $(e^{-t} - e^{-2t})/t$,   (b) $\displaystyle\int_0^t \frac{e^{-u} - e^{-2u}}{u}\,du$

68. Find $\mathcal{L}^{-1}\{\tan^{-1}(2/s^2)\}$.   *Ans.* $2\sin t\sinh t/t$

69. Find $\mathcal{L}^{-1}\left\{\dfrac{1}{s}\ln\left(\dfrac{s^2+a^2}{s^2+b^2}\right)\right\}$.   *Ans.* $\displaystyle\int_0^t \dfrac{\cos au-\cos bu}{u}\,du$

MULTIPLICATION AND DIVISION BY POWERS OF s

70. Prove that $\mathcal{L}^{-1}\left\{\dfrac{f(s)}{s^3}\right\} = \displaystyle\int_0^t\int_0^v\int_0^w F(u)\,du\,dv\,dw.$

Can the integral be written as $\displaystyle\int_0^t\int_0^t\int_0^t F(t)\,dt^3$?   Explain.

71. Evaluate   (a) $\mathcal{L}^{-1}\left\{\dfrac{1}{s^3(s+1)}\right\}$,   (b) $\mathcal{L}^{-1}\left\{\dfrac{s+2}{s^2(s+3)}\right\}$,   (c) $\mathcal{L}^{-1}\left\{\dfrac{1}{s(s+1)^3}\right\}$.

Ans. (a) $1-t+\frac{1}{2}t^2-e^{-t}$,   (b) $\frac{2}{3}t+\frac{1}{9}-\frac{1}{9}e^{-3t}$,   (c) $1-e^{-t}(1+t+\frac{1}{2}t^2)$

72. Find   (a) $\mathcal{L}^{-1}\left\{\dfrac{1}{s\sqrt{s+4}}\right\}$,   (b) $\mathcal{L}^{-1}\left\{\dfrac{1}{s\sqrt{s^2+a^2}}\right\}$.

Ans. (a) $\frac{1}{2}\operatorname{erf}(2\sqrt{t})$,   (b) $\displaystyle\int_0^t J_0(au)\,du$

73. Find   (a) $\mathcal{L}^{-1}\left\{\dfrac{1}{(s-1)^5(s+2)}\right\}$,   (b) $\mathcal{L}^{-1}\left\{\dfrac{s}{(s-2)^5(s+1)}\right\}$ and discuss the relationship between these inverse transforms.

Ans. (a) $\dfrac{e^t}{72}\left(t^4-\dfrac{4}{3}t^3+\dfrac{4}{3}t^2-\dfrac{8}{9}t+\dfrac{8}{27}\right)-\dfrac{e^{-2t}}{243}$

(b) $e^{2t}\left(\dfrac{t^4}{36}+\dfrac{t^3}{54}-\dfrac{t^2}{54}+\dfrac{t}{81}-\dfrac{1}{243}\right)+\dfrac{e^{-t}}{243}$

74. If $F(t)=\mathcal{L}^{-1}\{f(s)\}$,   show that

(a) $\mathcal{L}^{-1}\{s\,f'(s)\} = -t\,F'(t)-F(t)$ (c) $\mathcal{L}^{-1}\{s^2 f''(s)\} = t^2\,F''(t)+4t\,F'(t)+2\,F(t)$

(b) $\mathcal{L}^{-1}\{s\,f''(s)\} = t^2\,F'(t)+2t\,F(t)$

75. Show that $\mathcal{L}^{-1}\{s^2 f'(s)+F(0)\} = -t\,F''(t)-2\,F'(t)$.

THE CONVOLUTION THEOREM

76. Use the convolution theorem to find   (a) $\mathcal{L}^{-1}\left\{\dfrac{1}{(s+3)(s-1)}\right\}$,   (b) $\mathcal{L}^{-1}\left\{\dfrac{1}{(s+2)^2(s-2)}\right\}$.

Ans. (a) $\frac{1}{4}(e^t-e^{-3t})$,   (b) $\frac{1}{16}(e^{2t}-e^{-2t}-4te^{-2t})$

77. Find $\mathcal{L}^{-1}\left\{\dfrac{1}{(s+1)(s^2+1)}\right\}$.   *Ans.* $\frac{1}{2}(\sin t-\cos t+e^{-t})$

78. Find $\mathcal{L}^{-1}\left\{\dfrac{s^2}{(s^2+4)^2}\right\}$.   *Ans.* $\frac{1}{2}t\cos 2t+\frac{1}{4}\sin 2t$

79. Find   (a) $\mathcal{L}^{-1}\left\{\dfrac{1}{(s^2+1)^3}\right\}$,   (b) $\mathcal{L}^{-1}\left\{\dfrac{s}{(s^2+4)^3}\right\}$.

Ans. (a) $\frac{1}{8}\{(3-t^2)\sin t-3t\cos t\}$,   (b) $\frac{1}{64}t(\sin 2t-2t\cos 2t)$

80. Prove that $F * \{G * H\} = \{F * G\} * H$, i.e. the *associative law* for convolutions.

81. Prove that (a) $F * \{G + H\} = F * G + F * H$, (b) $\{F + G\} * H = F * H + G * H$.

82. Show that $1 * 1 * 1 * \ldots * 1$ (n ones) $= t^{n-1}/(n-1)!$ where $n = 1, 2, 3, \ldots$.

83. Show that $\displaystyle \int_0^t \int_0^t \int_0^t F(t)\, dt^3 = \int_0^t \frac{(t-u)^2}{2!}\, F(u)\, du$.

84. Show that $\displaystyle \int_0^t \int_0^t \cdots \int_0^t F(t)\, dt^n = \int_0^t \frac{(t-u)^{n-1}}{(n-1)!}\, F(u)\, du$.

85. Prove the convolution theorem directly by showing that

$$f(s)\, g(s) = \left\{ \int_0^\infty e^{-su}\, F(u)\, du \right\} \left\{ \int_0^\infty e^{-sv}\, G(v)\, dv \right\}$$

$$= \int_0^\infty \int_0^\infty e^{-s(u+v)}\, F(u)\, G(v)\, du\, dv$$

$$= \int_0^\infty e^{-st} \left\{ \int_0^t F(u)\, G(t-u)\, du \right\}\, dt.$$

86. Using the convolution theorem, verify that

$$\int_0^t \sin u \cos (t-u)\, du = \tfrac{1}{2} t \sin t$$

87. Show that $\displaystyle \frac{1}{\pi} \int_0^t \frac{e^{(a-b)u}}{\sqrt{u(t-u)}}\, du = e^{(a-b)t/2}\, I_0\{\tfrac{1}{2}(a-b)t\}$.

PARTIAL FRACTIONS

88. Use partial fractions to find (a) $\mathcal{L}^{-1}\left\{ \dfrac{3s + 16}{s^2 - s - 6} \right\}$, (b) $\mathcal{L}^{-1}\left\{ \dfrac{2s - 1}{s^3 - s} \right\}$.

   Ans. (a) $5e^{3t} - 2e^{-2t}$, (b) $1 - \tfrac{3}{2}e^{-t} + \tfrac{1}{2}e^t$

89. Find (a) $\mathcal{L}^{-1}\left\{ \dfrac{s + 1}{6s^2 + 7s + 2} \right\}$, (b) $\mathcal{L}^{-1}\left\{ \dfrac{11s^2 - 2s + 5}{(s - 2)(2s - 1)(s + 1)} \right\}$.

   Ans. (a) $\tfrac{1}{2}e^{-t/2} - \tfrac{1}{3}e^{-2t/3}$, (b) $5e^{2t} - \tfrac{3}{2}e^{t/2} + 2e^{-t}$

90. Find (a) $\mathcal{L}^{-1}\left\{ \dfrac{27 - 12s}{(s + 4)(s^2 + 9)} \right\}$, (b) $\mathcal{L}^{-1}\left\{ \dfrac{s^3 + 16s - 24}{s^4 + 20s^2 + 64} \right\}$.

   Ans. (a) $3e^{-4t} - 3 \cos 3t$, (b) $\tfrac{1}{2} \sin 4t + \cos 2t - \sin 2t$

91. Find $\mathcal{L}^{-1}\left\{ \dfrac{s - 1}{(s + 3)(s^2 + 2s + 2)} \right\}$.   *Ans.* $\tfrac{1}{5}e^{-t}(4 \cos t - 3 \sin t) - \tfrac{4}{5}e^{-3t}$

92. Find (a) $\mathcal{L}^{-1}\left\{ \dfrac{s^2 - 2s + 3}{(s - 1)^2 (s + 1)} \right\}$, (b) $\mathcal{L}^{-1}\left\{ \dfrac{3s^3 - 3s^2 - 40s + 36}{(s^2 - 4)^2} \right\}$.

   Ans. (a) $\tfrac{1}{2}(2t - 1)e^t + \tfrac{3}{2}e^{-t}$, (b) $(5t + 3)e^{-2t} - 2te^{2t}$

93. Find $\mathcal{L}^{-1}\left\{\dfrac{s^2-3}{(s+2)(s-3)(s^2+2s+5)}\right\}$.

    Ans. $\frac{3}{50}e^{3t} - \frac{1}{25}e^{-2t} - \frac{1}{50}e^{-t}\cos 2t + \frac{9}{25}e^{-t}\sin 2t$

94. Find $\mathcal{L}^{-1}\left\{\dfrac{s}{(s^2-2s+2)(s^2+2s+2)}\right\}$.   *Ans.* $\frac{1}{2}\sin t \sinh t$

95. Find $\mathcal{L}^{-1}\left\{\dfrac{2s^3-s^2-1}{(s+1)^2(s^2+1)^2}\right\}$.   *Ans.* $\frac{1}{2}\sin t + \frac{1}{2}t\cos t - te^{-t}$

96. Use partial fractions to work (*a*) Problem 44, (*b*) Problem 71, (*c*) Problem 73, (*d*) Problem 76, (*e*) Problem 77.

97. Can Problems 79(*a*) and 79(*b*) be worked by partial fractions? Explain.

HEAVISIDE'S EXPANSION FORMULA

98. Using Heaviside's expansion formula find (*a*) $\mathcal{L}^{-1}\left\{\dfrac{2s-11}{(s+2)(s-3)}\right\}$, (*b*) $\mathcal{L}^{-1}\left\{\dfrac{19s+37}{(s-2)(s+1)(s+3)}\right\}$.

    Ans. (*a*) $3e^{-2t} - e^{3t}$, (*b*) $5e^{2t} - 3e^{-t} - 2e^{-3t}$

99. Find $\mathcal{L}^{-1}\left\{\dfrac{2s^2-6s+5}{s^3-6s^2+11s-6}\right\}$.   *Ans.* $\frac{1}{2}e^t - e^{2t} + \frac{5}{2}e^{3t}$

100. Find $\mathcal{L}^{-1}\left\{\dfrac{s+5}{(s+1)(s^2+1)}\right\}$.   *Ans.* $2e^{-t} + 3\sin t - 2\cos t$

101. Use Heaviside's expansion formula to work (*a*) Problem 76(*a*), (*b*) Problem 77, (*c*) Problem 88, (*d*) Problem 89, (*e*) Problem 90.

102. Find $\mathcal{L}^{-1}\left\{\dfrac{s-1}{(s+3)(s^2+2s+2)}\right\}$. Compare with Problem 91.

103. Find $\mathcal{L}^{-1}\left\{\dfrac{s^2-3}{(s+2)(s-3)(s^2+2s+5)}\right\}$. Compare with Problem 93.

104. Find $\mathcal{L}^{-1}\left\{\dfrac{s}{(s^2-2s+2)(s^2+2s+2)}\right\}$. Compare with Problem 94.

105. Suppose that $f(s) = P(s)/Q(s)$ where $P(s)$ and $Q(s)$ are polynomials as in Problem 29 but that $Q(s) = 0$ has a repeated root a of multiplicity m while the remaining roots, $b_1, b_2, \ldots, b_n$ do not repeat.

(*a*) Show that

$$f(s) = \frac{P(s)}{Q(s)} = \frac{A_1}{(s-a)^m} + \frac{A_2}{(s-a)^{m-1}} + \cdots + \frac{A_m}{s-a} + \frac{B_1}{s-b_1} + \frac{B_2}{s-b_2} + \cdots + \frac{B_n}{s-b_n}$$

(*b*) Show that $A_k = \lim\limits_{s \to a} \dfrac{1}{(k-1)!} \dfrac{d^{k-1}}{ds^{k-1}}\{(s-a)^m f(s)\}, \quad k = 1, 2, \ldots, m.$

(*c*) Show that $\mathcal{L}^{-1}\{f(s)\} = e^{at}\left\{\dfrac{A_1 t^{m-1}}{(m-1)!} + \dfrac{A_2 t^{m-2}}{(m-2)!} + \cdots + A_m\right\} + B_1 e^{b_1 t} + \cdots + B_n e^{b_n t}.$

106. Use Problem 105 to find   (a) $\mathcal{L}^{-1}\left\{\dfrac{2s^2 - 9s + 19}{(s-1)^2\,(s+3)}\right\}$,   (b) $\mathcal{L}^{-1}\left\{\dfrac{2s+3}{(s+1)^2\,(s+2)^2}\right\}$.

   Ans. (a) $(3t-2)e^t + 4e^{-3t}$,   (b) $t(e^{-t} - e^{-2t})$

107. Find $\mathcal{L}^{-1}\left\{\dfrac{11s^3 - 47s^2 + 56s + 4}{(s-2)^3\,(s+2)}\right\}$.   *Ans.* $(2t^2 - t + 5)e^{2t} + 6e^{-2t}$

108. Use Problem 105 to work   (a) Problem 26,   (b) Problem 44,   (c) Problem 71,   (d) Problem 73, (e) Problem 76(b).

109. Can the method of Problem 105 be used to work Problems 79(a) and 79(b)? Explain.

110. Find $\mathcal{L}^{-1}\left\{\dfrac{2s^3 - s^2 - 1}{(s+1)^2\,(s^2+1)^2}\right\}$ using Problem 105.   Compare with Problem 95.

111. Develop a Heaviside expansion formula which will work for the case of repeated quadratic factors.

112. Find $\mathcal{L}^{-1}\left\{\dfrac{4s^4 + 5s^3 + 6s^2 + 8s + 2}{(s-1)(s^2+2s+2)^2}\right\}$ using the method developed in Problem 111.

   Ans. $e^t + e^{-t}\{(3-2t)\cos t - 3\sin t\}$

THE BETA FUNCTION

113. Evaluate each of the following: (a) $\displaystyle\int_0^1 x^{3/2}\,(1-x)^2\,dx$, (b) $\displaystyle\int_0^4 x^3(4-x)^{-1/2}\,dx$, (c) $\displaystyle\int_0^2 y^4\sqrt{4-y^2}\,dy$

   Ans. (a) 16/315, (b) 4096/35, (c) 2π

114. Show that $\displaystyle\int_0^1 \sqrt{1-x^2}\,dx = \pi/4$.

115. Evaluate each of the following: (a) $\displaystyle\int_0^{\pi/2} \cos^6\theta\,d\theta$, (b) $\displaystyle\int_0^{\pi/2} \sin^2\theta\,\cos^4\theta\,d\theta$, (c) $\displaystyle\int_0^\pi \sin^4\theta\,\cos^4\theta\,d\theta$.

   Ans. (a) $5\pi/32$, (b) $\pi/32$, (c) $3\pi/128$

116. Prove that

$$\int_0^{\pi/2} \sin^p\theta\,d\theta = \int_0^{\pi/2} \cos^p\theta\,d\theta = \begin{cases} (a)\ \dfrac{1\cdot 3\cdot 5\,\cdots\,(p-1)}{2\cdot 4\cdot 6\,\cdots\, p}\,\dfrac{\pi}{2} & \text{if } p \text{ is an even positive integer,} \\[2ex] (b)\ \dfrac{2\cdot 4\cdot 6\,\cdots\,(p-1)}{1\cdot 3\cdot 5\,\cdots\, p} & \text{if } p \text{ is an odd positive integer.} \end{cases}$$

117. Given that $\displaystyle\int_0^\infty \dfrac{x^{p-1}}{1+x}\,dx = \dfrac{\pi}{\sin p\pi}$,   show that $\Gamma(p)\,\Gamma(1-p) = \dfrac{\pi}{\sin p\pi}$ where $0 < p < 1$.

   [*Hint.* Let $x/(1+x) = y$.]

118. Use Problem 117 to show that $\displaystyle\int_0^\infty \dfrac{y^2\,dy}{1+y^4} = \dfrac{\pi}{2\sqrt{2}}$.

119. Show that $\int_0^{\pi/2} \sqrt{\tan\theta}\, d\theta \;=\; \dfrac{\pi\sqrt{2}}{2}$.

EVALUATION OF INTEGRALS

120. Show that $\int_0^\infty \sin x^2\, dx \;=\; \tfrac{1}{2}\sqrt{\pi/2}$.

121. Evaluate $\int_0^\infty \dfrac{\sin x}{x}\, dx$. *Ans.* $\pi/2$

122. Show that $\int_0^\infty x \cos x^3\, dx \;=\; \dfrac{\pi}{3\sqrt{3}\ \Gamma(1/3)}$.

123. Prove that if $0 < p < 1$, $(a)\;\displaystyle\int_0^\infty \frac{\sin x}{x^p}\, dx \;=\; \frac{\pi}{2\,\Gamma(p)\,\sin\,(p\pi/2)}$

$(b)\;\displaystyle\int_0^\infty \frac{\cos x}{x^p}\, dx \;=\; \frac{\pi}{2\,\Gamma(p)\,\cos\,(p\pi/2)}$.

124. Use the results in Problem 123 to verify the results of Problems 120, 121 and 122.

125. (a) Show that $\int_0^\infty x^2 e^{-x^2}\, dx$ converges.

(b) If $t > 0$, is $\mathcal{L}\left\{\displaystyle\int_0^\infty x^2 e^{-tx^2}\, dx\right\} \;=\; \displaystyle\int_0^\infty \mathcal{L}\left\{x^2 e^{-tx^2}\right\} dx$?

(c) Can the method of Problem 37 be used to evaluate the integral in (a)? Explain.

126. Evaluate $\int_0^t J_0(u)\, J_1(t-u)\, du$. *Ans.* $J_0(t) - \cos t$

MISCELLANEOUS PROBLEMS

127. Find $\mathcal{L}^{-1}\left\{\dfrac{1}{s^3+1}\right\}$. *Ans.* $\dfrac{1}{3}\left\{e^{-t} - e^{t/2}\left(\cos\dfrac{\sqrt{3}}{2}t - \sqrt{3}\sin\dfrac{\sqrt{3}}{2}t\right)\right\}$

128. Prove that $\int_a^b (x-a)^p (b-x)^q\, dx \;=\; (b-a)^{p+q+1} B(p+1, q+1)$ where $p > -1$, $q > -1$ and $b > a$.

[*Hint.* Let $x - a = (b-a)y$.]

129. Evaluate $(a)\;\displaystyle\int_2^4 \frac{dx}{\sqrt{(x-2)(4-x)}}$, $(b)\;\displaystyle\int_1^5 \sqrt[4]{(5-x)(x-1)}\, dx$. *Ans.* (a) π, (b) $\dfrac{2\{\Gamma(1/4)\}^2}{3\sqrt{\pi}}$

130. Find $\mathcal{L}^{-1}\left\{\dfrac{e^{-s}(1 - e^{-s})}{s(s^2+1)}\right\}$. *Ans.* $\{1 - \cos\,(t-1)\}\,\mathcal{U}(t-1) - \{1 - \cos\,(t-2)\}\,\mathcal{U}(t-2)$

131. Show that $\mathcal{L}^{-1}\left\{\dfrac{e^{-x\sqrt{s}}}{\sqrt{s}}\right\} \;=\; \dfrac{e^{-x^2/4t}}{\sqrt{\pi t}}$.

132. Prove that $\int_0^t J_0(u)\, \sin\,(t-u)\, du \;=\; \tfrac{1}{2}t\, J_1(t)$.

133. (a) Show that the function $f(s) = \dfrac{1 - e^{-2\pi s}}{s}$ is zero for infinitely many complex values of s. What are these values? (b) Find the inverse Laplace transform of $f(s)$.

Ans. (a) $s = \pm i, \pm 2i, \pm 3i, \ldots$ (b) $F(t) = \begin{cases} 1 & t > 2\pi \\ 0 & 0 < t < 2\pi \end{cases}$ or $F(t) = \mathcal{U}(t - 2\pi)$

134. Find $\mathcal{L}^{-1}\left\{\ln\left(\dfrac{s + \sqrt{s^2 + 1}}{2s}\right)\right\}$.   Ans. $\dfrac{1 - J_0(t)}{t}$

135. Show that $\displaystyle\int_0^2 u(8 - u^3)^{1/3}\, du = \dfrac{16\sqrt{3}\,\pi}{27}$.

136. Let $F(t) = t^2$ at all values of t which are irrational, and $F(t) = t$ at all values of t which are rational. (a) Prove that $\mathcal{L}\{F(t)\} = 2/s^3$, $s > 0$. (b) Discuss the significance of the result in (a) from the viewpoint of the uniqueness of inverse Laplace transforms.

137. Show how series methods can be used to evaluate (a) $\mathcal{L}^{-1}\{1/(s^2 + 1)\}$, (b) $\mathcal{L}^{-1}\{\ln(1 + 1/s)\}$, (c) $\mathcal{L}^{-1}\{\tan^{-1}(1/s)\}$.

138. Find $\mathcal{L}^{-1}\{e^{-3s - 2\sqrt{s}}\}$.   Ans. $\dfrac{1}{\sqrt{\pi(t-3)^3}}\, e^{-1/(t-3)}\, \mathcal{U}(t - 3)$

139. Show that $\displaystyle\int_0^\infty \dfrac{u \sin tu}{1 + u^2}\, du = \dfrac{\pi}{2} e^{-t}, \quad t > 0$.

140. If $F(t) = t^{-1/2}$, $t > 0$ and $G(t) = \begin{cases} t^{-1/2} & 0 < t < 1 \\ 0 & t > 1 \end{cases}$, show that

$$F(t) * G(t) = \begin{cases} \pi & 0 < t < 1 \\ \pi - 2\tan^{-1}\sqrt{t-1} & t > 1 \end{cases}$$

141. Show that $\mathcal{L}^{-1}\left\{\dfrac{\sqrt{s+1} - \sqrt{s}}{\sqrt{s+1} + \sqrt{s}}\right\} = \dfrac{e^{-t/2}\, I_1(t/2)}{t}$.

142. Find $\mathcal{L}^{-1}\left\{\dfrac{\sqrt{s}}{s - 1}\right\}$.   Ans. $t^{-1/2}/\sqrt{\pi} + e^t\, \mathrm{erf}\,\sqrt{t}$

143. Show that (a) $\displaystyle\int_0^{\pi/2} \sin(t \sin^2 \theta)\, d\theta = \tfrac{1}{2}\sin(t/2)\, J_0(t/2)$

(b) $\displaystyle\int_0^{\pi/2} \cos(t \cos^2 \theta)\, d\theta = \tfrac{1}{2}\cos(t/2)\, J_0(t/2)$.

144. Let $\mathcal{L}^{-1}\{f(s)\} = F(t)$ have period $T > 0$. Prove that

$$\mathcal{L}^{-1}\{f(s)(1 - e^{-sT})\} = F(t) \text{ if } 0 < t < T \text{ and zero if } t > T.$$

145. (a) Show that $\mathcal{L}^{-1}\left\{\dfrac{1}{s^3 + 1}\right\} = \dfrac{t^2}{2!} - \dfrac{t^5}{5!} + \dfrac{t^8}{8!} - \dfrac{t^{11}}{11!} + \cdots$.

(b) Discuss the relationship of the result in (a) to that of Problem 127.

146. Can Heaviside's expansion formula be applied to the function $f(s) = 1/(s \cosh s)$?   Explain.

147. Prove that $\displaystyle\int_0^\infty J_0(x^2)\, dx = 1/4\sqrt{\pi}$.

148. Show that

$$\mathcal{L}^{-1}\left\{\frac{1}{s}\sin\frac{1}{s}\right\} = t - \frac{t^3}{(3!)^2} + \frac{t^5}{(5!)^2} - \frac{t^7}{(7!)^2} + \cdots$$

$$= \frac{i}{2}\{J_0(2e^{\pi i/4}\sqrt{t}) - J_0(2e^{-\pi i/4}\sqrt{t})\}$$

149. Show that

$$\mathcal{L}^{-1}\left\{\frac{1}{s}\cos\frac{1}{s}\right\} = 1 - \frac{t^2}{(2!)^2} + \frac{t^4}{(4!)^2} - \frac{t^6}{(6!)^2} + \cdots$$

150. Find $\mathcal{L}^{-1}\left\{\dfrac{1}{1+\sqrt{s}}\right\}$.   *Ans.* $t^{-1/2}/\sqrt{\pi} - e^t \operatorname{erfc}(\sqrt{t})$

151. Show that

$$\mathcal{L}^{-1}\left\{\frac{1}{s+e^{-s}}\right\} = \sum_{n=0}^{[t]} \frac{(-1)^n (t-n)^n}{n!}$$

where $[t]$ denotes the greatest integer less than or equal to t.

152. Show that $\mathcal{L}^{-1}\left\{\dfrac{1}{s} J_0\left(\dfrac{2}{\sqrt{s}}\right)\right\} = 1 - \dfrac{t}{(1!)^3} + \dfrac{t^2}{(2!)^3} - \dfrac{t^3}{(3!)^3} + \cdots$

Chapter 3

Applications To
Differential Equations

ORDINARY DIFFERENTIAL EQUATIONS WITH CONSTANT COEFFICIENTS

The Laplace transform is useful in solving linear ordinary differential equations with constant coefficients. For example, suppose we wish to solve the second order linear differential equation

$$\frac{d^2Y}{dt^2} + \alpha\frac{dY}{dt} + \beta Y = F(t) \qquad \text{or} \qquad Y'' + \alpha Y' + \beta Y = F(t) \tag{1}$$

where α and β are constants, subject to the *initial* or *boundary conditions*

$$Y(0) = A, \qquad Y'(0) = B \tag{2}$$

where A and B are given constants. On taking the Laplace transform of both sides of (*1*) and using (*2*), we obtain an algebraic equation for determination of $\mathcal{L}\{Y(t)\} = y(s)$. The required solution is then obtained by finding the inverse Laplace transform of $y(s)$. The method is easily extended to higher order differential equations. See Problems 1-8.

ORDINARY DIFFERENTIAL EQUATIONS WITH VARIABLE COEFFICIENTS

The Laplace transform can also be used in solving some ordinary differential equations in which the coefficients are variable. A particular differential equation where the method proves useful is one in which the terms have the form

$$t^m\, Y^{(n)}(t) \tag{3}$$

the Laplace transform of which is

$$(-1)^m \frac{d^m}{ds^m} \mathcal{L}\{Y^{(n)}(t)\} \tag{4}$$

See *Theorem 1-10*, Page 4, and *Theorem 1-12*, Page 5.

For details of solution see Problems 9-11.

SIMULTANEOUS ORDINARY DIFFERENTIAL EQUATIONS

The Laplace transform can be used to solve two or more simultaneous ordinary differential equations. The procedure is essentially the same as that described above. See Problems 12 and 13.

APPLICATIONS TO MECHANICS

Suppose a mass m, attached to a flexible spring fixed at O, is free to move on a frictionless plane PQ [see Fig. 3-1]. If $X(t)$, or briefly X, denotes the instantaneous displacement of m at time t from the *equilibrium* or *rest position*, there will be a *restoring force* acting on m equal to $-kX$, where k is a constant depending on the spring, and called the *spring constant*. This follows from *Hooke's law* which, on the basis of experiment, states that the restoring force acting on a spring is proportional to the stretch or extension of the spring from the equilibrium position. According to Newton's law which states that the net force acting on m is equal to the mass times the acceleration, the equation of motion is

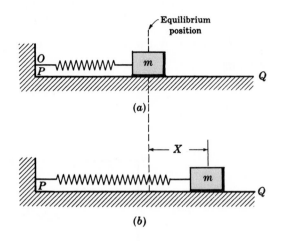

Fig. 3-1

$$m\frac{d^2X}{dt^2} = -kX \qquad \text{or} \qquad mX'' + kX = 0 \tag{5}$$

If in addition, there is a *damping force* proportional to the instantaneous speed of m, the equation of motion is

$$m\frac{d^2X}{dt^2} = -kX - \beta\frac{dX}{dt} \qquad \text{or} \qquad mX'' + \beta X' + kX = 0 \tag{6}$$

where the proportionality constant β is called the *damping constant*.

A further modification takes place when some prescribed time-varying external force $\mathcal{F}(t)$ also acts on m. In such case the equation of motion is

$$m\frac{d^2X}{dt^2} = -kX - \beta\frac{dX}{dt} + \mathcal{F}(t) \qquad \text{or} \qquad mX'' + \beta X' + kx = \mathcal{F}(t) \tag{7}$$

By using Laplace transforms to solve equations (5), (6) or (7) subject to various appropriate initial conditions of physical interest, the displacement $X(t)$ can be found. See Problems 14, 15, 27 and 28.

APPLICATIONS TO ELECTRICAL CIRCUITS

A simple electrical circuit [Fig. 3-2] consists of the following *circuit elements* connected in *series* with a *switch* or *key K*:

1. a *generator* or *battery*, supplying an *electromotive force* or *e.m.f.* E (volts),

2. a *resistor* having *resistance* R (ohms),

3. an *inductor* having *inductance* L (henrys),

4. a *capacitor* having *capacitance* C (farads).

These circuit elements are represented symbolically as in Fig. 3-2.

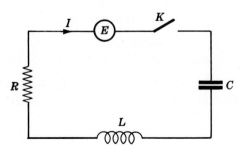

Fig. 3-2

When the switch or key K is closed, so that the circuit is completed, a charge Q (coulombs) will flow to the capacitor plates. The time rate of flow of charge, given by $\frac{dQ}{dt} = I$, is called the *current* and is measured in amperes when time t is measured in seconds.

More complex electrical circuits, as shown for example in Fig. 3-3, can occur in practice.

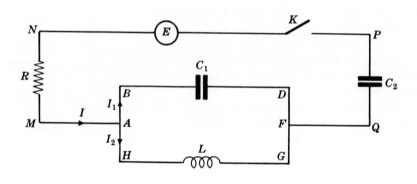

Fig. 3-3

An important problem is to determine the charges on the capacitors and currents as functions of time. To do this we define the *potential drop* or *voltage drop* across a circuit element.

(*a*) Voltage drop across a resistor $= RI = R\dfrac{dQ}{dt}$

(*b*) Voltage drop across an inductor $= L\dfrac{dI}{dt} = L\dfrac{d^2Q}{dt^2}$

(*c*) Voltage drop across a capacitor $= \dfrac{Q}{C}$

(*d*) Voltage drop across a generator $= -\text{Voltage rise} = -E$

The differential equations can then be found by using the following laws due to Kirchhoff.

Kirchhoff's Laws

1. The algebraic sum of the currents flowing toward any junction point [for example A in Fig. 3-3] is equal to zero.

2. The algebraic sum of the potential drops, or voltage drops, around any closed loop [such as $ABDFGHA$ or $ABDFQPNMA$ in Fig. 3-3] is equal to zero.

For the simple circuit of Fig. 3-2 application of these laws is particularly easy [the first law is actually not necessary in this case]. We find that the equation for determination of Q is

$$L\frac{d^2Q}{dt^2} + R\frac{dQ}{dt} + \frac{Q}{C} = E \tag{8}$$

By applying the laws to the circuit of Fig. 3-3, two simultaneous equations are obtained [see Problem 17].

Note the analogy of equation (8) with equation (7). It is at once apparent that *mass m* corresponds to *inductance L, displacement X* corresponds to *charge Q, damping factor β* to *resistance R, spring constant k* to *reciprocal of capacitance 1/C,* and *force F* to *electromotive force E.* Such analogies are often useful in practice.

APPLICATIONS TO BEAMS

Suppose that a beam whose ends are at $x = 0$ and $x = l$ is coincident with the x axis [Fig. 3-4]. Suppose also that a vertical load, given by $W(x)$ per unit length, acts transversely on the beam. Then the axis of the beam has a transverse deflection $Y(x)$ at the point x which satisfies the differential equation

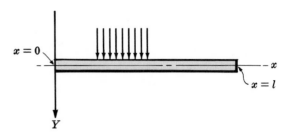

Fig. 3-4

$$\frac{d^4Y}{dx^4} = \frac{W(x)}{EI} \qquad 0 < x < l \qquad (9)$$

This transverse deflection is sometimes called the *deflection curve* or *elastic curve*. The quantity EI is called the *flexural rigidity* of the beam and we shall assume it to be constant. [Actually, E is *Young's modulus of elasticity* for the beam and I is the moment of inertia of a cross section of the beam about the axis.] The quantities $EI\,Y''(x)$ and $EI\,Y'''(x)$ are called respectively the *bending moment* and *vertical shear* at x. Note that the Y axis is taken as positive downward so that deflections are positive downward.

The boundary conditions associated with the differential equation (9) depend on the manner in which the beam is supported. The following are most common.

1. **Clamped, Built-In or Fixed End:** $Y = Y' = 0$

2. **Hinged or Simply-Supported End:** $Y = Y'' = 0$

3. **Free End:** $Y'' = Y''' = 0$

PARTIAL DIFFERENTIAL EQUATIONS

The Laplace transform is also useful in solving various partial differential equations subject to boundary conditions. Such problems are often referred to as *boundary-value problems.* We consider a few such simple problems in this chapter [see Problems 22-26 and 31]. A more complete discussion of boundary-value problems is given in Chapter 8 where advantage can be taken of the complex inversion formula of Chapter 6.

Solved Problems

ORDINARY DIFFERENTIAL EQUATIONS WITH CONSTANT COEFFICIENTS

1. Solve $Y'' + Y = t$, $Y(0) = 1$, $Y'(0) = -2$.

Taking the Laplace transform of both sides of the differential equation and using the given conditions, we have

$$\mathcal{L}\{Y''\} + \mathcal{L}\{Y\} = \mathcal{L}\{t\}, \qquad s^2 y - s\,Y(0) - Y'(0) + y = \frac{1}{s^2}$$

$$s^2 y - s + 2 + y = \frac{1}{s^2}$$

Then
$$y = \mathcal{L}\{Y\} = \frac{1}{s^2(s^2+1)} + \frac{s-2}{s^2+1}$$

$$= \frac{1}{s^2} - \frac{1}{s^2+1} + \frac{s}{s^2+1} - \frac{2}{s^2+1}$$

$$= \frac{1}{s^2} + \frac{s}{s^2+1} - \frac{3}{s^2+1}$$

and
$$Y = \mathcal{L}^{-1}\left\{\frac{1}{s^2} + \frac{s}{s^2+1} - \frac{3}{s^2+1}\right\} = t + \cos t - 3\sin t$$

Check: $Y = t + \cos t - 3\sin t$, $Y' = 1 - \sin t - 3\cos t$, $Y'' = -\cos t + 3\sin t$. Then $Y'' + Y = t$, $Y(0) = 1$, $Y'(0) = -2$ and the function obtained is the required solution.

For another method, using the convolution integral, see Problem 7 and let $a = 1$, $F(t) = t$.

2. Solve $Y'' - 3Y' + 2Y = 4e^{2t}$, $Y(0) = -3$, $Y'(0) = 5$.

We have
$$\mathcal{L}\{Y''\} - 3\mathcal{L}\{Y'\} + 2\mathcal{L}\{Y\} = 4\mathcal{L}\{e^{2t}\}$$

$$\{s^2 y - s\,Y(0) - Y'(0)\} - 3\{sy - Y(0)\} + 2y = \frac{4}{s-2}$$

$$\{s^2 y + 3s - 5\} - 3\{sy + 3\} + 2y = \frac{4}{s-2}$$

$$(s^2 - 3s + 2)y + 3s - 14 = \frac{4}{s-2}$$

$$y = \frac{4}{(s^2-3s+2)(s-2)} + \frac{14-3s}{s^2-3s+2}$$

$$= \frac{-3s^2 + 20s - 24}{(s-1)(s-2)^2}$$

$$= \frac{-7}{s-1} + \frac{4}{s-2} + \frac{4}{(s-2)^2}$$

Thus
$$Y = \mathcal{L}^{-1}\left\{\frac{-7}{s-1} + \frac{4}{s-2} + \frac{4}{(s-2)^2}\right\} = -7e^t + 4e^{2t} + 4te^{2t}$$

which can be verified as the solution.

3. Solve $Y'' + 2Y' + 5Y = e^{-t} \sin t$, $Y(0) = 0$, $Y'(0) = 1$.

We have $\mathcal{L}\{Y''\} + 2\mathcal{L}\{Y'\} + 5\mathcal{L}\{Y\} = \mathcal{L}\{e^{-t}\sin t\}$

$$\{s^2 y - s\,Y(0) - Y'(0)\} + 2\{sy - Y(0)\} + 5y = \frac{1}{(s+1)^2 + 1} = \frac{1}{s^2 + 2s + 2}$$

$$\{s^2 y - s(0) - 1\} + 2\{sy - 0\} + 5y = \frac{1}{s^2 + 2s + 2}$$

$$(s^2 + 2s + 5)y - 1 = \frac{1}{s^2 + 2s + 2}$$

$$y = \frac{1}{s^2 + 2s + 5} + \frac{1}{(s^2 + 2s + 2)(s^2 + 2s + 5)}$$

$$= \frac{s^2 + 2s + 3}{(s^2 + 2s + 2)(s^2 + 2s + 5)}$$

Then [see Problem 28, Page 60]

$$Y = \mathcal{L}^{-1}\left\{\frac{s^2 + 2s + 3}{(s^2 + 2s + 2)(s^2 + 2s + 5)}\right\} = \frac{1}{3} e^{-t}(\sin t + \sin 2t)$$

4. Solve $Y''' - 3Y'' + 3Y' - Y = t^2 e^t$, $Y(0) = 1$, $Y'(0) = 0$, $Y''(0) = -2$.

We have $\mathcal{L}\{Y'''\} - 3\mathcal{L}\{Y''\} + 3\mathcal{L}\{Y'\} - \mathcal{L}\{Y\} = \mathcal{L}\{t^2 e^t\}$

$$\{s^3 y - s^2\,Y(0) - s\,Y'(0) - Y''(0)\} - 3\{s^2 y - s\,Y(0) - Y'(0)\} + 3\{sy - Y(0)\} - y = \frac{2}{(s-1)^3}$$

Thus $(s^3 - 3s^2 + 3s - 1)y - s^2 + 3s - 1 = \dfrac{2}{(s-1)^3}$

$$y = \frac{s^2 - 3s + 1}{(s-1)^3} + \frac{2}{(s-1)^6}$$

$$= \frac{s^2 - 2s + 1 - s}{(s-1)^3} + \frac{2}{(s-1)^6}$$

$$= \frac{(s-1)^2 - (s-1) - 1}{(s-1)^3} + \frac{2}{(s-1)^6}$$

$$= \frac{1}{s-1} - \frac{1}{(s-1)^2} - \frac{1}{(s-1)^3} + \frac{2}{(s-1)^6}$$

and $Y = e^t - te^t - \dfrac{t^2 e^t}{2} + \dfrac{t^5 e^t}{60}$

5. Find the general solution of the differential equation in Problem 4.

In this case, the initial conditions are arbitrary. If we assume $Y(0) = A$, $Y'(0) = B$, $Y''(0) = C$, we find as in Problem 4,

$$(s^3 y - As^2 - Bs - C) - 3(s^2 y - As - B) + 3(sy - A) - y = \frac{2}{(s-1)^3}$$

or $y = \dfrac{As^2 + (B - 3A)s + 3A - 3B + C}{(s-1)^3} + \dfrac{2}{(s-1)^6}$

Since A, B and C are arbitrary, so also is the polynomial in the numerator of the first term on the right. We can thus write

$$y = \frac{c_1}{(s-1)^3} + \frac{c_2}{(s-1)^2} + \frac{c_3}{s-1} + \frac{2}{(s-1)^6}$$

and invert to find the required general solution

$$y = \frac{c_1 t^2}{2} e^t + c_2 t e^t + c_3 e^t + \frac{t^5 e^t}{60}$$

$$= c_4 t^2 + c_5 t e^t + c_6 e^t + \frac{t^5 e^t}{60}$$

where the c_k's are arbitrary constants.

It should be noted that finding the general solution is easier than finding the particular solution since we avoid the necessity of determining the constants in the partial fraction expansion.

6. Solve $Y'' + 9Y = \cos 2t$ if $Y(0) = 1$, $Y(\pi/2) = -1$.

Since $Y'(0)$ is not known, let $Y'(0) = c$. Then

$$\mathcal{L}\{Y''\} + 9\mathcal{L}\{Y\} = \mathcal{L}\{\cos 2t\}$$

$$s^2 y - s Y(0) - Y'(0) + 9y = \frac{s}{s^2 + 4}$$

$$(s^2 + 9)y - s - c = \frac{s}{s^2 + 4}$$

and

$$y = \frac{s + c}{s^2 + 9} + \frac{s}{(s^2 + 9)(s^2 + 4)}$$

$$= \frac{s}{s^2 + 9} + \frac{c}{s^2 + 9} + \frac{s}{5(s^2 + 4)} - \frac{s}{5(s^2 + 9)}$$

$$= \frac{4}{5}\left(\frac{s}{s^2 + 9}\right) + \frac{c}{s^2 + 9} + \frac{s}{5(s^2 + 4)}$$

Thus

$$Y = \frac{4}{5}\cos 3t + \frac{c}{3}\sin 3t + \frac{1}{5}\cos 2t$$

To determine c, note that $Y(\pi/2) = -1$ so that $-1 = -c/3 - 1/5$ or $c = 12/5$. Then

$$Y = \frac{4}{5}\cos 3t + \frac{4}{5}\sin 3t + \frac{1}{5}\cos 2t$$

7. Solve $Y'' + a^2 Y = F(t)$, $Y(0) = 1$, $Y'(0) = -2$.

We have

$$\mathcal{L}\{Y''\} + a^2 \mathcal{L}\{Y\} = \mathcal{L}\{F(t)\} = f(s)$$

$$s^2 y - s Y(0) - Y'(0) + a^2 y = f(s)$$

$$s^2 y - s + 2 + a^2 y = f(s)$$

and so

$$y = \frac{s - 2}{s^2 + a^2} + \frac{f(s)}{s^2 + a^2}$$

Then using the convolution theorem,

$$Y = \mathcal{L}^{-1}\left\{\frac{s-2}{s^2+a^2}\right\} + \mathcal{L}^{-1}\left\{\frac{f(s)}{s^2+a^2}\right\}$$

$$= \cos at - \frac{2\sin at}{a} + F(t) * \frac{\sin at}{a}$$

$$= \cos at - \frac{2\sin at}{a} + \frac{1}{a}\int_0^t F(u)\sin a(t-u)\,du$$

Note that in this case the actual Laplace transform of $F(t)$ does not enter into the final solution.

8.   Find the general solution of $Y'' - a^2 Y = F(t)$.

Let $Y(0) = c_1$, $Y'(0) = c_2$.   Then taking the Laplace transform, we find

$$s^2 y - sc_1 - c_2 - a^2 y = f(s)$$

or

$$y = \frac{sc_1 + c_2}{s^2 - a^2} + \frac{f(s)}{s^2 - a^2}$$

Thus

$$Y = c_1 \cosh at + \frac{c_2}{a}\sinh at + \frac{1}{a}\int_0^t F(u)\sinh a(t-u)\,du$$

$$= A\cosh at + B\sinh at + \frac{1}{a}\int_0^t F(u)\sinh a(t-u)\,du$$

which is the required general solution.

ORDINARY DIFFERENTIAL EQUATIONS WITH VARIABLE COEFFICIENTS

9.   Solve $tY'' + Y' + 4tY = 0$, $Y(0) = 3$, $Y'(0) = 0$.

We have

$$\mathcal{L}\{tY''\} + \mathcal{L}\{Y'\} + \mathcal{L}\{4tY\} = 0$$

or

$$-\frac{d}{ds}\{s^2 y - s\,Y(0) - Y'(0)\} + \{sy - Y(0)\} - 4\frac{dy}{ds} = 0$$

i.e.,

$$(s^2 + 4)\frac{dy}{ds} + sy = 0$$

Then

$$\frac{dy}{y} + \frac{s\,ds}{s^2 + 4} = 0$$

and integrating

$$\ln y + \tfrac{1}{2}\ln(s^2 + 4) = c_1 \quad \text{or} \quad y = \frac{c}{\sqrt{s^2 + 4}}$$

Inverting, we find

$$Y = c\,J_0(2t)$$

To determine c note that $Y(0) = c\,J_0(0) = c = 3$.   Thus

$$Y = 3\,J_0(2t)$$

10. Solve $tY'' + 2Y' + tY = 0,\ Y(0+) = 1,\ Y(\pi) = 0.$

Let $Y'(0+) = c.$ Then taking the Laplace transform of each term

$$-\frac{d}{ds}\{s^2 y - s\,Y(0+) - Y'(0+)\} + 2\{sy - Y(0+)\} - \frac{d}{ds}y = 0$$

or

$$-s^2 y' - 2sy + 1 + 2sy - 2 - y' = 0$$

i.e.,

$$-(s^2 + 1)y' - 1 = 0 \quad\text{or}\quad y' = \frac{-1}{s^2 + 1}$$

Integrating,

$$y = -\tan^{-1} s + A$$

Since $y \to 0$ as $s \to \infty$, we must have $A = \pi/2.$ Thus

$$y = \frac{\pi}{2} - \tan^{-1} s = \tan^{-1}\frac{1}{s}$$

Then by the Example following *Theorem 1-13* on Page 5,

$$Y = \mathcal{L}^{-1}\left\{\tan^{-1}\frac{1}{s}\right\} = \frac{\sin t}{t}$$

This satisfies $Y(\pi) = 0$ and is the required solution.

11. Solve $Y'' - tY' + Y = 1,\ Y(0) = 1,\ Y'(0) = 2.$

We have

$$\mathcal{L}\{Y''\} - \mathcal{L}\{tY'\} + \mathcal{L}\{Y\} = \mathcal{L}\{1\} = \frac{1}{s}$$

i.e.,

$$s^2 y - s\,Y(0) - Y'(0) + \frac{d}{ds}\{sy - Y(0)\} + y = \frac{1}{s}$$

or

$$s^2 y - s - 2 + sy' + y + y = \frac{1}{s}$$

Then

$$sy' + (s^2 + 2)y = s + 2 + \frac{1}{s}$$

or

$$\frac{dy}{ds} + \left(s + \frac{2}{s}\right)y = 1 + \frac{2}{s} + \frac{1}{s^2}$$

An integrating factor is $e^{\int\left(s + \frac{2}{s}\right)ds} = e^{\frac{1}{2}s^2 + 2\ln s} = s^2\,e^{\frac{1}{2}s^2}.$ Then

$$\frac{d}{ds}\{s^2\,e^{\frac{1}{2}s^2}\,y\} = \left(1 + \frac{2}{s} + \frac{1}{s^2}\right)s^2\,e^{\frac{1}{2}s^2}$$

or integrating,

$$\begin{aligned}
y &= \frac{1}{s^2}\,e^{-\frac{1}{2}s^2}\int\left(1 + \frac{2}{s} + \frac{1}{s^2}\right)s^2\,e^{\frac{1}{2}s^2}\,ds \\[2mm]
&= \frac{1}{s^2}\,e^{-\frac{1}{2}s^2}\int(s^2 + 2s + 1)\,e^{\frac{1}{2}s^2}\,ds \\[2mm]
&= \frac{1}{s^2}\,e^{-\frac{1}{2}s^2}[se^{\frac{1}{2}s^2} + 2e^{\frac{1}{2}s^2} + c] \\[2mm]
&= \frac{1}{s} + \frac{2}{s^2} + \frac{c}{s^2}\,e^{-\frac{1}{2}s^2}
\end{aligned}$$

To determine c, note that by series expansion,

$$y = \frac{1}{s} + \frac{2}{s^2} + \frac{c}{s^2}(1 - \tfrac{1}{2}s^2 + \tfrac{1}{8}s^4 - \cdots)$$

$$= \frac{1}{s} + \frac{c+2}{s^2} - c(\tfrac{1}{2} - \tfrac{1}{8}s^2 + \cdots)$$

Then since $\mathcal{L}^{-1}\{s^k\} = 0$, $k = 0, 1, 2, \ldots$, we obtain on inverting,

$$Y = 1 + (c+2)t$$

But $Y'(0) = 2$, so that $c = 0$ and we have the required solution

$$Y = 1 + 2t$$

SIMULTANEOUS ORDINARY DIFFERENTIAL EQUATIONS

12. Solve $\begin{cases} \dfrac{dX}{dt} = 2X - 3Y \\[2mm] \dfrac{dY}{dt} = Y - 2X \end{cases}$ subject to $X(0) = 8$, $Y(0) = 3$.

Taking the Laplace transform, we have, if $\mathcal{L}\{X\} = x$, $\mathcal{L}\{Y\} = y$,

$$sx - 8 = 2x - 3y \qquad \text{or} \qquad (1) \quad (s-2)x + 3y = 8$$

$$sy - 3 = y - 2x \qquad \text{or} \qquad (2) \quad 2x + (s-1)y = 3$$

Solving (1) and (2) simultaneously,

$$x = \frac{\begin{vmatrix} 8 & 3 \\ 3 & s-1 \end{vmatrix}}{\begin{vmatrix} s-2 & 3 \\ 2 & s-1 \end{vmatrix}} = \frac{8s-17}{s^2-3s-4} = \frac{8s-17}{(s+1)(s-4)} = \frac{5}{s+1} + \frac{3}{s-4}$$

$$y = \frac{\begin{vmatrix} s-2 & 8 \\ 2 & 3 \end{vmatrix}}{\begin{vmatrix} s-2 & 3 \\ 2 & s-1 \end{vmatrix}} = \frac{3s-22}{s^2-3s-4} = \frac{3s-22}{(s+1)(s-4)} = \frac{5}{s+1} - \frac{2}{s-4}$$

Then

$$X = \mathcal{L}^{-1}\{x\} = 5e^{-t} + 3e^{4t}$$

$$Y = \mathcal{L}^{-1}\{y\} = 5e^{-t} - 2e^{4t}$$

13. Solve $\begin{cases} X'' + Y' + 3X = 15e^{-t} \\ Y'' - 4X' + 3Y = 15\sin 2t \end{cases}$ subject to $X(0) = 35$, $X'(0) = -48$, $Y(0) = 27$, $Y'(0) = -55$.

Taking the Laplace transform, we have

$$s^2x - s(35) - (-48) + sy - 27 + 3x = \frac{15}{s+1}$$

$$s^2y - s(27) - (-55) - 4\{sx - 35\} + 3y = \frac{30}{s^2+4}$$

or
$$(s^2 + 3)x + sy = 35s - 21 + \frac{15}{s+1} \qquad (1)$$

$$-4sx + (s^2 + 3)y = 27s - 195 + \frac{30}{s^2 + 4} \qquad (2)$$

Solving (1) and (2) simultaneously,

$$x = \frac{\begin{vmatrix} 35s - 21 + \dfrac{15}{s+1} & s \\[4mm] 27s - 195 + \dfrac{30}{s^2+4} & s^2 + 3 \end{vmatrix}}{\begin{vmatrix} s^2 + 3 & s \\[2mm] -4s & s^2 + 3 \end{vmatrix}}$$

$$= \frac{35s^3 - 48s^2 + 300s - 63}{(s^2+1)(s^2+9)} + \frac{15(s^2+3)}{(s+1)(s^2+1)(s^2+9)} - \frac{30s}{(s^2+1)(s^2+4)(s^2+9)}$$

$$= \frac{30s}{s^2+1} - \frac{45}{s^2+9} + \frac{3}{s+1} + \frac{2s}{s^2+4}$$

$$y = \frac{\begin{vmatrix} s^2 + 3 & 35s - 21 + \dfrac{15}{s+1} \\[4mm] -4s & 27s - 195 + \dfrac{30}{s^2+4} \end{vmatrix}}{\begin{vmatrix} s^2 + 3 & s \\[2mm] -4s & s^2 + 3 \end{vmatrix}}$$

$$= \frac{27s^3 - 55s^2 - 3s - 585}{(s^2+1)(s^2+9)} + \frac{60s}{(s+1)(s^2+1)(s^2+9)} + \frac{30(s^2+3)}{(s^2+1)(s^2+4)(s^2+9)}$$

$$= \frac{30s}{s^2+9} - \frac{60}{s^2+1} - \frac{3}{s+1} + \frac{2}{s^2+4}$$

Then
$$X = \mathcal{L}^{-1}\{x\} = 30 \cos t - 15 \sin 3t + 3e^{-t} + 2 \cos 2t$$

$$Y = \mathcal{L}^{-1}\{y\} = 30 \cos 3t - 60 \sin t - 3e^{-t} + \sin 2t$$

APPLICATIONS TO MECHANICS

14. A particle P of mass 2 grams moves on the X axis and is attracted toward origin O with a force numerically equal to $8X$. If it is initially at rest at $X = 10$, find its position at any subsequent time assuming (a) no other forces act, (b) a damping force numerically equal to 8 times the instantaneous velocity acts.

(a) Choose the positive direction to the right [see Fig. 3-5]. When $X > 0$, the net force is to the left (i.e. is negative) and must be given by $-8X$. When $X < 0$ the net force is to the right (i.e. is positive) and must be given by $-8X$. Hence in either case the net force is $-8X$. Then by Newton's law,

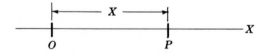

Fig. 3-5

$$(\text{Mass}) \cdot (\text{Acceleration}) = \text{Net force}$$

$$2 \cdot \frac{d^2X}{dt^2} = -8X$$

or
$$\frac{d^2X}{dt^2} + 4X = 0 \qquad (1)$$

The initial conditions are: (2) $X(0) = 10$, (3) $X'(0) = 0$.

Taking the Laplace transform of (1) and using conditions (2) and (3), we have, if $x = \mathcal{L}\{X\}$,

$$s^2 x - 10s + 4x = 0 \qquad \text{or} \qquad x = \frac{10s}{s^2 + 4}$$

Then $$X = \mathcal{L}^{-1}\{x\} = 10\cos 2t$$

The graph of the motion is shown in Fig. 3-6 below. The *amplitude* [maximum displacement from O] is 10. The *period* [time for a complete cycle] is π. The *frequency* [number of cycles per second] is $1/\pi$.

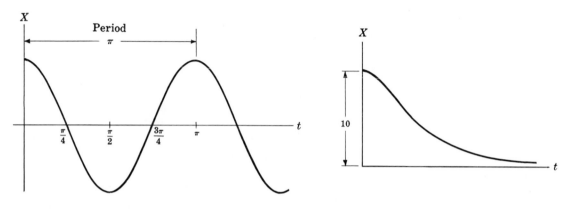

Fig. 3-6   Fig. 3-7

(b) When $X > 0$ and $dX/dt > 0$, P is on the right of O and moving to the right. Then the damping force is to the left (i.e. is negative) and must be given by $-8\,dX/dt$. Similarly when $X < 0$ and $dX/dt < 0$, P is on the left and moving to the left so the damping force is to the right (i.e. is positive) and must also be given by $-8\,dX/dt$. The damping force is also $-8\,dX/dt$ for the cases $X > 0$, $dX/dt < 0$ and $X < 0$, $dX/dt > 0$. Then

$$(\text{Mass})(\text{Acceleration}) = \text{Net force}$$

or $$2\frac{d^2X}{dt^2} = -8X - 8\frac{dX}{dt}$$

i.e., $$\frac{d^2X}{dt^2} + 4\frac{dX}{dt} + 4X = 0 \tag{4}$$

with initial conditions (5) $X(0) = 10$, (6) $X'(0) = 0$.

Taking the Laplace transform of (4) and using conditions (5) and (6), we have

$$s^2 x - 10s + 4(sx - 10) + 4x = 0$$

or $$x = \frac{10s + 40}{s^2 + 4s + 4}$$

Then $$X = \mathcal{L}^{-1}\{x\} = \mathcal{L}^{-1}\left\{\frac{10s + 40}{(s+2)^2}\right\} = \mathcal{L}^{-1}\left\{\frac{10(s+2) + 20}{(s+2)^2}\right\}$$

$$= 10\,\mathcal{L}^{-1}\left\{\frac{1}{s+2}\right\} + 20\,\mathcal{L}^{-1}\left\{\frac{1}{(s+2)^2}\right\}$$

$$= 10e^{-2t} + 20te^{-2t} = 10e^{-2t}(1 + 2t)$$

The graph of X vs. t is shown in Fig. 3-7 above. Note that the motion is *non-oscillatory*. The particle approaches O but never reaches it.

15. A particle of mass m moves along the X axis and is attracted toward origin O with a force numerically equal to kx, $k > 0$. A damping force given by $\beta\, dX/dt$, $\beta > 0$, also acts. Discuss the motion, treating all cases, assuming that $X(0) = X_0$, $X'(0) = V_0$.

The equation of motion is

$$m \frac{d^2X}{dt^2} = -kX - \beta \frac{dX}{dt}$$

or

$$\frac{d^2X}{dt^2} + 2\alpha \frac{dX}{dt} + \omega^2 X = 0 \tag{1}$$

where $\alpha = \beta/2m$, $\omega^2 = k/m$.

The Laplace transform of (1), using the initial conditions, yields

$$s^2 x - X_0 s - V_0 + 2\alpha(sx - X_0) + \omega^2 x = 0$$

or

$$x = \frac{sX_0 + (V_0 + 2\alpha X_0)}{s^2 + 2\alpha s + \omega^2}$$

$$= \frac{(s+\alpha)X_0}{(s+\alpha)^2 + \omega^2 - \alpha^2} + \frac{V_0 + \alpha X_0}{(s+\alpha)^2 + \omega^2 - \alpha^2}$$

Case 1, $\omega^2 - \alpha^2 > 0$.

In this case,

$$X = \mathcal{L}^{-1}\{x\} = X_0 e^{-\alpha t} \cos \sqrt{\omega^2 - \alpha^2}\, t + \frac{(V_0 + \alpha X_0)}{\sqrt{\omega^2 - \alpha^2}} e^{-\alpha t} \sin \sqrt{\omega^2 - \alpha^2}\, t$$

The motion is called *damped oscillatory* [see Fig. 3-8 below]. The particle oscillates about O, the magnitude of each oscillation becoming smaller with each swing. The period of the oscillations is given by $2\pi/\sqrt{\omega^2 - \alpha^2}$, and the frequency is $\sqrt{\omega^2 - \alpha^2}/2\pi$. The quantity $\omega/2\pi$ (corresponding to $\alpha = 0$, i.e. no damping) is called the *natural frequency*.

Case 2, $\omega^2 - \alpha^2 = 0$.

In this case,

$$X = \mathcal{L}^{-1}\{x\} = \mathcal{L}^{-1}\left\{ \frac{X_0}{s+\alpha} + \frac{V_0 + \alpha X_0}{(s+\alpha)^2} \right\}$$

$$= X_0 e^{-\alpha t} + (V_0 + \alpha X_0) t\, e^{-\alpha t}$$

Here the particle does not oscillate indefinitely about O. Instead, it approaches O gradually but never reaches it. The motion is called *critically damped motion* since any decrease in the damping constant β would produce oscillations [see Fig. 3-9 below].

Case 3, $\omega^2 - \alpha^2 < 0$.

In this case,

$$X = \mathcal{L}^{-1}\{x\} = \mathcal{L}^{-1}\left\{ \frac{(s+\alpha)X_0}{(s+\alpha)^2 - (\alpha^2 - \omega^2)} + \frac{V_0 + \alpha X_0}{(s+\alpha)^2 - (\alpha^2 - \omega^2)} \right\}$$

$$= X_0 \cosh \sqrt{\alpha^2 - \omega^2}\, t + \frac{V_0 + \alpha X_0}{\sqrt{\alpha^2 - \omega^2}} \sinh \sqrt{\alpha^2 - \omega^2}\, t$$

The motion is called *overdamped motion* and is non-oscillatory. The graph is similar to that of critically damped motion [see Fig. 3-10 below].

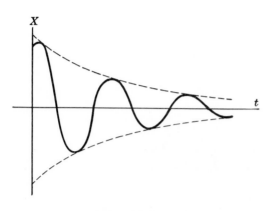

Damped oscillatory motion
Fig. 3-8

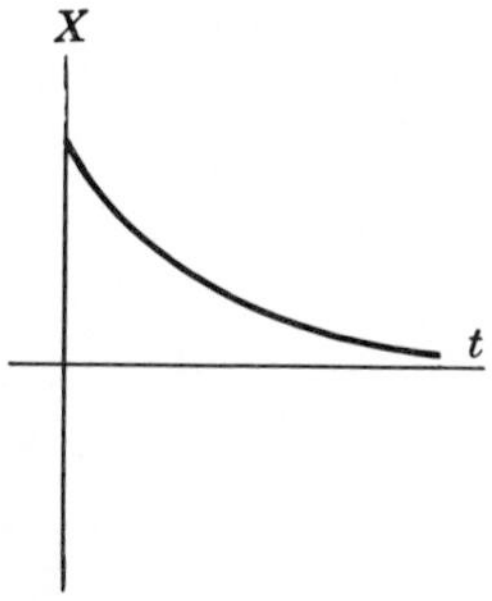

Critically damped motion
Fig. 3-9

Overdamped motion
Fig. 3-10

APPLICATIONS TO ELECTRICAL CIRCUITS

16. An inductor of 2 henrys, a resistor of 16 ohms and a capacitor of .02 farads are connected in series with an e.m.f. of E volts.   At $t = 0$ the charge on the capacitor and current in the circuit are zero.   Find the charge and current at any time $t > 0$ if (a) $E = 300$ (volts), (b) $E = 100 \sin 3t$ (volts).

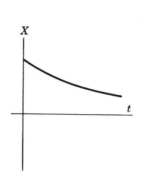

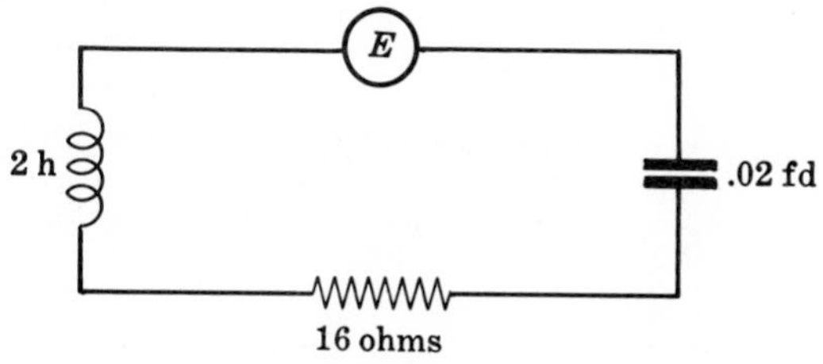

Fig. 3-11

Let Q and I be the instantaneous charge and current respectively at time t. By Kirchhoff's laws, we have

$$2 \frac{dI}{dt} + 16I + \frac{Q}{.02} = E \qquad (1)$$

or since $I = dQ/dt$,

$$2 \frac{d^2Q}{dt^2} + 16 \frac{dQ}{dt} + 50Q = E \qquad (2)$$

with the initial conditions $Q(0) = 0$, $I(0) = Q'(0) = 0$.

(a) If $E = 300$, then (2) becomes

$$\frac{d^2Q}{dt^2} + 8 \frac{dQ}{dt} + 25Q = 150 .$$

Then taking the Laplace transform, we find

$$\{s^2q - s\,Q(0) - Q'(0)\} + 8\{sq - Q(0)\} + 25q = \frac{150}{s}$$

or

$$q = \frac{150}{s(s^2 + 8s + 25)} = \frac{6}{s} - \frac{6s + 48}{s^2 + 8s + 25}$$

$$= \frac{6}{s} - \frac{6(s+4) + 24}{(s+4)^2 + 9}$$

$$= \frac{6}{s} - \frac{6(s+4)}{(s+4)^2 + 9} - \frac{24}{(s+4)^2 + 9}$$

Then

$$Q = 6 - 6e^{-4t} \cos 3t - 8e^{-4t} \sin 3t$$

$$I = \frac{dQ}{dt} = 50e^{-4t} \sin 3t$$

(b) If $E = 100 \sin 3t$, then (2) becomes

$$\frac{d^2Q}{dt^2} + 8\frac{dQ}{dt} + 25Q = 50 \sin 3t$$

Taking the Laplace transform, we find

$$(s^2 + 8s + 25)q = \frac{150}{s^2 + 9}$$

and

$$q = \frac{150}{(s^2 + 9)(s^2 + 8s + 25)}$$

$$= \frac{75}{26}\frac{1}{s^2 + 9} - \frac{75}{52}\frac{s}{s^2 + 9} + \frac{75}{26}\frac{1}{(s+4)^2 + 9} + \frac{75}{52}\frac{s+4}{(s+4)^2 + 9}$$

Thus

$$Q = \frac{25}{26}\sin 3t - \frac{75}{52}\sin 3t + \frac{25}{26}e^{-4t}\sin 3t + \frac{75}{52}e^{-4t}\cos 3t$$

$$= \frac{25}{52}(2\sin 3t - 3\cos 3t) + \frac{25}{52}e^{-4t}(3\cos 3t + 2\sin 3t)$$

and

$$I = \frac{dQ}{dt} = \frac{75}{52}(2\cos 3t + 3\sin 3t) - \frac{25}{52}e^{-4t}(17\sin 3t + 6\cos 3t)$$

For large t, those terms of Q or I which involve e^{-4t} are negligible and these are called the *transient terms* or *transient part* of the solution. The other terms are called the *steady-state terms* or *steady-state part* of the solution.

17. Given the electric network of Fig. 3-12, determine the currents in the various branches if the initial currents are zero.

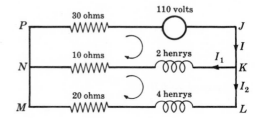

Fig. 3-12

Kirchhoff's second law [see Page 80] states that the algebraic sum of the voltage or potential drops around a closed loop is zero. Let us traverse loops *KLMNK* and *JKNPJ* in a clockwise fashion as shown. In traversing these loops we shall consider voltage drops as positive when we travel against the current. A voltage rise is considered as the negative of a voltage drop.

Let I be the current in *NPJK*. This current divides at the junction point K into I_1 and I_2 so that $I = I_1 + I_2$. This is equivalent to Kirchhoff's first law [see Page 80].

Applying Kirchhoff's second law to loops *KLMNK* and *JKNPJ*, we then have respectively

$$-10I_1 - 2\frac{dI_1}{dt} + 4\frac{dI_2}{dt} + 20I_2 = 0$$

$$30I - 110 + 2\frac{dI_1}{dt} + 10I_1 = 0$$

or

$$-5I_1 - \frac{dI_1}{dt} + 2\frac{dI_2}{dt} + 10I_2 = 0$$

$$\frac{dI_1}{dt} + 20I_1 + 15I_2 = 55$$

subject to the conditions $I_1(0) = I_2(0) = 0$.

Taking the Laplace transform of the system and using the initial conditions, we find

$$-5i_1 - \{si_1 - I_1(0)\} + 2\{si_2 - I_2(0)\} + 10i_2 = 0$$

$$\{si_1 - I_1(0)\} + 20i_1 + 15i_2 = 55/s$$

or

$$(s+5)i_1 - (2s+10)i_2 = 0$$

$$(s+20)i_1 + 15i_2 = 55/s$$

From the first equation, $i_1 = 2i_2$, so that the second equation yields

$$(2s+55)i_2 = \frac{55}{s} \quad \text{or} \quad i_2 = \frac{55}{s(2s+55)} = \frac{1}{s} - \frac{2}{2s+55}$$

Then

$$I_2 = 1 - e^{-55t/2}$$

$$I_1 = 2I_2 = 2 - 2e^{-55t/2}$$

$$I = I_1 + I_2 = 3 - 3e^{-55t/2}$$

APPLICATIONS TO BEAMS

18. A beam which is hinged at its ends $x = 0$ and $x = l$ [see Fig. 3-13] carries a uniform load W_0 per unit length. Find the deflection at any point.

The differential equation and boundary conditions are

$$\frac{d^4Y}{dx^4} = \frac{W_0}{EI} \qquad 0 < x < l \qquad (1)$$

$$Y(0) = 0, \ Y''(0) = 0, \ Y(l) = 0, \ Y''(l) = 0 \qquad (2)$$

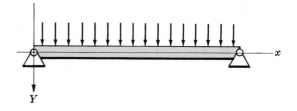

Fig. 3-13

Taking Laplace transforms of both sides of (1), we have, if $y = y(s) = \mathcal{L}\{Y(x)\}$,

$$s^4y - s^3Y(0) - s^2Y'(0) - sY''(0) - Y'''(0) = \frac{W_0}{EIs} \qquad (3)$$

Using the first two conditions in (2) and the unknown conditions $Y'(0) = c_1$, $Y'''(0) = c_2$, we find

$$y = \frac{c_1}{s^2} + \frac{c_2}{s^4} + \frac{W_0}{EIs^5}$$

Then inverting,

$$Y(x) = c_1x + \frac{c_2x^3}{3!} + \frac{W_0}{EI}\frac{x^4}{4!} = c_1x + \frac{c_2x^3}{6} + \frac{W_0x^4}{24EI}$$

From the last two conditions in (2), we find

$$c_1 = \frac{W_0l^3}{24EI}, \qquad c_2 = -\frac{W_0l}{2EI}$$

Thus the required deflection is

$$Y(x) = \frac{W_0}{24EI}(l^3x - 2lx^3 + x^4) = \frac{W_0}{24EI}x(l-x)(l^2 + lx - x^2)$$

19. A *cantilever beam* [Fig. 3-14] is clamped at the end $x = 0$ and is free at the end $x = l$. It carries a load per unit length given by

$$W(x) \;=\; \begin{cases} W_0 & 0 < x < l/2 \\ 0 & l/2 < x < l \end{cases}$$

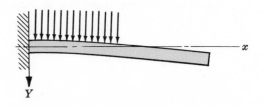

Find the deflection.

Fig. 3-14

The differential equation and boundary conditions are

$$\frac{d^4 Y}{dx^4} \;=\; \frac{W(x)}{EI} \qquad 0 < x < l \tag{1}$$

$$Y(0) = 0, \quad Y'(0) = 0, \quad Y''(l) = 0, \quad Y'''(l) = 0 \tag{2}$$

In order to apply Laplace transforms, we extend the definition of $W(x)$ as follows:

$$W(x) \;=\; \begin{cases} W_0 & 0 < x < l/2 \\ 0 & x > l/2 \end{cases} \tag{3}$$

This can be written in terms of Heaviside's unit function as

$$W(x) \;=\; W_0 \{ \mathcal{U}(x) - \mathcal{U}(x - l/2) \} \tag{4}$$

Taking Laplace transforms of (1), we have, if $y = y(s) = \mathcal{L}\{Y(x)\}$,

$$s^4 y \;-\; s^3 Y(0) \;-\; s^2 Y'(0) \;-\; s Y''(0) \;-\; Y'''(0) \;=\; \frac{W_0}{EI} \left\{ \frac{1 - e^{-sl/2}}{s} \right\}$$

From the first two of conditions (2) and the unknown conditions $Y''(0) = c_1$, $Y'''(0) = c_2$, we find

$$y \;=\; \frac{c_1}{s^3} + \frac{c_2}{s^4} + \frac{W_0}{EI s^5} \{1 - e^{-sl/2}\}$$

Inverting, we find

$$Y(x) \;=\; \frac{c_1 x^2}{2!} + \frac{c_2 x^3}{3!} + \frac{W_0}{EI} \frac{x^4}{4!} - \frac{W_0}{EI} \frac{(x - l/2)^4}{4!} \, \mathcal{U}(x - l/2)$$

This is equivalent to

$$Y(x) \;=\; \begin{cases} \dfrac{c_1 x^2}{2!} + \dfrac{1}{6} c_2 x^3 + \dfrac{W_0}{24EI} x^4 & 0 < x < l/2 \\[3mm] \dfrac{c_1 x^2}{2!} + \dfrac{1}{6} c_2 x^3 + \dfrac{W_0}{24EI} x^4 - \dfrac{W_0}{24EI} (x - l/2)^4 & x > l/2 \end{cases}$$

We now use the conditions $Y''(l) = 0$, $Y'''(l) = 0$ to find

$$c_1 \;=\; \frac{W_0 l^2}{8EI}, \qquad c_2 \;=\; -\frac{W_0 l}{2EI}$$

Thus the required deflection is

$$Y(x) \;=\; \frac{W_0 l^2}{16EI} x^2 - \frac{W_0 l}{12EI} x^3 + \frac{W_0}{24EI} x^4 - \frac{W_0}{24EI} (x - l/2)^4 \, \mathcal{U}(x - l/2)$$

or

$$Y(x) \;=\; \begin{cases} \dfrac{W_0 l^2}{16EI} x^2 - \dfrac{W_0 l}{12EI} x^3 + \dfrac{W_0}{24EI} x^4 & 0 < x < l/2 \\[3mm] \dfrac{W_0 l^2}{16EI} x^2 - \dfrac{W_0 l}{12EI} x^3 + \dfrac{W_0}{24EI} x^4 - \dfrac{W_0}{24EI} (x - l/2)^4 & l/2 < x < l \end{cases}$$

20. A beam has a concentrated load P_0 acting at the point $x = a$. Show that we can represent this loading by $W(x) = P_0 \delta(x - a)$ where δ is the Dirac delta function or impulse function.

Consider a uniform loading W_0 per unit length over the portion of the beam between a and $a + \epsilon$ [see Fig. 3-15]. Then the total loading on this portion is

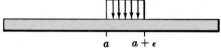

$$W_0 [a + \epsilon - a] = W_0 \epsilon$$

Since this total loading is to equal P_0, we must have

Fig. 3-15

$$W(x) = \begin{cases} P_0/\epsilon & a < x < a + \epsilon \\ 0 & \text{otherwise} \end{cases}$$

But we have already agreed to represent this in the limit as $\epsilon \to 0$ by

$$W(x) = P_0 \delta(x - a)$$

Thus the required result is demonstrated.

21. A beam has its ends clamped at $x = 0$ and $x = l$ [see Fig. 3-16]. A concentrated load P_0 acts vertically downward at the point $x = l/3$. Find the resulting deflection.

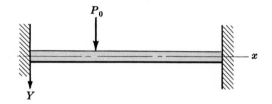

By Problem 20, the concentrated load at $x = l/3$ can be represented by $P_0 \delta(x - l/3)$ where δ is the Dirac delta function or impulse function. Then the differential equation for the deflection and the associated boundary conditions are given by

Fig. 3-16

$$\frac{d^4Y}{dx^4} = \frac{P_0}{EI} \delta(x - l/3) \tag{1}$$

$$Y(0) = 0, \qquad Y'(0) = 0, \qquad Y(l) = 0, \qquad Y'(l) = 0 \tag{2}$$

Taking Laplace transforms, we have, if $y = \mathcal{L}\{Y(x)\}$,

$$s^4 y - s^3 Y(0) - s^2 Y'(0) - s Y''(0) - Y'''(0) = \frac{P_0}{EI} e^{-ls/3} \tag{3}$$

Using the first two conditions in (2) and calling $Y''(0) = c_1$, $Y'''(0) = c_2$, we find

$$y = \frac{c_1}{s^3} + \frac{c_2}{s^4} + \frac{P_0}{EI} \frac{e^{-ls/3}}{s^4} \tag{4}$$

Inverting, we obtain

$$Y(x) = \frac{c_1 x^2}{2!} + \frac{c_2 x^3}{3!} + \frac{P_0}{EI} \frac{(x - l/3)^3}{3!} u(x - l/3) \tag{5}$$

or equivalently,

$$Y(x) = \begin{cases} \frac{1}{2}c_1 x^2 + \frac{1}{6}c_2 x^3 & 0 < x < l/3 \\ \frac{1}{2}c_1 x^2 + \frac{1}{6}c_2 x^3 + \frac{P_0}{6EI}(x - l/3)^3 & l/3 < x < l \end{cases}$$

From the last two conditions in (2), we find

$$c_1 = \frac{4P_0 l}{27EI}, \qquad c_2 = \frac{-20P_0}{27EI}$$

Then the required deflection is

$$Y(x) = \frac{2P_0 \, lx^2}{27EI} - \frac{10P_0 \, x^3}{81EI} + \frac{P_0}{6EI}(x - l/3)^3 \, u(x - l/3)$$

or

$$Y(x) = \begin{cases} \dfrac{2P_0 \, x^2(3l - 5x)}{81EI} & 0 < x < l/3 \\[3mm] \dfrac{2P_0 \, x^2(3l - 5x)}{81EI} + \dfrac{P_0}{6EI}(x - l/3)^3 & l/3 < x < l \end{cases}$$

PARTIAL DIFFERENTIAL EQUATIONS

22. Given the function $U(x, t)$ defined for $a \leqq x \leqq b$, $t > 0$. Find

$$(a) \quad \mathcal{L}\left\{\frac{\partial U}{\partial t}\right\} = \int_0^\infty e^{-st} \frac{\partial U}{\partial t} \, dt, \qquad (b) \quad \mathcal{L}\left\{\frac{\partial U}{\partial x}\right\} = \int_0^\infty e^{-st} \frac{\partial U}{\partial x} \, dt$$

assuming suitable restrictions on $U = U(x, t)$.

(a) Integrating by parts, we have

$$\begin{aligned} \mathcal{L}\left\{\frac{\partial U}{\partial t}\right\} &= \int_0^\infty e^{-st} \frac{\partial U}{\partial t} \, dt = \lim_{P \to \infty} \int_0^P e^{-st} \frac{\partial U}{\partial t} \, dt \\[2mm] &= \lim_{P \to \infty} \left\{ e^{-st} U(x, t) \Big|_0^P + s \int_0^P e^{-st} U(x, t) \, dt \right\} \\[2mm] &= s \int_0^\infty e^{-st} U(x, t) \, dt - U(x, 0) \\[2mm] &= s \, u(x, s) - U(x, 0) = s \, u - U(x, 0) \end{aligned}$$

where $u = u(x, s) = \mathcal{L}\{U(x, t)\}$.

We have assumed that $U(x, t)$ satisfies the restrictions of *Theorem 1-1*, Page 2, when regarded as a function of t.

(b) We have, using Leibnitz's rule for differentiating under the integral sign,

$$\mathcal{L}\left\{\frac{\partial U}{\partial x}\right\} = \int_0^\infty e^{-st} \frac{\partial U}{\partial x} \, dt = \frac{d}{dx} \int_0^\infty e^{-st} U \, dt = \frac{du}{dx}$$

23. Referring to Problem 22, show that

$$(a) \quad \mathcal{L}\left\{\frac{\partial^2 U}{\partial t^2}\right\} = s^2 \, u(x, s) - s \, U(x, 0) - U_t(x, 0)$$

$$(b) \quad \mathcal{L}\left\{\frac{\partial^2 U}{\partial x^2}\right\} = \frac{d^2 u}{dx^2}$$

where $U_t(x, 0) = \dfrac{\partial U}{\partial t}\Big|_{t=0}$ and $u = u(x, s) = \mathcal{L}\{U(x, t)\}$.

Let $V = \partial U/\partial t$. Then as in part (a) of Problem 22, we have

$$\begin{aligned} \mathcal{L}\left\{\frac{\partial^2 U}{\partial t^2}\right\} &= \mathcal{L}\left\{\frac{\partial V}{\partial t}\right\} = s \, \mathcal{L}\{V\} - V(x, 0) \\[2mm] &= s \, [s \, \mathcal{L}\{U\} - U(x, 0)] - U_t(x, 0) \\[2mm] &= s^2 u - s \, U(x, 0) - U_t(x, 0) \end{aligned}$$

Note the similarity of the results of this problem and part (a) of Problem 22 with *Theorems 1-6* and *1-9*, Page 4. Extensions are easily made.

24. Find the solution of

$$\frac{\partial U}{\partial x} \;=\; 2\frac{\partial U}{\partial t} \,+\, U, \qquad U(x,0) \;=\; 6e^{-3x}$$

which is bounded for $x > 0$, $t > 0$.

Taking the Laplace transform of the given partial differential equation with respect to t and using Problem 22, we find

$$\frac{du}{dx} \;=\; 2\{su - U(x,0)\} \,+\, u$$

or

$$\frac{du}{dx} \,-\, (2s+1)u \;=\; -12e^{-3x} \tag{1}$$

from the given boundary condition. Note that the Laplace transformation has transformed the partial differential equation into an ordinary differential equation *(1)*.

To solve *(1)* multiply both sides by the integrating factor $e^{\int -(2s+1)\,dx} = e^{-(2s+1)x}$. Then *(1)* can be written

$$\frac{d}{dx}\{u\,e^{-(2s+1)x}\} \;=\; -12\,e^{-(2s+4)x}$$

Integration yields

$$u\,e^{-(2s+1)x} \;=\; \frac{6}{s+2}\,e^{-(2s+4)x} + c \qquad \text{or} \qquad u \;=\; \frac{6}{s+2}\,e^{-3x} + c\,e^{(2s+1)x}$$

Now since $U(x,t)$ must be bounded as $x \to \infty$, we must have $u(x,s)$ also bounded as $x \to \infty$ and it follows that we must choose $c = 0$. Then

$$u \;=\; \frac{6}{s+2}\,e^{-3x}$$

and so, on taking the inverse, we find

$$U(x,t) \;=\; 6\,e^{-2t-3x}$$

This is easily checked as the required solution.

25. Solve $\dfrac{\partial U}{\partial t} = \dfrac{\partial^2 U}{\partial x^2}$, $\;U(x,0) = 3\sin 2\pi x$, $\;U(0,t) = 0$, $\;U(1,t) = 0\;$ where $0 < x < 1$, $t > 0$.

Taking the Laplace transform of the partial differential equation using Problems 22 and 23, we find

$$su - U(x,0) \;=\; \frac{d^2u}{dx^2} \qquad \text{or} \qquad \frac{d^2u}{dx^2} - su \;=\; -3\sin 2\pi x \tag{1}$$

where $u = u(x,s) = \mathcal{L}\{U(x,t)\}$. The general solution of *(1)* is

$$u \;=\; c_1\,e^{\sqrt{s}\,x} \,+\, c_2\,e^{-\sqrt{s}\,x} \,+\, \frac{3}{s+4\pi^2}\sin 2\pi x \tag{2}$$

Taking the Laplace transform of those boundary conditions which involve t, we have

$$\mathcal{L}\{U(0,t)\} \;=\; u(0,s) \;=\; 0 \qquad \text{and} \qquad \mathcal{L}\{U(1,t)\} \;=\; u(1,s) \;=\; 0 \tag{3}$$

Using the first condition $[u(0, s) = 0]$ of (3) in (2), we have

$$c_1 + c_2 = 0 \tag{4}$$

Using the second condition $[u(1, s) = 0]$ of (3) in (2), we have

$$c_1 e^{\sqrt{s}} + c_2 e^{-\sqrt{s}} = 0 \tag{5}$$

From (4) and (5) we find $c_1 = 0$, $c_2 = 0$ and so (2) becomes

$$u = \frac{3}{s + 4\pi^2} \sin 2\pi x \tag{6}$$

from which we obtain on inversion

$$U(x, t) = 3 e^{-4\pi^2 t} \sin 2\pi x \tag{7}$$

This problem has an interesting physical interpretation. If we consider a solid bounded by the infinite plane faces $x = 0$ and $x = 1$, the equation

$$\frac{\partial U}{\partial t} = k \frac{\partial^2 U}{\partial x^2}$$

is the *equation for heat conduction* in this solid where $U = U(x, t)$ is the *temperature* at any plane face x at any time t and k is a constant called the *diffusivity*, which depends on the material of the solid. The boundary conditions $U(0, t) = 0$ and $U(1, t) = 0$ indicate that the temperatures at $x = 0$ and $x = 1$ are kept at temperature zero, while $U(x, 0) = 3 \sin 2\pi x$ represents the initial temperature everywhere in $0 < x < 1$. The result (7) then is the temperature everywhere in the solid at time $t > 0$. Further applications are considered in Chapter 8.

26. Find the bounded solution of $\dfrac{\partial U}{\partial t} = \dfrac{\partial^2 U}{\partial x^2}$, $x > 0$, $t > 0$ such that $U(0, t) = 1$, $U(x, 0) = 0$.

Taking the Laplace transform of the partial differential equation and the condition $U(0, t) = 1$, we find respectively

$$su - U(x, 0) = \frac{d^2u}{dx^2} \quad \text{or} \quad \frac{d^2u}{dx^2} - su = 0 \tag{1}$$

and

$$u(0, s) = \frac{1}{s} \tag{2}$$

From (1), $u = u(x, s) = c_1 e^{\sqrt{s}\, x} + c_2 e^{-\sqrt{s}\, x}$. Since $U(x, t)$ must be bounded as $x \to \infty$, $u(x, s) = \mathcal{L}\{U(x, t)\}$ must also be bounded as $x \to \infty$. Then we must have $c_1 = 0$, assuming $\sqrt{s} > 0$, so that

$$u(x, s) = c_2 e^{-\sqrt{s}\, x} \tag{3}$$

From (2) and (3) we find $c_2 = 1/s$, so that

$$u(x, s) = \frac{e^{-\sqrt{s}\, x}}{s}$$

Thus using Problem 43, Page 67, we find

$$U(x, t) = \operatorname{erfc}\left(\frac{x}{2\sqrt{t}}\right) = \frac{2}{\sqrt{\pi}} \int_{x/(2\sqrt{t})}^{\infty} e^{-v^2}\, dv$$

Physically, this represents the temperature at any point of a semi-infinite solid $x > 0$ whose face $x = 0$ is kept at unit temperature and whose initial temperature is zero [see Problem 25].

MISCELLANEOUS PROBLEMS

27. Suppose that in Problem 14, Page 88, an external force $\mathcal{F}(t)$ acts on the particle but there is no damping force. (*a*) Find the position of the particle at any time if $\mathcal{F}(t) = F_0 \cos \omega t$. (*b*) Discuss the physical significance of your results.

(*a*) If the external force $\mathcal{F}(t)$ is taken into account, the equation of motion becomes

$$2\frac{d^2X}{dt^2} = -8X + \mathcal{F}(t) \tag{1}$$

or

$$2X'' + 8X = \mathcal{F}(t) \tag{2}$$

As before, the initial conditions are

$$X(0) = 10, \qquad X'(0) = 0 \tag{3}$$

If $\mathcal{F}(t) = F_0 \cos \omega t$, (*2*) becomes

$$2X'' + 8X = F_0 \cos \omega t \tag{4}$$

Taking Laplace transforms and using conditions (*3*), we find, if $x = \mathcal{L}\{X\}$,

$$2\{s^2 x - s(10) - 0\} + 8x = \frac{F_0\, s}{s^2 + \omega^2}$$

Then if $\omega^2 \neq 4$,

$$x = \frac{10s}{s^2 + 4} + \frac{(F_0/2)s}{(s^2 + 4)(s^2 + \omega^2)} \tag{5}$$

or

$$x = \frac{10s}{s^2 + 4} + \frac{F_0}{2(\omega^2 - 4)} \left\{ \frac{s}{s^2 + 4} - \frac{s}{s^2 + \omega^2} \right\} \tag{6}$$

and so

$$X = \mathcal{L}^{-1}\{x\} = 10 \cos 2t + \frac{F_0}{2(\omega^2 - 4)}(\cos 2t - \cos \omega t) \tag{7}$$

If $\omega^2 = 4$, then (*5*) becomes

$$x = \frac{10s}{s^2 + 4} + \frac{(F_0/2)s}{(s^2 + 4)^2} \tag{8}$$

and so using Problem 13, Page 53,

$$X = \mathcal{L}^{-1}\{x\} = 10 \cos 2t + \frac{F_0}{8} t \sin 2t \tag{9}$$

(*b*) If $\omega^2 = 4$ or $\omega = 2$, i.e. if the frequency of the applied external force is equal to the natural frequency of the system, it is seen from (*9*) that the oscillations about the equilibrium position increase indefinitely. This phenomenon is called *resonance* and the frequency corresponding to $\omega = 2$ is called the *resonant frequency*. If in such case the particle is attached to a spring, the spring will break.

28. Work Problem 27 if (*a*) $\mathcal{F}(t) = F_0\, \mathcal{U}(t - a)$, (*b*) $\mathcal{F}(t) = F_0\, \delta(t)$.

(*a*) In this case the equation of motion is [equation (*2*) of Problem 27]

$$2X'' + 8X = F_0\, \mathcal{U}(t - a)$$

where $X(0) = 10$, $X'(0) = 0$. Then taking Laplace transforms, we find

$$2(s^2 x - 10s) + 8x = \frac{F_0\, e^{-as}}{s}$$

and
$$x \;=\; \frac{10s}{s^2+4} \;+\; \frac{F_0\,e^{-as}}{2s(s^2+4)}$$

$$=\; \frac{10s}{s^2+4} \;+\; \frac{F_0\,e^{-as}}{8}\left\{\frac{1}{s}-\frac{s}{s^2+4}\right\}$$

Hence
$$X \;=\; \begin{cases} 10\cos 2t \;+\; \frac{1}{8}F_0\,\{1-\cos 2(t-a)\} & \text{if } t>a \\ 10\cos 2t & \text{if } t<a \end{cases}$$

Thus the displacement of the particle is the same as in Problem 27 until the time $t=a$, after which it changes.

(b) In this case the equation of motion is

$$2X'' + 8X \;=\; F_0\,\delta(t), \qquad X(0)=10, \;\; X'(0)=0$$

Then taking the Laplace transform, we find

$$2(s^2x - 10s) \;+\; 8x \;=\; F_0$$

or
$$x \;=\; \frac{10s}{s^2+4} \;+\; \frac{F_0}{2(s^2+4)}$$

Thus
$$X \;=\; 10\cos 2t \;+\; \tfrac{1}{4}F_0\sin 2t \tag{1}$$

Physically, applying the external force $F_0\,\delta(t)$ is equivalent to applying a very large force for a very short time and applying no force at all thereafter. The effect is to produce a displacement of larger amplitude than that produced in Problem 14. This is seen by writing (1) in the form

$$X \;=\; \sqrt{100+F_0^2/16}\,\cos\,(2t-\phi) \tag{2}$$

where
$$\cos\phi \;=\; \frac{10}{\sqrt{100+F_0^2/16}}\,, \qquad \sin\phi \;=\; \frac{F_0/4}{\sqrt{100+F_0^2/16}}$$

or $\tan\phi = F_0/40$, so that the amplitude is $\sqrt{100+F_0^2/16}$.

29. Let $Y = Y_1(t)$ be a solution of the equation

$$Y''(t) \;+\; P(t)\,Y'(t) \;+\; Q(t)\,Y(t) \;=\; 0$$

Find the general solution of $\;\;Y''(t) + P(t)\,Y'(t) + Q(t)\,Y(t) \;=\; R(t)$.

The differential equation whose general solution is sought is given by

$$Y'' \;+\; PY' \;+\; QY \;=\; R \tag{1}$$

Since $Y = Y_1$ is a solution of this equation with the right hand side equal to zero, we have

$$Y_1'' \;+\; PY_1' \;+\; QY_1 \;=\; 0 \tag{2}$$

Multiplying equation (1) by Y_1, equation (2) by Y, and subtracting, we find

$$Y_1 Y'' \;-\; YY_1'' \;+\; P(Y_1 Y' - YY_1') \;=\; RY_1 \tag{3}$$

which can be written

$$\frac{d}{dt}(Y_1 Y' - YY_1') \;+\; P(Y_1 Y' - YY_1') \;=\; RY_1 \tag{4}$$

An integrating factor of this equation is

$$e^{\int P\,dt}$$

Multiplying (4) by this factor, it can be written as

$$\frac{d}{dt}\left\{ e^{\int P\,dt}(Y_1 Y' - YY'_1) \right\} = RY_1 e^{\int P\,dt} \tag{5}$$

Then by integrating,

$$e^{\int P\,dt}(Y_1 Y' - YY'_1) = \int RY_1 e^{\int P\,dt}\,dt + c_1 \tag{6}$$

or

$$Y_1 Y' - YY'_1 = e^{-\int P\,dt} \int RY_1 e^{\int P\,dt}\,dt + c_1 e^{-\int P\,dt} \tag{7}$$

where c_1 is a constant of integration.

Dividing both sides of (7) by Y_1^2, it can be written as

$$\frac{d}{dt}\left(\frac{Y}{Y_1}\right) = \frac{e^{-\int P\,dt}}{Y_1^2} \int RY_1 e^{\int P\,dt}\,dt + c_1 \frac{e^{-\int P\,dt}}{Y_1^2} \tag{8}$$

Integrating both sides of (8) and multiplying by Y_1, we find, if c_2 is a constant integration,

$$Y = c_1 Y_1 \int \frac{e^{-\int P\,dt}}{Y_1^2}\,dt + c_2 Y_1 + Y_1 \int \left\{ \frac{e^{-\int P\,dt}}{Y_1^2} \int RY_1 e^{\int P\,dt}\,dt \right\}\,dt \tag{9}$$

This is the required general solution.　For another method, see Problem 103.

30. Find the general solution of　(a) $tY'' + 2Y' + tY = 0$,　(b) $tY'' + 2Y' + tY = \csc t$.

(a) According to Problem 10, a particular solution of the given differential equation is

$$Y_1(t) = \frac{\sin t}{t}$$

Since the given differential equation can be written in the form (1) of Problem 29 with

$$P = 2/t, \quad Q = 1, \quad R = 0$$

we see from equation (9) of Problem 29 that the general solution is

$$Y = c_1 \frac{\sin t}{t} \int \frac{e^{-\int (2/t)\,dt}}{\sin^2 t/t^2}\,dt + c_2 \frac{\sin t}{t}$$

$$= c_1 \frac{\sin t}{t} \int \csc^2 t\,dt + c_2 \frac{\sin t}{t}$$

$$= c_1 \frac{\sin t}{t}(-\cot t) + c_2 \frac{\sin t}{t} = \frac{A\cos t + B\sin t}{t}$$

where we have written　$c_1 = -A$, $c_2 = B$　as the arbitrary constants.

(b) In this case we use equation (9) of Problem 29 with

$$P = 2/t, \quad Q = 1, \quad R = (\csc t)/t$$

and we find

$$Y = \frac{A\cos t + B\sin t}{t} - \cos t + \frac{\sin t \ln \sin t}{t}$$

31. Solve the partial differential equation

$$\frac{\partial^2 Y}{\partial t^2} - 4\frac{\partial^2 Y}{\partial x^2} + Y = 16x + 20\sin x$$

subject to the conditions

$$Y(0,t) = 0, \quad Y(\pi,t) = 16\pi, \quad Y_t(x,0) = 0, \quad Y(x,0) = 16x + 12\sin 2x - 8\sin 3x$$

Taking Laplace transforms, we find

$$s^2 y - s\,Y(x,0) - Y_t(x,0) - 4\frac{d^2 y}{dx^2} + y = \frac{16x}{s} + \frac{20\sin x}{s} \tag{1}$$

or, on using the given conditions,

$$\frac{d^2 y}{dx^2} - \frac{1}{4}(s^2+1)y = \frac{-4(s^2+1)x}{s} - \frac{5\sin x}{s} - 3s\sin 2x + 2s\sin 3x \tag{2}$$

$$y(0,s) = 0, \qquad y(\pi,s) = \frac{16\pi}{s} \tag{3}$$

A particular solution of (2) has the form

$$y_p = ax + b\sin x + c\sin 2x + d\sin 3x \tag{4}$$

Then substituting and equating coefficients of like terms, we find the particular solution

$$y_p = \frac{16x}{s} + \frac{20\sin x}{s(s^2+5)} + \frac{12s\sin 2x}{s^2+17} - \frac{8s\sin 3x}{s^2+37} \tag{5}$$

The general solution of the equation (2) with right hand side replaced by zero [i.e. the *complementary solution*] is

$$y_c = c_1 e^{-\frac{1}{2}\sqrt{s^2+1}\,x} + c_2 e^{\frac{1}{2}\sqrt{s^2+1}\,x} \tag{6}$$

Thus the general solution of (2) is

$$y = y_p + y_c \tag{7}$$

Using the conditions (3) in (7), we find

$$c_1 + c_2 = 0, \qquad c_1 e^{-\frac{1}{2}\sqrt{s^2+1}\,\pi} + c_2 e^{\frac{1}{2}\sqrt{s^2+1}\,\pi} = 0$$

from which $c_1 = c_2 = 0$. Thus

$$y = \frac{16x}{s} + \frac{20\sin x}{s(s^2+5)} + \frac{12s\sin 2x}{s^2+17} - \frac{8s\sin 3x}{s^2+37}$$

Then taking the inverse Laplace transform, we find the required solution

$$Y(x,t) = 16x + 4\sin x\,(1 - \cos\sqrt{5}\,t) + 12\sin 2x\cos\sqrt{17}\,t - 8\sin 3x\cos\sqrt{37}\,t$$

Supplementary Problems

ORDINARY DIFFERENTIAL EQUATIONS WITH CONSTANT COEFFICIENTS

Solve each of the following by using Laplace transforms and check solutions.

32. $Y''(t) + 4Y(t) = 12t$, $Y(0) = 0$, $Y'(0) = 7$.   *Ans.* $Y(t) = \frac{9}{4}t + \frac{19}{8}\sin 2t$

33. $Y''(t) - 3Y'(t) + 2Y(t) = 4t + 12e^{-t}$, $Y(0) = 6$, $Y'(0) = -1$.
   Ans. $Y(t) = 3e^t - 2e^{2t} + 2t + 3 + 2e^{-t}$

34. $Y''(t) - 4Y'(t) + 5Y(t) = 125t^2$, $Y(0) = Y'(0) = 0$.

    Ans. $Y(t) = 25t^2 + 40t + 22 + 2e^{2t}(2 \sin t - 11 \cos t)$

35. $Y''(t) + Y(t) = 8 \cos t$, $Y(0) = 1$, $Y'(0) = -1$.

    Ans. $Y(t) = \cos t - \sin t + 4t \sin t$

36. $Y'''(t) - Y(t) = e^t$, $Y(0) = 0$, $Y'(0) = 0$, $Y''(0) = 0$.

    Ans. $Y(t) = \frac{1}{3} e^t(t-1) + \frac{1}{3} e^{-t/2}(\cos \frac{\sqrt{3}}{2} t + \frac{1}{\sqrt{3}} \sin \frac{\sqrt{3}}{2} t)$

37. $Y^{iv}(t) + 2Y''(t) + Y(t) = \sin t$, $Y(0) = Y'(0) = Y''(0) = Y'''(0) = 0$.

    Ans. $Y(t) = \frac{1}{8}\{(3 - t^2) \sin t - 3t \cos t\}$

38. Find the general solution of the differential equations of:

    (*a*) Problem 2, Page 82; (*b*) Problem 3, Page 83; (*c*) Problem 6, Page 84.

    Ans. (*a*) $Y = c_1 e^t + c_2 e^{2t} + 4te^{2t}$ (*c*) $Y = c_1 \sin 3t + c_2 \cos 3t + \frac{1}{5} \cos 2t$

        (*b*) $Y = e^{-t}(c_1 \sin 2t + c_2 \cos 2t) + \frac{1}{3}e^{-t} \sin t$

39. Solve $Y''(t) + 9Y(t) = 18t$ if $Y(0) = 0$, $Y(\pi/2) = 0$.   *Ans.* $Y(t) = 2t + \pi \sin 3t$

40. Solve $Y^{iv}(t) - 16Y(t) = 30 \sin t$ if $Y(0) = 0$, $Y'(0) = 2$, $Y''(\pi) = 0$, $Y'''(\pi) = -18$.

    Ans. $Y = 2(\sin 2t - \sin t)$

41. Solve $Y'' - 4Y' + 3Y = F(t)$ if $Y(0) = 1$, $Y'(0) = 0$.

    Ans. $Y = \frac{3}{2}e^t - \frac{1}{2}e^{3t} + \frac{1}{2} \int_0^t (e^{3u} - e^u) F(t-u) \, du$

42. Solve the differential equation

$$Y'' + 4Y = F(t), \quad Y(0) = 0, \ Y'(0) = 1$$

    where $F(t) = \begin{cases} 1 & 0 < t < 1 \\ 0 & t > 1 \end{cases}$.

    Ans. $Y(t) = \frac{1}{2} \sin 2t + \frac{1}{4}\{\cos(2t-2) - \cos 2t\}$ for $t > 1$

       and $Y(t) = \frac{1}{2} \sin 2t + \frac{1}{4}(1 - \cos 2t)$ for $t < 1$

43. Solve Problem 42 if: (*a*) $F(t) = U(t-2)$, [Heaviside's unit step function];   (*b*) $F(t) = \delta(t)$, [Dirac delta function];   (*c*) $F(t) = \delta(t-2)$.

    Ans. (*a*) $Y(t) = \frac{1}{2} \sin 2t$ if $t < 2$, $\frac{1}{2} \sin 2t + \frac{1}{4}\{1 - \cos(2t-4)\}$ if $t > 2$

       (*b*) $Y(t) = \sin 2t$, $t > 0$

       (*c*) $Y(t) = \frac{1}{2} \sin 2t$ if $t < 2$, $\frac{1}{2}\{\sin 2t + \sin(2t-4)\}$ if $t > 2$

ORDINARY DIFFERENTIAL EQUATIONS WITH VARIABLE COEFFICIENTS

Solve each of the following by using Laplace transforms and check solutions.

44. $Y'' + tY' - Y = 0$, $Y(0) = 0$, $Y'(0) = 1$.   *Ans.* $Y = t$

45. $tY'' + (1 - 2t)Y' - 2Y = 0$, $Y(0) = 1$, $Y'(0) = 2$.   *Ans.* $Y = e^{2t}$

46. $tY'' + (t - 1)Y' - Y = 0$, $Y(0) = 5$, $Y(\infty) = 0$.   *Ans.* $Y = 5e^{-t}$

47. Find the bounded solution of the equation

$$t^2 Y'' + tY' + (t^2 - 1)Y = 0$$

    which is such that $Y(1) = 2$.   *Ans.* $2J_1(t)/J_1(1)$

SIMULTANEOUS ORDINARY DIFFERENTIAL EQUATIONS

48. Solve $\begin{cases} Y' + Z' = t \\ Y'' - Z = e^{-t} \end{cases}$ subject to the conditions $Y(0) = 3,\ Y'(0) = -2,\ Z(0) = 0$.

    Ans. $Y = 2 + \frac{1}{2}t^2 + \frac{1}{2}e^{-t} - \frac{3}{2}\sin t + \frac{1}{2}\cos t,\quad Z = 1 - \frac{1}{2}e^{-t} + \frac{3}{2}\sin t - \frac{1}{2}\cos t$

49. Solve $\begin{cases} Y' - Z' - 2Y + 2Z = \sin t \\ Y'' + 2Z' + Y = 0 \end{cases}$ if $Y(0) = Y'(0) = Z(0) = 0$.

    Ans. $Y = \frac{1}{9}e^{-t} + \frac{4}{45}e^{2t} - \frac{1}{5}\cos t - \frac{2}{3}\sin t + \frac{1}{3}te^{-t},\quad Z = \frac{1}{9}e^{-t} - \frac{1}{9}e^{2t} + \frac{1}{3}te^{-t}$

50. Solve $\begin{cases} X' + 2Y'' = e^{-t} \\ X' + 2X - Y = 1 \end{cases}$ if $X(0) = Y(0) = Y'(0) = 0$.

    Ans. $X = 1 + e^{-t} - e^{-at} - e^{-bt},\ Y = 1 + e^{-t} - be^{-at} - ae^{-bt}$ where $a = \frac{1}{2}(2 - \sqrt{2}),\ b = \frac{1}{2}(2 + \sqrt{2})$

51. Solve Problem 49 with the conditions $Y(0) = 0,\ Y'(\pi) = 1,\ Z(0) = 0$.

52. Solve $\begin{cases} tY + Z + tZ' = (t-1)e^{-t} \\ Y' - Z = e^{-t} \end{cases}$ given that $Y(0) = 1,\ Z(0) = -1$.

    Ans. $Y = J_0(t),\ Z = -J_1(t) - e^{-t}$

53. Solve $\begin{cases} -3Y'' + 3Z'' = te^{-t} - 3\cos t \\ tY'' - Z' = \sin t \end{cases}$ given that $Y(0) = -1,\ Y'(0) = 2,\ Z(0) = 4,\ Z''(0) = 0$.

    Ans. $Y = \frac{2}{3}t^2 + \frac{5}{3}t - \frac{2}{3} - \frac{1}{3}e^{-t},\quad Z = \frac{2}{3}t^2 + \frac{8}{3} + \frac{1}{3}e^{-t} + \frac{1}{3}te^{-t} + \cos t$

54. Find the general solution of the system of equations in Problem 49.

    Ans. $Y = c_1 + c_2\sin t + c_3\cos t + \frac{1}{2}t^2 + \frac{1}{2}e^{-t}$

            $Z = 1 - c_2\sin t - c_3\cos t - \frac{1}{2}e^{-t}$

APPLICATIONS TO MECHANICS

55. Referring to Fig. 3-1, Page 79, suppose that mass m has a force $\mathcal{F}(t),\ t > 0$ acting on it but that no damping forces are present.

    (*a*) Show that if the mass starts from rest at a distance $X = a$ from the equilibrium position $(X = 0)$, then the displacement X at any time $t > 0$ can be determined from the equation of motion

$$mX'' + kX = \mathcal{F}(t),\quad X(0) = a,\quad X'(0) = 0$$

    where primes denote derivatives with respect to t.

    (*b*) Find X at any time if $\mathcal{F}(t) = F_0$ (a constant) for $t > 0$.

    (*c*) Find X at any time if $\mathcal{F}(t) = F_0 e^{-\alpha t}$ where $\alpha > 0$.

    Ans.   (*b*) $X = a + \dfrac{F_0}{k}\left(1 - \cos\sqrt{\dfrac{k}{m}}\,t\right)$

           (*c*) $X = a + \dfrac{F_0}{m\alpha^2 + k}\,(e^{-\alpha t} - \cos\sqrt{k/m}\,t) + \dfrac{\alpha F_0\sqrt{m/k}}{m\alpha^2 + k}\,\sin\sqrt{k/m}\,t$

56. Work Problem 55 if $\mathcal{F}(t) = F_0\sin\omega t$, treating the two cases: (*a*) $\omega \neq \sqrt{k/m}$, (*b*) $\omega = \sqrt{k/m}$. Discuss the physical significance of each case.

57. A particle moves along a line so that its displacement X from a fixed point O at any time t is given by

$$X''(t) + 4X'(t) + 5X(t) = 80\sin 5t$$

(a) If at $t = 0$ the particle is at rest at $X = 0$, find its displacement at any time $t > 0$.

(b) Find the amplitude, period and frequency of the motion after a long time.

(c) Which term in the result of (a) is the transient term and which the steady-state term?

(d) Is the motion overdamped, critically damped or damped oscillatory?

  Ans.   (a) $X(t) = 2e^{-2t}(\cos t + 7 \sin t) - 2(\sin 5t + \cos 5t)$

   (b) Amplitude $= 2\sqrt{2}$, period $= 2\pi/5$, frequency $= 5/2\pi$

   (c) Transient term, $2e^{-2t}(\cos t + 7 \sin t)$; steady-state term, $-2(\sin 5t + \cos 5t)$

   (d) Damped oscillatory

58. Suppose that at $t = 0$, the mass m of Fig. 3-1, Page 79, is at rest at the equilibrium position $X = 0$. Suppose further that a force is suddenly applied to it so as to give it an instantaneous velocity V_0 in a direction toward the right and that the force is then removed. Show that the displacement of the mass from the equilibrium position at any time $t > 0$ is

(a)
$$V_0 \sqrt{\frac{m}{k}} \sin \sqrt{\frac{k}{m}} t$$

if there is no damping force, and

(b)
$$\frac{V_0}{\alpha} e^{-\beta t/2m} \quad \text{where} \quad \gamma = \sqrt{\frac{k}{m} - \frac{\beta^2}{4m^2}}$$

if there is a damping force of magnitude $\beta X'(t)$ where $\beta < 2\sqrt{km}$.

59. Work Problem 55 if: (a) $\mathcal{F}(t) = F_0 \, \mathcal{U}(t - T)$, [Heaviside's unit step function]; (b) $\mathcal{F}(t) = F_0 \, \delta(t - T)$ [Dirac delta function]. Discuss the physical significance in each case.

  Ans.   (a) $X = aF_0 \cos \sqrt{k/m} \, t$ if $t < T$ and

   $X = aF_0 \cos \sqrt{k/m} \, t + (F_0/k)\{1 - \cos \sqrt{k/m} \, (t - T)\}$ if $t > T$

   (b) $X = aF_0 \cos \sqrt{k/m} \, t$ if $t < T$ and

   $X = aF_0 \cos \sqrt{k/m} \, t + (F_0/\sqrt{km}) \sin \sqrt{k/m} \, (t - T)$ if $t > T$

60. Suppose that at $t = 0$ the mass m of Fig. 3-1, Page 79, is at rest at the equilibrium position and that a force $F_0 \, \delta(t)$ is applied. Find the displacement at any time $t > 0$ if (a) the system is undamped, (b) the system is critically damped. Discuss the physical significance of each case.

  Ans. (a) $\dfrac{F_0}{\sqrt{km}} \sin \sqrt{k/m} \, t$, (b) $\dfrac{F_0}{m} t \, e^{-\beta t/2m}$

61. A ball of mass m is thrown upward from the earth's surface with velocity V_0. Show that it will rise to a maximum height equal to $V_0^2/2g$, where g is the acceleration due to gravity.

62. A mass m moves along the x axis under the influence of a force which is proportional to its instantaneous speed and in a direction opposite to the direction of motion. Assuming that at $t = 0$ the particle is located at $X = a$ and moving to the right with speed V_0, find the position where the mass comes to rest.

63. A particle moves in the xy plane so that its position (X, Y) at any time is given by
$$X'' + k_1^2 Y = 0, \qquad Y'' + k_2^2 X = 0$$
If at time $t = 0$ the particle is released from rest at (a, b), find its position at any time $t > 0$.

  Ans. $X = \left(\dfrac{ak_2 + bk_1}{2k_2}\right) \cos \sqrt{k_1 k_2} \, t + \left(\dfrac{ak_2 - bk_1}{2k_2}\right) \cosh \sqrt{k_1 k_2} \, t$

   $Y = \left(\dfrac{ak_2 + bk_1}{2k_1}\right) \cos \sqrt{k_1 k_2} \, t - \left(\dfrac{ak_2 - bk_1}{2k_1}\right) \cosh \sqrt{k_1 k_2} \, t$

APPLICATIONS TO ELECTRICAL CIRCUITS

64. A resistor of R ohms and a capacitor of C farads are connected in series with a generator supplying E volts [see Fig. 3-17]. At $t = 0$ the charge on the capacitor is zero. Find the charge and current at any time $t > 0$ if: (a) $E = E_0$, a constant; (b) $E = E_0 e^{-\alpha t}$, $\alpha > 0$.

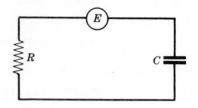

Ans. (a) $Q = CE_0(1 - e^{-t/RC})$, $\quad I = (E_0/R)e^{-t/RC}$

   (b) $Q = \dfrac{CE_0}{1 - \alpha RC}(e^{-\alpha t} - e^{-t/RC})$,

   $I = \dfrac{CE_0}{1 - \alpha RC}\left(\dfrac{e^{-t/RC}}{RC} - \alpha e^{-\alpha t}\right)$ if $\alpha \neq 1/RC$

Fig. 3-17

65. Work Problem 64 if $E = E_0 \sin \omega t$ and the initial charge on the capacitor is Q_0.

   Ans. $Q = \left\{Q_0 + \dfrac{\omega E_0}{R(\omega^2 + 1/R^2C^2)}\right\}e^{-t/RC} - \dfrac{E_0}{R}\left\{\dfrac{\omega \cos \omega t - (1/RC)\sin \omega t}{\omega^2 + 1/R^2C^2}\right\}$, $\quad I = dQ/dt$

66. An inductor of L henrys and a capacitor of C farads are in series with a generator of E volts. At $t = 0$ the charge on the capacitor and current in the circuit are zero. Find the charge on the capacitor at any time $t > 0$ if: (a) $E = E_0$, a constant; (b) $E = E_0 e^{-\alpha t}$, $\alpha > 0$.

   Ans. (a) $Q = CE_0\{1 - \cos(t/\sqrt{LC})\}$

   (b) $Q = \dfrac{E_0}{L(\alpha^2 + 1/LC)}\{e^{-\alpha t} - \cos(t/\sqrt{LC})\} + \dfrac{\alpha E_0 \sqrt{C/L}}{\alpha^2 + 1/LC}\sin(t/\sqrt{LC})$

67. Work Problem 66 if $E = E_0 \sin \omega t$, discussing the cases (a) $\omega \neq 1/\sqrt{LC}$ and (b) $\omega = 1/\sqrt{LC}$ and explaining the physical significance.

68. Work Problem 66 if $E(t)$ is (a) $E_0 \mathcal{U}(t - a)$ where $\mathcal{U}(t - a)$ is Heaviside's unit step function, (b) $E_0 \delta(t)$ where $\delta(t)$ is the Dirac delta function.

   Ans. (a) $Q = 0$ if $t < a$, and $CE_0\left\{1 - \cos\left(\dfrac{t - a}{LC}\right)\right\}$ if $t > a$

   (b) $Q = E_0\sqrt{C/L}\sin(t/\sqrt{LC})$

69. An inductor of 3 henrys is in series with a resistor of 30 ohms and an e.m.f. of 150 volts. Assuming that at $t = 0$ the current is zero, find the current at any time $t > 0$.   *Ans.* $I = 5(1 - e^{-10t})$

70. Work Problem 69 if the e.m.f. is given by $150 \sin 20t$.   *Ans.* $I = \sin 20t - 2 \cos 20t + 2e^{-10t}$

71. Find the charge on the capacitor and the current in the circuit [Fig. 3-18] at any time t after the key K is closed at $t = 0$. Assume that L, R, C and E are constants and that the charge and current are zero at $t = 0$. Treat all cases.

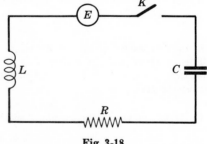

72. (a) Work Problem 71 if $E = E_0 \sin \omega t$. (b) Show that resonance occurs if we choose $\omega = \sqrt{\dfrac{1}{LC} - \dfrac{R^2}{2L^2}}$. (c) Discuss the case $R = 0$.

Fig. 3-18

73. An electric circuit consists of an inductor of L henrys in series with a capacitor of C farads. At $t = 0$ an e.m.f. given by

$$E(t) = \begin{cases} E_0 t/T_0 & 0 < t < T_0 \\ 0 & t > T_0 \end{cases}$$

is applied. Assuming that the current and charge on the capacitor are zero at $t = 0$, find the charge at any time $t > 0$.

Ans. $Q = \dfrac{CE_0}{T_0} \{ t - \sqrt{LC} \sin (t/\sqrt{LC}) \}$ if $0 < t < T_0$ and

$$Q = \frac{CE_0}{T_0} \left\{ T_0 \cos \left(\frac{t - T_0}{\sqrt{LC}} \right) + \sqrt{LC} \sin \left(\frac{t - T_0}{\sqrt{LC}} \right) - \sqrt{LC} \sin \frac{t}{\sqrt{LC}} \right\}   \text{ if } t > T_0$$

74. In the electric circuit of Fig. 3-19,

$$E \ = \ 500 \sin 10t$$
$$R_1 \ = \ 10 \text{ ohms}$$
$$R_2 \ = \ 10 \text{ ohms}$$
$$L \ = \ 1 \text{ henry}$$
$$C \ = \ .01 \text{ farad}$$

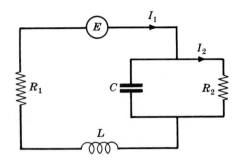

If the charge on the capacitor and the currents I_1 and I_2 are zero at $t = 0$, find the charge on the capacitor at any time $t > 0$.

Ans. $Q = \sin 10t - 2 \cos 10t + e^{-10t}(\sin 10t + 2 \cos 10t)$

Fig. 3-19

APPLICATIONS TO BEAMS

75. A beam which is clamped at its ends $x = 0$ and $x = l$ carries a uniform load W_0 per unit length. Show that the deflection at any point is $Y(x) = \dfrac{W_0\, x^2(l - x)^2}{24EI}$

76. Work Problem 75 if the end $x = 0$ is clamped while the end $x = l$ is hinged.

77. A cantilever beam, clamped at $x = 0$ and free at $x = l$, carries a uniform load W_0 per unit length. Show that the deflection is $Y(x) = \dfrac{W_0\, x^2}{24EI}\,(x^2 - 4lx + 6l^2)$.

78. A beam whose ends are hinged at $x = 0$ and $x = l$ has a load given by

$$W(x) \ = \ \begin{cases} 0 & 0 < x < l/3 \\ W_0 & l/3 < x < l \end{cases}$$

Find the deflection.

79. A cantilever beam, clamped at $x = 0$ and free at $x = l$, carries a concentrated load P_0 at $x = l$. Show that the deflection is given by $Y(x) = \dfrac{P_0\, x^2}{6EI}\,(3l - x)$.

80. Work Problem 79 if the load is at $x = l/2$.

81. A beam has its ends hinged at $x = 0$ and $x = l$. If a concentrated load P_0 acts vertically downward at $x = l/2$, show that the deflection is

$$Y(x) \ = \ \frac{P_0\, x}{48EI}(3l^2 - 4x^2) \qquad 0 < x < l/2$$

The deflection for $l/2 < x < l$ is obtained by symmetry or by replacing x by $l - x$.

82. Work Problem 81 if the ends of the beam are clamped.

83. A beam has its ends hinged at $x = 0$ and $x = l$. A concentrated load P_0 acts vertically downward at the point $x = l/3$. Show that the deflection is given by

$$Y(x) \ = \ \frac{P_0\, x(5l^2 - 9x^2)}{81EI} + \frac{P_0}{6EI}\,(x - l/3)^3\, u(x - l/3)$$

84. A beam has its ends hinged at $x = 0$ and $x = l$. The beam carries a uniform load W_0 per unit length and also has a concentrated load P_0 acting at $x = l/2$. (a) Find the deflection. (b) Discuss how the solution in (a) can be obtained from the solutions to Problems 18 and 81. Explain.

85. A beam whose ends are clamped at $x = 0$ and $x = l$ carries a load $W(x)$ per unit length given by

$$W(x) \;=\; \begin{cases} 0 & 0 < x < l/2 \\ W_0\, x & l/2 < x < l \end{cases}$$

and also a concentrated load at $x = l/3$. Find the deflection.

PARTIAL DIFFERENTIAL EQUATIONS

86. Solve $\dfrac{\partial U}{\partial t} = 2\dfrac{\partial^2 U}{\partial x^2}$, $\;U(0,t) = 0$, $\;U(5,t) = 0$, $\;U(x,0) = 10\sin 4\pi x$.

   Ans. $U(x,t) = 10\,e^{-32\pi^2 t}\sin 4\pi x$

87. **Work Problem 86 if** $\;U(x,0) = 10\sin 4\pi x - 5\sin 6\pi x$.

   Ans. $U(x,t) = 10\,e^{-32\pi^2 t}\sin 4\pi x - 5\,e^{-72\pi^2 t}\sin 6\pi x$

88. Solve $\dfrac{\partial^2 Y}{\partial t^2} = 9\dfrac{\partial^2 Y}{\partial x^2}$, $\;Y(0,t) = 0$, $\;Y(2,t) = 0$, $\;Y(x,0) = 20\sin 2\pi x - 10\sin 5\pi x$, $\;Y_t(x,0) = 0$.

   Ans. $Y(x,t) = 20\sin 2\pi x \cos 6\pi t - 10\sin 5\pi x \cos 15\pi t$

89. Give physical interpretations to (a) Problem 86, (b) Problem 87, (c) Problem 88.

90. Solve $\dfrac{\partial U}{\partial t} = 3\dfrac{\partial^2 U}{\partial x^2}$, $\;U_x(0,t) = 0$, $\;U(\pi/2, t) = 0$ if:

   (a) $U(x,0) = 30\cos 5x$,   (b) $U(x,0) = 20\cos 3x - 5\cos 9x$

   Ans.   (a) $30\,e^{-75t}\cos 5x$,   (b) $U(x,t) = 20\,e^{-27t}\cos 3x - 5\,e^{-243t}\cos 9x$

91. Present a physical interpretation of Problem 90.

92. (a) Find the solution of $\dfrac{\partial U}{\partial t} = \dfrac{\partial^2 U}{\partial x^2} - 4U$, $\;U(0,t) = 0$, $\;U(\pi,t) = 0$, $\;U(x,0) = 6\sin x - 4\sin 2x$.

   (b) Give a possible physical interpretation to the solution.

   Ans.   (a) $U(x,t) = 6\,e^{-5t}\sin x - 4\,e^{-8t}\sin 2x$

93. Solve $\dfrac{\partial^2 Y}{\partial t^2} = 16\dfrac{\partial^2 Y}{\partial x^2}$, $\;Y_x(0,t) = 0$, $\;Y(3,t) = 0$, $\;Y(x,0) = 0$, $\;Y_t(x,0) = 12\cos \pi x + 16\cos 3\pi x - 8\cos 5\pi x$.

   Ans. $Y(x,t) = 12\cos \pi x \sin 4\pi t + 16\cos 3\pi x \sin 12\pi t - 8\cos 5\pi x \sin 20\pi t$

94. Find the bounded solution $Y(x,t)$, $0 < x < 1$, $t > 0$ of the boundary-value problem

$$\frac{\partial Y}{\partial x} - \frac{\partial Y}{\partial t} \;=\; 1 - e^{-t}, \qquad Y(x,0) = x$$

   Ans. $Y(x,t) = x + 1 - e^{-t}$

95. Solve the equation

$$\frac{\partial^2 Y}{\partial t^2} \;=\; \frac{\partial^2 Y}{\partial x^2} \qquad x > 0, \; t > 0$$

   subject to the conditions

$$Y(0,t) = 10\sin 2t, \quad Y(x,0) = 0, \quad Y_t(x,0) = 0, \quad \lim_{x \to \infty} Y(x,t) = 0$$

MISCELLANEOUS PROBLEMS

96. Show that the solution of the differential equation

$$Y''(t) - k^2 Y(t) = F(t)$$

subject to $Y(0) = a$, $Y'(0) = b$ is

$$Y(t) = a \cosh kt + (b/k) \sinh kt + \frac{1}{k} \int_0^t F(u) \sinh k(t-u)\, du$$

97. Solve $Y^{iv}(t) + Y'''(t) = 2 \sin t$, $Y(0) = Y'(0) = 0$, $Y''(0) = 1$, $Y'''(0) = -2$.

Ans. $Y = \frac{1}{2}t^2 - 2 + e^{-t} + \sin t + \cos t$

98. Find the general solution of the differential equation of Problem 45.

Ans. $Y(t) = c_1 e^{2t} \int \frac{e^{-2t}}{t} dt + c_2 e^{2t}$

99. Find that solution of the equation

$$tY'' - (t+2)Y' + 3Y = t - 1$$

which has a Laplace transform and is such that $Y(0) = 0$.

100. What is the general solution of the differential equation in Problem 99?

101. (*a*) Use Laplace transforms to show that the solution of

$$\frac{d^2Y}{dt^2} + k^2Y = A \cos \omega t, \qquad Y(0) = \alpha, \ Y'(0) = \beta$$

is $Y(t) = \frac{A(\cos \omega t - \cos kt)}{\omega^2 - k^2} + \alpha \cos kt + (\beta/k) \sin kt$.

(*b*) Give a physical interpretation of the results of part (*a*).

102. Solve for X: $\begin{cases} X' + Y' = Y + Z \\ Y' + Z' = X + Z \\ X' + Z' = X + Y \end{cases}$ if $X(0) = 2$, $Y(0) = -3$, $Z(0) = 1$.

Ans. $X = \frac{2}{3}e^{-t/2}\{3 \cos(\sqrt{3}\,t/2) - 2\sqrt{3} \sin(\sqrt{3}\,t/2)\}$

103. Work Problem 29 by letting $Y = VY_1$, where V is a new dependent variable.

104. Can the method of Laplace transforms be used to find the general solution of

$$Y'' + Y = \sec t$$

Explain.

105. (*a*) Find a bounded solution of

$$(t-1)Y'' + (5-4t)Y' - 4Y = 0$$

such that $Y(0) = 3$. (*b*) What is the general solution of the equation in (*a*)?

Ans. (*a*) $Y = 3e^{4t}$, (*b*) $Y = c_1 e^{4t} \int \frac{e^{-4t}}{t-1} dt + c_2 e^{4t}$

106. (a) Show that
$$I(t) = \int_0^\infty \frac{e^{-tx^2}}{1 + x^2}\, dx$$
satisfies the differential equation
$$\frac{dI}{dt} - I = -\frac{1}{2}\sqrt{\frac{\pi}{t}}, \qquad I(0) = \pi/2$$

(b) By solving the differential equation in (a), show that
$$I(t) = \frac{\pi}{2} e^t \operatorname{erfc} \sqrt{t}$$

107. A particle moving on a straight line (the x axis) is acted upon by a force of repulsion which is proportional to its instantaneous distance from a fixed point O on the line. If the particle is placed at a distance a from O and is given a velocity toward O of magnitude V_0, find the distance of closest approach to O.

108. If the ball of Problem 61 encounters air resistance proportional to its instantaneous velocity, show that the maximum height reached is
$$\frac{m}{k^2}(kV_0 + mg - kg) - \frac{m^2 g}{k^2}$$
where k is a constant of proportionality.

109. In the circuit of Fig. 3-18, Page 106, suppose that the e.m.f. E is a function of t while L, R and C are constants. At the instant $t = 0$ that the key K is closed, assume that the charge Q on the capacitor and current I are zero. Show that if $R^2 < 4L/C$, then the current at any time $t > 0$ is given by
$$I(t) = \frac{1}{L} \int_0^t E(t - u)\, e^{-Ru/2L} \left(\cos \alpha u - \frac{R}{2L\alpha} \sin \alpha u \right) du$$
where $\alpha = \sqrt{1/LC - R^2/4L^2}$.

110. Work Problem 109 if   (a) $R^2 = 4L/C$,   (b) $R^2 > 4L/C$.

111. Present a mechanical analog to   (a) Problem 64, (b) Problem 66, (c) Problem 71.

112. Give an electrical analog to   (a) Problem 55, (b) Problem 57.

113. Give a mechanical analog to Problem 74 involving masses connected by springs.

114. A particle of mass m moves along the x axis under the influence of a force $\mathcal{F}(t)$ as indicated in Fig. 3-20. If the particle starts from rest at $t = 0$ determine its position and speed at any time $t > 0$.

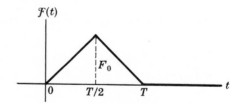

Fig. 3-20

115. A beam which is clamped at $x = 0$ and $x = l$ carries a concentrated load P_0 at a point $x = a$ where $0 < a < l$. Show that the deflection is
$$Y(x) = \begin{cases} \dfrac{P_0\, x^2 (l - a)^2}{6EI l^3} \{3al - (2a + l)x\} & 0 < x < a \\[2ex] \dfrac{P_0\, x^2 (l - a)^2}{6EI l^3} \{3al - (2a + l)x\} + \dfrac{P_0\, (x - a)^3}{6EI} & a < x < l \end{cases}$$

116. Work Problem 115 if the beam is clamped at $x = 0$ but free at $x = l$.

   Ans. $Y(x) = \begin{cases} \dfrac{P_0\, x^2}{6EI}(3a - x) & 0 < x < a \\[2ex] \dfrac{P_0\, a^2}{6EI}(3x - a) & a < x < l \end{cases}$

117. A beam which is hinged at $x = 0$ and $x = l$ carries concentrated loads P_0 at $x = l/3$ and $x = 2l/3$. Find the deflection.

118. If a beam carrying a load $W(x)$ per unit length rests on an elastic foundation, the differential equation for the deflection is

$$EI \frac{d^4 Y}{dx^4} + kY = W(x)$$

where k is called the *elastic constant of the foundation.* Suppose that such a beam, clamped at both ends $x = 0$ and $x = l$, carries a uniform load W_0 per unit length. Show that the bending moment at $x = 0$ is given by

$$\frac{W_0}{2a} \left(\frac{\sinh al - \sin al}{\sinh al + \sin al} \right)$$

where $a = \sqrt[4]{k/4EI}$.

119. Two electric circuits, called the *primary* and *secondary circuits,* are coupled inductively as shown in Fig. 3-21.

   (a) If M is the mutual inductance, show that the currents I_1 and I_2 are given by

$$L_1 \frac{dI_1}{dt} + R_1 I_1 + M \frac{dI_2}{dt} = E$$

$$L_2 \frac{dI_2}{dt} + R_2 I_2 + M \frac{dI_1}{dt} = 0$$

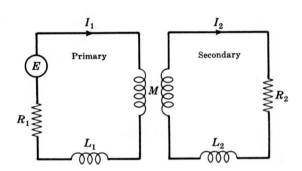

Fig. 3-21

   (b) If the currents I_1 and I_2 in the circuits are zero at time $t = 0$, show that at time $t > 0$ they are given by

$$I_1 = \frac{EL_2}{L_1 L_2 - M^2} \left(\frac{e^{\alpha_1 t} - e^{\alpha_2 t}}{\alpha_1 - \alpha_2} \right) + \frac{ER_2}{\alpha_1 - \alpha_2} \left(\frac{e^{\alpha_1 t}}{\alpha_1} - \frac{e^{\alpha_2 t}}{\alpha_2} \right) + \frac{E}{R_1}$$

$$I_2 = \frac{EM}{L_1 L_2 - M^2} \left(\frac{e^{\alpha_1 t} - e^{\alpha_2 t}}{\alpha_2 - \alpha_1} \right)$$

where α_1 and α_2 are the roots of the equation

$$(L_1 L_2 - M^2)\alpha^2 + (L_1 R_2 + L_2 R_1)\alpha + R_1 R_2 = 0$$

120. Discuss Problem 119 if $L_1 L_2 = M^2$.

Chapter 4

INTEGRAL EQUATIONS

An *integral equation* is an equation having the form

$$Y(t) \;=\; F(t) \;+\; \int_a^b K(u, t)\, Y(u)\, du \tag{1}$$

where $F(t)$ and $K(u, t)$ are known, a and b are either given constants or functions of t, and the function $Y(t)$ which appears under the integral sign is to be determined.

The function $K(u, t)$ is often called the *kernel* of the integral equation. If a and b are constants, the equation is often called a *Fredholm integral equation*. If a is a constant while $b = t$, it is called a *Volterra integral equation*.

It is possible to convert a linear differential equation into an integral equation. See Problems 1-3 and 25.

INTEGRAL EQUATIONS OF CONVOLUTION TYPE

A special integral equation of importance in applications is

$$Y(t) \;=\; F(t) \;+\; \int_0^t K(t-u)\, Y(u)\, du \tag{2}$$

This equation is of *convolution type* and can be written as

$$Y(t) \;=\; F(t) \;+\; K(t) * Y(t)$$

Taking the Laplace transform of both sides, assuming $\mathcal{L}\{F(t)\} = f(s)$ and $\mathcal{L}\{K(t)\} = k(s)$ both exist, we find

$$y(s) \;=\; f(s) + k(s)\, y(s) \quad \text{or} \quad y(s) = \frac{f(s)}{1 - k(s)}$$

The required solution may then be found by inversion. See Problems 5 and 6.

ABEL'S INTEGRAL EQUATION. THE TAUTOCHRONE PROBLEM.

An important integral equation of convolution type is *Abel's integral equation*

$$\int_0^t \frac{Y(u)}{(t-u)^\alpha}\, du \;=\; G(t) \tag{3}$$

where $G(t)$ is given and α is a constant such that $0 < \alpha < 1$.

An application of Abel's integral equation is that of finding the shape of a frictionless wire lying in a vertical plane such that a bead placed on the wire slides to the lowest point in the same time T regardless of where the bead is placed initially. This problem is called the *tautochrone* problem and the shape of the wire can be shown to be a cycloid. [See Problems 7-9.]

INTEGRO-DIFFERENTIAL EQUATIONS

An *integro-differential equation* is an integral equation in which various derivatives of the unknown function $Y(t)$ can also be present. For example,

$$Y''(t) \;=\; Y(t) \;+\; \sin t \;+\; \int_0^t \cos(t-u)\, Y(u)\, du \tag{4}$$

is an integro-differential equation. The solution of such equations subject to given initial conditions can often be obtained by Laplace transformation [see Problem 10].

DIFFERENCE EQUATIONS

An equation which relates the function $Y(t)$ with one or more functions $Y(t-\alpha)$, where α is constant, is called a *difference equation*.

Example. $Y(t) - 4Y(t-1) + 3Y(t-2) = t$ is a difference equation.

In various applications it is possible to formulate a difference equation from which we seek the unknown function $Y(t)$ subject to specified conditions. Determination of this function, which is called *solving* the difference equation, can often be accomplished by the Laplace transformation. See Problem 11.

Difference equations involving relations of terms of the sequence $a_0, a_1, a_2, \ldots$, such as for example $a_{n+2} - 5a_{n+1} + 6a_n = 0$ where $a_0 = 0$, $a_1 = 1$, can also be solved by Laplace transforms. See Problems 18, 19 and 24.

DIFFERENTIAL-DIFFERENCE EQUATIONS

A *differential-difference equation* is a difference equation in which various derivatives of the function $Y(t)$ can be present. Thus, for example,

$$Y'(t) \;=\; Y(t-1) \;+\; 2t \tag{5}$$

is a differential-difference equation. See Problem 12.

It is also possible to have an integro-differential difference equation which is a differential-difference equation in which the unknown function $Y(t)$ can also appear under an integral sign.

Solved Problems

INTEGRAL EQUATIONS

1. Convert the differential equation

$$Y''(t) - 3Y'(t) + 2Y(t) = 4 \sin t, \quad Y(0) = 1, \quad Y'(0) = -2$$

into an integral equation.

Method 1.

Let $Y''(t) = V(t)$. Then using Problem 23, Page 57, and the conditions $Y'(0) = -2$ and $Y(0) = 1$,

$$Y'(t) = \int_0^t V(u) \, du - 2, \qquad Y(t) = \int_0^t (t-u) V(u) \, du - 2t + 1$$

Thus the differential equation becomes

$$V(t) - 3 \int_0^t V(u) \, du + 6 + 2 \int_0^t (t-u) V(u) \, du - 4t + 2 = 4 \sin t$$

from which we obtain

$$V(t) = 4 \sin t + 4t - 8 + \int_0^t \{3 - 2(t-u)\} V(u) \, du$$

Method 2.

Integrating both sides of the given differential equation, we have

$$\int_0^t \{Y''(u) - 3Y'(u) + 2Y(u)\} \, du = \int_0^t 4 \sin u \, du$$

or

$$Y'(t) - Y'(0) - 3Y(t) + 3Y(0) + 2 \int_0^t Y(u) \, du = 4 - 4 \cos t$$

This becomes, using $Y'(0) = -2$ and $Y(0) = 1$,

$$Y'(t) - 3Y(t) + 2 \int_0^t Y(u) \, du = -1 - 4 \cos t$$

Integrating again from 0 to t as before, we find

$$Y(t) - Y(0) - 3 \int_0^t Y(u) \, du + 2 \int_0^t (t-u) Y(u) \, du = -t - 4 \sin t$$

or

$$Y(t) + \int_0^t \{2(t-u) - 3\} Y(u) \, du = 1 - t - 4 \sin t$$

2. Convert the differential equation

$$Y''(t) + (1-t)\,Y'(t) + e^{-t}\,Y(t) \;=\; t^3 - 5t, \qquad Y(0) = -3, \qquad Y'(0) = 4$$

into an integral equation.

Method 1.

Letting $Y''(t) = V(t)$ and using $Y'(0) = 4$, $Y(0) = -3$ we have as in Problem 1, Method 1,

$$Y'(t) \;=\; \int_0^t V(u)\,du + 4, \qquad Y(t) \;=\; \int_0^t (t-u)\,V(u)\,du + 4t - 3$$

Thus the differential equation becomes

$$V(t) + (1-t)\int_0^t V(u)\,du + 4(1-t) + e^{-t}\int_0^t (t-u)\,V(u)\,du + 4t\,e^{-t} - 3e^{-t} \;=\; t^3 - 5t$$

which can be written

$$V(t) \;=\; t^3 - t - 4 + 3e^{-t} - 4t\,e^{-t} + \int_0^t \{t - 1 - e^{-t}\,(t-u)\}\,V(u)\,du$$

Method 2.

Integrating both sides of the differential equation as in Problem 1, Method 2, we find

$$\int_0^t Y''(u)\,du + \int_0^t (1-u)\,Y'(u)\,du + \int_0^t e^{-u}\,Y(u)\,du \;=\; \int_0^t (u^3 - 5u)\,du$$

Then integrating by parts in the second integral, we find

$$Y'(t) - Y'(0) + \left\{(1-u)\,Y(u)\Big|_0^t + \int_0^t Y(u)\,du\right\} + \int_0^t e^{-u}\,Y(u)\,du \;=\; \frac{t^4}{4} - \frac{5t^2}{2}$$

i.e.,

$$Y'(t) - Y'(0) + (1-t)\,Y(t) - Y(0) + \int_0^t Y(u)\,du + \int_0^t e^{-u}\,Y(u)\,du \;=\; \frac{t^4}{4} - \frac{5t^2}{2}$$

or

$$Y'(t) + (1-t)\,Y(t) + \int_0^t Y(u)\,du + \int_0^t e^{-u}\,Y(u)\,du \;=\; \frac{t^4}{4} - \frac{5t^2}{2} + 1$$

Another integration from 0 to t yields

$$Y(t) - Y(0) + \int_0^t (1-u)\,Y(u)\,du + \int_0^t (t-u)\,Y(u)\,du + \int_0^t (t-u)\,e^{-u}\,Y(u)\,du \;=\; \frac{t^5}{20} - \frac{5t^3}{6} + t$$

which can be written

$$Y(t) + \int_0^t \{1 + t - 2u + (t-u)\,e^{-u}\}\,Y(u)\,du \;=\; \frac{t^5}{20} - \frac{5t^3}{6} + t - 3$$

3. Express as an integral equation the differential equation

$$Y^{\text{iv}}(t) - 4Y'''(t) + 6Y''(t) - 4Y'(t) + Y(t) \;=\; 3\cos 2t$$

subject to the conditions $Y(0) = -1$, $Y'(0) = 4$, $Y''(0) = 0$, $Y'''(0) = 2$.

Method 1.

Let $Y^{\text{iv}}(t) = V(t)$. Then as in Problems 1 and 2, we find

$$Y'''(t) \;=\; \int_0^t V(u)\,du + 2, \qquad Y''(t) \;=\; \int_0^t (t-u)\,V(u)\,du + 2t$$

$$Y'(t) \;=\; \int_0^t \frac{(t-u)^2}{2!}\,V(u)\,du + t^2 + 4, \qquad Y(t) \;=\; \int_0^t \frac{(t-u)^3}{3!}\,V(u)\,du + \frac{t^3}{3} + 4t - 1$$

Substituting these into the given differential equation, it becomes

$$V(t) \;=\; 25 \;-\; 16t \;+\; 4t^2 \;-\; \tfrac{1}{3}t^3 \;+\; 3\cos 2t \;+\; \int_0^t \{4 - 6(t-u) + 2(t-u)^2 - \tfrac{1}{6}(t-u)^3\}\, V(u)\, du$$

Method 2.

Integrating successively from 0 to t as in the second methods of Problems 1 and 2, we find the integral equation

$$Y(t) \;-\; \int_0^t \{4 - 6(t-u) + 2(t-u)^2 - \tfrac{1}{6}(t-u)^3\}\, Y(u)\, du \;=\; -\frac{19}{16} \;+\; 8t \;-\; \frac{85t^2}{8} \;+\; 5t^3 \;+\; \frac{3}{16}\cos 2t$$

These integral equations, as well as those obtained in Problems 1 and 2, are *Volterra integral equations*; the limits of integration are from 0 to t. In general this type of integral equation arises from linear differential equations where conditions are specified at one point. For an example of a *Fredholm integral equation* which arises from linear differential equations in which conditions are specified at two points, see Problem 25.

4. Convert the integral equation

$$Y(t) \;=\; 3t \;-\; 4 \;-\; 2\sin t \;+\; \int_0^t \{(t-u)^2 - 3(t-u) + 2\}\, Y(u)\, du$$

into a differential equation.

We make use of Leibnitz's rule,

$$\frac{d}{dt}\int_{a(t)}^{b(t)} K(u,t)\, du \;=\; \int_{a(t)}^{b(t)} \frac{\partial K}{\partial t}\, du \;+\; K\{b(t),t\}\frac{db}{dt} \;-\; K\{a(t),t\}\frac{da}{dt} \tag{1}$$

Thus we have on differentiating both sides of the given integral equation,

$$Y'(t) \;=\; 3 \;-\; 2\cos t \;+\; \int_0^t 2(t-u)\, Y(u)\, du \;-\; 3\int_0^t Y(u)\, du \;+\; 2Y(t) \tag{2}$$

Another differentiation yields,

$$Y''(t) \;=\; 2\sin t \;+\; 2\int_0^t Y(u)\, du \;-\; 3Y(t) \;+\; 2Y'(t) \tag{3}$$

and a final differentiation yields the required differential equation

$$Y'''(t) \;=\; 2\cos t \;+\; 2\,Y(t) \;-\; 3\,Y'(t) \;+\; 2\,Y''(t) \tag{4}$$

or $$Y''' \;-\; 2Y'' \;+\; 3Y' \;-\; 2Y \;=\; 2\cos t$$

The initial conditions obtained by letting $t=0$ in the given integral equation and also in equations (2) and (3), are

$$Y(0) \;=\; -4, \quad Y'(0) \;=\; -7, \quad Y''(0) \;=\; -2$$

Note that the initial conditions are contained in the integral equation.

It is possible to convert every linear differential equation into an integral equation. However, not every integral equation can be converted into a differential equation, as, for example,

$$Y(t) \;=\; \cos t \;+\; \int_0^t \ln(u+t)\, Y(u)\, du$$

INTEGRAL EQUATIONS OF CONVOLUTION TYPE

5. Solve the integral equation $Y(t) = t^2 + \displaystyle\int_0^t Y(u) \sin(t-u)\, du.$

The integral equation can be written

$$Y(t) = t^2 + Y(t) * \sin t$$

Then taking the Laplace transform and using the convolution theorem, we find, if $y = \mathcal{L}\{Y\}$,

$$y = \frac{2}{s^3} + \frac{y}{s^2+1}$$

solving, $y = \dfrac{2(s^2+1)}{s^5} = \dfrac{2}{s^3} + \dfrac{2}{s^5}$

and so $Y = 2\left(\dfrac{t^2}{2!}\right) + 2\left(\dfrac{t^4}{4!}\right) = t^2 + \dfrac{1}{12} t^4$

This can be checked by direct substitution in the integral equation.

6. Solve the integral equation $\displaystyle\int_0^t Y(u)\, Y(t-u)\, du = 16 \sin 4t.$

The equation can be written as

$$Y(t) * Y(t) = 16 \sin 4t$$

Taking the Laplace transform, we find

$$\{y(s)\}^2 = \frac{64}{s^2+16} \qquad \text{or} \qquad y(s) = \frac{\pm 8}{\sqrt{s^2+16}}$$

Then $Y(t) = \mathcal{L}^{-1}\{y(s)\} = \pm\, 8\, J_0(4t)$

Thus $Y(t) = 8\, J_0(4t)$ and $Y(t) = -8\, J_0(4t)$ are both solutions.

ABEL'S INTEGRAL EQUATION. THE TAUTOCHRONE PROBLEM.

7. Solve $\displaystyle\int_0^t \frac{Y(u)}{\sqrt{t-u}}\, du = 1 + t + t^2.$

The equation can be written

$$Y(t) * t^{-1/2} = 1 + t + t^2$$

Then taking the Laplace transform, we find

$$\mathcal{L}\{Y\}\, \mathcal{L}\{t^{-1/2}\} = \mathcal{L}\{1+t+t^2\}$$

or $\dfrac{y\, \Gamma(1/2)}{s^{1/2}} = \dfrac{1}{s} + \dfrac{1}{s^2} + \dfrac{2}{s^3}$

and $y = \dfrac{1}{\Gamma(1/2)}\left\{\dfrac{1}{s^{1/2}} + \dfrac{1}{s^{3/2}} + \dfrac{2}{s^{5/2}}\right\}$

Inverting,
$$Y = \frac{1}{\Gamma(1/2)} \left\{ \frac{t^{-1/2}}{\Gamma(1/2)} + \frac{t^{1/2}}{\Gamma(3/2)} + \frac{2t^{3/2}}{\Gamma(5/2)} \right\}$$

$$= \frac{1}{\pi}(t^{-1/2} + 2t^{1/2} + \tfrac{8}{3}t^{3/2}) = \frac{t^{-1/2}}{3\pi}(3 + 6t + 8t^2)$$

The integral equation is a special case of *Abel's integral equation*.

8. A bead is constrained to move on a frictionless wire which lies in a vertical plane. If the particle starts from rest at any point of the wire and falls under the influence of gravity, find the time of descent to the lowest point of the wire.

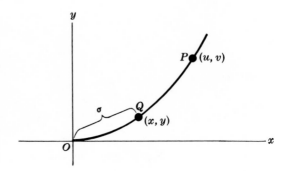

Fig. 4-1

Assume that the bead has mass m and starts from rest at point P with coordinates (u, v) as shown in Fig. 4-1. Let point Q, having coordinates (x, y), be some intermediate point in the motion and suppose that the lowest point of the wire is taken to be the origin O. Let σ be the arc length OQ. From the conservation of energy, we have

Potential energy at P + Kinetic energy at P = Potential energy at Q + Kinetic energy at Q

$$\tfrac{1}{2}mgv + 0 = \tfrac{1}{2}mgy + \tfrac{1}{2}m\left(\frac{d\sigma}{dt}\right)^2$$

where $d\sigma/dt$ is the instantaneous speed of the particle at Q. Then

$$\left(\frac{d\sigma}{dt}\right)^2 = 2g(v - y)$$

or using the fact that σ decreases as time t increases,

$$\frac{d\sigma}{dt} = -\sqrt{2g(v - y)} \tag{1}$$

The total time T taken for the bead to go from P to O is given by

$$T = \int_0^T dt = \int_v^0 \frac{-d\sigma}{\sqrt{2g(v - y)}} = \int_0^v \frac{d\sigma}{\sqrt{2g(v - y)}} \tag{2}$$

When the shape of the curve is given, the arc length can be expressed in terms of y and we find

$$d\sigma = F(y)\, dy \tag{3}$$

Thus (2) becomes

$$T = \frac{1}{\sqrt{2g}} \int_0^v \frac{F(y)\, dy}{\sqrt{v - y}} \tag{4}$$

In general T is a function of v, i.e. of the starting position.

9. Find the shape which the wire of Problem 8 must have if the time taken to reach the lowest point is a constant, i.e. is independent of the starting position.

In this case we have to find $F(y)$ such that

$$T = \frac{1}{\sqrt{2g}} \int_0^v \frac{F(y)}{\sqrt{v - y}}\, dy \tag{1}$$

where T is a constant. This integral equation of convolution type is a special case of *Abel's integral equation* [see Page 113] and can be written

$$\sqrt{2g}\ T \quad = \quad F(y) * y^{-1/2} \tag{2}$$

Taking Laplace transforms and noting that $\mathcal{L}\{F(y)\} = f(s)$, $\mathcal{L}\{y^{-1/2}\} = \Gamma(\tfrac{1}{2})/s^{1/2} = \sqrt{\pi}/s^{1/2}$, we have

$$\frac{\sqrt{2g}\ T}{s} \quad = \quad f(s)\,\frac{\sqrt{\pi}}{s^{1/2}} \qquad \text{or} \qquad f(s) \quad = \quad \frac{T\sqrt{2g}}{\sqrt{\pi}\ s^{1/2}}$$

The inverse Laplace transform is given by

$$F(y) \quad = \quad \frac{T\sqrt{2g}}{\sqrt{\pi}}\,\mathcal{L}^{-1}\left\{\frac{1}{s^{1/2}}\right\} \quad = \quad \frac{T\sqrt{2g}}{\sqrt{\pi}}\,\frac{y^{-1/2}}{\Gamma(1/2)} \quad = \quad \frac{T\sqrt{2g}}{\pi}\,y^{-1/2}$$

Since

$$\frac{d\sigma}{dy} \quad = \quad \frac{\sqrt{dx^2 + dy^2}}{dy} \quad = \quad \sqrt{1 + \left(\frac{dx}{dy}\right)^2}$$

we have

$$\sqrt{1 + \left(\frac{dx}{dy}\right)^2} \quad = \quad \frac{T\sqrt{2g}}{\pi}\,y^{-1/2} \tag{3}$$

If we let

$$\sqrt{b} \ = \ \frac{T\sqrt{2g}}{\pi} \qquad \text{or} \qquad b \ = \ \frac{2gT^2}{\pi^2} \tag{4}$$

(3) can be written

$$1 + \left(\frac{dx}{dy}\right)^2 \ = \ \frac{b}{y} \qquad \text{or} \qquad \frac{dx}{dy} \ = \ \sqrt{\frac{b-y}{y}}$$

since the slope must be positive. From this we find on integrating,

$$x \quad = \quad \int \sqrt{\frac{b-y}{y}}\ dy \ + \ c \tag{5}$$

Letting $y = b\sin^2\theta$, this can be written

$$x \quad = \quad \int \sqrt{\frac{b\cos^2\theta}{b\sin^2\theta}} \cdot 2b\sin\theta\cos\theta\ d\theta \ + \ c$$

$$= \quad 2b\int \cos^2\theta\ d\theta \ + \ c \quad = \quad b\int (1 + \cos 2\theta)\ d\theta \ + \ c \quad = \quad \frac{b}{2}(2\theta + \sin 2\theta) \ + \ c$$

Thus the parametric equations of the required curve are

$$x \ = \ \frac{b}{2}(2\theta + \sin 2\theta) + c, \qquad y \ = \ b\sin^2\theta \ = \ \frac{b}{2}(1 - \cos 2\theta)$$

Since the curve must pass through the point $x = 0$, $y = 0$, we have $c = 0$. Then letting

$$a \ = \ \frac{b}{2} \ = \ \frac{gT^2}{\pi^2} \qquad \text{and} \qquad \phi \ = \ 2\theta$$

the parametric equations are

$$x \ = \ a(\phi + \sin\phi), \qquad y \ = \ a(1 - \cos\phi)$$

These are the parametric equations of a cycloid [see Fig. 4-2 below]. For a given constant T, the wire has the shape of the curve shown heavy in the figure. The cycloid is the path taken by a fixed point on a circle as it rolls along a given line [see Problem 44].

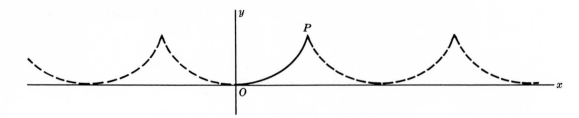

Fig. 4-2

INTEGRO-DIFFERENTIAL EQUATIONS

10. Solve $Y'(t) + 5 \int_0^t \cos 2(t-u)\, Y(u)\, du = 10$ if $Y(0) = 2$.

The equation can be written

$$Y'(t) + 5 \cos 2t * Y(t) = 10$$

Then taking the Laplace transform, we find

$$sy - Y(0) + \frac{5sy}{s^2+4} = \frac{10}{s}$$

or
$$y = \frac{2s^3 + 10s^2 + 8s + 40}{s^2(s^2+9)}$$

Hence by Problem 44, Page 67,

$$Y = \frac{1}{27}(24 + 120t + 30 \cos 3t + 50 \sin 3t)$$

Note that by integration from 0 to t using $Y(0) = 2$, the given integro-differential equation can be converted into the integral equation

$$Y(t) + 5 \int_0^t (t-u) \cos 2(t-u)\, Y(u)\, du = 10t + 2$$

DIFFERENCE AND DIFFERENTIAL-DIFFERENCE EQUATIONS

11. Solve $3Y(t) - 4Y(t-1) + Y(t-2) = t$ if $Y(t) = 0$ for $t < 0$.

Taking the Laplace transform of both sides yields

$$3 \mathcal{L}\{Y(t)\} - 4 \mathcal{L}\{Y(t-1)\} + \mathcal{L}\{Y(t-2)\} = \mathcal{L}\{t\} = \frac{1}{s^2} \qquad (1)$$

Now
$$\mathcal{L}\{Y(t-1)\} = \int_0^\infty e^{-st}\, Y(t-1)\, dt$$

$$= \int_{-1}^\infty e^{-s(u+1)}\, Y(u)\, du \qquad [\text{letting } t = u+1]$$

$$= e^{-s} \int_{-1}^0 e^{-su}\, Y(u)\, du + e^{-s} \int_0^\infty e^{-su}\, Y(u)\, du$$

$$= e^{-s} y$$

and
$$\mathcal{L}\{Y(t-2)\} = \int_0^\infty e^{-st} \, Y(t-2) \, dt$$

$$= \int_{-2}^\infty e^{-s(u+2)} \, Y(u) \, du \qquad [\text{letting } t = u + 2]$$

$$= e^{-2s} \int_{-2}^0 e^{-su} \, Y(u) \, du \; + \; e^{-2s} \int_0^\infty e^{-su} \, Y(u) \, du$$

$$= e^{-2s} \, y$$

since $Y(u) = 0$ if $u < 0$, so that

$$\int_{-1}^0 e^{-su} \, Y(u) \, du = 0 \qquad \text{and} \qquad \int_{-2}^0 e^{-su} \, Y(u) \, du = 0$$

Then (1) becomes
$$3y \; - \; 4e^{-s} \, y \; + \; e^{-2s} \, y \; = \; \frac{1}{s^2}$$

and
$$y = \frac{1}{s^2(3 - 4e^{-s} + e^{-2s})} = \frac{1}{s^2(1 - e^{-s})(3 - e^{-s})}$$

$$= \frac{1}{2s^2} \left\{ \frac{1}{1 - e^{-s}} - \frac{1}{3 - e^{-s}} \right\}$$

$$= \frac{1}{2s^2} \left\{ \frac{1}{1 - e^{-s}} - \frac{1}{3(1 - e^{-s}/3)} \right\}$$

$$= \frac{1}{2s^2} \left\{ (1 + e^{-s} + e^{-2s} + e^{-3s} + \cdots) - \frac{1}{3}\left(1 + \frac{e^{-s}}{3} + \frac{e^{-2s}}{3^2} + \frac{e^{-3s}}{3^3} + \cdots \right) \right\}$$

$$= \frac{1}{3s^2} + \frac{1}{2} \sum_{n=1}^\infty \left(1 - \frac{1}{3^n} \right) \frac{e^{-ns}}{s^2}$$

Hence
$$Y = \frac{t}{3} + \frac{1}{2} \sum_{n=1}^{[t]} \left(1 - \frac{1}{3^n} \right)(t - n)$$

where $[t]$ is the greatest integer less than or equal to t.

12. Solve $Y'(t) + Y(t-1) = t^2$ if $Y(t) = 0$ for $t \leqq 0$.

Taking the Laplace transform of both sides yields
$$\mathcal{L}\{Y'(t)\} \; + \; \mathcal{L}\{Y(t-1)\} \; = \; 2/s^3 \tag{1}$$

Now
$$\mathcal{L}\{Y'(t)\} = s \, \mathcal{L}\{Y\} - Y(0) = sy - 0 = sy$$

and
$$\mathcal{L}\{Y(t-1)\} = \int_0^\infty e^{-st} \, Y(t-1) \, dt$$

$$= \int_{-1}^\infty e^{-s(u+1)} \, Y(u) \, du \qquad [\text{letting } t = u + 1]$$

$$= e^{-s} \int_{-1}^0 e^{-su} \, Y(u) \, du \; + \; e^{-s} \int_0^\infty e^{-su} \, Y(u) \, du$$

$$= e^{-s} \, y$$

since $Y(u) = 0$ for $u \leq 0$ so that $\int_{-1}^{0} e^{-su} Y(u)\, du = 0$. Then (1) can be written

$$sy + e^{-s} y = \frac{2}{s^3} \quad \text{or} \quad y = \frac{2}{s^3(s + e^{-s})}$$

By use of series, we have

$$y = \frac{2}{s^3(s + e^{-s})} = \frac{2}{s^4(1 + e^{-s}/s)}$$

$$= \frac{2}{s^4}\left(1 - \frac{e^{-s}}{s} + \frac{e^{-2s}}{s^2} - \frac{e^{-3s}}{s^3} + \cdots\right)$$

$$= \frac{2}{s^4} - \frac{2e^{-s}}{s^5} + \frac{2e^{-2s}}{s^6} - \frac{2e^{-3s}}{s^7} + \cdots$$

$$= 2 \sum_{n=0}^{\infty} \frac{e^{-ns}}{s^{n+4}}$$

Now
$$\mathcal{L}^{-1}\left\{\frac{e^{-ns}}{s^{n+4}}\right\} = \begin{cases} \dfrac{(t-n)^{n+3}}{(n+3)!} & t \geq n \\[2ex] 0 & \text{otherwise} \end{cases}$$

Thus if $[t]$ denotes the greatest integer less than or equal to t, we find that

$$Y(t) = 2 \sum_{n=0}^{[t]} \frac{(t-n)^{n+3}}{(n+3)!} \tag{2}$$

13. In Problem 12 find (a) $Y(4)$, (b) $Y(\pi)$.

(a) Since $[4] = 4$, we have

$$Y(4) = 2 \sum_{n=0}^{4} \frac{(4-n)^{n+3}}{(n+3)!} = 2\left\{\frac{4^3}{3!} + \frac{3^4}{4!} + \frac{2^5}{5!} + \frac{1^6}{6!}\right\} = 28.62 \text{ (approx.)}$$

(b) Since $[\pi] = 3$, we have

$$Y(\pi) = 2 \sum_{n=0}^{3} \frac{(\pi-n)^{n+3}}{(n+3)!} = 2\left\{\frac{\pi^3}{3!} + \frac{(\pi-1)^4}{4!} + \frac{(\pi-2)^5}{5!} + \frac{(\pi-3)^6}{6!}\right\} = 12.12 \text{ (approx.)}$$

14. If $F(t) = r^n$ for $n \leq t < n+1$, $n = 0, 1, 2, 3, \ldots$,   find $\mathcal{L}\{F(t)\}$.

$$\mathcal{L}\{F(t)\} = \int_{0}^{\infty} e^{-st} F(t)\, dt$$

$$= \int_{0}^{1} e^{-st} r^0 \, dt + \int_{1}^{2} e^{-st} r^1 \, dt + \int_{2}^{3} e^{-st} r^2 \, dt + \cdots$$

$$= \frac{1 - e^{-s}}{s} + r\left(\frac{e^{-s} - e^{-2s}}{s}\right) + r^2\left(\frac{e^{-2s} - e^{-3s}}{s}\right) + \cdots$$

$$= \frac{1 - e^{-s}}{s}(1 + re^{-s} + r^2 e^{-2s} + \cdots)$$

$$= \frac{1 - e^{-s}}{s} \cdot \frac{1}{1 - re^{-s}} = \frac{1 - e^{-s}}{s(1 - re^{-s})}$$

15. Find $\mathcal{L}^{-1}\left\{\dfrac{1-e^{-s}}{s(1-re^{-s})}\right\}$.

By Problem 14, we have $\mathcal{L}^{-1}\left\{\dfrac{1-e^{-s}}{s(1-re^{-s})}\right\} = F(t) = r^n$ for $n \leqq t < n+1$.

Another method.

We have

$$\frac{1-e^{-s}}{s(1-re^{-s})} \quad = \quad \frac{1-e^{-s}}{s} \cdot \frac{1}{1-re^{-s}}$$

$$= \quad \frac{1-e^{-s}}{s}(1 + re^{-s} + r^2e^{-2s} + \cdots)$$

$$= \quad \int_0^1 e^{-st}\, r^0\, dt \;+\; \int_1^2 e^{-st}\, r^1\, dt \;+\; \int_2^3 e^{-st}\, r^2\, dt \;+\; \cdots$$

$$= \quad \int_0^\infty e^{-st}\, F(t)\, dt$$

where $F(t) = r^n$ for $n \leqq t < n+1$, $n = 0,1,2,3,\ldots$.

16. Find $\mathcal{L}^{-1}\left\{\dfrac{(1-e^{-s})e^{-s}}{s(1-re^{-s})}\right\}$.

If $\mathcal{L}^{-1}\{f(s)\} = F(t)$, then by *Theorem 2-4*, Page 44,

$$\mathcal{L}^{-1}\{e^{-s}f(s)\} \quad = \quad \begin{cases} F(t-1) & t > 1 \\ 0 & t < 1 \end{cases}$$

Thus by Problem 15,

$$\mathcal{L}^{-1}\left\{\frac{(1-e^{-s})e^{-s}}{s(1-re^{-s})}\right\} \;=\; F(t-1) \;=\; r^n \quad \text{for} \quad n \leqq t-1 < n+1, \ n = 0,1,2,3,\ldots$$

or, equivalently,

$$\mathcal{L}^{-1}\left\{\frac{(1-e^{-s})e^{-s}}{s(1-re^{-s})}\right\} \;=\; r^{n-1} \quad \text{for} \quad n \leqq t < n+1, \ n = 1,2,3,\ldots$$

17. Let $Y(t) = a_n$ for $n \leqq t < n+1$ where $n = 0,1,2,\ldots$. Find (a) $\mathcal{L}\{Y(t+1)\}$ and (b) $\mathcal{L}\{Y(t+2)\}$ in terms of $\mathcal{L}\{Y(t)\} = y(s)$.

(a) Letting $t+1 = u$, we have

$$\mathcal{L}\{Y(t+1)\} \quad = \quad \int_0^\infty e^{-st}\, Y(t+1)\, dt \quad = \quad e^s\int_1^\infty e^{-su}\, Y(u)\, du$$

$$= \quad e^s\int_0^\infty e^{-su}\, Y(u)\, du \;-\; e^s\int_0^1 e^{-su}\, Y(u)\, du$$

$$= \quad e^s\, y(s) \;-\; e^s\int_0^1 e^{-su}\, a_0\, du \quad = \quad e^s\, y(s) \;-\; \frac{a_0\, e^s(1-e^{-s})}{s}$$

using the fact that $Y(t) = a_0$ for $0 \leqq t < 1$.

(b) Letting $t + 2 = u$, we have

$$\mathcal{L}\{Y(t+2)\} = \int_0^\infty e^{-st} Y(t+2) \, dt$$

$$= e^{2s} \int_2^\infty e^{-su} Y(u) \, du$$

$$= e^{2s} \left\{ \int_0^\infty e^{-su} Y(u) \, du - \int_0^1 e^{-su} Y(u) \, du - \int_1^2 e^{-su} Y(u) \, du \right\}$$

$$= e^{2s} y(s) - e^{2s} \int_0^1 e^{-su} a_0 \, du - e^{2s} \int_1^2 e^{-su} a_1 \, du$$

$$= e^{2s} y(s) - \frac{a_0 e^{2s}(1 - e^{-s})}{s} - \frac{a_1 e^{2s}(e^{-s} - e^{-2s})}{s}$$

$$= e^{2s} y(s) - \frac{e^s(1 - e^{-s})(a_0 e^s + a_1)}{s}$$

using the fact that $Y(t) = a_0$ for $0 \leqq t < 1$ and $Y(t) = a_1$ for $1 \leqq t < 2$.

18. Let $\{a_n\}$, $n = 0, 1, 2, \ldots$, denote the sequence of constants $a_0, a_1, a_2, \ldots$ and suppose that we have the *recursion formula* defined by the difference equation

$$a_{n+2} - 5a_{n+1} + 6a_n = 0, \qquad a_0 = 0, \ a_1 = 1$$

Find a formula for a_n, i.e. solve this difference equation for a_n.

Define the function

$$Y(t) = a_n, \qquad n \leqq t < n+1 \qquad \text{where } n = 0, 1, 2, \ldots$$

Then the given recursion formula becomes

$$Y(t+2) - 5Y(t+1) + 6Y(t) = 0 \tag{1}$$

Taking the Laplace transform of (1) using the results of Problem 17 with $a_0 = 0$, $a_1 = 1$, we find

$$e^{2s} y(s) - \frac{e^s(1 - e^{-s})}{s} - 5e^s y(s) + 6y(s) = 0$$

or

$$(e^{2s} - 5e^s + 6) y(s) = \frac{e^s(1 - e^{-s})}{s}$$

Then

$$y(s) = \frac{e^s(1 - e^{-s})}{s(e^{2s} - 5e^s + 6)} = \frac{e^s(1 - e^{-s})}{s} \left\{ \frac{1}{(e^s - 3)(e^s - 2)} \right\}$$

$$= \frac{e^s(1 - e^{-s})}{s} \left\{ \frac{1}{e^s - 3} - \frac{1}{e^s - 2} \right\} = \frac{1 - e^{-s}}{s} \left\{ \frac{1}{1 - 3e^{-s}} - \frac{1}{1 - 2e^{-s}} \right\}$$

Hence by Problem 15 we find on inverting,

$$a_n = 3^n - 2^n, \qquad n = 0, 1, 2, \ldots$$

Check: If $a_n = 3^n - 2^n$, then $a_0 = 0$, $a_1 = 1$. Also,

$$a_{n+2} - 5a_{n+1} + 6a_n = (3^{n+2} - 2^{n+2}) - 5(3^{n+1} - 2^{n+1}) + 6(3^n - 2^n)$$

$$= 9 \cdot 3^n - 4 \cdot 2^n - 15 \cdot 3^n + 10 \cdot 2^n + 6 \cdot 3^n - 6 \cdot 2^n = 0$$

19. Solve the difference equation

$$a_{n+2} - 5a_{n+1} + 6a_n = 4^n, \quad a_0 = 0, \ a_1 = 1$$

The only difference between this problem and Problem 18 is the presence of the right hand term 4^n. We write the equation as

$$Y(t+2) - 5Y(t+1) + 6Y(t) = F(t) \tag{1}$$

where $Y(t) = a_n$, $F(t) = 4^n$ for $n \leqq t < n+1$, $n = 0, 1, 2, \ldots$.

Taking the Laplace transform of both sides of (1) using the results in Problems 14 and 17, we find if $y(s) = \mathcal{L}\{Y(t)\}$,

$$e^{2s}\,y(s) - \frac{e^s}{s}(1 - e^{-s}) - 5e^s\,y(s) + 6y(s) = \frac{1 - e^{-s}}{s(1 - 4e^{-s})}$$

Then

$$
\begin{aligned}
y(s) &= \frac{e^s(1 - e^{-s})}{s(e^s - 2)(e^s - 3)} + \frac{1 - e^{-s}}{s(e^s - 2)(e^s - 3)(1 - 4e^{-s})} \\[2mm]
&= \frac{e^s(1 - e^{-s})}{s}\left\{\frac{1}{e^s - 3} - \frac{1}{e^s - 2}\right\} + \frac{e^s - 1}{s(e^s - 2)(e^s - 3)(e^s - 4)} \\[2mm]
&= \frac{1 - e^{-s}}{s}\left\{\frac{1}{1 - 3e^{-s}} - \frac{1}{1 - 2e^{-s}}\right\} + \frac{e^s - 1}{s}\left\{\frac{1/2}{e^s - 2} - \frac{1}{e^s - 3} + \frac{1/2}{e^s - 4}\right\} \\[2mm]
&= \frac{1 - e^{-s}}{s}\left\{\frac{1}{1 - 3e^{-s}} - \frac{1}{1 - 2e^{-s}}\right\} + \frac{1 - e^{-s}}{s}\left\{\frac{1/2}{1 - 2e^{-s}} - \frac{1}{1 - 3e^{-s}} + \frac{1/2}{1 - 4e^{-s}}\right\}
\end{aligned}
$$

Hence on inverting, using the results of Problem 15, we find

$$
\begin{aligned}
Y(t) = a_n &= 3^n - 2^n + \tfrac{1}{2}\cdot 2^n - 3^n + \tfrac{1}{2}\cdot 4^n \tag{2} \\[2mm]
&= \tfrac{1}{2}\cdot 4^n - \tfrac{1}{2}\cdot 2^n = \tfrac{1}{2}(4^n - 2^n)
\end{aligned}
$$

20. In Problem 19, find a_5.

Method 1.   From the solution (2) in Problem 19, we have

$$a_5 = \tfrac{1}{2}(4^5 - 2^5) = 496$$

Method 2.   From the given difference equation in Problem 19, we have for $n = 0$

$$a_2 - 5a_1 + 6a_0 = 1$$

or using $a_0 = 0$, $a_1 = 1$

$$a_2 = 1 + 5a_1 - 6a_0 = 6$$

If $n = 1$, $a_3 - 5a_2 + 6a_1 = 4$ so that

$$a_3 = 4 + 5a_2 - 6a_1 = 28$$

If $n = 2$, $a_4 - 5a_3 + 6a_2 = 16$ or

$$a_4 = 16 + 5a_3 - 6a_2 = 16 + 5(28) - 6(6) = 120$$

Finally if $n = 3$, $a_5 - 5a_4 + 6a_3 = 64$ so that

$$a_5 = 64 + 5a_4 - 6a_3 = 64 + 5(120) - 6(28) = 496$$

MISCELLANEOUS PROBLEMS

21. Solve the integral equation

$$Y(t) = \tfrac{1}{2}\sin 2t + \int_0^t Y(u)\, Y(t-u)\, du$$

The integral equation can be written in the form

$$Y(t) = \tfrac{1}{2}\sin 2t + Y(t) * Y(t)$$

Then taking the Laplace transform, using the convolution theorem, we find

$$y(s) = \frac{1}{s^2+4} + \{y(s)\}^2 \quad\text{or}\quad \{y(s)\}^2 - y(s) + \frac{1}{s^2+4} = 0$$

Solving, we obtain

$$y(s) = \frac{1}{2} \pm \frac{1}{2}\sqrt{1 - \frac{4}{s^2+4}} = \frac{1}{2} \pm \frac{1}{2}\frac{s}{\sqrt{s^2+4}}$$

Thus

$$y(s) = \frac{1}{2}\left(\frac{\sqrt{s^2+4}+s}{\sqrt{s^2+4}}\right) \tag{1}$$

and

$$y(s) = \frac{1}{2}\left(\frac{\sqrt{s^2+4}-s}{\sqrt{s^2+4}}\right) \tag{2}$$

From (2) we find the solution

$$Y(t) = \mathcal{L}^{-1}\left\{\frac{1}{2}\left(\frac{\sqrt{s^2+4}-s}{\sqrt{s^2+4}}\right)\right\} = J_1(2t) \tag{3}$$

The result (1) can be written

$$y(s) = -\frac{1}{2}\left(\frac{\sqrt{s^2+4}-s}{\sqrt{s^2+4}} - 2\right) = 1 - \frac{1}{2}\left(\frac{\sqrt{s^2+4}-s}{\sqrt{s^2+4}}\right)$$

Hence a second solution is

$$Y(t) = \delta(t) - J_1(2t) \tag{4}$$

where $\delta(t)$ is the Dirac delta function.

The solution (3) is continuous and bounded for $t \geqq 0$.

22. Find $\mathcal{L}\{F(t)\}$ if $F(t) = n,\ n \leqq t < n+1,\ n = 0,1,2,3,\ldots$.

We have

$$\mathcal{L}\{F(t)\} = \int_0^\infty e^{-st}\, F(t)\, dt$$

$$= \int_0^1 e^{-st}\,(0)\, dt + \int_1^2 e^{-st}\,(1)\, dt + \int_2^3 e^{-st}\,(2)\, dt + \cdots$$

$$= (1)\left(\frac{e^{-s}-e^{-2s}}{s}\right) + (2)\left(\frac{e^{-2s}-e^{-3s}}{s}\right) + (3)\left(\frac{e^{-3s}-e^{-4s}}{s}\right) + \cdots$$

$$= \frac{e^{-s}(1-e^{-s})}{s}(1 + 2e^{-s} + 3e^{-2s} + 4e^{-3s} + \cdots)$$

Now since for $|x| < 1$,

$$1 + x + x^2 + x^3 + \cdots = \frac{1}{1-x}$$

we have by differentiation,

$$1 + 2x + 3x^2 + \cdots = \frac{1}{(1-x)^2}$$

Then if $x = e^{-s}$, we find

$$1 + 2e^{-s} + 3e^{-2s} + \cdots = \frac{1}{(1-e^{-s})^2}$$

Thus

$$\mathcal{L}\{F(t)\} = \frac{e^{-s}}{s(1-e^{-s})}$$

23. Find $\mathcal{L}^{-1}\left\{\dfrac{e^{-s}}{s(1-re^{-s})}\right\}$ for (a) $r \neq 1$, (b) $r = 1$.

(a) By the binomial formula,

$$\frac{e^{-s}}{s(1-re^{-s})} = \frac{e^{-s}}{s}(1 + re^{-s} + r^2e^{-2s} + \cdots)$$

$$= \frac{e^{-s}}{s} + \frac{re^{-2s}}{s} + \frac{r^2e^{-2s}}{s} + \cdots$$

$$= u(t-1) + r\,u(t-2) + r^2\,u(t-3) + \cdots$$

Thus

$$\mathcal{L}^{-1}\left\{\frac{e^{-s}}{s(1-re^{-s})}\right\} = F(t) = \sum_{k=1}^{[t]} r^k \qquad (1)$$

if $t \geqq 1$, and 0 if $t < 1$.

If $n \leqq t < n+1$, (1) becomes if $r \neq 1$,

$$r + r^2 + \cdots + r^n = \frac{r(r^n - 1)}{r - 1} \qquad (2)$$

(b) If $r = 1$ we find that $F(t) = n$, $n \leqq t < n+1$. This agrees with Problem 22.

24. Solve the difference equation

$$a_{n+2} - 7a_{n+1} + 10a_n = 16n, \qquad a_0 = 6,\ a_1 = 2$$

The given equation can be written

$$Y(t+2) - 7Y(t+1) + 10Y(t) = F(t) \qquad (1)$$

where $Y(t) = a_n$, $F(t) = 16n$ for $n \leqq t < n+1$, $n = 0, 1, 2, \ldots$.

Using Problems 17 and 22, the Laplace transform of (1) is

$$e^{2s}y(s) - \frac{e^s(1-e^{-s})(6e^s + 2)}{s} - 7e^s y(s) + \frac{42e^s(1-e^{-s})}{s} + 10y(s) = \frac{16e^{-s}}{s(1-e^{-s})}$$

Then $\quad y(s) \quad = \quad \dfrac{e^s(1 - e^{-s})(6e^s + 2)}{s(e^s - 5)(e^s - 2)} \; - \; \dfrac{42e^s(1 - e^{-s})}{s(e^s - 5)(e^s - 2)} \; + \; \dfrac{16e^{-s}}{s(1 - e^{-s})(e^s - 5)(e^s - 2)}$

$$= \quad e^s \left(\frac{1 - e^{-s}}{s} \right) \left\{ \frac{6e^s + 2}{(e^s - 5)(e^s - 2)} \right\}$$

$$- \; 42 \left(\frac{1 - e^{-s}}{s} \right) \left\{ \frac{e^s}{(e^s - 5)(e^s - 2)} \right\}$$

$$+ \; \frac{16}{s} \left\{ \frac{1}{(e^s - 1)(e^s - 5)(e^s - 2)} \right\}$$

$$= \quad e^s \left(\frac{1 - e^{-s}}{s} \right) \left\{ \frac{32/3}{e^s - 5} - \frac{14/3}{e^s - 2} \right\}$$

$$- \; 42 \left(\frac{1 - e^{-s}}{s} \right) \left\{ \frac{5/3}{e^s - 5} - \frac{2/3}{e^s - 2} \right\}$$

$$+ \; \frac{1}{s} \left\{ \frac{4}{e^s - 1} + \frac{4/3}{e^s - 5} - \frac{16/3}{e^s - 2} \right\}$$

$$= \quad \left(\frac{1 - e^{-s}}{s} \right) \left\{ \frac{32/3}{1 - 5e^{-s}} - \frac{14/3}{1 - 2e^{-s}} \right\}$$

$$- \; \left(\frac{1 - e^{-s}}{s} \right) \left\{ \frac{70e^{-s}}{1 - 5e^{-s}} - \frac{28e^{-s}}{1 - 2e^{-s}} \right\}$$

$$+ \; \frac{1}{s} \left\{ \frac{4e^{-s}}{1 - e^{-s}} + \frac{(4/3)e^{-s}}{1 - 5e^{-s}} - \frac{(16/3)e^{-s}}{1 - 2e^{-s}} \right\}$$

Now by Problems 14 and 22, we find for $n \geqq 1$,

$$a_n \quad = \quad \frac{32}{3} \cdot 5^n \; - \; \frac{14}{3} \cdot 2^n \; - \; 70 \cdot 5^{n-1} \; + \; 28 \cdot 2^{n-1} \; + \; 4(n-1) \; + \; \frac{4}{3} \cdot \frac{5}{4}(5^n - 1) \; - \; \frac{16}{3} \cdot \frac{2}{1}(2^n - 1)$$

$$= \quad 4 \cdot 2^n \; - \; 3 \cdot 5^n \; + \; 4n \; + \; 5$$

25. Express the differential equation

$$Y''(t) \; + \; \lambda \, Y(t) \quad = \quad 0, \qquad Y(0) = 0, \; Y(1) = 0$$

where λ is a constant, as an integral equation.

Method 1.

Letting $Y''(t) = V(t)$, we find, if $Y'(0) = c$,

$$Y'(t) \quad = \quad \int_0^t V(u) \, du \, + \, c, \qquad Y(t) \quad = \quad \int_0^t (t - u) \, V(u) \, du \, + \, ct \tag{1}$$

Since $Y(1) = 0$, we must have

$$\int_0^1 (1 - u) \, V(u) \, du \, + \, c \quad = \quad 0 \qquad \text{or} \qquad c \quad = \quad \int_0^1 (u - 1) \, V(u) \, du$$

Then from (*1*), we find

$$Y(t) \;=\; \int_0^t (t-u)\,V(u)\,du \;+\; \int_0^1 (tu-t)\,V(u)\,du$$

$$=\; \int_0^t (t-u)\,V(u)\,du \;+\; \int_0^t (tu-t)\,V(u)\,du \;+\; \int_t^1 (tu-t)\,V(u)\,du$$

$$=\; \int_0^t (t-1)\,u\,V(u)\,du \;+\; \int_t^1 (u-1)\,t\,V(u)\,du$$

This can be written
$$Y(t) \;=\; \int_0^1 K(t,u)\,V(u)\,du$$

where $K(t,u) = \begin{cases} (t-1)\,u & u < t \\ (u-1)\,t & u > t \end{cases}$.   [Note that $K(t,u) = K(u,t)$, i.e. $K(t,u)$ is *symmetric*.]

Thus the required integral equation is

$$V(t) \;+\; \lambda \int_0^1 K(t,u)\,V(u)\,du \;=\; 0$$

or
$$V(t) \;=\; -\lambda \int_0^1 K(t,u)\,V(u)\,du$$

Method 2.

Integrating both sides of the given differential equation from 0 to t, we find

$$Y'(t) \;-\; Y'(0) \;+\; \lambda \int_0^t Y(u)\,du \;=\; 0$$

Another integration from 0 to t yields

$$Y(t) \;-\; Y(0) \;-\; Y'(0)\,t \;+\; \lambda \int_0^t (t-u)\,Y(u)\,du \;=\; 0 \qquad (1)$$

Since $Y(0) = 0$, (*1*) becomes

$$Y(t) \;=\; Y'(0)\,t \;-\; \lambda \int_0^t (t-u)\,Y(u)\,du \qquad (2)$$

Letting $t = 1$ and using $Y(1) = 0$, we find from (*2*)

$$Y'(0) \;=\; \lambda \int_0^1 (1-u)\,Y(u)\,du$$

Thus (*2*) becomes

$$Y(t) \;=\; \lambda \int_0^1 (t-tu)\,Y(u)\,du \;-\; \lambda \int_0^t (t-u)\,Y(u)\,du$$

$$=\; \lambda \int_0^t (t-tu)\,Y(u)\,du \;+\; \lambda \int_t^1 (t-tu)\,Y(u)\,du \;-\; \lambda \int_0^t (t-u)\,Y(u)\,du$$

$$=\; \lambda \int_0^t u(1-t)\,Y(u)\,du \;+\; \lambda \int_t^1 t(1-u)\,Y(u)\,du$$

$$=\; -\lambda \int_0^1 K(t,u)\,Y(u)\,du$$

where $K(t,u) = \begin{cases} (t-1)\,u & u < t \\ (u-1)\,t & u > t \end{cases}$.

The integral equations obtained here are examples of a *Fredholm integral equation* with a symmetric kernel.

Supplementary Problems

INTEGRAL EQUATIONS

Convert each of the following differential equations into integral equations.

26. $Y''(t) + 2Y'(t) - 8Y(t) = 5t^2 - 3t,$ $Y(0) = -2,\ Y'(0) = 3.$

Ans. $V(t) + \int_0^t (2 - 8t + 8u)\ V(u)\ du = 5t^2 + 21t - 22,$ $V(t) = Y''(t)$

or $Y(t) + \int_0^t (2 - 8t + 8u)\ Y(u)\ du = -2 - t + 5t^4/12 - t^3$

27. $2Y''(t) - 3Y'(t) - 2Y(t) = 4e^{-t} + 2\cos t,$ $Y(0) = 4,\ Y'(0) = -1.$

Ans. $2V(t) + \int_0^t (2u - 2t - 3)\ V(u)\ du = 4e^{-t} + 2\cos t + 5 - 2t,$ $V(t) = Y''(t)$

or $2Y(t) + \int_0^t (2u - 2t - 3)\ Y(u)\ du = 6 - 10t + 4e^{-t} - 2\cos t$

28. $Y'''(t) + 8Y(t) = 3\sin t + 2\cos t,$ $Y(0) = 0,\ Y'(0) = -1,\ Y''(0) = 2.$

Ans. $V(t) + 4\int_0^t (t - u)^2\ V(u)\ du = 3\sin t + 2\cos t - 4t^2 + 4t,$ $V(t) = Y'''(t)$

or $Y(t) + 4\int_0^t (t - u)^2\ Y(u)\ du = 5t^2/2 + t - 3 + 3\cos t - 2\sin t$

29. $Y''(t) + \cos t\ Y(t) = e^{-t},$ $Y(0) = -2,\ Y'(0) = 0.$

Ans. $V(t) + \int_0^t (t - u)\cos t\ V(u)\ du = e^{-t} + 2\cos t,$ $V(t) = Y''(t)$

or $Y(t) + \int_0^t (t - u)\cos u\ Y(u)\ du = t - 3 + e^{-t}$

30. $Y''(t) - t\ Y'(t) + t^2\ Y(t) = 1 + t,$ $Y(0) = 4,\ Y'(0) = 2.$

Ans. $V(t) + \int_0^t (t^3 - t - ut^2)\ V(u)\ du = 1 + 3t - 4t^2 - 2t^3,$ $V(t) = Y''(t)$

or $Y(t) - \int_0^t (t - 2u + tu^2 - u^3)\ Y(u)\ du = t^2/2 + t^3/6 + 2t + 4$

31. $Y^{iv}(t) - 2t\ Y''(t) + (1 - t^2)\ Y(t) = 1 + 4t - 2t^2 + t^4,$ $Y(0) = 1,\ Y'(0) = 0,\ Y''(0) = -2,\ Y'''(0) = 0.$

Ans. $V(t) + \int_0^t \{\tfrac{1}{6}(t - u)^3(1 - t^2) - 2t(t - u)\}\ V(u)\ du = 0,$ $V(t) = Y^{iv}(t)$

or $Y(t) - \int_0^t \{2u(t - u) + 2(t - u)^2 + \tfrac{1}{6}(t - u)^3(1 - u^2)\}\ Y(u)\ du$

$$= 1 - t^2 + \frac{t^3}{3} + \frac{t^4}{24} - \frac{t^6}{180} + \frac{t^8}{1680}$$

Convert each of the following integral equations into differential equations and associated conditions.

32. $Y(t) = 5\cos t + \int_0^t (t - u)\ Y(u)\ du$

Ans. $Y''(t) - Y(t) = -5\sin t,$ $Y(0) = 5,\ Y'(0) = 0$

33. $Y(t) = t^2 - 3t + 4 - 3 \int_0^t (t-u)^2 \, Y(u) \, du$

    Ans. $Y'''(t) + 6\,Y(t) = 0, \quad Y(0) = 4, \ Y'(0) = -3, \ Y''(0) = 2$

34. $Y(t) + \int_0^t \{(t-u)^2 + 4(t-u) - 3\} \, Y(u) \, du = e^{-t}$

    Ans. $Y'''(t) - 3\,Y''(t) + 4\,Y'(t) + 2\,Y(t) = -e^{-t}, \ Y(0) = 1, \ Y'(0) = 2, \ Y''(0) = 3$

35. $Y(t) - \int_0^t (t-u) \sec t \, Y(u) \, du = t$

    Ans. $Y''(t) - 2 \tan t \, Y'(t) - (1 + \sec t) \, Y(t) = -t - 2 \tan t, \quad Y(0) = 0, \ Y'(0) = 1$

36. $Y(t) + \int_0^t (t^2 + 4t - ut - u - 2) \, Y(u) \, du = 0$

    Ans. $Y'''(t) + (3t - 2) \, Y''(t) + (t + 10) \, Y'(t) + Y(t) = 0, \quad Y(0) = 0, \ Y'(0) = 0, \ Y''(0) = 0$

INTEGRAL EQUATIONS OF CONVOLUTION TYPE

37. Solve $Y(t) = t + 2 \int_0^t \cos(t - u) \, Y(u) \, du$.

    Ans. $Y(t) = t + 2 + 2(t-1)e^t$

38. (*a*) Show that the integral equation

    $$Y(t) = t + \tfrac{1}{6} \int_0^t (t-u)^3 \, Y(u) \, du$$

    has solution $Y(t) = \tfrac{1}{2}(\sin t + \sinh t)$.

    (*b*) Is the solution in (*a*) unique?   Explain.

39. Find the continuous solution of the integral equation $\int_0^t Y(u) \, Y(t-u) \, du = 2\,Y(t) + t - 2$.

    Ans. $Y(t) = 1$

40. Show that the only solution of the integral equation $\int_0^t Y(u) \sin(t-u) \, du = Y(t)$ is the *trivial solution* $Y(t) = 0$.

41. Discuss the solutions of the integral equation $\int_0^t Y(u) \, G(t-u) \, du = Y(t)$.

ABEL'S INTEGRAL EQUATION AND THE TAUTOCHRONE PROBLEM

42. Solve the integral equation $\int_0^t \dfrac{Y(u)}{\sqrt{t-u}} \, du = \sqrt{t}.$ *Ans.* $Y(t) = \tfrac{1}{2}$

43. Show that the solution of the integral equation $\int_0^t \dfrac{Y(u)}{(t-u)^{1/3}} \, du = t(1+t)$ is $\dfrac{3\sqrt{3}}{4\pi} \, t^{1/3} \, (3t + 2)$.

44. A circular wheel of radius a [see Fig. 4-3] rolls on a straight line, taken to be the x axis. Show that a fixed point O' on its rim, originally in contact with the line at O describes the cycloid

$$x = a(\phi - \sin \phi), \quad y = a(1 - \cos \phi)$$

shown dashed in Fig. 4-3.

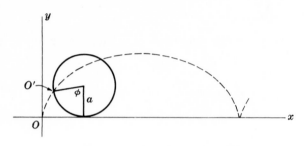

Fig. 4-3

45. Prove that the curve in the tautochrone problem, Page 118, is a cycloid and discuss the relationship to the curve of Problem 44.

46. Show that the time required for the bead of Problems 8 and 9 to slide from the top P of the wire to the bottom O [lowest point on the cycloid] is $\pi\sqrt{a/g}$.

47. If $0 < \alpha < 1$, show that the solution of $\displaystyle\int_0^t \frac{Y(u)}{(t-u)^\alpha}\,du = F(t)$, assuming $F(0) = 0$, is

$$Y(t) = \frac{\sin \alpha\pi}{\pi} \int_0^t F'(u)\,(t-u)^{\alpha-1}\,du$$

48. Discuss the solutions of the integral equation in Problem 47 if $F(0) \neq 0$. Illustrate your remarks by considering

$$\int_0^t \frac{Y(u)}{(t-u)^{1/2}}\,du = 1 + t$$

INTEGRO-DIFFERENTIAL EQUATIONS

49. Solve $\displaystyle\int_0^t Y(u)\cos(t-u)\,du = Y'(t)$ if $Y(0) = 1$.

   Ans. $Y(t) = 1 + \tfrac{1}{2}t^2$

50. Solve $\displaystyle\int_0^t Y'(u)\,Y(t-u)\,du = 24t^3$ if $Y(0) = 0$.

   Ans. $Y(t) = \pm 16t^{3/2}/\sqrt{\pi}$

51. The current $I(t)$ in a certain electric circuit is given by

$$L\,I'(t) + R\int_0^t I(u)\cos \omega(t-u)\,du = 0$$

where L, R, and ω are constants. Find $I(t)$ if $I(0) = I_0$.

52. *Ans.* $I(t) = \dfrac{\omega^2 L I_0}{\omega^2 L + R} + \dfrac{I_0 R}{\omega^2 L + R}\cos\sqrt{\dfrac{\omega^2 L + R}{L}}\,t$

DIFFERENCE AND DIFFERENTIAL-DIFFERENCE EQUATIONS

53. Solve $Y(t) - 3Y(t-1) + 2Y(t-2) = 1$ if $Y(t) = 0, \ t < 0$.

   Ans. $Y(t) = 2^{[t]+2} - [t] - 3$

54. Show that the solution of $Y'(t) = 2Y(t-1) + t$ if $Y(t) = 0$, $t < 0$ is

$$Y(t) = \sum_{n=0}^{[t]} \frac{2^n(t-n)^{n+2}}{(n+2)!}$$

55. Solve $Y''(t) - Y(t-1) = F(t)$ where $Y(t) = 0$, $Y'(t) = 0$ for $t \leqq 0$, and

$$F(t) = \begin{cases} 0 & t \leqq 0 \\ 2t & t > 0 \end{cases}$$

Ans. $Y(t) = 2\sum_{n=0}^{[t]} \frac{(t-n)^{2n+3}}{(2n+3)!}$

56. Solve $3Y(t) - 5Y(t-1) + 2Y(t-2) = F(t)$ if $Y(t) = 0$, $t < 0$, and

$$F(t) = \begin{cases} 0 & t < 0 \\ t^2 & t > 0 \end{cases}$$

Ans. $Y(t) = \sum_{n=0}^{[t]} \{1 - (\tfrac{2}{3})^{n+1}\}(t-n)^2$

57. Solve the difference equations

(a) $3a_{n+2} - 5a_{n+1} + 2a_n = 0$ if $a_0 = 1$, $a_1 = 0$.

(b) $a_{n+2} + 2a_{n+1} - 3a_n = 0$ if $a_0 = 0$, $a_1 = 1$.

Ans. (a) $3(2/3)^n - 2$, (b) $\tfrac{1}{4}\{1 - (-3)^n\}$

58. The *Fibonacci numbers* $a_0, a_1, a_2, \ldots$ are defined by the relation $a_{n+2} = a_{n+1} + a_n$ where $a_0 = 0$, $a_1 = 1$. (a) Find the first ten Fibonacci numbers. (b) Find a formula for a_n.

Ans. (a) 0, 1, 1, 2, 3, 5, 8, 13, 21, 34 (b) $a_n = \dfrac{1}{\sqrt{5}}\left\{\left(\dfrac{1+\sqrt{5}}{2}\right)^n - \left(\dfrac{1-\sqrt{5}}{2}\right)^n\right\}$

59. Solve the equation $a_{n+2} - 4a_{n+1} + 4a_n = 0$ where $a_0 = 1$, $a_1 = 4$.   *Ans.* $a_n = 2^n(n+1)$

60. Solve the equation $a_{n+2} - 2a_{n+1} + 2a_n = 0$ where $a_0 = 0$, $a_1 = 1$.

Ans. $a_n = \{(1+i)^n - (1-i)^n\}/2i$

61. (a) Solve $a_{n+3} - 2a_{n+2} - a_{n+1} + 2a_n = 0$ if $a_0 = 0$, $a_1 = 1$, $a_2 = 1$. (b) Find a_{10}.

Ans. (a) $a_n = \tfrac{1}{3}\{2^n - (-1)^n\}$, (b) $a_{10} = 341$

62. (a) Show how a solution to $a_{n+2} - 6a_{n+1} + 8a_n = 0$ can be obtained by assuming $a_n = r^n$ where r is an unknown constant. (b) Use this method to solve Problems 57-61.

MISCELLANEOUS PROBLEMS

63. Show that the non-linear differential equation

$$Y''(t) + \{Y(t)\}^2 = t \sin t, \qquad Y(0) = 1, \ Y'(0) = -1$$

can be written as the integral equation

$$Y(t) + \int_0^t (t-u)\{Y(u)\}^2\, du = 3 - t - 2\cos t - t \sin t$$

64. Solve $\displaystyle\int_0^t Y(u)\, Y(t-u)\, du = 2Y(t) + \tfrac{1}{6}t^3 - 2t$.

Ans. $Y(t) = t$ or $Y(t) = 2\delta(t) - t$

65. Express as an integral equation: $Y''(t) - Y(t) = 3 \cos t - \sin t$, $Y(\pi) = 1$, $Y'(\pi) = -2$.

Ans. $V(t) = 2\pi + 1 - 2t + 3 \cos t - \sin t + \displaystyle\int_{\pi}^{t} (t-u) V(u) \, du$,   where $V(t) = Y''(t)$

66. Solve $Y(t) = t + \displaystyle\int_{0}^{t} Y(u) J_1(t-u) \, du$.

Ans. $Y(t) = \tfrac{1}{2}(t^2 + 1) \displaystyle\int_{0}^{t} J_0(u) \, du + \tfrac{1}{2} t J_0(t) - \tfrac{1}{2} t^2 J_1(t)$

67. Find $G(x)$ such that $\displaystyle\int_{0}^{x} G(u) \, G(x-u) \, du = 8(\sin x - x \cos x)$.

Ans. $G(x) = \pm 4 \sin x$

68. Solve $\displaystyle\int_{0}^{t} Y(u) \, Y(t-u) \, du = t + 2Y(t)$.

Ans. $Y(t) = J_1(t) - \displaystyle\int_{0}^{t} J_0(u) \, du$ or $Y(t) = 2 \delta(t) - J_1(t) + \displaystyle\int_{0}^{t} J_0(u) \, du$

69. Solve the following difference equations using Laplace transform methods.

(a) $a_{n+2} - 5a_{n+1} + 6a_n = 2n + 1$, $a_0 = 0$, $a_1 = 1$.

(b) $a_{n+2} + 4a_{n+1} - 5a_n = 24n - 8$, $a_0 = 3$, $a_1 = -5$.

Ans.   (a) $a_n = \tfrac{5}{2} \cdot 3^n - 5 \cdot 2^n + n + \tfrac{5}{2}$ (b) $a_n = 2n^2 - 4n + 2 + (-5)^n$

70. Solve   (a) $a_{n+2} + 2a_{n+1} + a_n = n + 2$, $a_0 = 0$, $a_1 = 0$.

(b) $a_{n+2} - 6a_{n+1} + 5a_n = 2^n$, $a_0 = 0$, $a_1 = 0$.

Ans.   (a) $a_n = \tfrac{1}{4}(3n - 1)(-1)^n + \tfrac{1}{4}(n+1)$ (b) $a_n = \tfrac{1}{4} + \tfrac{1}{12} \cdot 5^n - \tfrac{1}{3} \cdot 2^n$

71. Solve $a_{n+3} - 2a_{n+2} - a_{n+1} + 2a_n = n^2 + 2^n$, $a_0 = 0$, $a_1 = 1$, $a_2 = 1$.

Ans. $a_n = \tfrac{1}{3} + \tfrac{5}{6}n - \tfrac{1}{6}n^3 + \tfrac{1}{6}n \cdot 2^n - \tfrac{2}{9} \cdot 2^n - \tfrac{1}{9}(-1)^n$

72. (a) Show how a particular solution to Problem 69(a) can be found by assuming $a_n = A + Bn$ where A and B are unknown constants. (b) Using the result of part (a) and the method of Problem 62, show how to obtain the solution of Problem 69(a). (c) How can the method indicated in parts (a) and (b) be revised to enable solution of Problems 69(b), 70(a), 70(b) and 71.

73. Find all continuous functions $F(t)$ for which $\displaystyle\int_{0}^{t} u F(u) \cos(t-u) \, du = te^{-t} - \sin t$.

Ans. $F(t) = -2e^{-t}$

74. Show that the non-linear differential equation

$$Y''(t) + 2Y'(t) = Y^3(t), \qquad Y(0) = 0, \ Y(1) = 0$$

can be written as the integral equations

$$Y(t) = \int_{0}^{t} (2t - 2) Y(u) \, du + \int_{t}^{1} 2t \, Y(u) \, du + \int_{0}^{1} K(t, u) Y^3(u) \, du$$

or $Y(t) = \displaystyle\int_{0}^{t} (2 - 2t)e^{2(u-t)} Y(u) \, du - \int_{t}^{1} 2te^{2(u-t)} Y(u) \, du + \int_{0}^{1} e^{-2t} K(t, u) Y^3(u) \, du$

where $K(t, u) = \begin{cases} u(t-1) & u < t \\ t(u-1) & u > t \end{cases}$.

75. Solve for $Y(t)$: $8Y(t) - 12Y(t-1) + 4Y(t-2) = F(t)$ where $Y(t) = 0$ for $t < 0$ and

$$F(t) = \begin{cases} 0 & t < 0 \\ e^{-t} & t > 0 \end{cases}$$

Ans. $Y(t) = \frac{1}{8} e^{-t} \left\{ 1 + \sum_{n=0}^{[t]} (2 - 2^{-n}) e^n \right\}$

76. If $Y'_n(t) = \beta \{ Y_{n-1}(t) - Y_n(t) \}$ $n = 1, 2, 3, \ldots$

$$Y'_0(t) = -\beta Y_0(t)$$

where $Y_n(0) = 0$ for $n = 1, 2, 3, \ldots,$ $Y_0(0) = 1$ and β is a constant, find $Y_n(t)$.

Ans. $Y_n(t) = \dfrac{(\beta t)^n e^{-\beta t}}{n!}$

77. Work Problem 76 if the first equation is replaced by

$$Y'_n(t) = \beta_n \{ Y_{n-1}(t) - Y_n(t) \}   n = 1, 2, 3, \ldots$$

where $\beta_1, \beta_2, \beta_3, \ldots$ are constants.

78. Give a direct proof of the tautochrone property of the cycloid.

79. The *brachistochrone problem* is that of finding the shape of a frictionless wire in a vertical plane, as shown in Fig. 4-1, Page 118, such that a bead placed at P will slide to O in the shortest time. The solution of this problem is the cycloid as in Fig. 4-2, Page 120. Demonstrate this property for the particular cases of (*a*) a straight line and (*b*) a parabola joining points O and P.

80. Find the shape of a frictionless wire in a vertical plane such that a bead placed on it will descend to the lowest point in a time proportional to the vertical component of its distance from the lowest point.

Ans. $x = a(1 - \cos^3 \theta)$, $y = \frac{3}{2} a \sin^2 \theta$

Chapter 5

Complex Variable Theory

THE COMPLEX NUMBER SYSTEM

Since there is no real number x which satisfies the polynomial equation $x^2 + 1 = 0$ or similar equations, the set of complex numbers is introduced.

We can consider a complex number as having the form $a + bi$ where a and b are real numbers called the *real* and *imaginary parts*, and $i = \sqrt{-1}$ is called the *imaginary unit*. Two complex numbers $a + bi$ and $c + di$ are *equal* if and only if $a = c$ and $b = d$. We can consider real numbers as a subset of the set of complex numbers with $b = 0$. The complex number $0 + 0i$ corresponds to the real number 0.

The *absolute value* or *modulus* of $a + bi$ is defined as $|a + bi| = \sqrt{a^2 + b^2}$. The *complex conjugate* of $a + bi$ is defined as $a - bi$. The complex conjugate of the complex number z is often indicated by $\bar{z}$ or z^*.

In performing operations with complex numbers we can operate as in the algebra of real numbers, replacing i^2 by -1 when it occurs. Inequalities for complex numbers are not defined.

From the point of view of an axiomatic foundation of complex numbers, it is desirable to treat a complex number as an ordered pair (a, b) of real numbers a and b subject to certain operational rules which turn out to be equivalent to those above. For example, we define $(a, b) + (c, d) = (a + c, b + d)$, $(a, b)(c, d) = (ac - bd, ad + bc)$, $m(a, b) = (ma, mb)$, etc. We then find that $(a, b) = a(1, 0) + b(0, 1)$ and we associate this with $a + bi$, where i is the symbol for $(0, 1)$.

POLAR FORM OF COMPLEX NUMBERS

If real scales are chosen on two mutually perpendicular axes $X'OX$ and $Y'OY$ (the x and y axes) as in Fig. 5-1 below, we can locate any point in the plane determined by these lines by the ordered pair of numbers (x, y) called *rectangular coordinates* of the point. Examples of the location of such points are indicated by P, Q, R, S and T in Fig. 5-1.

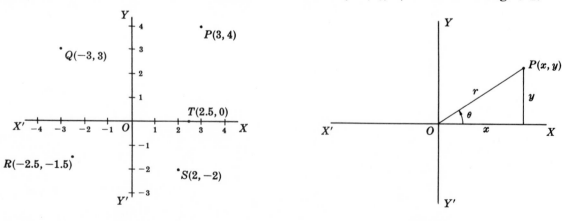

Fig. 5-1   Fig. 5-2

Since a complex number $x + iy$ can be considered as an ordered pair (x, y), we can represent such numbers by points in an xy plane called the *complex plane* or *Argand diagram*. Referring to Fig. 5-2 above we see that

$$x = r \cos \theta, \qquad y = r \sin \theta \tag{1}$$

where $r = \sqrt{x^2 + y^2} = |x + iy|$ and θ, called the *amplitude* or *argument*, is the angle which line OP makes with the positive x axis OX. It follows that

$$z = x + iy = r(\cos \theta + i \sin \theta) \tag{2}$$

called the *polar form* of the complex number, where r and θ are called *polar coordinates*. It is sometimes convenient to write $\operatorname{cis} \theta$ instead of $\cos \theta + i \sin \theta$.

OPERATIONS IN POLAR FORM. DE MOIVRE'S THEOREM

If $z_1 = x_1 + iy_1 = r_1(\cos \theta_1 + i \sin \theta_1)$ and $z_2 = x_2 + iy_2 = r_2(\cos \theta_2 + i \sin \theta_2)$, we can show that

$$z_1 z_2 = r_1 r_2 \{\cos(\theta_1 + \theta_2) + i \sin(\theta_1 + \theta_2)\} \tag{3}$$

$$\frac{z_1}{z_2} = \frac{r_1}{r_2} \{\cos(\theta_1 - \theta_2) + i \sin(\theta_1 - \theta_2)\} \tag{4}$$

$$z^n = \{r(\cos \theta + i \sin \theta)\}^n = r^n(\cos n\theta + i \sin n\theta) \tag{5}$$

where n is any real number. Equation (5) is often called *De Moivre's theorem*.

In terms of *Euler's formula*

$$e^{i\theta} = \cos \theta + i \sin \theta$$

we can write (3), (4) and (5) in the suggestive forms

$$z_1 z_2 = (r_1 e^{i\theta_1})(r_2 e^{i\theta_2}) = r_1 r_2 e^{i(\theta_1 + \theta_2)} \tag{6}$$

$$\frac{z_1}{z_2} = \frac{r_1 e^{i\theta_1}}{r_2 e^{i\theta_2}} = \frac{r_1}{r_2} e^{i(\theta_1 - \theta_2)} \tag{7}$$

$$z^n = (r e^{i\theta})^n = r^n e^{in\theta} \tag{8}$$

ROOTS OF COMPLEX NUMBERS

If n is a positive integer, we have using De Moivre's theorem,

$$z^{1/n} = \{r(\cos \theta + i \sin \theta)\}^{1/n}$$

$$= r^{1/n} \left\{ \cos\left(\frac{\theta + 2k\pi}{n}\right) + i \sin\left(\frac{\theta + 2k\pi}{n}\right) \right\} \qquad k = 0, 1, 2, 3, \ldots \tag{9}$$

or equivalently

$$z^{1/n} = (r e^{i\theta})^{1/n} = \{r e^{i(\theta + 2k\pi)}\}^{1/n} = r^{1/n} e^{i(\theta + 2k\pi)/n} \tag{10}$$

from which it follows that there are n different values for $z^{1/n}$, $z \neq 0$. Extensions are easily made to $z^{m/n}$.

FUNCTIONS

If to each of a set of complex numbers which a variable z may assume there corresponds one or more values of a variable w, then w is called a *function of the complex variable z*, written $w = f(z)$.

A function is *single-valued* if for each value of z there corresponds only one value of w; otherwise it is *multiple-valued* or *many-valued*. In general we can write $w = f(z) = u(x, y) + i\,v(x, y)$, where u and v are real functions of x and y.

Example. $w = z^2 = (x + iy)^2 = x^2 - y^2 + 2ixy = u + iv$ so that $u(x, y) = x^2 - y^2$, $v(x, y) = 2xy$. These are called the *real* and *imaginary parts* of $w = z^2$ respectively.

Unless otherwise specified we shall assume that $f(z)$ is single-valued. A function which is multiple-valued can be considered as a collection of single-valued functions.

LIMITS AND CONTINUITY

Definitions of limits and continuity for functions of a complex variable are analogous to those for a real variable. Thus $f(z)$ is said to have the *limit l* as z approaches z_0 if, given any $\epsilon > 0$, there exists a $\delta > 0$ such that $|f(z) - l| < \epsilon$ whenever $0 < |z - z_0| < \delta$.

Similarly, $f(z)$ is said to be *continuous* at z_0 if, given any $\epsilon > 0$, there exists a $\delta > 0$ such that $|f(z) - f(z_0)| < \epsilon$ whenever $|z - z_0| < \delta$. Alternatively, $f(z)$ is continuous at z_0 if $\lim_{z \to z_0} f(z) = f(z_0)$.

DERIVATIVES

If $f(z)$ is single-valued in some region of the z plane the *derivative* of $f(z)$, denoted by $f'(z)$, is defined as

$$\lim_{\Delta z \to 0} \frac{f(z + \Delta z) - f(z)}{\Delta z} \tag{11}$$

provided the limit exists independent of the manner in which $\Delta z \to 0$. If the limit (11) exists for $z = z_0$, then $f(z)$ is called *differentiable at z_0*. If the limit exists for all z such that $|z - z_0| < \delta$ for some $\delta > 0$, then $f(z)$ is called *analytic at z_0*. If the limit exists for all z in a region $\mathcal{R}$, then $f(z)$ is called *analytic in $\mathcal{R}$*. In order to be analytic, $f(z)$ must be single-valued and continuous. The converse, however, is not necessarily true.

We define elementary functions of a complex variable by a natural extension of the corresponding functions of a real variable. Where series expansions for real functions $f(x)$ exist, we can use as definition the series with x replaced by z.

Example 1. We define $e^z = 1 + z + \dfrac{z^2}{2!} + \dfrac{z^3}{3!} + \cdots$, $\sin z = z - \dfrac{z^3}{3!} + \dfrac{z^5}{5!} - \dfrac{z^7}{7!} + \cdots$, $\cos z = 1 - \dfrac{z^2}{2!} + \dfrac{z^4}{4!} - \dfrac{z^6}{6!} + \cdots$. From these we can show that $e^z = e^{x+iy} = e^x(\cos y + i \sin y)$, as well as numerous other relations.

Example 2. We define a^b as $e^{b \ln a}$ even when a and b are complex numbers. Since $e^{2k\pi i} = 1$, it follows that $e^{i\theta} = e^{i(\theta + 2k\pi)}$ and we define $\ln z = \ln(re^{i\theta}) = \ln r + i(\theta + 2k\pi)$. Thus $\ln z$ is a many-valued function. The various single-valued functions of which this many-valued function is composed are called its *branches*.

Rules for differentiating functions of a complex variable are much the same as for those of real variables. Thus $\frac{d}{dz}(z^n) = nz^{n-1}$, $\frac{d}{dz}(\sin z) = \cos z$, etc.

CAUCHY-RIEMANN EQUATIONS

A necessary condition that $w = f(z) = u(x, y) + i\,v(x, y)$ be analytic in a region $\mathcal{R}$ is that u and v satisfy the *Cauchy-Riemann equations*

$$\frac{\partial u}{\partial x} = \frac{\partial v}{\partial y}, \qquad \frac{\partial u}{\partial y} = -\frac{\partial v}{\partial x} \tag{12}$$

(see Problem 12). If the partial derivatives in (12) are continuous in $\mathcal{R}$, the equations are sufficient conditions that $f(z)$ be analytic in $\mathcal{R}$.

If the second derivatives of u and v with respect to x and y exist and are continuous, we find by differentiating (12) that

$$\frac{\partial^2 u}{\partial x^2} + \frac{\partial^2 u}{\partial y^2} = 0, \qquad \frac{\partial^2 v}{\partial x^2} + \frac{\partial^2 v}{\partial y^2} = 0 \tag{13}$$

Thus the real and imaginary parts satisfy Laplace's equation in two dimensions. Functions satisfying Laplace's equation are called *harmonic functions*.

LINE INTEGRALS

Let C be a curve in the xy plane joining points (x_1, y_1) and (x_2, y_2). The integral

$$\int_C P\,dx + Q\,dy \qquad \text{or} \qquad \int_{(x_1, y_1)}^{(x_2, y_2)} P\,dx + Q\,dy$$

where P and Q are functions of x and y, is called a *line integral* along curve C. This is a generalization of the integral of elementary calculus to curves. As in elementary calculus it can be defined as the limit of a sum.

Two important properties of line integrals are:

1. $$\int_{(x_1, y_1)}^{(x_2, y_2)} P\,dx + Q\,dy = -\int_{(x_2, y_2)}^{(x_1, y_1)} P\,dx + Q\,dy$$

2. If (x_3, y_3) is any other point on C, then

$$\int_{(x_1, y_1)}^{(x_2, y_2)} P\,dx + Q\,dy = \int_{(x_1, y_1)}^{(x_3, y_3)} P\,dx + Q\,dy + \int_{(x_3, y_3)}^{(x_2, y_2)} P\,dx + Q\,dy$$

If C is a *simple closed curve* (one which does not cross itself anywhere) as in Fig. 5-3, the line integral around C, traversed in the positive or counterclockwise direction, is denoted by

$$\oint_C P\,dx + Q\,dy$$

For evaluation of line integrals, see Problem 15.

GREEN'S THEOREM IN THE PLANE

Let C be a simple closed curve bounding a region $\mathcal{R}$ [see Fig. 5-3]. Suppose that P, Q and their first partial derivatives with respect to x and y are continuous in $\mathcal{R}$ and on C. Then we have

$$\oint_C P\,dx + Q\,dy = \iint_{\mathcal{R}} \left(\frac{\partial Q}{\partial x} - \frac{\partial P}{\partial y}\right) dx\,dy$$

which is often called *Green's theorem in the plane.*

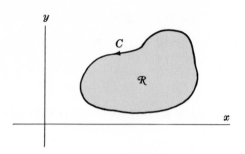

Fig. 5-3

INTEGRALS

If $f(z)$ is defined, single-valued and continuous in a region $\mathcal{R}$, we define the *integral* of $f(z)$ along some path C in $\mathcal{R}$ from point z_1 to point z_2, where $z_1 = x_1 + iy_1$, $z_2 = x_2 + iy_2$, as

$$\int_C f(z)\,dz = \int_{(x_1,y_1)}^{(x_2,y_2)} (u+iv)(dx + i\,dy) = \int_{(x_1,y_1)}^{(x_2,y_2)} u\,dx - v\,dy + i\int_{(x_1,y_1)}^{(x_2,y_2)} v\,dx + u\,dy$$

With this definition the integral of a function of a complex variable can be made to depend on line integrals. An alternative definition based on the limit of a sum, as for functions of a real variable, can also be formulated and turns out to be equivalent to the one above.

The rules for complex integration are similar to those for real integrals. An important result is

$$\left|\int_C f(z)\,dz\right| \leqq \int_C |f(z)|\,|dz| \leqq M\int_C ds = ML \tag{14}$$

where M is an upper bound of $|f(z)|$ on C, i.e. $|f(z)| \leqq M$, and L is the length of the path C.

CAUCHY'S THEOREM

Let C be a simple closed curve. If $f(z)$ is analytic within the region bounded by C as well as on C, then we have *Cauchy's theorem* that

$$\oint_C f(z)\,dz = 0 \tag{15}$$

See Problem 19.

Expressed in another way, (15) is equivalent to the statement that $\displaystyle\int_{z_1}^{z_2} f(z)\,dz$ has a value *independent of the path* joining z_1 and z_2. Such integrals can be evaluated as $F(z_2) - F(z_1)$ where $F'(z) = f(z)$.

Example. Since $f(z) = 2z$ is analytic everywhere, we have for any simple closed curve C

$$\oint_C 2z\,dz = 0$$

Also,
$$\int_{2i}^{1+i} 2z\,dz = z^2\Big|_{2i}^{1+i} = (1+i)^2 - (2i)^2 = 2i + 4$$

CAUCHY'S INTEGRAL FORMULAS

If $f(z)$ is analytic within and on a simple closed curve C and a is any point interior to C, then

$$f(a) \;=\; \frac{1}{2\pi i} \oint_C \frac{f(z)}{z-a}\, dz \tag{16}$$

where C is traversed in the positive (counterclockwise) sense.

Also, the nth derivative of $f(z)$ at $z = a$ is given by

$$f^{(n)}(a) \;=\; \frac{n!}{2\pi i} \oint_C \frac{f(z)}{(z-a)^{n+1}}\, dz \tag{17}$$

These are called *Cauchy's integral formulas*. They are quite remarkable because they show that if the function $f(z)$ is known *on* the closed curve C then it is also known *within* C, and the various derivatives at points within C can be calculated. Thus if a function of a complex variable has a first derivative, it has all higher derivatives as well. This of course is not necessarily true for functions of real variables.

TAYLOR'S SERIES

Let $f(z)$ be analytic inside and on a circle having its center at $z = a$. Then for all points z in the circle we have the *Taylor series* representation of $f(z)$ given by

$$f(z) \;=\; f(a) \,+\, f'(a)(z-a) \,+\, \frac{f''(a)}{2!}(z-a)^2 \,+\, \frac{f'''(a)}{3!}(z-a)^3 \,+\, \cdots \tag{18}$$

See Problem 29.

SINGULAR POINTS

A singular point of a function $f(z)$ is a value of z at which $f(z)$ fails to be analytic. If $f(z)$ is analytic everywhere in some region except at an interior point $z = a$, we call $z = a$ an *isolated singularity* of $f(z)$.

Example. If $f(z) = \dfrac{1}{(z-3)^2}$, then $z = 3$ is an isolated singularity of $f(z)$.

POLES

If $f(z) = \dfrac{\phi(z)}{(z-a)^n}$, $\phi(a) \neq 0$, where $\phi(z)$ is analytic everywhere in a region including $z = a$, and if n is a positive integer, then $f(z)$ has an isolated singularity at $z = a$ which is called a *pole of order n*. If $n = 1$, the pole is often called a *simple pole*; if $n = 2$ it is called a *double pole*, etc.

Example 1. $f(z) = \dfrac{z}{(z-3)^2 (z+1)}$ has two singularities: a pole of order 2 or double pole at $z = 3$, and a pole of order 1 or simple pole at $z = -1$.

Example 2. $f(z) = \dfrac{3z-1}{z^2+4} = \dfrac{3z-1}{(z+2i)(z-2i)}$ has two simple poles at $z = \pm 2i$.

A function can have other types of singularities besides poles. For example, $f(z) = \sqrt{z}$ has a *branch point* at $z = 0$ (see Problem 45). The function $f(z) = \dfrac{\sin z}{z}$ has a singularity at $z = 0$. However, due to the fact that $\lim\limits_{z \to 0} \dfrac{\sin z}{z}$ is finite, we call such a singularity a *removable singularity*.

LAURENT'S SERIES

If $f(z)$ has a pole of order n at $z = a$ but is analytic at every other point inside and on a circle C with center at a, then $(z - a)^n f(z)$ is analytic at all points inside and on C and has a Taylor series about $z = a$ so that

$$f(z) \;=\; \frac{a_{-n}}{(z-a)^n} + \frac{a_{-n+1}}{(z-a)^{n-1}} + \cdots + \frac{a_{-1}}{z-a} + a_0 + a_1(z-a) + a_2(z-a)^2 + \cdots \qquad (19)$$

This is called a *Laurent series* for $f(z)$. The part $a_0 + a_1(z-a) + a_2(z-a)^2 + \cdots$ is called the *analytic part*, while the remainder consisting of inverse powers of $z - a$ is called the *principal part*. More generally, we refer to the series $\sum_{k=-\infty}^{\infty} a_k(z-a)^k$ as a Laurent series where the terms with $k < 0$ constitute the principal part. A function which is analytic in a region bounded by two concentric circles having center at $z = a$ can always be expanded into such a Laurent series (see Problem 119).

It is possible to define various types of singularities of a function $f(z)$ from its Laurent series. For example, when the principal part of a Laurent series has a finite number of terms and $a_{-n} \neq 0$ while $a_{-n-1}, a_{-n-2}, \ldots$ are all zero, then $z = a$ is a pole of order n. If the principal part has infinitely many non-zero terms, $z = a$ is called an *essential singularity* or sometimes a *pole of infinite order*.

> **Example.** The function $e^{1/z} = 1 + \dfrac{1}{z} + \dfrac{1}{2!\,z^2} + \cdots$ has an essential singularity at $z = 0$.

RESIDUES

The coefficients in *(19)* can be obtained in the customary manner by writing the coefficients for the Taylor series corresponding to $(z - a)^n f(z)$. In further developments, the coefficient a_{-1}, called the *residue* of $f(z)$ at the pole $z = a$, is of considerable importance. It can be found from the formula

$$a_{-1} \;=\; \lim_{z \to a} \frac{1}{(n-1)!} \frac{d^{n-1}}{dz^{n-1}} \{(z-a)^n f(z)\} \qquad (20)$$

where n is the order of the pole. For simple poles the calculation of the residue is of particular simplicity since it reduces to

$$a_{-1} \;=\; \lim_{z \to a} (z-a) f(z) \qquad (21)$$

RESIDUE THEOREM

If $f(z)$ is analytic in a region $\mathcal{R}$ except for a pole of order n at $z = a$ and if C is any simple closed curve in $\mathcal{R}$ containing $z = a$, then $f(z)$ has the form *(19)*. Integrating *(19)*, using the fact that

$$\oint_C \frac{dz}{(z-a)^n} \;=\; \begin{cases} 0 & \text{if } n \neq 1 \\ 2\pi i & \text{if } n = 1 \end{cases} \qquad (22)$$

(see Problem 21), it follows that

$$\oint_C f(z)\, dz \;=\; 2\pi i a_{-1} \qquad (23)$$

i.e. the integral of $f(z)$ around a closed path enclosing a single pole of $f(z)$ is $2\pi i$ times the residue at the pole.

More generally, we have the following important

Theorem. If $f(z)$ is analytic within and on the boundary C of a region $\mathcal{R}$ except at a finite number of poles $a, b, c, \ldots$ within $\mathcal{R}$, having residues $a_{-1}, b_{-1}, c_{-1}, \ldots$ respectively, then

$$\oint_C f(z)\, dz \;=\; 2\pi i(a_{-1} + b_{-1} + c_{-1} + \cdots) \tag{24}$$

i.e. the integral of $f(z)$ is $2\pi i$ times the sum of the residues of $f(z)$ at the poles enclosed by C. Cauchy's theorem and integral formulas are special cases of this result which we call the *residue theorem*.

EVALUATION OF DEFINITE INTEGRALS

The evaluation of various definite integrals can often be achieved by using the residue theorem together with a suitable function $f(z)$ and a suitable path or *contour C*, the choice of which may require great ingenuity. The following types are most common in practice.

1. $\displaystyle\int_0^\infty F(x)\, dx,\quad F(x)$ is an even function.

   Consider $\displaystyle\oint_C F(z)\, dz$ along a contour C consisting of the line along the x axis from $-R$ to $+R$ and the semi-circle above the x axis having this line as diameter. Then let $R \to \infty$. See Problems 37, 38.

2. $\displaystyle\int_0^{2\pi} G(\sin\theta, \cos\theta)\, d\theta,\quad G$ is a rational function of $\sin\theta$ and $\cos\theta$.

   Let $z = e^{i\theta}$. Then $\sin\theta = \dfrac{z - z^{-1}}{2i}$, $\cos\theta = \dfrac{z + z^{-1}}{2}$ and $dz = ie^{i\theta}\, d\theta$ or $d\theta = dz/iz$. The given integral is equivalent to $\displaystyle\oint_C F(z)\, dz$ where C is the unit circle with center at the origin. See Problems 39, 40.

3. $\displaystyle\int_{-\infty}^\infty F(x) \begin{Bmatrix} \cos mx \\ \sin mx \end{Bmatrix} dx,\quad F(x)$ is a rational function.

   Here we consider $\displaystyle\oint_C F(z)\, e^{imz}\, dz$ where C is the same contour as that in Type 1. See Problem 42.

4. Miscellaneous integrals involving particular contours. See Problems 43, 46.

Solved Problems

COMPLEX NUMBERS

1. Perform the indicated operations.

(a) $(4 - 2i) + (-6 + 5i) = 4 - 2i - 6 + 5i = 4 - 6 + (-2 + 5)i = -2 + 3i$

(b) $(-7 + 3i) - (2 - 4i) = -7 + 3i - 2 + 4i = -9 + 7i$

(c) $(3 - 2i)(1 + 3i) = 3(1 + 3i) - 2i(1 + 3i) = 3 + 9i - 2i - 6i^2 = 3 + 9i - 2i + 6 = 9 + 7i$

(d) $\dfrac{-5 + 5i}{4 - 3i} = \dfrac{-5 + 5i}{4 - 3i} \cdot \dfrac{4 + 3i}{4 + 3i} = \dfrac{(-5 + 5i)(4 + 3i)}{16 - 9i^2} = \dfrac{-20 - 15i + 20i + 15i^2}{16 + 9}$

$= \dfrac{-35 + 5i}{25} = \dfrac{5(-7 + i)}{25} = \dfrac{-7}{5} + \dfrac{1}{5}i$

(e) $\dfrac{i + i^2 + i^3 + i^4 + i^5}{1 + i} = \dfrac{i - 1 + (i^2)(i) + (i^2)^2 + (i^2)^2 i}{1 + i} = \dfrac{i - 1 - i + 1 + i}{1 + i}$

$= \dfrac{i}{1 + i} \cdot \dfrac{1 - i}{1 - i} = \dfrac{i - i^2}{1 - i^2} = \dfrac{i + 1}{2} = \dfrac{1}{2} + \dfrac{1}{2}i$

(f) $|3 - 4i|\,|4 + 3i| = \sqrt{(3)^2 + (-4)^2}\,\sqrt{(4)^2 + (3)^2} = (5)(5) = 25$

(g) $\left| \dfrac{1}{1 + 3i} - \dfrac{1}{1 - 3i} \right| = \left| \dfrac{1 - 3i}{1 - 9i^2} - \dfrac{1 + 3i}{1 - 9i^2} \right| = \left| \dfrac{-6i}{10} \right| = \sqrt{(0)^2 + (-\tfrac{6}{10})^2} = \dfrac{3}{5}$

2. If z_1 and z_2 are two complex numbers, prove that $|z_1 z_2| = |z_1|\,|z_2|$.

Let $z_1 = x_1 + iy_1$, $z_2 = x_2 + iy_2$. Then

$\begin{aligned}
|z_1 z_2| &= |(x_1 + iy_1)(x_2 + iy_2)| = |x_1 x_2 - y_1 y_2 + i(x_1 y_2 + x_2 y_1)| \\
&= \sqrt{(x_1 x_2 - y_1 y_2)^2 + (x_1 y_2 + x_2 y_1)^2} = \sqrt{x_1^2 x_2^2 + y_1^2 y_2^2 + x_1^2 y_2^2 + x_2^2 y_1^2} \\
&= \sqrt{(x_1^2 + y_1^2)(x_2^2 + y_2^2)} = \sqrt{x_1^2 + y_1^2}\,\sqrt{x_2^2 + y_2^2} = |x_1 + iy_1|\,|x_2 + iy_2| = |z_1|\,|z_2|
\end{aligned}$

3. Solve $z^3 - 2z - 4 = 0$.

The possible rational roots are $\pm 1, \pm 2, \pm 4$. By trial we find $z = 2$ is a root. Then the given equation can be written $(z - 2)(z^2 + 2z + 2) = 0$. The solutions to the *quadratic equation* $az^2 + bz + c = 0$ are $z = \dfrac{-b \pm \sqrt{b^2 - 4ac}}{2a}$. For $a = 1$, $b = 2$, $c = 2$ this gives $z = \dfrac{-2 \pm \sqrt{4 - 8}}{2} = \dfrac{-2 \pm \sqrt{-4}}{2} = \dfrac{-2 \pm 2i}{2} = -1 \pm i$.

The set of solutions is $2, -1 + i, -1 - i$.

POLAR FORM OF COMPLEX NUMBERS

4. Express in polar form (a) $3 + 3i$, (b) $-1 + \sqrt{3}\,i$, (c) -1, (d) $-2 - 2\sqrt{3}\,i$. [See Fig. 5-4.]

(a) Amplitude $\theta = 45° = \pi/4$ radians. Modulus $r = \sqrt{3^2 + 3^2} = 3\sqrt{2}$. Then

$3 + 3i = r(\cos\theta + i\sin\theta) = 3\sqrt{2}\,(\cos \pi/4 + i\sin \pi/4) = 3\sqrt{2}\,\operatorname{cis} \pi/4 = 3\sqrt{2}\,e^{\pi i/4}$

(b) Amplitude $\theta = 120° = 2\pi/3$ radians. Modulus $r = \sqrt{(-1)^2 + (\sqrt{3})^2} = \sqrt{4} = 2$. Then

$-1 + \sqrt{3}\,i = 2(\cos 2\pi/3 + i\sin 2\pi/3) = 2\operatorname{cis} 2\pi/3 = 2e^{2\pi i/3}$

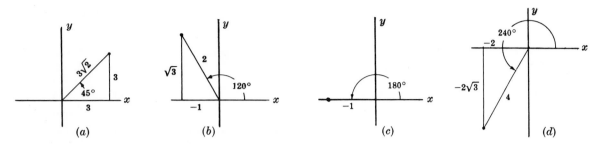

Fig. 5-4

(c) Amplitude $\theta = 180° = \pi$ radians. Modulus $r = \sqrt{(-1)^2 + (0)^2} = 1$. Then

$$-1 = 1(\cos\pi + i\sin\pi) = \text{cis}\,\pi = e^{\pi i}$$

(d) Amplitude $\theta = 240° = 4\pi/3$ radians. Modulus $r = \sqrt{(-2)^2 + (-2\sqrt{3})^2} = 4$. Then

$$-2 - 2\sqrt{3} = 4(\cos 4\pi/3 + i\sin 4\pi/3) = 4\,\text{cis}\,4\pi/3 = 4e^{4\pi i/3}$$

5. Evaluate $\quad$ (a) $(-1 + \sqrt{3}\,i)^{10}$, $\quad$ (b) $(-1 + i)^{1/3}$.

(a) By Problem 4(b) and De Moivre's theorem,

$$(-1 + \sqrt{3}\,i)^{10} = [2(\cos 2\pi/3 + i\sin 2\pi/3)]^{10} = 2^{10}(\cos 20\pi/3 + i\sin 20\pi/3)$$

$$= 1024[\cos(2\pi/3 + 6\pi) + i\sin(2\pi/3 + 6\pi)] = 1024(\cos 2\pi/3 + i\sin 2\pi/3)$$

$$= 1024(-\tfrac{1}{2} + \tfrac{1}{2}\sqrt{3}\,i) = -512 + 512\sqrt{3}\,i$$

(b) $-1 + i = \sqrt{2}(\cos 135° + i\sin 135°) = \sqrt{2}[\cos(135° + k\cdot 360°) + i\sin(135° + k\cdot 360°)]$

Then

$$(-1 + i)^{1/3} = (\sqrt{2})^{1/3}\left[\cos\left(\frac{135° + k\cdot 360°}{3}\right) + i\sin\left(\frac{135° + k\cdot 360°}{3}\right)\right]$$

The results for $k = 0, 1, 2$ are

$$\sqrt[6]{2}\,(\cos 45° + i\sin 45°),$$

$$\sqrt[6]{2}\,(\cos 165° + i\sin 165°),$$

$$\sqrt[6]{2}\,(\cos 285° + i\sin 285°)$$

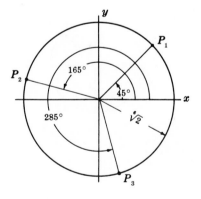

The results for $k = 3, 4, 5, 6, 7, \ldots$ give repetitions of these. These complex roots are represented geometrically in the complex plane by points P_1, P_2, P_3 on the circle of Fig. 5-5.

Fig. 5-5

6. Determine the locus represented by

(a) $|z - 2| = 3$, $\quad$ (b) $|z - 2| = |z + 4|$, $\quad$ (c) $|z - 3| + |z + 3| = 10$.

(a) *Method 1.* $|z - 2| = |x + iy - 2| = |x - 2 + iy| = \sqrt{(x-2)^2 + y^2} = 3$ or $(x-2)^2 + y^2 = 9$, a circle with center at $(2, 0)$ and radius 3.

Method 2. $|z - 2|$ is the distance between the complex numbers $z = x + iy$ and $2 + 0i$. If this distance is always 3, the locus is a circle of radius 3 with center at $2 + 0i$ or $(2, 0)$.

(b) **Method 1.** $|x + iy - 2| = |x + iy + 4|$ or $\sqrt{(x-2)^2 + y^2} = \sqrt{(x+4)^2 + y^2}$. Squaring, we find $x = -1$, a straight line.

Method 2. The locus is such that the distances from any point on it to $(2, 0)$ and $(-4, 0)$ are equal. Thus the locus is the perpendicular bisector of the line joining $(2, 0)$ and $(-4, 0)$, or $x = -1$.

(c) **Method 1.** The locus is given by $\sqrt{(x-3)^2 + y^2} + \sqrt{(x+3)^2 + y^2} = 10$ or $\sqrt{(x-3)^2 + y^2} = 10 - \sqrt{(x+3)^2 + y^2}$. Squaring and simplifying, $25 + 3x = 5\sqrt{(x+3)^2 + y^2}$. Squaring and simplifying again yields $\dfrac{x^2}{25} + \dfrac{y^2}{16} = 1$, an ellipse with semi-major and semi-minor axes of lengths 5 and 4 respectively.

Method 2. The locus is such that the sum of the distances from any point on it to $(3, 0)$ and $(-3, 0)$ is 10. Thus the locus is an ellipse whose foci are at $(-3, 0)$ and $(3, 0)$ and whose major axis has length 10.

7. Determine the region in the z plane represented by each of the following.

(a) $|z| < 1$.

Interior of a circle of radius 1. See Fig. 5-6(a) below.

(b) $1 < |z + 2i| \leqq 2$.

$|z + 2i|$ is the distance from z to $-2i$, so that $|z + 2i| = 1$ is a circle of radius 1 with center at $-2i$, i.e. $(0, -2)$; and $|z + 2i| = 2$ is a circle of radius 2 with center at $-2i$. Then $1 < |z + 2i| \leqq 2$ represents the region *exterior* to $|z + 2i| = 1$ but *interior* to or on $|z + 2i| = 2$. See Fig. 5-6(b) below.

(c) $\pi/3 \leqq \arg z \leqq \pi/2$.

Note that $\arg z = \theta$, where $z = re^{i\theta}$. The required region is the infinite region bounded by the lines $\theta = \pi/3$ and $\theta = \pi/2$, including these lines. See Fig. 5-6(c) below.

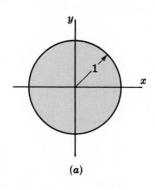 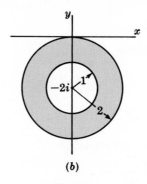 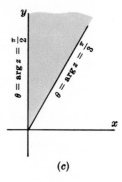

(a)   (b)   (c)

Fig. 5-6

8. Express each function in the form $u(x, y) + i\, v(x, y)$, where u and v are real:

(a) z^3, (b) $1/(1 - z)$, (c) e^{3z}, (d) $\ln z$.

(a) $w = z^3 = (x + iy)^3 = x^3 + 3x^2(iy) + 3x(iy)^2 + (iy)^3 = x^3 + 3ix^2y - 3xy^2 - iy^3$

$\qquad = x^3 - 3xy^2 + i(3x^2y - y^3)$

Then $u(x, y) = x^3 - 3xy^2,$ $v(x, y) = 3x^2y - y^3$.

(b) $w = \dfrac{1}{1 - z} = \dfrac{1}{1 - (x + iy)} = \dfrac{1}{1 - x - iy} \cdot \dfrac{1 - x + iy}{1 - x + iy} = \dfrac{1 - x + iy}{(1 - x)^2 + y^2}$

Then $u(x, y) = \dfrac{1 - x}{(1 - x)^2 + y^2},$ $v(x, y) = \dfrac{y}{(1 - x)^2 + y^2}.$

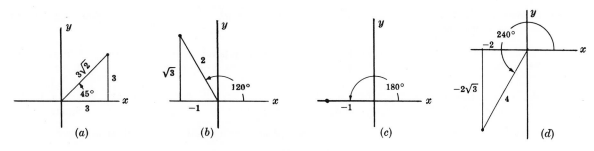

Fig. 5-4

(c) Amplitude $\theta = 180° = \pi$ radians. Modulus $r = \sqrt{(-1)^2 + (0)^2} = 1$. Then

$$-1 = 1(\cos \pi + i \sin \pi) = \operatorname{cis} \pi = e^{\pi i}$$

(d) Amplitude $\theta = 240° = 4\pi/3$ radians. Modulus $r = \sqrt{(-2)^2 + (-2\sqrt{3})^2} = 4$. Then

$$-2 - 2\sqrt{3} = 4(\cos 4\pi/3 + i \sin 4\pi/3) = 4 \operatorname{cis} 4\pi/3 = 4e^{4\pi i/3}$$

5. **Evaluate**   (a) $(-1 + \sqrt{3}\,i)^{10}$,   (b) $(-1 + i)^{1/3}$.

(a) By Problem 4(b) and De Moivre's theorem,

$$\begin{aligned}
(-1 + \sqrt{3}\,i)^{10} &= [2(\cos 2\pi/3 + i \sin 2\pi/3)]^{10} = 2^{10}(\cos 20\pi/3 + i \sin 20\pi/3) \\
&= 1024[\cos(2\pi/3 + 6\pi) + i \sin(2\pi/3 + 6\pi)] = 1024(\cos 2\pi/3 + i \sin 2\pi/3) \\
&= 1024(-\tfrac{1}{2} + \tfrac{1}{2}\sqrt{3}\,i) = -512 + 512\sqrt{3}\,i
\end{aligned}$$

(b) $-1 + i = \sqrt{2}(\cos 135° + i \sin 135°) = \sqrt{2}[\cos(135° + k \cdot 360°) + i \sin(135° + k \cdot 360°)]$

Then

$$\begin{aligned}
(-1 + i)^{1/3} = (\sqrt{2})^{1/3}\Big[&\cos\Big(\frac{135° + k \cdot 360°}{3}\Big) \\
&+ i \sin\Big(\frac{135° + k \cdot 360°}{3}\Big)\Big]
\end{aligned}$$

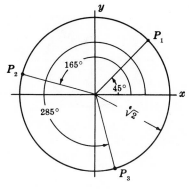

The results for $k = 0, 1, 2$ are

$$\sqrt[6]{2}\,(\cos 45° + i \sin 45°),$$

$$\sqrt[6]{2}\,(\cos 165° + i \sin 165°),$$

$$\sqrt[6]{2}\,(\cos 285° + i \sin 285°)$$

The results for $k = 3, 4, 5, 6, 7, \ldots$ give repetitions of these. These complex roots are represented geometrically in the complex plane by points P_1, P_2, P_3 on the circle of Fig. 5-5.

Fig. 5-5

6. **Determine the locus represented by**

(a) $|z - 2| = 3$,   (b) $|z - 2| = |z + 4|$,   (c) $|z - 3| + |z + 3| = 10$.

(a) *Method 1.* $|z - 2| = |x + iy - 2| = |x - 2 + iy| = \sqrt{(x - 2)^2 + y^2} = 3$ or $(x - 2)^2 + y^2 = 9$, a circle with center at $(2, 0)$ and radius 3.

Method 2. $|z - 2|$ is the distance between the complex numbers $z = x + iy$ and $2 + 0i$. If this distance is always 3, the locus is a circle of radius 3 with center at $2 + 0i$ or $(2, 0)$.

(b) *Method 1.* $|x + iy - 2| = |x + iy + 4|$ or $\sqrt{(x-2)^2 + y^2} = \sqrt{(x+4)^2 + y^2}$. Squaring, we find $x = -1$, a straight line.

Method 2. The locus is such that the distances from any point on it to $(2, 0)$ and $(-4, 0)$ are equal. Thus the locus is the perpendicular bisector of the line joining $(2, 0)$ and $(-4, 0)$, or $x = -1$.

(c) *Method 1.* The locus is given by $\sqrt{(x-3)^2 + y^2} + \sqrt{(x+3)^2 + y^2} = 10$ or $\sqrt{(x-3)^2 + y^2} = 10 - \sqrt{(x+3)^2 + y^2}$. Squaring and simplifying, $25 + 3x = 5\sqrt{(x+3)^2 + y^2}$. Squaring and simplifying again yields $\dfrac{x^2}{25} + \dfrac{y^2}{16} = 1$, an ellipse with semi-major and semi-minor axes of lengths 5 and 4 respectively.

Method 2. The locus is such that the sum of the distances from any point on it to $(3, 0)$ and $(-3, 0)$ is 10. Thus the locus is an ellipse whose foci are at $(-3, 0)$ and $(3, 0)$ and whose major axis has length 10.

7. Determine the region in the z plane represented by each of the following.

(a) $|z| < 1$.

   Interior of a circle of radius 1. See Fig. 5-6(a) below.

(b) $1 < |z + 2i| \leqq 2$.

   $|z + 2i|$ is the distance from z to $-2i$, so that $|z + 2i| = 1$ is a circle of radius 1 with center at $-2i$, i.e. $(0, -2)$; and $|z + 2i| = 2$ is a circle of radius 2 with center at $-2i$. Then $1 < |z + 2i| \leqq 2$ represents the region *exterior* to $|z + 2i| = 1$ but *interior* to or *on* $|z + 2i| = 2$. See Fig. 5-6(b) below.

(c) $\pi/3 \leqq \arg z \leqq \pi/2$.

   Note that $\arg z = \theta$, where $z = re^{i\theta}$. The required region is the infinite region bounded by the lines $\theta = \pi/3$ and $\theta = \pi/2$, including these lines. See Fig. 5-6(c) below.

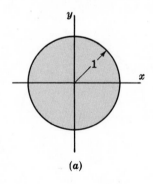   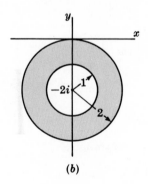   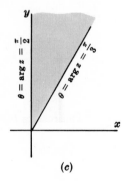

(a)   (b)   (c)

Fig. 5-6

8. Express each function in the form $u(x, y) + i\,v(x, y)$, where u and v are real:

(a) z^3, (b) $1/(1 - z)$, (c) e^{3z}, (d) $\ln z$.

(a) $w = z^3 = (x + iy)^3 = x^3 + 3x^2(iy) + 3x(iy)^2 + (iy)^3 = x^3 + 3ix^2 y - 3xy^2 - iy^3$

   $= x^3 - 3xy^2 + i(3x^2 y - y^3)$

   Then $u(x, y) = x^3 - 3xy^2$, $v(x, y) = 3x^2 y - y^3$.

(b) $w = \dfrac{1}{1-z} = \dfrac{1}{1 - (x + iy)} = \dfrac{1}{1 - x - iy} \cdot \dfrac{1 - x + iy}{1 - x + iy} = \dfrac{1 - x + iy}{(1-x)^2 + y^2}$

   Then $u(x, y) = \dfrac{1 - x}{(1-x)^2 + y^2}$, $v(x, y) = \dfrac{y}{(1-x)^2 + y^2}$.

(c) $e^{3z} = e^{3(x+iy)} = e^{3x} e^{3iy} = e^{3x}(\cos 3y + i \sin 3y)$ and $u = e^{3x} \cos 3y$, $v = e^{3x} \sin 3y$

(d) $\ln z = \ln (re^{i\theta}) = \ln r + i\theta = \ln \sqrt{x^2+y^2} + i \tan^{-1} y/x$ and

$$u = \tfrac{1}{2} \ln (x^2+y^2), \qquad v = \tan^{-1} y/x$$

Note that $\ln z$ is a multiple-valued function (in this case it is *infinitely* many-valued) since θ can be increased by any multiple of 2π. The *principal value* of the logarithm is defined as that value for which $0 \leqq \theta < 2\pi$ and is called the *principal branch* of $\ln z$.

9. Prove   (a) $\sin (x+iy) = \sin x \cosh y + i \cos x \sinh y$

   (b) $\cos (x+iy) = \cos x \cosh y - i \sin x \sinh y$.

We use the relations $e^{iz} = \cos z + i \sin z$, $e^{-iz} = \cos z - i \sin z$,   from which

$$\sin z = \frac{e^{iz} - e^{-iz}}{2i}, \qquad \cos z = \frac{e^{iz} + e^{-iz}}{2}$$

Then

$$\sin z = \sin (x+iy) = \frac{e^{i(x+iy)} - e^{-i(x+iy)}}{2i} = \frac{e^{ix-y} - e^{-ix+y}}{2i}$$

$$= \frac{1}{2i}\{e^{-y}(\cos x + i \sin x) - e^{y}(\cos x - i \sin x)\}$$

$$= (\sin x)\left(\frac{e^{y} + e^{-y}}{2}\right) + i(\cos x)\left(\frac{e^{y} - e^{-y}}{2}\right) = \sin x \cosh y + i \cos x \sinh y$$

Similarly,

$$\cos z = \cos (x+iy) = \frac{e^{i(x+iy)} + e^{-i(x+iy)}}{2}$$

$$= \tfrac{1}{2}\{e^{ix-y} + e^{-ix+y}\} = \tfrac{1}{2}\{e^{-y}(\cos x + i \sin x) + e^{y}(\cos x - i \sin x)\}$$

$$= (\cos x)\left(\frac{e^{y} + e^{-y}}{2}\right) - i(\sin x)\left(\frac{e^{y} - e^{-y}}{2}\right) = \cos x \cosh y - i \sin x \sinh y$$

DERIVATIVES. CAUCHY-RIEMANN EQUATIONS

10. Prove that $\dfrac{d}{dz}\bar{z}$, where $\bar{z}$ is the conjugate of z, does not exist anywhere.

By definition, $\dfrac{d}{dz}f(z) = \lim\limits_{\Delta z \to 0} \dfrac{f(z+\Delta z) - f(z)}{\Delta z}$ if this limit exists independent of the manner in which $\Delta z = \Delta x + i\,\Delta y$ approaches zero.   Then

$$\frac{d}{dz}\bar{z} = \lim_{\Delta z \to 0} \frac{\overline{z+\Delta z} - \bar{z}}{\Delta z} = \lim_{\substack{\Delta x \to 0 \\ \Delta y \to 0}} \frac{\overline{x+iy+\Delta x + i\,\Delta y} - \overline{x+iy}}{\Delta x + i\,\Delta y}$$

$$= \lim_{\substack{\Delta x \to 0 \\ \Delta y \to 0}} \frac{x - iy + \Delta x - i\,\Delta y - (x - iy)}{\Delta x + i\,\Delta y} = \lim_{\substack{\Delta x \to 0 \\ \Delta y \to 0}} \frac{\Delta x - i\,\Delta y}{\Delta x + i\,\Delta y}$$

If $\Delta y = 0$, the required limit is $\lim\limits_{\Delta x \to 0} \dfrac{\Delta x}{\Delta x} = 1$.

If $\Delta x = 0$, the required limit is $\lim\limits_{\Delta y \to 0} \dfrac{-i\,\Delta y}{i\,\Delta y} = -1$.

These two possible approaches show that the limit depends on the manner in which $\Delta z \to 0$, so that the derivative does not exist; i.e. $\bar{z}$ is *non-analytic* anywhere.

11. (a) If $w = f(z) = \dfrac{1+z}{1-z}$, find $\dfrac{dw}{dz}$. (b) Determine where w is non-analytic.

(a) **Method 1.**

$$\frac{dw}{dz} = \lim_{\Delta z \to 0} \frac{\dfrac{1 + (z + \Delta z)}{1 - (z + \Delta z)} - \dfrac{1+z}{1-z}}{\Delta z} = \lim_{\Delta z \to 0} \frac{2}{(1 - z - \Delta z)(1 - z)}$$

$$= \frac{2}{(1-z)^2} \quad \text{provided } z \neq 1, \text{ independent of the manner in which } \Delta z \to 0.$$

Method 2. The usual rules of differentiation apply provided $z \neq 1$. Thus by the quotient rule for differentiation,

$$\frac{d}{dz}\left(\frac{1+z}{1-z}\right) = \frac{(1-z)\dfrac{d}{dz}(1+z) - (1+z)\dfrac{d}{dz}(1-z)}{(1-z)^2} = \frac{(1-z)(1) - (1+z)(-1)}{(1-z)^2} = \frac{2}{(1-z)^2}$$

(b) The function is analytic everywhere except at $z = 1$, where the derivative does not exist; i.e. the function is non-analytic at $z = 1$.

12. Prove that a necessary condition for $w = f(z) = u(x, y) + i\,v(x, y)$ to be analytic in a region is that the Cauchy-Riemann equations $\dfrac{\partial u}{\partial x} = \dfrac{\partial v}{\partial y}$, $\dfrac{\partial u}{\partial y} = -\dfrac{\partial v}{\partial x}$ be satisfied in the region.

Since $f(z) = f(x + iy) = u(x, y) + i\,v(x, y)$, we have

$$f(z + \Delta z) = f[x + \Delta x + i(y + \Delta y)] = u(x + \Delta x, y + \Delta y) + i\,v(x + \Delta x, y + \Delta y)$$

Then

$$\lim_{\Delta z \to 0} \frac{f(z + \Delta z) - f(z)}{\Delta z} = \lim_{\substack{\Delta x \to 0 \\ \Delta y \to 0}} \frac{u(x + \Delta x, y + \Delta y) - u(x, y) + i\{v(x + \Delta x, y + \Delta y) - v(x, y)\}}{\Delta x + i\,\Delta y}$$

If $\Delta y = 0$, the required limit is

$$\lim_{\Delta x \to 0} \frac{u(x + \Delta x, y) - u(x, y)}{\Delta x} + i\left\{\frac{v(x + \Delta x, y) - v(x, y)}{\Delta x}\right\} = \frac{\partial u}{\partial x} + i\frac{\partial v}{\partial x}$$

If $\Delta x = 0$, the required limit is

$$\lim_{\Delta y \to 0} \frac{u(x, y + \Delta y) - u(x, y)}{i\,\Delta y} + \left\{\frac{v(x, y + \Delta y) - v(x, y)}{\Delta y}\right\} = \frac{1}{i}\frac{\partial u}{\partial y} + \frac{\partial v}{\partial y}$$

If the derivative is to exist, these two special limits must be equal, i.e.,

$$\frac{\partial u}{\partial x} + i\frac{\partial v}{\partial x} = \frac{1}{i}\frac{\partial u}{\partial y} + \frac{\partial v}{\partial y} = -i\frac{\partial u}{\partial y} + \frac{\partial v}{\partial y}$$

so that we must have $\dfrac{\partial u}{\partial x} = \dfrac{\partial v}{\partial y}$ and $\dfrac{\partial v}{\partial x} = -\dfrac{\partial u}{\partial y}$.

Conversely, we can prove that if the first partial derivatives of u and v with respect to x and y are continuous in a region, then the Cauchy-Riemann equations provide sufficient conditions for $f(z)$ to be analytic.

13. (a) If $f(z) = u(x, y) + i\,v(x, y)$ is analytic in a region $\mathcal{R}$, prove that the one parameter families of curves $u(x, y) = C_1$ and $v(x, y) = C_2$ are orthogonal families. (b) Illustrate by using $f(z) = z^2$.

(a) Consider any two particular members of these families $u(x, y) = u_0$, $v(x, y) = v_0$ which intersect at the point (x_0, y_0).

Since $du = u_x\,dx + u_y\,dy = 0$, we have $\dfrac{dy}{dx} = -\dfrac{u_x}{u_y}$.

Also since $dv = v_x\,dx + v_y\,dy = 0$, $\dfrac{dy}{dx} = -\dfrac{v_x}{v_y}$.

When evaluated at (x_0, y_0), these represent respectively the slopes of the two curves at this point of intersection.

By the Cauchy-Riemann equations, $u_x = v_y$, $u_y = -v_x$, we have the product of the slopes at the point (x_0, y_0) equal to

$$\left(-\frac{u_x}{u_y}\right)\left(-\frac{v_x}{v_y}\right) = -1$$

so that any two members of the respective families are orthogonal, and thus the two families are orthogonal.

(b) If $f(z) = z^2$, then $u = x^2 - y^2$, $v = 2xy$. The graphs of several members of $x^2 - y^2 = C_1$, $2xy = C_2$ are shown in Fig. 5-7.

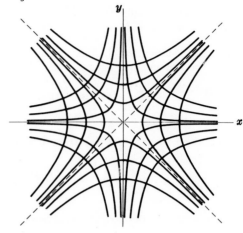

Fig. 5-7

14. In aerodynamics and fluid mechanics, the functions ϕ and ψ in $f(z) = \phi + i\psi$, where $f(z)$ is analytic, are called the *velocity potential* and *stream function* respectively. If $\phi = x^2 + 4x - y^2 + 2y$, (a) find ψ and (b) find $f(z)$.

(a) By the Cauchy-Riemann equations, $\dfrac{\partial\phi}{\partial x} = \dfrac{\partial\psi}{\partial y}$, $\dfrac{\partial\psi}{\partial x} = -\dfrac{\partial\phi}{\partial y}$. Then

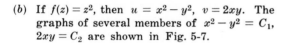

$$(1) \quad \frac{\partial\psi}{\partial y} = 2x + 4 \qquad (2) \quad \frac{\partial\psi}{\partial x} = 2y - 2$$

Method 1. Integrating (1), $\psi = 2xy + 4y + F(x)$.

Integrating (2), $\psi = 2xy - 2x + G(y)$.

These are identical if $F(x) = -2x + c$, $G(y) = 4y + c$ where c is any real constant. Thus $\psi = 2xy + 4y - 2x + c$.

Method 2.

Integrating (1), $\psi = 2xy + 4y + F(x)$. Then substituting in (2), $2y + F'(x) = 2y - 2$ or $F'(x) = -2$ and $F(x) = -2x + c$. Hence $\psi = 2xy + 4y - 2x + c$.

(b) From (a),

$$\begin{aligned}
f(z) &= \phi + i\psi = x^2 + 4x - y^2 + 2y + i(2xy + 4y - 2x + c) \\
&= (x^2 - y^2 + 2ixy) + 4(x + iy) - 2i(x + iy) + ic \\
&= z^2 + 4z - 2iz + c_1
\end{aligned}$$

where c_1 is a pure imaginary constant.

This can also be accomplished by noting that $z = x + iy$, $\bar{z} = x - iy$ so that $x = \dfrac{z + \bar{z}}{2}$, $y = \dfrac{z - \bar{z}}{2i}$. The result is then obtained by substitution; the terms involving $\bar{z}$ drop out.

LINE INTEGRALS

15. Evaluate $\displaystyle\int_{(0,1)}^{(1,2)} (x^2 - y)\, dx + (y^2 + x)\, dy$ along   (a) a straight line from $(0, 1)$ to $(1, 2)$,

(b) straight lines from $(0, 1)$ to $(1, 1)$ and then from $(1, 1)$ to $(1, 2)$,   (c) the parabola $x = t$, $y = t^2 + 1$.

(a) An equation for the line joining $(0, 1)$ and $(1, 2)$ in the xy plane is $y = x + 1$. Then $dy = dx$ and the line integral equals

$$\int_{x=0}^{1} \{x^2 - (x+1)\}\, dx + \{(x+1)^2 + x\}\, dx = \int_{0}^{1} (2x^2 + 2x)\, dx = 5/3$$

(b) Along the straight line from $(0, 1)$ to $(1, 1)$, $y = 1$, $dy = 0$ and the line integral equals

$$\int_{x=0}^{1} (x^2 - 1)\, dx + (1 + x)(0) = \int_{0}^{1} (x^2 - 1)\, dx = -2/3$$

Along the straight line from $(1, 1)$ to $(1, 2)$, $x = 1$, $dx = 0$ and the line integral equals

$$\int_{y=1}^{2} (1 - y)(0) + (y^2 + 1)\, dy = \int_{1}^{2} (y^2 + 1)\, dy = 10/3$$

Then the required value $= -2/3 + 10/3 = 8/3$.

(c) Since $t = 0$ at $(0, 1)$ and $t = 1$ at $(1, 2)$, the line integral equals

$$\int_{t=0}^{1} \{t^2 - (t^2 + 1)\}\, dt + \{(t^2 + 1)^2 + t\}\, 2t\, dt = \int_{0}^{1} (2t^5 + 4t^3 + 2t^2 + 2t - 1)\, dt = 2$$

GREEN'S THEOREM IN THE PLANE

16. Prove Green's theorem in the plane if C is a simple closed curve which has the property that any straight line parallel to the coordinate axes cuts C in at most two points.

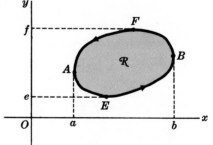

Fig. 5-8

Let the equations of the curves AEB and AFB (see adjoining Fig. 5-8) be $y = Y_1(x)$ and $y = Y_2(x)$ respectively. If $\mathcal{R}$ is the region bounded by C, we have

$$\iint_{\mathcal{R}} \frac{\partial P}{\partial y}\, dx\, dy = \int_{x=a}^{b} \left[\int_{y=Y_1(x)}^{Y_2(x)} \frac{\partial P}{\partial y}\, dy \right] dx$$

$$= \int_{x=a}^{b} P(x, y) \Big|_{y=Y_1(x)}^{Y_2(x)} dx = \int_{a}^{b} [P(x, Y_2) - P(x, Y_1)]\, dx$$

$$= -\int_{a}^{b} P(x, Y_1)\, dx - \int_{b}^{a} P(x, Y_2)\, dx = -\oint_{C} P\, dx$$

Then   (1) $\displaystyle\oint_{C} P\, dx = -\iint_{\mathcal{R}} \frac{\partial P}{\partial y}\, dx\, dy$

Similarly let the equations of curves EAF and EBF be $x = X_1(y)$ and $x = X_2(y)$ respectively. Then

$$\iint\limits_{\mathcal{R}} \frac{\partial Q}{\partial x}\, dx\, dy \;=\; \int_{y=e}^{f}\left[\int_{x=X_1(y)}^{X_2(y)} \frac{\partial Q}{\partial x}\, dx\right] dy \;=\; \int_{e}^{f}\left[Q(X_2,y) - Q(X_1,y)\right] dy$$

$$=\; \int_{f}^{e} Q(X_1,y)\, dy \;+\; \int_{e}^{f} Q(X_2,y)\, dy \;=\; \oint_{C} Q\, dy$$

Then
$$(2) \qquad \oint_{C} Q\, dy \;=\; \iint\limits_{\mathcal{R}} \frac{\partial Q}{\partial x}\, dx\, dy$$

Adding (1) and (2),
$$\oint_{C} P\, dx \;+\; Q\, dy \;=\; \iint\limits_{\mathcal{R}}\left(\frac{\partial Q}{\partial x} - \frac{\partial P}{\partial y}\right) dx\, dy.$$

Extensions to other simple closed curves are easily made.

17. Verify Green's theorem in the plane for

$$\oint_{C} (2xy - x^2)\, dx \;+\; (x + y^2)\, dy$$

where C is the closed curve of the region bounded by $y = x^2$ and $y^2 = x$.

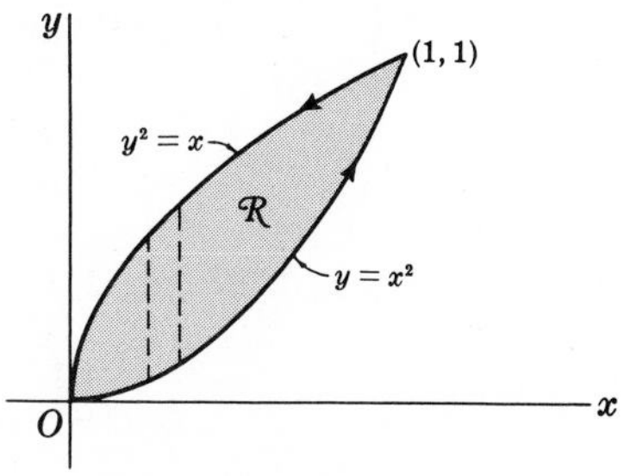

The plane curves $y = x^2$ and $y^2 = x$ intersect at $(0,0)$ and $(1,1)$. The positive direction in traversing C is as shown in Fig. 5-9.

Fig. 5-9

Along $y = x^2$, the line integral equals

$$\int_{x=0}^{1} \{(2x)(x^2) - x^2\}\, dx \;+\; \{x + (x^2)^2\}\, d(x^2) \;=\; \int_{0}^{1} (2x^3 + x^2 + 2x^5)\, dx \;=\; 7/6$$

Along $y^2 = x$ the line integral equals

$$\int_{y=1}^{0} \{2(y^2)(y) - (y^2)^2\}\, d(y^2) \;+\; \{y^2 + y^2\}\, dy \;=\; \int_{1}^{0} (4y^4 - 2y^5 + 2y^2)\, dy \;=\; -17/15$$

Then the required line integral $= 7/6 - 17/15 = 1/30$.

$$\iint\limits_{\mathcal{R}}\left(\frac{\partial Q}{\partial x} - \frac{\partial P}{\partial y}\right) dx\, dy \;=\; \iint\limits_{\mathcal{R}}\left\{\frac{\partial}{\partial x}(x + y^2) - \frac{\partial}{\partial y}(2xy - x^2)\right\} dx\, dy$$

$$=\; \iint\limits_{\mathcal{R}} (1 - 2x)\, dx\, dy \;=\; \int_{x=0}^{1}\int_{y=x^2}^{\sqrt{x}} (1 - 2x)\, dy\, dx$$

$$=\; \int_{x=0}^{1} (y - 2xy)\Big|_{y=x^2}^{\sqrt{x}}\, dx \;=\; \int_{0}^{1} (x^{1/2} - 2x^{3/2} - x^2 + 2x^3)\, dx \;=\; 1/30$$

Hence Green's theorem is verified.

INTEGRALS, CAUCHY'S THEOREM, CAUCHY'S INTEGRAL FORMULAS

18. Evaluate $\displaystyle\int_{1+i}^{2+4i} z^2\, dz$

(a) along the parabola $x = t$, $y = t^2$ where $1 \leqq t \leqq 2$,

(b) along the straight line joining $1 + i$ and $2 + 4i$,

(c) along straight lines from $1 + i$ to $2 + i$ and then to $2 + 4i$.

We have

$$\int_{1+i}^{2+4i} z^2 \, dz \;=\; \int_{(1,1)}^{(2,4)} (x+iy)^2 \, (dx+i\,dy) \;=\; \int_{(1,1)}^{(2,4)} (x^2-y^2+2ixy)(dx+i\,dy)$$

$$=\; \int_{(1,1)}^{(2,4)} (x^2-y^2)\,dx \;-\; 2xy\,dy \;+\; i\int_{(1,1)}^{(2,4)} 2xy\,dx \;+\; (x^2-y^2)\,dy$$

Method 1.

(a) The points $(1,1)$ and $(2,4)$ correspond to $t=1$ and $t=2$ respectively. Then the above line integrals become

$$\int_{t=1}^{2} \{(t^2-t^4)\,dt \,-\, 2(t)(t^2)2t\,dt\} \;+\; i\int_{t=1}^{2} \{2(t)(t^2)\,dt \,+\, (t^2-t^4)(2t)\,dt\} \;=\; -\frac{86}{3} - 6i$$

(b) The line joining $(1,1)$ and $(2,4)$ has the equation $y-1 = \dfrac{4-1}{2-1}(x-1)$ or $y=3x-2$. Then we find

$$\int_{x=1}^{2} \{[x^2-(3x-2)^2]\,dx \,-\, 2x(3x-2)3\,dx\}$$

$$+\; i\int_{x=1}^{2} \{2x(3x-2)\,dx \,+\, [x^2-(3x-2)^2]3\,dx\} \;=\; -\frac{86}{3} - 6i$$

(c) From $1+i$ to $2+i$ [or $(1,1)$ to $(2,1)$], $y=1$, $dy=0$ and we have

$$\int_{x=1}^{2} (x^2-1)\,dx \;+\; i\int_{x=1}^{2} 2x\,dx \;=\; \frac{4}{3} + 3i$$

From $2+i$ to $2+4i$ [or $(2,1)$ to $(2,4)$], $x=2$, $dx=0$ and we have

$$\int_{y=1}^{4} -4y\,dy \;+\; i\int_{y=1}^{4} (4-y^2)\,dy \;=\; -30 - 9i$$

Adding, $\left(\dfrac{4}{3}+3i\right) + (-30-9i) \;=\; -\dfrac{86}{3} - 6i.$

Method 2.

The line integrals are independent of the path [see Problem 19], thus accounting for the same values obtained in (a), (b) and (c) above. In such case the integral can be evaluated directly, as for real variables, as follows:

$$\int_{1+i}^{2+4i} z^2 \, dz \;=\; \frac{z^3}{3}\Big|_{1+i}^{2+4i} \;=\; \frac{(2+4i)^3}{3} - \frac{(1+i)^3}{3} \;=\; -\frac{86}{3} - 6i$$

19. (a) Prove Cauchy's theorem: If $f(z)$ is analytic inside and on a simple closed curve C, then $\displaystyle\oint_C f(z)\,dz \,=\, 0.$

(b) Under these conditions prove that $\displaystyle\int_{P_1}^{P_2} f(z)\,dz$ is independent of the path joining P_1 and P_2.

(a)

$$\oint_C f(z)\,dz \;=\; \oint_C (u+iv)(dx+i\,dy) \;=\; \oint_C u\,dx - v\,dy \;+\; i\oint_C v\,dx + u\,dy$$

By Green's theorem,

$$\oint_C u\,dx - v\,dy \;=\; \iint_{\mathcal{R}} \left(-\frac{\partial v}{\partial x}-\frac{\partial u}{\partial y}\right)dx\,dy, \qquad \oint_C v\,dx + u\,dy \;=\; \iint_{\mathcal{R}} \left(\frac{\partial u}{\partial x}-\frac{\partial v}{\partial y}\right)dx\,dy$$

where $\mathcal{R}$ is the region bounded by C.

Since $f(z)$ is analytic, $\dfrac{\partial u}{\partial x} = \dfrac{\partial v}{\partial y}$, $\dfrac{\partial v}{\partial x} = -\dfrac{\partial u}{\partial y}$ (Problem 12), and so the above integrals are zero. Then $\displaystyle\oint_C f(z)\,dz = 0$. We are assuming in this derivation that $f'(z)$ [and thus the partial derivatives] are continuous. This restriction can be removed.

(b) Consider any two paths joining points P_1 and P_2 (see Fig. 5-10). By Cauchy's theorem,

$$\int_{P_1 A P_2 B P_1} f(z)\,dz = 0$$

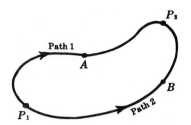

Then $$\int_{P_1 A P_2} f(z)\,dz + \int_{P_2 B P_1} f(z)\,dz = 0$$

or $$\int_{P_1 A P_2} f(z)\,dz = -\int_{P_2 B P_1} f(z)\,dz = \int_{P_1 B P_2} f(z)\,dz$$

i.e. the integral along $P_1 A P_2$ (path 1) = integral along $P_1 B P_2$ (path 2), and so the integral is independent of the path joining P_1 and P_2.

Fig. 5-10

This explains the results of Problem 18, since $f(z) = z^2$ is analytic.

20. If $f(z)$ is analytic within and on the boundary of a region bounded by two closed curves C_1 and C_2 (see Fig. 5-11), prove that

$$\oint_{C_1} f(z)\,dz = \oint_{C_2} f(z)\,dz$$

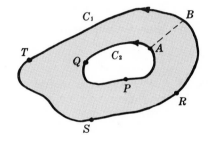

As in Fig. 5-11, construct line AB (called a *cross-cut*) connecting any point on C_2 and a point on C_1. By Cauchy's theorem (Problem 19),

$$\int_{AQPABRSTBA} f(z)\,dz = 0$$

Fig. 5-11

since $f(z)$ is analytic within the region shaded and also on the boundary. Then

$$\int_{AQPA} f(z)\,dz + \int_{AB} f(z)\,dz + \int_{BRSTB} f(z)\,dz + \int_{BA} f(z)\,dz = 0 \tag{1}$$

But $\displaystyle\int_{AB} f(z)\,dz = -\int_{BA} f(z)\,dz$. Hence (1) gives

$$\int_{AQPA} f(z)\,dz = -\int_{BRSTB} f(z)\,dz = \int_{BTSRB} f(z)\,dz$$

i.e. $$\oint_{C_1} f(z)\,dz = \oint_{C_2} f(z)\,dz$$

Note that $f(z)$ need not be analytic *within* curve C_2.

21. (a) Prove that $\displaystyle\oint_C \frac{dz}{(z-a)^n} = \begin{cases} 2\pi i & \text{if } n = 1 \\ 0 & \text{if } n = 2, 3, 4, \ldots \end{cases}$ where C is a simple closed curve bounding a region having $z = a$ as interior point.

(b) What is the value of the integral if $n = 0, -1, -2, -3, \ldots$?

(a) Let C_1 be a circle of radius ϵ having center at $z = a$ (see Fig. 5-12). Since $(z - a)^{-n}$ is analytic within and on the boundary of the region bounded by C and C_1, we have by Problem 20,

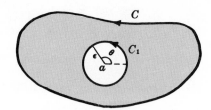

Fig. 5-12

$$\oint_C \frac{dz}{(z - a)^n} = \oint_{C_1} \frac{dz}{(z - a)^n}$$

To evaluate this last integral, note that on C_1, $|z - a| = \epsilon$ or $z - a = \epsilon e^{i\theta}$ and $dz = i\epsilon e^{i\theta}\, d\theta$. The integral equals

$$\int_0^{2\pi} \frac{i\epsilon e^{i\theta}\, d\theta}{\epsilon^n e^{in\theta}} = \frac{i}{\epsilon^{n-1}} \int_0^{2\pi} e^{(1-n)i\theta}\, d\theta = \frac{i}{\epsilon^{n-1}} \frac{e^{(1-n)i\theta}}{(1-n)i}\Big|_0^{2\pi} = 0 \qquad \text{if } n \neq 1$$

If $n = 1$, the integral equals $i \int_0^{2\pi} d\theta = 2\pi i$.

(b) For $n = 0, -1, -2, \ldots$ the integrand is $1, (z - a), (z - a)^2, \ldots$ and is analytic everywhere inside C_1, including $z = a$. Hence by Cauchy's theorem the integral is zero.

---

22. Evaluate $\oint_C \dfrac{dz}{z - 3}$ where C is   (a) the circle $|z| = 1$,   (b) the circle $|z + i| = 4$.

(a) Since $z = 3$ is not interior to $|z| = 1$, the integral equals zero (Problem 19).

(b) Since $z = 3$ is interior to $|z + i| = 4$, the integral equals $2\pi i$ (Problem 21).

---

23. If $f(z)$ is analytic inside and on a simple closed curve C, and a is any point within C, prove that

$$f(a) = \frac{1}{2\pi i} \oint_C \frac{f(z)}{z - a}\, dz$$

Referring to Problem 20 and the figure of Problem 21, we have

$$\oint_C \frac{f(z)}{z - a}\, dz = \oint_{C_1} \frac{f(z)}{z - a}\, dz$$

Letting $z - a = \epsilon e^{i\theta}$, the last integral becomes $i \int_0^{2\pi} f(a + \epsilon e^{i\theta})\, d\theta$. But since $f(z)$ is analytic, it is continuous. Hence

$$\lim_{\epsilon \to 0} i \int_0^{2\pi} f(a + \epsilon e^{i\theta})\, d\theta = i \int_0^{2\pi} \lim_{\epsilon \to 0} f(a + \epsilon e^{i\theta})\, d\theta = i \int_0^{2\pi} f(a)\, d\theta = 2\pi i\, f(a)$$

and the required result follows.

---

24. Evaluate   (a) $\oint_C \dfrac{\cos z}{z - \pi}\, dz$,   (b) $\oint_C \dfrac{e^z}{z(z + 1)}\, dz$ where C is the circle $|z - 1| = 3$.

(a) Since $z = \pi$ lies within C, $\dfrac{1}{2\pi i} \oint_C \dfrac{\cos z}{z - \pi}\, dz = \cos \pi = -1$ by Problem 23 with $f(z) = \cos z$, $a = \pi$. Then $\oint_C \dfrac{\cos z}{z - \pi}\, dz = -2\pi i$.

(b)
$$\oint_C \frac{e^z}{z(z + 1)}\, dz = \oint_C e^z \left(\frac{1}{z} - \frac{1}{z + 1}\right) dz = \oint_C \frac{e^z}{z}\, dz - \oint_C \frac{e^z}{z + 1}\, dz$$
$$= 2\pi i e^0 - 2\pi i e^{-1} = 2\pi i (1 - e^{-1})$$

by Problem 23, since $z = 0$ and $z = -1$ are both interior to C.

25. Evaluate $\oint_C \dfrac{5z^2 - 3z + 2}{(z-1)^3}\, dz$ where C is any simple closed curve enclosing $z = 1$.

Method 1.   By Cauchy's integral formula, $f^{(n)}(a) = \dfrac{n!}{2\pi i} \oint_C \dfrac{f(z)}{(z-a)^{n+1}}\, dz$.

If $n = 2$ and $f(z) = 5z^2 - 3z + 2$, then $f''(1) = 10$.   Hence

$$10 = \frac{2!}{2\pi i} \oint_C \frac{5z^2 - 3z + 2}{(z-1)^3}\, dz \qquad \text{or} \qquad \oint_C \frac{5z^2 - 3z + 2}{(z-1)^3}\, dz = 10\pi i$$

Method 2. $5z^2 - 3z + 2 = 5(z-1)^2 + 7(z-1) + 4$.   Then

$$\oint_C \frac{5z^2 - 3z + 2}{(z-1)^3}\, dz = \oint_C \frac{5(z-1)^2 + 7(z-1) + 4}{(z-1)^3}\, dz$$

$$= 5 \oint_C \frac{dz}{z-1} + 7 \oint_C \frac{dz}{(z-1)^2} + 4 \oint_C \frac{dz}{(z-1)^3} = 5(2\pi i) + 7(0) + 4(0)$$

$$= 10\pi i$$

By Problem 21.

SERIES AND SINGULARITIES

26. For what values of z does each series converge?

(a) $\displaystyle\sum_{n=1}^{\infty} \frac{z^n}{n^2\, 2^n}$.   The nth term $= u_n = \dfrac{z^n}{n^2\, 2^n}$.   Then

$$\lim_{n\to\infty} \left| \frac{u_{n+1}}{u_n} \right| = \lim_{n\to\infty} \left| \frac{z^{n+1}}{(n+1)^2\, 2^{n+1}} \cdot \frac{n^2\, 2^n}{z^n} \right| = \frac{|z|}{2}$$

By the ratio test the series converges if $|z| < 2$ and diverges if $|z| > 2$. If $|z| = 2$ the ratio test fails.

However, the series of absolute values $\displaystyle\sum_{n=1}^{\infty} \left| \frac{z^n}{n^2\, 2^n} \right| = \sum_{n=1}^{\infty} \frac{|z|^n}{n^2\, 2^n}$ converges if $|z| = 2$, since $\displaystyle\sum_{n=1}^{\infty} \frac{1}{n^2}$ converges.

Thus the series converges (absolutely) for $|z| \leqq 2$, i.e. at all points inside and on the circle $|z| = 2$.

(b) $\displaystyle\sum_{n=1}^{\infty} \frac{(-1)^{n-1} z^{2n-1}}{(2n-1)!} = z - \frac{z^3}{3!} + \frac{z^5}{5!} - \cdots$.   We have

$$\lim_{n\to\infty} \left| \frac{u_{n+1}}{u_n} \right| = \lim_{n\to\infty} \left| \frac{(-1)^n z^{2n+1}}{(2n+1)!} \cdot \frac{(2n-1)!}{(-1)^{n-1} z^{2n-1}} \right| = \lim_{n\to\infty} \left| \frac{-z^2}{2n(2n+1)} \right| = 0$$

Then the series, which represents $\sin z$, converges for all values of z.

(c) $\displaystyle\sum_{n=1}^{\infty} \frac{(z-i)^n}{3^n}$.   We have $\displaystyle\lim_{n\to\infty} \left| \frac{u_{n+1}}{u_n} \right| = \lim_{n\to\infty} \left| \frac{(z-i)^{n+1}}{3^{n+1}} \cdot \frac{3^n}{(z-i)^n} \right| = \frac{|z-i|}{3}$.

The series converges if $|z - i| < 3$, and diverges if $|z - i| > 3$.

If $|z - i| = 3$, then $z - i = 3e^{i\theta}$ and the series becomes $\displaystyle\sum_{n=1}^{\infty} e^{in\theta}$. This series diverges since the nth term does not approach zero as $n \to \infty$.

Thus the series converges within the circle $|z - i| = 3$ but not on the boundary.

27. If $\displaystyle\sum_{n=0}^{\infty} a_n z^n$ is absolutely convergent for $|z| \leqq R$, show that it is uniformly convergent for these values of z.

The definitions, theorems and proofs for series of complex numbers and functions are analogous to those for real series.

In particular, a series $\displaystyle\sum_{n=0}^{\infty} u_n(z)$ is said to be *absolutely convergent* in a region $\mathcal{R}$ if $\displaystyle\sum_{n=0}^{\infty} |u_n(z)|$ converges in $\mathcal{R}$. We can also show that if $\displaystyle\sum_{n=0}^{\infty} |u_n(z)|$ converges in $\mathcal{R}$, then so also does $\displaystyle\sum_{n=0}^{\infty} u_n(z)$, i.e. an absolutely convergent series is convergent.

Also, a series $\displaystyle\sum_{n=0}^{\infty} u_n(z)$ convergent to a sum function $S(z)$ in a region $\mathcal{R}$ is said to be *uniformly convergent* in $\mathcal{R}$ if for any $\epsilon > 0$, we can find N such that

$$|S_n(z) - S(z)| < \epsilon \qquad \text{for all } n > N$$

where N depends only on ϵ and not on the particular z in $\mathcal{R}$, and where

$$S_n(z) = u_0(z) + u_1(z) + \cdots + u_n(z)$$

An important test for uniform convergence is the following. If for all z in $\mathcal{R}$ we can find constants M_n such that

$$|u_n(z)| \leqq M_n, \quad n = 0, 1, 2, \ldots \qquad \text{and} \qquad \sum_{n=0}^{\infty} M_n \text{ converges}$$

then $\displaystyle\sum_{n=0}^{\infty} u_n(z)$ converges uniformly in $\mathcal{R}$. This is called the *Weierstrass M test*.

For this particular problem, we have

$$|a_n z^n| \leqq |a_n| R^n = M_n \qquad n = 0, 1, 2, \ldots$$

Since by hypothesis $\displaystyle\sum_{n=0}^{\infty} M_n$ converges, it follows by the Weierstrass M test that $\displaystyle\sum_{n=0}^{\infty} a_n z^n$ converges uniformly for $|z| \leqq R$.

28. Locate in the finite z plane all the singularities, if any, of each function and name them.

(a) $\dfrac{z^2}{(z+1)^3}$. $z = -1$ is a pole of order 3.

(b) $\dfrac{2z^3 - z + 1}{(z-4)^2\,(z-i)(z-1+2i)}$. $z = 4$ is a pole of order 2 (double pole); $z = i$ and $z = 1 - 2i$ are poles of order 1 (simple poles).

(c) $\dfrac{\sin mz}{z^2 + 2z + 2}$, $m \neq 0$.   Since $z^2 + 2z + 2 = 0$ when $z = \dfrac{-2 \pm \sqrt{4-8}}{2} = \dfrac{-2 \pm 2i}{2} = -1 \pm i$, we can write $z^2 + 2z + 2 = \{z - (-1+i)\}\{z - (-1-i)\} = (z+1-i)(z+1+i)$.

The function has the two simple poles: $z = -1 + i$ and $z = -1 - i$.

(d) $\dfrac{1 - \cos z}{z}$. $z = 0$ appears to be a singularity. However, since $\displaystyle\lim_{z \to 0} \frac{1 - \cos z}{z} = 0$, it is a removable singularity.

Another method.

Since $\dfrac{1 - \cos z}{z} = \dfrac{1}{z}\left\{1 - \left(1 - \dfrac{z^2}{2!} + \dfrac{z^4}{4!} - \dfrac{z^6}{6!} + \cdots\right)\right\} = \dfrac{z}{2!} - \dfrac{z^3}{4!} + \cdots$, we see that

$z = 0$ is a removable singularity.

(e) $e^{-1/(z-1)^2} = 1 - \dfrac{1}{(z-1)^2} + \dfrac{1}{2!\,(z-1)^4} - \cdots$.

This is a Laurent series where the principal part has an infinite number of non-zero terms. Then $z = 1$ is an *essential singularity.*

(f) e^z.

This function has no finite singularity. However, letting $z = 1/u$, we obtain $e^{1/u}$ which has an essential singularity at $u = 0$. We conclude that $z = \infty$ is an essential singularity of e^z.

In general, to determine the nature of a possible singularity of $f(z)$ at $z = \infty$, we let $z = 1/u$ and then examine the behavior of the new function at $u = 0$.

29. If $f(z)$ is analytic at all points inside and on a circle of radius R with center at a, and if $a + h$ is any point inside C, prove *Taylor's theorem* that

$$f(a + h) = f(a) + h\,f'(a) + \dfrac{h^2}{2!}f''(a) + \dfrac{h^3}{3!}f'''(a) + \cdots$$

By Cauchy's integral formula (Problem 23), we have

$$f(a + h) = \dfrac{1}{2\pi i}\oint_C \dfrac{f(z)\,dz}{z - a - h} \tag{1}$$

By division,

$$\dfrac{1}{z - a - h} = \dfrac{1}{(z - a)\,[1 - h/(z - a)]}$$

$$= \dfrac{1}{(z - a)}\left\{1 + \dfrac{h}{(z - a)} + \dfrac{h^2}{(z - a)^2} + \cdots + \dfrac{h^n}{(z - a)^n} + \dfrac{h^{n+1}}{(z - a)^n\,(z - a - h)}\right\} \tag{2}$$

Substituting (2) in (1) and using Cauchy's integral formulas, we have

$$f(a + h) = \dfrac{1}{2\pi i}\oint_C \dfrac{f(z)\,dz}{z - a} + \dfrac{h}{2\pi i}\oint_C \dfrac{f(z)\,dz}{(z - a)^2} + \cdots + \dfrac{h^n}{2\pi i}\oint_C \dfrac{f(z)\,dz}{(z - a)^{n+1}} + R_n$$

$$= f(a) + h\,f'(a) + \dfrac{h^2}{2!}f''(a) + \cdots + \dfrac{h^n}{n!}f^{(n)}(a) + R_n$$

where $$R_n = \dfrac{h^{n+1}}{2\pi i}\oint_C \dfrac{f(z)\,dz}{(z - a)^{n+1}\,(z - a - h)}$$

Now when z is on C, $\left|\dfrac{f(z)}{z - a - h}\right| \leqq M$ and $|z - a| = R$, so that by *(14)*, Page 140, we have, since $2\pi R$ is the length of C,

$$|R_n| \leqq \dfrac{|h|^{n+1}\,M}{2\pi\,R^{n+1}} \cdot 2\pi R$$

As $n \to \infty$, $|R_n| \to 0$. Then $R_n \to 0$ and the required result follows.

If $f(z)$ is analytic in an annular region $r_1 \leqq |z - a| \leqq r_2$, we can generalize the Taylor series to a Laurent series (see Problem 119). In some cases, as shown in Problem 30, the Laurent series can be obtained by use of known Taylor series.

30. Find Laurent series about the indicated singularity for each of the following functions. Name the singularity in each case and give the region of convergence of each series.

(a) $\dfrac{e^z}{(z-1)^2}$; $z = 1$.   Let $z - 1 = u$.   Then $z = 1 + u$ and

$$\frac{e^z}{(z-1)^2} \;=\; \frac{e^{1+u}}{u^2} \;=\; e \cdot \frac{e^u}{u^2} \;=\; \frac{e}{u^2}\left\{1 + u + \frac{u^2}{2!} + \frac{u^3}{3!} + \frac{u^4}{4!} + \cdots\right\}$$

$$\;=\; \frac{e}{(z-1)^2} + \frac{e}{z-1} + \frac{e}{2!} + \frac{e(z-1)}{3!} + \frac{e(z-1)^2}{4!} + \cdots$$

$z = 1$ is a *pole of order 2*, or *double pole*.

The series converges for all values of $z \neq 1$.

(b) $z \cos \dfrac{1}{z}$; $z = 0$.

$$z \cos \frac{1}{z} \;=\; z\left(1 - \frac{1}{2!\,z^2} + \frac{1}{4!\,z^4} - \frac{1}{6!\,z^6} + \cdots\right) \;=\; z - \frac{1}{2!\,z} + \frac{1}{4!\,z^3} - \frac{1}{6!\,z^5} + \cdots$$

$z = 0$ is an *essential singularity*.

The series converges for all values of $z \neq 0$.

(c) $\dfrac{\sin z}{z - \pi}$; $z = \pi$.   Let $z - \pi = u$.   Then $z = u + \pi$ and

$$\frac{\sin z}{z - \pi} \;=\; \frac{\sin(u + \pi)}{u} \;=\; -\frac{\sin u}{u} \;=\; -\frac{1}{u}\left(u - \frac{u^3}{3!} + \frac{u^5}{5!} - \cdots\right)$$

$$\;=\; -1 + \frac{u^2}{3!} - \frac{u^4}{5!} + \cdots \;=\; -1 + \frac{(z-\pi)^2}{3!} - \frac{(z-\pi)^4}{5!} + \cdots$$

$z = \pi$ is a *removable singularity*.

The series converges for all values of z.

(d) $\dfrac{z}{(z+1)(z+2)}$; $z = -1$.   Let $z + 1 = u$.   Then

$$\frac{z}{(z+1)(z+2)} \;=\; \frac{u-1}{u(u+1)} \;=\; \frac{u-1}{u}(1 - u + u^2 - u^3 + u^4 - \cdots)$$

$$\;=\; -\frac{1}{u} + 2 - 2u + 2u^2 - 2u^3 + \cdots$$

$$\;=\; -\frac{1}{z+1} + 2 - 2(z+1) + 2(z+1)^2 - \cdots$$

$z = -1$ is a *pole of order 1*, or *simple pole*.

The series converges for values of z such that $0 < |z+1| < 1$.

(e) $\dfrac{1}{z(z+2)^3}$; $z = 0, -2$.

Case 1, $z = 0$.   Using the binomial theorem,

$$\frac{1}{z(z+2)^3} \;=\; \frac{1}{8z(1+z/2)^3} \;=\; \frac{1}{8z}\left\{1 + (-3)\left(\frac{z}{2}\right) + \frac{(-3)(-4)}{2!}\left(\frac{z}{2}\right)^2 + \frac{(-3)(-4)(-5)}{3!}\left(\frac{z}{2}\right)^3 + \cdots\right\}$$

$$\;=\; \frac{1}{8z} - \frac{3}{16} + \frac{3}{16}z - \frac{5}{32}z^2 + \cdots$$

$z = 0$ is a *pole of order 1*, or *simple pole*.

The series converges for $0 < |z| < 2$.

Case 2, $z = -2$. Let $z + 2 = u$. Then

$$\frac{1}{z(z+2)^3} = \frac{1}{(u-2)u^3} = \frac{1}{-2u^3(1-u/2)} = -\frac{1}{2u^3}\left\{1 + \frac{u}{2} + \left(\frac{u}{2}\right)^2 + \left(\frac{u}{2}\right)^3 + \left(\frac{u}{2}\right)^4 + \cdots\right\}$$

$$= -\frac{1}{2u^3} - \frac{1}{4u^2} - \frac{1}{8u} - \frac{1}{16} - \frac{1}{32}u - \cdots$$

$$= -\frac{1}{2(z+2)^3} - \frac{1}{4(z+2)^2} - \frac{1}{8(z+2)} - \frac{1}{16} - \frac{1}{32}(z+2) - \cdots$$

$z = -2$ is a *pole of order 3.*

The series converges for $0 < |z+2| < 2$.

RESIDUES AND THE RESIDUE THEOREM

31. If $f(z)$ is analytic everywhere inside and on a simple closed curve C except at $z = a$ which is a pole of order n so that

$$f(z) = \frac{a_{-n}}{(z-a)^n} + \frac{a_{-n+1}}{(z-a)^{n-1}} + \cdots + a_0 + a_1(z-a) + a_2(z-a)^2 + \cdots$$

where $a_{-n} \neq 0$, prove that

(a) $\displaystyle\oint_C f(z)\,dz = 2\pi i\, a_{-1}$

(b) $\displaystyle a_{-1} = \lim_{z \to a} \frac{1}{(n-1)!} \frac{d^{n-1}}{dz^{n-1}}\{(z-a)^n f(z)\}.$

(a) By integration, we have on using Problem 21

$$\oint_C f(z)\,dz = \oint_C \frac{a_{-n}}{(z-a)^n}\,dz + \cdots + \oint_C \frac{a_{-1}}{z-a}\,dz + \oint_C \{a_0 + a_1(z-a) + a_2(z-a)^2 + \cdots\}\,dz$$

$$= 2\pi i\, a_{-1}$$

Since only the term involving a_{-1} remains, we call a_{-1} the *residue* of $f(z)$ at the pole $z = a$.

(b) Multiplication by $(z-a)^n$ gives the Taylor series

$$(z-a)^n f(z) = a_{-n} + a_{-n+1}(z-a) + \cdots + a_{-1}(z-a)^{n-1} + \cdots$$

Taking the $(n-1)$st derivative of both sides and letting $z \to a$, we find

$$(n-1)!\, a_{-1} = \lim_{z \to a} \frac{d^{n-1}}{dz^{n-1}}\{(z-a)^n f(z)\}$$

from which the required result follows.

32. Determine the residues of each function at the indicated poles.

(a) $\dfrac{z^2}{(z-2)(z^2+1)}$; $z = 2, i, -i$. These are simple poles. Then:

Residue at $z = 2$ is $\displaystyle\lim_{z \to 2}(z-2)\left\{\frac{z^2}{(z-2)(z^2+1)}\right\} = \frac{4}{5}.$

Residue at $z = i$ is $\displaystyle\lim_{z \to i}(z-i)\left\{\frac{z^2}{(z-2)(z-i)(z+i)}\right\} = \frac{i^2}{(i-2)(2i)} = \frac{1-2i}{10}.$

Residue at $z = -i$ is $\displaystyle\lim_{z \to -i}(z+i)\left\{\frac{z^2}{(z-2)(z-i)(z+i)}\right\} = \frac{i^2}{(-i-2)(-2i)} = \frac{1+2i}{10}.$

(b) $\dfrac{1}{z(z+2)^3}$; $z = 0, -2$. $z = 0$ is a simple pole, $z = -2$ is a pole of order 3.   Then:

Residue at $z = 0$ is $\lim\limits_{z \to 0} z \cdot \dfrac{1}{z(z+2)^3} = \dfrac{1}{8}$

Residue at $z = -2$ is $\lim\limits_{z \to -2} \dfrac{1}{2!} \dfrac{d^2}{dz^2} \left\{ (z+2)^3 \cdot \dfrac{1}{z(z+2)^3} \right\}$

$$= \lim\limits_{z \to -2} \frac{1}{2} \frac{d^2}{dz^2}\left(\frac{1}{z}\right) = \lim\limits_{z \to -2} \frac{1}{2}\left(\frac{2}{z^3}\right) = -\frac{1}{8}$$

Note that these residues can also be obtained from the coefficients of $1/z$ and $1/(z+2)$ in the respective Laurent series [see Problem 30(e)].

(c) $\dfrac{ze^{zt}}{(z-3)^2}$; $z = 3$, a pole of order 2 or double pole.   Then:

Residue is $\lim\limits_{z \to 3} \dfrac{d}{dz}\left\{ (z-3)^2 \cdot \dfrac{ze^{zt}}{(z-3)^2} \right\} = \lim\limits_{z \to 3} \dfrac{d}{dz}(ze^{zt}) = \lim\limits_{z \to 3}(e^{zt} + zte^{zt})$

$$= e^{3t} + 3te^{3t}$$

(d) $\cot z$; $z = 5\pi$, a pole of order 1.   Then:

Residue is $\lim\limits_{z \to 5\pi}(z - 5\pi) \cdot \dfrac{\cos z}{\sin z} = \left(\lim\limits_{z \to 5\pi} \dfrac{z - 5\pi}{\sin z}\right)\left(\lim\limits_{z \to 5\pi} \cos z\right) = \left(\lim\limits_{z \to 5\pi} \dfrac{1}{\cos z}\right)(-1)$

$$= (-1)(-1) = 1$$

where we have used L'Hospital's rule, which can be shown applicable for functions of a complex variable.

33. If $f(z)$ is analytic within and on a simple closed curve C except at a number of poles $a, b, c, \ldots$ interior to C, prove that

$$\oint_C f(z)\, dz = 2\pi i \,\{\text{sum of residues of } f(z) \text{ at poles } a, b, c, \text{ etc.}\}$$

Refer to Fig. 5-13.

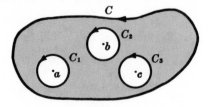

By reasoning similar to that of Problem 20 (i.e. by constructing cross cuts from C to C_1, C_2, C_3, etc.), we have

$$\oint_C f(z)\, dz = \oint_{C_1} f(z)\, dz + \oint_{C_2} f(z)\, dz + \cdots$$

Fig. 5-13

For pole a,

$$f(z) = \frac{a_{-m}}{(z-a)^m} + \cdots + \frac{a_{-1}}{(z-a)} + a_0 + a_1(z-a) + \cdots$$

hence, as in Problem 31, $\oint_{C_1} f(z)\, dz = 2\pi i\, a_{-1}$.

Similarly for pole b, $f(z) = \dfrac{b_{-n}}{(z-b)^n} + \cdots + \dfrac{b_{-1}}{(z-b)} + b_0 + b_1(z-b) + \cdots$

so that $\oint_{C_2} f(z)\, dz = 2\pi i\, b_{-1}$

Continuing in this manner, we see that

$$\oint_C f(z)\, dz = 2\pi i(a_{-1} + b_{-1} + \cdots) = 2\pi i\,(\text{sum of residues})$$

34. Evaluate $\displaystyle\oint_C \frac{e^z\,dz}{(z-1)(z+3)^2}$ where C is given by $\;(a)\;|z|=3/2,\;\;(b)\;|z|=10.$

Residue at simple pole $z=1$ is $\displaystyle\lim_{z\to 1}\left\{(z-1)\,\frac{e^z}{(z-1)(z+3)^2}\right\} \;=\; \frac{e}{16}$

Residue at double pole $z=-3$ is

$$\lim_{z\to -3}\frac{d}{dz}\left\{(z+3)^2\,\frac{e^z}{(z-1)(z+3)^2}\right\} \;=\; \lim_{z\to -3}\frac{(z-1)e^z-e^z}{(z-1)^2} \;=\; \frac{-5e^{-3}}{16}$$

(a) Since $|z|=3/2$ encloses only the pole $z=1$,

the required integral $\;=\; 2\pi i\left(\dfrac{e}{16}\right) \;=\; \dfrac{\pi i e}{8}$

(b) Since $|z|=10$ encloses both poles $z=1$ and $z=-3$,

the required integral $\;=\; 2\pi i\left(\dfrac{e}{16}-\dfrac{5e^{-3}}{16}\right) \;=\; \dfrac{\pi i(e-5e^{-3})}{8}$

EVALUATION OF DEFINITE INTEGRALS

35. If $|f(z)| \leqq \dfrac{M}{R^k}$ for $z=Re^{i\theta}$, where $k>1$ and M are constants, prove that $\displaystyle\lim_{R\to\infty}\int_\Gamma f(z)\,dz \;=\; 0$ where Γ is the semi-circular arc of radius R shown in Fig. 5-14.

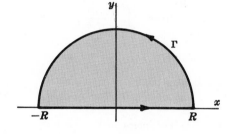

By the result (14), Page 140, we have

$$\left|\int_\Gamma f(z)\,dz\right| \;\leqq\; \int_\Gamma |f(z)|\,|dz| \;\leqq\; \frac{M}{R^k}\cdot \pi R \;=\; \frac{\pi M}{R^{k-1}}$$

Fig. 5-14

since the length of arc $L=\pi R$. Then

$$\lim_{R\to\infty}\left|\int_\Gamma f(z)\,dz\right| \;=\; 0 \qquad\text{and so}\qquad \lim_{R\to\infty}\int_\Gamma f(z)\,dz \;=\; 0$$

36. Show that for $z=Re^{i\theta}$, $\;|f(z)|\leqq\dfrac{M}{R^k}$, $\;k>1\;$ if $\;f(z)=\dfrac{1}{1+z^4}$.

If $z=Re^{i\theta}$, $\;|f(z)| \;=\; \left|\dfrac{1}{1+R^4e^{4i\theta}}\right| \;\leqq\; \dfrac{1}{|R^4e^{4i\theta}|-1} \;=\; \dfrac{1}{R^4-1} \;\leqq\; \dfrac{2}{R^4}$ if R is large enough (say $R>2$, for example) so that $M=2,\;k=4$.

Note that we have made use of the inequality $\;|z_1+z_2|\geqq|z_1|-|z_2|\;$ with $\;z_1=R^4e^{4i\theta}\;$ and $\;z_2=1$.

37. Evaluate $\displaystyle\int_0^\infty \frac{dx}{x^4+1}$.

Consider $\displaystyle\oint_C \frac{dz}{z^4+1}$, where C is the closed contour of Problem 35 consisting of the line from $-R$ to R and the semi-circle Γ, traversed in the positive (counterclockwise) sense.

Since $z^4+1=0$ when $z=e^{\pi i/4},\,e^{3\pi i/4},\,e^{5\pi i/4},\,e^{7\pi i/4}$, these are simple poles of $1/(z^4+1)$. Only the poles $e^{\pi i/4}$ and $e^{3\pi i/4}$ lie within C. Then using L'Hospital's rule,

$$\text{Residue at } e^{\pi i/4} = \lim_{z \to e^{\pi i/4}} \left\{ (z - e^{\pi i/4}) \frac{1}{z^4 + 1} \right\}$$

$$= \lim_{z \to e^{\pi i/4}} \frac{1}{4z^3} = \frac{1}{4} e^{-3\pi i/4}$$

$$\text{Residue at } e^{3\pi i/4} = \lim_{z \to e^{3\pi i/4}} \left\{ (z - e^{3\pi i/4}) \frac{1}{z^4 + 1} \right\}$$

$$= \lim_{z \to e^{3\pi i/4}} \frac{1}{4z^3} = \frac{1}{4} e^{-9\pi i/4}$$

Thus
$$\oint_C \frac{dz}{z^4 + 1} = 2\pi i \{ \tfrac{1}{4} e^{-3\pi i/4} + \tfrac{1}{4} e^{-9\pi i/4} \} = \frac{\pi \sqrt{2}}{2} \tag{1}$$

i.e.
$$\int_{-R}^{R} \frac{dx}{x^4 + 1} + \int_{\Gamma} \frac{dz}{z^4 + 1} = \frac{\pi \sqrt{2}}{2} \tag{2}$$

Taking the limit of both sides of (2) as $R \to \infty$ and using the results of Problem 36, we have

$$\lim_{R \to \infty} \int_{-R}^{R} \frac{dx}{x^4 + 1} = \int_{-\infty}^{\infty} \frac{dx}{x^4 + 1} = \frac{\pi \sqrt{2}}{2}$$

Since $\displaystyle\int_{-\infty}^{\infty} \frac{dx}{x^4 + 1} = 2\int_{0}^{\infty} \frac{dx}{x^4 + 1}$, the required integral has the value $\dfrac{\pi \sqrt{2}}{4}$.

38. Show that $\displaystyle\int_{-\infty}^{\infty} \frac{x^2 \, dx}{(x^2 + 1)^2 (x^2 + 2x + 2)} = \frac{7\pi}{50}$.

The poles of $\dfrac{z^2}{(z^2 + 1)^2 (z^2 + 2z + 2)}$ enclosed by the contour C of Problem 35 are $z = i$ of order 2 and $z = -1 + i$ of order 1.

Residue at $z = i$ is $\displaystyle\lim_{z \to i} \frac{d}{dz} \left\{ (z - i)^2 \frac{z^2}{(z + i)^2 (z - i)^2 (z^2 + 2z + 2)} \right\} = \frac{9i - 12}{100}$

Residue at $z = -1 + i$ is $\displaystyle\lim_{z \to -1 + i} (z + 1 - i) \frac{z^2}{(z^2 + 1)^2 (z + 1 - i)(z + 1 + i)} = \frac{3 - 4i}{25}$

Then
$$\oint_C \frac{z^2 \, dz}{(z^2 + 1)^2 (z^2 + 2z + 2)} = 2\pi i \left\{ \frac{9i - 12}{100} + \frac{3 - 4i}{25} \right\} = \frac{7\pi}{50}$$

or
$$\int_{-R}^{R} \frac{x^2 \, dx}{(x^2 + 1)^2 (x^2 + 2x + 2)} + \int_{\Gamma} \frac{z^2 \, dz}{(z^2 + 1)^2 (z^2 + 2z + 2)} = \frac{7\pi}{50}$$

Taking the limit as $R \to \infty$ and noting that the second integral approaches zero by Problem 35, we obtain the required result.

39. Evaluate $\displaystyle\int_{0}^{2\pi} \frac{d\theta}{5 + 3 \sin \theta}$.

Let $z = e^{i\theta}$. Then $\sin \theta = \dfrac{e^{i\theta} - e^{-i\theta}}{2i} = \dfrac{z - z^{-1}}{2i}$, $dz = ie^{i\theta} \, d\theta = iz \, d\theta$ so that

$$\int_{0}^{2\pi} \frac{d\theta}{5 + 3 \sin \theta} = \oint_C \frac{dz/iz}{5 + 3 \left(\dfrac{z - z^{-1}}{2i} \right)} = \oint_C \frac{2 \, dz}{3z^2 + 10iz - 3}$$

where C is the circle of unit radius with center at the origin, as shown in Fig. 5-15 below.

The poles of $\dfrac{2}{3z^2 + 10iz - 3}$ are the simple poles

$$z = \frac{-10i \pm \sqrt{-100 + 36}}{6}$$

$$= \frac{-10i \pm 8i}{6}$$

$$= -3i, \ -i/3.$$

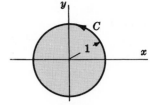

Fig. 5-15

Only $-i/3$ lies inside C.

Residue at $-i/3$ = $\displaystyle\lim_{z \to -i/3} \left(z + \frac{i}{3}\right)\left(\frac{2}{3z^2 + 10iz - 3}\right)$ = $\displaystyle\lim_{z \to -i/3} \frac{2}{6z + 10i}$ = $\dfrac{1}{4i}$ by L'Hospital's rule.

Then $\displaystyle\oint_C \frac{2\,dz}{3z^2 + 10iz - 3}$ = $2\pi i\left(\dfrac{1}{4i}\right)$ = $\dfrac{\pi}{2}$, the required value.

40. Show that $\displaystyle\int_0^{2\pi} \frac{\cos 3\theta}{5 - 4\cos\theta}\,d\theta$ = $\dfrac{\pi}{12}$.

If $z = e^{i\theta}$, $\cos\theta = \dfrac{z + z^{-1}}{2}$, $\cos 3\theta = \dfrac{e^{3i\theta} + e^{-3i\theta}}{2} = \dfrac{z^3 + z^{-3}}{2}$, $dz = iz\,d\theta$.

Then $\displaystyle\int_0^{2\pi} \frac{\cos 3\theta}{5 - 4\cos\theta}\,d\theta$ = $\displaystyle\oint_C \frac{(z^3 + z^{-3})/2}{5 - 4\left(\dfrac{z + z^{-1}}{2}\right)}\,\frac{dz}{iz}$ = $-\dfrac{1}{2i}\displaystyle\oint_C \frac{z^6 + 1}{z^3(2z - 1)(z - 2)}\,dz$

where C is the contour of Problem 39.

The integrand has a pole of order 3 at $z = 0$ and a simple pole $z = \frac{1}{2}$ within C.

Residue at $z = 0$ is $\displaystyle\lim_{z \to 0} \frac{1}{2!}\frac{d^2}{dz^2}\left\{z^3 \cdot \frac{z^6 + 1}{z^3(2z - 1)(z - 2)}\right\}$ = $\dfrac{21}{8}$.

Residue at $z = \frac{1}{2}$ is $\displaystyle\lim_{z \to 1/2}\left\{(z - \tfrac{1}{2}) \cdot \frac{z^6 + 1}{z^3(2z - 1)(z - 2)}\right\}$ = $-\dfrac{65}{24}$.

Then $-\dfrac{1}{2i}\displaystyle\oint_C \frac{z^6 + 1}{z^3(2z - 1)(z - 2)}\,dz$ = $-\dfrac{1}{2i}(2\pi i)\left\{\dfrac{21}{8} - \dfrac{65}{24}\right\}$ = $\dfrac{\pi}{12}$ as required.

41. If $|f(z)| \leqq \dfrac{M}{R^k}$ for $z = Re^{i\theta}$, where $k > 0$ and M are constants, prove that

$$\lim_{R \to \infty} \int_\Gamma e^{imz} f(z)\,dz = 0$$

where Γ is the semi-circular arc of the contour in Problem 35 and m is a positive constant.

If $z = Re^{i\theta}$, $\displaystyle\int_\Gamma e^{imz} f(z)\,dz$ = $\displaystyle\int_0^\pi e^{imRe^{i\theta}} f(Re^{i\theta})\,iRe^{i\theta}\,d\theta$.

Then $\left|\displaystyle\int_0^\pi e^{imRe^{i\theta}} f(Re^{i\theta})\,iRe^{i\theta}\,d\theta\right|$ $\leqq$ $\displaystyle\int_0^\pi \left|e^{imRe^{i\theta}} f(Re^{i\theta})\,iRe^{i\theta}\right|\,d\theta$

$= \displaystyle\int_0^\pi \left|e^{imR\cos\theta - mR\sin\theta} f(Re^{i\theta})\,iRe^{i\theta}\right|\,d\theta$

$= \displaystyle\int_0^\pi e^{-mR\sin\theta}\,|f(Re^{i\theta})|\,R\,d\theta$

$\leqq \dfrac{M}{R^{k-1}}\displaystyle\int_0^\pi e^{-mR\sin\theta}\,d\theta$ = $\dfrac{2M}{R^{k-1}}\displaystyle\int_0^{\pi/2} e^{-mR\sin\theta}\,d\theta$

Now $\sin \theta \geqq 2\theta/\pi$ for $0 \leqq \theta \leqq \pi/2$ (see Problem 3, Chapter 7). Then the last integral is less than or equal to

$$\frac{2M}{R^{k-1}} \int_0^{\pi/2} e^{-2mR\theta/\pi} \, d\theta \;\; = \;\; \frac{\pi M}{mR^k}(1 - e^{-mR})$$

As $R \to \infty$ this approaches zero, since m and k are positive, and the required result is proved.

42. Show that $\displaystyle\int_0^\infty \frac{\cos mx}{x^2+1} \, dx \;\; = \;\; \frac{\pi}{2} e^{-m}, \quad m > 0.$

Consider $\displaystyle\oint_C \frac{e^{imz}}{z^2+1} \, dz$ where C is the contour of Problem 35.

The integrand has simple poles at $z = \pm i$, but only $z = i$ lies within C.

Residue at $z = i$ is $\displaystyle\lim_{z \to i} \left\{ (z-i)\, \frac{e^{imz}}{(z-i)(z+i)} \right\} \;\; = \;\; \frac{e^{-m}}{2i}.$

Then $$\oint_C \frac{e^{imz}}{z^2+1} \, dz \;\; = \;\; 2\pi i \left(\frac{e^{-m}}{2i} \right) \;\; = \;\; \pi e^{-m}$$

or $$\int_{-R}^R \frac{e^{imx}}{x^2+1} \, dx \;+\; \int_\Gamma \frac{e^{imz}}{z^2+1} \, dz \;\; = \;\; \pi e^{-m}$$

i.e. $$\int_{-R}^R \frac{\cos mx}{x^2+1} \, dx \;+\; i\int_{-R}^R \frac{\sin mx}{x^2+1} \, dx \;+\; \int_\Gamma \frac{e^{imz}}{z^2+1} \, dz \;\; = \;\; \pi e^{-m}$$

and so $$2\int_0^R \frac{\cos mx}{x^2+1} \, dx \;+\; \int_\Gamma \frac{e^{imz}}{z^2+1} \, dz \;\; = \;\; \pi e^{-m}$$

Taking the limit as $R \to \infty$ and using Problem 41 to show that the integral around Γ approaches zero, we obtain the required result.

43. Show that $\displaystyle\int_0^\infty \frac{\sin x}{x} \, dx \;\; = \;\; \frac{\pi}{2}.$

The method of Problem 42 leads us to consider the integral of e^{iz}/z around the contour of Problem 35. However, since $z = 0$ lies on this path of integration and since we cannot integrate through a singularity, we modify that contour by indenting the path at $z = 0$, as shown in Fig. 5-16, which we call contour C' or $ABDEFGHJA$.

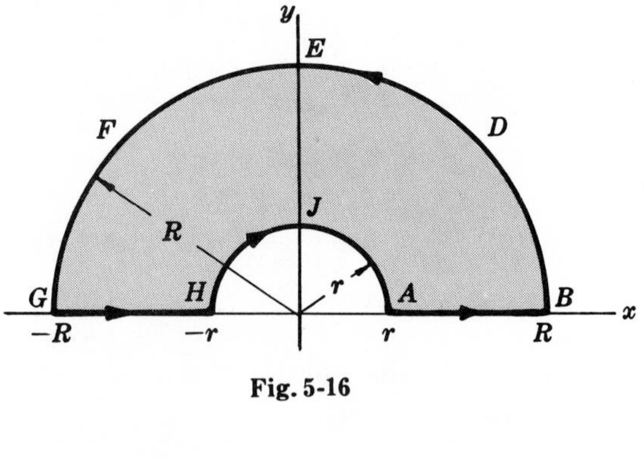

Since $z = 0$ is outside C', we have

Fig. 5-16

$$\int_{C'} \frac{e^{iz}}{z} \, dz \;\; = \;\; 0$$

or $$\int_{-R}^{-r} \frac{e^{ix}}{x} \, dx \;+\; \int_{HJA} \frac{e^{iz}}{z} \, dz \;+\; \int_r^R \frac{e^{ix}}{x} \, dx \;+\; \int_{BDEFG} \frac{e^{iz}}{z} \, dz \;\; = \;\; 0$$

Replacing x by $-x$ in the first integral and combining with the third integral, we find,

$$\int_r^R \frac{e^{ix} - e^{-ix}}{x} \, dx \;+\; \int_{HJA} \frac{e^{iz}}{z} \, dz \;+\; \int_{BDEFG} \frac{e^{iz}}{z} \, dz \;\; = \;\; 0$$

or $$2i\int_r^R \frac{\sin x}{x} \, dx \;\; = \;\; -\int_{HJA} \frac{e^{iz}}{z} \, dz \;-\; \int_{BDEFG} \frac{e^{iz}}{z} \, dz$$

Let $r \to 0$ and $R \to \infty$. By Problem 41, the second integral on the right approaches zero. The first integral on the right approaches

$$- \lim_{r \to 0} \int_{\pi}^{0} \frac{e^{ire^{i\theta}}}{re^{i\theta}} \, ire^{i\theta} \, d\theta \;=\; - \lim_{r \to 0} \int_{\pi}^{0} ie^{ire^{i\theta}} \, d\theta \;=\; \pi i$$

since the limit can be taken under the integral sign.

Then we have

$$\lim_{\substack{R \to \infty \\ r \to 0}} 2i \int_{r}^{R} \frac{\sin x}{x} \, dx \;=\; \pi i \qquad \text{or} \qquad \int_{0}^{\infty} \frac{\sin x}{x} \, dx \;=\; \frac{\pi}{2}$$

MISCELLANEOUS PROBLEMS

44. Let $w = z^2$ define a transformation from the z plane (xy plane) to the w plane (uv plane). Consider a triangle in the z plane with vertices at $A(2,1)$, $B(4,1)$, $C(4,3)$. (a) Show that the *image* or *mapping* of this triangle is a curvilinear triangle in the uv plane. (b) Find the angles of this curvilinear triangle and compare with those of the original triangle.

(a) Since $w = z^2$, we have $u = x^2 - y^2$, $v = 2xy$ as the transformation equations. Then point $A(2,1)$ in the xy plane maps into point $A'(3,4)$ of the uv plane (see figures below). Similarly, points B and C map into points B' and C' respectively. The line segments AC, BC, AB of triangle ABC map respectively into parabolic segments $A'C', B'C', A'B'$ of curvilinear triangle $A'B'C'$ with equations as shown in Figures 5-17(a) and (b).

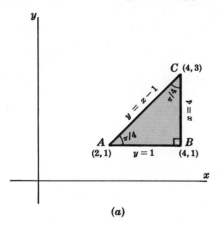

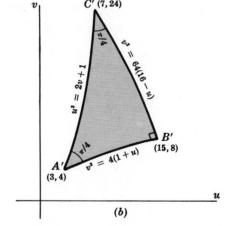

(a)   (b)

Fig. 5-17

(b) The slope of the tangent to the curve $v^2 = 4(1 + u)$ at $(3,4)$ is $m_1 = \left. \dfrac{dv}{du} \right|_{(3,4)} = \left. \dfrac{2}{v} \right|_{(3,4)} = \dfrac{1}{2}$.

The slope of the tangent to the curve $u^2 = 2v + 1$ at $(3,4)$ is $m_2 = \left. \dfrac{dv}{du} \right|_{(3,4)} = u = 3$.

Then the angle θ between the two curves at A' is given by

$$\tan \theta \;=\; \frac{m_2 - m_1}{1 + m_1 m_2} \;=\; \frac{3 - \frac{1}{2}}{1 + (3)(\frac{1}{2})} \;=\; 1, \quad \text{and} \quad \theta = \pi/4$$

Similarly we can show that the angle between $A'C'$ and $B'C'$ is $\pi/4$, while the angle between $A'B'$ and $B'C'$ is $\pi/2$. Therefore the angles of the curvilinear triangle are equal to the corresponding ones of the given triangle. In general, if $w = f(z)$ is a transformation where $f(z)$ is analytic, the angle between two curves in the z plane intersecting at $z = z_0$ has the same magnitude and sense (orientation) as the angle between the images of the two curves, so long as $f'(z_0) \neq 0$. This property is called the *conformal property* of analytic functions and for this reason the transformation $w = f(z)$ is often called a *conformal transformation* or *conformal mapping function*.

45. Let $w = \sqrt{z}$ define a transformation from the z plane to the w plane. A point moves counterclockwise along the circle $|z| = 1$. Show that when it has returned to its starting position for the first time its image point has not yet returned, but that when it has returned for the second time its image point returns for the first time.

Let $z = e^{i\theta}$. Then $w = \sqrt{z} = e^{i\theta/2}$. Let $\theta = 0$ correspond to the starting position. Then $z = 1$ and $w = 1$ [corresponding to A and P in Figures 5-18(a) and (b)].

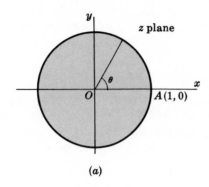

Fig. 5-18

When one complete revolution in the z plane has been made, $\theta = 2\pi$, $z = 1$ but $w = e^{i\theta/2} = e^{i\pi} = -1$ so the image point has not yet returned to its starting position.

However, after two complete revolutions in the z plane have been made, $\theta = 4\pi$, $z = 1$ and $w = e^{i\theta/2} = e^{2\pi i} = 1$ so the image point has returned for the first time.

It follows from the above that w is not a single-valued function of z but is a *double-valued function* of z; i.e. given z, there are two values of w. If we wish to consider it a single-valued function, we must restrict θ. We can, for example, choose $0 \le \theta < 2\pi$, although other possibilities exist. This represents one branch of the double-valued function $w = \sqrt{z}$. In continuing beyond this interval we are on the second branch, e.g. $2\pi \le \theta < 4\pi$. The point $z = 0$ about which the rotation is taking place is called a *branch point*. Equivalently, we can insure that $f(z) = \sqrt{z}$ will be single-valued by agreeing not to cross the line Ox, called a *branch line*.

46. Show that $\displaystyle\int_0^\infty \frac{x^{p-1}}{1+x}\,dx = \frac{\pi}{\sin p\pi}, \quad 0 < p < 1.$

Consider $\displaystyle\oint_C \frac{z^{p-1}}{1+z}\,dz$. Since $z = 0$ is a branch point, choose C as the contour of Fig. 5-19 where AB and GH are actually coincident with the x axis but are shown separated for visual purposes.

The integrand has the pole $z = -1$ lying within C.

Residue at $z = -1 = e^{\pi i}$ is

$$\lim_{z \to -1} (z+1)\frac{z^{p-1}}{1+z} = (e^{\pi i})^{p-1} = e^{(p-1)\pi i}$$

Then $\displaystyle\oint_C \frac{z^{p-1}}{1+z}\,dz = 2\pi i\, e^{(p-1)\pi i}$

or, omitting the integrand,

$$\int_{AB} + \int_{BDEFG} + \int_{GH} + \int_{HJA} = 2\pi i\, e^{(p-1)\pi i}$$

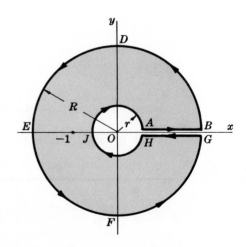

Fig. 5-19

We thus have

$$\int_r^R \frac{x^{p-1}}{1+x}dx \;+\; \int_0^{2\pi} \frac{(Re^{i\theta})^{p-1}\,iRe^{i\theta}\,d\theta}{1+Re^{i\theta}} \;+\; \int_R^r \frac{(xe^{2\pi i})^{p-1}}{1+xe^{2\pi i}}dx \;+\; \int_{2\pi}^0 \frac{(re^{i\theta})^{p-1}\,ire^{i\theta}\,d\theta}{1+re^{i\theta}} \;=\; 2\pi i\,e^{(p-1)\pi i}$$

where we have to use $z = xe^{2\pi i}$ for the integral along GH, since the argument of z is increased by 2π in going around the circle $BDEFG$.

Taking the limit as $r \to 0$ and $R \to \infty$ and noting that the second and fourth integrals approach zero, we find

$$\int_0^\infty \frac{x^{p-1}}{1+x}dx \;+\; \int_\infty^0 \frac{e^{2\pi i(p-1)}\,x^{p-1}}{1+x}dx \;=\; 2\pi\,e^{(p-1)\pi i}$$

or

$$(1 - e^{2\pi i(p-1)})\int_0^\infty \frac{x^{p-1}}{1+x}dx \;=\; 2\pi i\,e^{(p-1)\pi i}$$

so that

$$\int_0^\infty \frac{x^{p-1}}{1+x}dx \;=\; \frac{2\pi i\,e^{(p-1)\pi i}}{1 - e^{2\pi i(p-1)}} \;=\; \frac{2\pi i}{e^{p\pi i} - e^{-p\pi i}} \;=\; \frac{\pi}{\sin p\pi}$$

Supplementary Problems

COMPLEX NUMBERS. POLAR FORM

47. Perform each of the indicated operations:

(a) $2(5 - 3i) - 3(-2 + i) + 5(i - 3)$

(c) $\dfrac{5}{3 - 4i} + \dfrac{10}{4 + 3i}$

(e) $\left|\dfrac{2 - 4i}{5 + 7i}\right|^2$

(b) $(3 - 2i)^3$

(d) $\left(\dfrac{1 - i}{1 + i}\right)^{10}$

(f) $\dfrac{(1 + i)(2 + 3i)(4 - 2i)}{(1 + 2i)^2(1 - i)}$

Ans. (a) $1 - 4i$, (b) $-9 - 46i$, (c) $\frac{11}{5} - \frac{2}{5}i$, (d) -1, (e) $\frac{10}{37}$, (f) $\frac{16}{5} - \frac{2}{5}i$

48. If z_1 and z_2 are complex numbers, prove (a) $\left|\dfrac{z_1}{z_2}\right| = \dfrac{|z_1|}{|z_2|}$, (b) $|z_1^2| = |z_1|^2$ giving any restrictions.

49. Prove (a) $|z_1 + z_2| \leqq |z_1| + |z_2|$, (b) $|z_1 + z_2 + z_3| \leqq |z_1| + |z_2| + |z_3|$, (c) $|z_1 - z_2| \geqq |z_1| - |z_2|$.

50. Find all solutions of $2z^4 - 3z^3 - 7z^2 - 8z + 6 = 0$.   Ans. $3, \frac{1}{2}, -1 \pm i$

51. Let z_1 and z_2 be represented by points P_1 and P_2 in the Argand diagram. Construct lines OP_1 and OP_2, where O is the origin. Show that $z_1 + z_2$ can be represented by the point P_3, where OP_3 is the diagonal of a parallelogram having sides OP_1 and OP_2. This is called the *parallelogram law* of addition of complex numbers. Because of this and other properties, complex numbers can be considered as *vectors* in two dimensions.

52. Interpret geometrically the inequalities of Problem 49.

53. Express in polar form   (a) $3\sqrt{3} + 3i$, (b) $-2 - 2i$, (c) $1 - \sqrt{3}\,i$, (d) 5, (e) $-5i$.
Ans.   (a) $6\text{ cis }\pi/6$, (b) $2\sqrt{2}\text{ cis }5\pi/4$, (c) $2\text{ cis }5\pi/3$, (d) $5\text{ cis }0$, (e) $5\text{ cis }3\pi/2$

54. Evaluate   (a) $[2(\cos 25° + i\sin 25°)]\,[5(\cos 110° + i\sin 110°)]$,   (b) $\dfrac{12\text{ cis }16°}{(3\text{ cis }44°)(2\text{ cis }62°)}$.
Ans.   (a) $-5\sqrt{2} + 5\sqrt{2}\,i$, (b) $-2i$

55. Determine all the indicated roots and represent them graphically:

(a) $(4\sqrt{2} + 4\sqrt{2}\,i)^{1/3}$, (b) $(-1)^{1/5}$, (c) $(\sqrt{3} - i)^{1/3}$, (d) $i^{1/4}$.

Ans. (a) $2 \operatorname{cis} 15°$, $2 \operatorname{cis} 135°$, $2 \operatorname{cis} 255°$

(b) $\operatorname{cis} 36°$, $\operatorname{cis} 108°$, $\operatorname{cis} 180° = -1$, $\operatorname{cis} 252°$, $\operatorname{cis} 324°$

(c) $\sqrt[3]{2} \operatorname{cis} 110°$, $\sqrt[3]{2} \operatorname{cis} 230°$, $\sqrt[3]{2} \operatorname{cis} 350°$

(d) $\operatorname{cis} 22.5°$, $\operatorname{cis} 112.5°$, $\operatorname{cis} 202.5°$, $\operatorname{cis} 292.5°$

56. If $z_1 = r_1 \operatorname{cis} \theta_1$ and $z_2 = r_2 \operatorname{cis} \theta_2$, prove (a) $z_1 z_2 = r_1 r_2 \operatorname{cis}(\theta_1 + \theta_2)$, (b) $z_1/z_2 = (r_1/r_2) \operatorname{cis}(\theta_1 - \theta_2)$. Interpret geometrically.

FUNCTIONS, LIMITS, CONTINUITY

57. Describe the locus represented by (a) $|z + 2 - 3i| = 5$, (b) $|z + 2| = 2|z - 1|$, (c) $|z + 5| - |z - 5| = 6$. Construct a figure in each case.

Ans. (a) Circle $(x + 2)^2 + (y - 3)^2 = 25$, center $(-2, 3)$, radius 5.

(b) Circle $(x - 2)^2 + y^2 = 4$, center $(2, 0)$, radius 2.

(c) Branch of hyperbola $x^2/9 - y^2/16 = 1$, where $x \geqq 3$.

58. Determine the region in the z plane represented by each of the following:

(a) $|z - 2 + i| \geqq 4$, (b) $|z| \leqq 3$, $0 \leqq \arg z \leqq \dfrac{\pi}{4}$, (c) $|z - 3| + |z + 3| < 10$. Construct a figure in each case.

Ans. (a) Boundary and exterior of circle $(x - 2)^2 + (y + 1)^2 = 16$.

(b) Region in the first quadrant bounded by $x^2 + y^2 = 9$, the x axis and the line $y = x$.

(c) Interior of ellipse $x^2/25 + y^2/16 = 1$.

59. Express each function in the form $u(x, y) + iv(x, y)$, where u and v are real.

(a) $z^3 + 2iz$, (b) $z/(3 + z)$, (c) e^{z^2}, (d) $\ln(1 + z)$.

Ans. (a) $u = x^3 - 3xy^2 - 2y$, $v = 3x^2y - y^3 + 2x$

(b) $u = \dfrac{x^2 + 3x + y^2}{x^2 + 6x + y^2 + 9}$, $v = \dfrac{3y}{x^2 + 6x + y^2 + 9}$

(c) $u = e^{x^2 - y^2} \cos 2xy$, $v = e^{x^2 - y^2} \sin 2xy$

(d) $u = \frac{1}{2} \ln\{(1 + x)^2 + y^2\}$, $v = \tan^{-1}\dfrac{y}{1 + x} + 2k\pi$, $k = 0, \pm 1, \pm 2, \ldots$

60. Prove that (a) $\lim\limits_{z \to z_0} z^2 = z_0^2$, (b) $f(z) = z^2$ is continuous at $z = z_0$ directly from the definition.

61. (a) If $z = \omega$ is any root of $z^5 = 1$ different from 1, prove that all roots are $1, \omega, \omega^2, \omega^3, \omega^4$.

(b) Show that $1 + \omega + \omega^2 + \omega^3 + \omega^4 = 0$.

(c) Generalize the results in (a) and (b) to the equation $z^n = 1$.

DERIVATIVES, CAUCHY-RIEMANN EQUATIONS

62. (a) If $w = f(z) = z + \dfrac{1}{z}$, find $\dfrac{dw}{dz}$ directly from the definition.

(b) For what finite values of z is $f(z)$ non-analytic?

Ans. (a) $1 - 1/z^2$, (b) $z = 0$

63. Given the function $w = z^4$. (a) Find real functions u and v such that $w = u + iv$. (b) Show that the Cauchy-Riemann equations hold at all points in the finite z plane. (c) Prove that u and v are harmonic functions. (d) Determine dw/dz. *Ans.* (a) $u = x^4 - 6x^2y^2 + y^4$, $v = 4x^3y - 4xy^3$ (d) $4z^3$

64. Prove that $f(z) = z|z|$ is not analytic anywhere.

65. Prove that $f(z) = \dfrac{1}{z-2}$ is analytic in any region not including $z = 2$.

66. If the imaginary part of an analytic function is $2x(1-y)$, determine (a) the real part, (b) the function.
    Ans. (a) $y^2 - x^2 - 2y + c$, (b) $2iz - z^2 + c$, where c is real

67. Construct an analytic function $f(z)$ whose real part is $e^{-x}(x\cos y + y\sin y)$ and for which $f(0) = 1$.
    Ans. $ze^{-z} + 1$

68. Prove that there is no analytic function whose imaginary part is $x^2 - 2y$.

69. Find $f(z)$ such that $f'(z) = 4z - 3$ and $f(1+i) = -3i$.   Ans. $f(z) = 2z^2 - 3z + 3 - 4i$

LINE INTEGRALS

70. Evaluate $\displaystyle\int_{(1,1)}^{(4,2)} (x+y)\,dx + (y-x)\,dy$ along (a) the parabola $y^2 = x$, (b) a straight line, (c) straight

    lines from $(1,1)$ to $(1,2)$ and then to $(4,2)$, (d) the curve $x = 2t^2 + t + 1$, $y = t^2 + 1$.
    Ans. (a) 34/3, (b) 11, (c) 14, (d) 32/3

71. Evaluate $\displaystyle\oint (2x - y + 4)\,dx + (5y + 3x - 6)\,dy$ around a triangle in the xy plane with vertices at
    $(0,0)$, $(3,0)$, $(3,2)$ traversed in a counterclockwise direction.   Ans. 12

72. Evaluate the line integral in the preceding problem around a circle of radius 4 with center at $(0,0)$.
    Ans. 64π

GREEN'S THEOREM IN THE PLANE. INDEPENDENCE OF THE PATH

73. Verify Green's theorem in the plane for $\displaystyle\oint_C (x^2 - xy^3)\,dx + (y^2 - 2xy)\,dy$ where C is a square with

    vertices at $(0,0)$, $(2,0)$, $(2,2)$, $(0,2)$.   Ans. common value = 8

74. (a) Let C be any simple closed curve bounding a region having area A. Prove that if $a_1, a_2, a_3, b_1, b_2, b_3$
    are constants,
    $$\oint_C (a_1x + a_2y + a_3)\,dx + (b_1x + b_2y + b_3)\,dy = (b_1 - a_2)A$$

    (b) Under what conditions will the line integral around any path C be zero?   Ans. (b) $a_2 = b_1$

75. Find the area bounded by the hypocycloid $x^{2/3} + y^{2/3} = a^{2/3}$.
    [Hint. Parametric equations are $x = a\cos^3 t$, $y = a\sin^3 t$, $0 \leqq t \leqq 2\pi$.]   Ans. $3\pi a^2/8$

76. If $x = r\cos\theta$, $y = r\sin\theta$, prove that $\frac{1}{2}\displaystyle\oint x\,dy - y\,dx = \frac{1}{2}\displaystyle\int r^2\,d\theta$ and interpret.

77. (a) Verify Green's theorem in the plane for $\displaystyle\oint_C (x^3 - x^2y)\,dx + xy^2\,dy$, where C is the boundary of

    the region enclosed by the circles $x^2 + y^2 = 4$ and $x^2 + y^2 = 16$. (b) Evaluate the line integrals of
    Problems 71 and 72 by Green's theorem.   Ans. (a) common value = 120π

78. (a) Prove that $\displaystyle\int_{(1,0)}^{(2,1)} (2xy - y^4 + 3)\,dx + (x^2 - 4xy^3)\,dy$ is independent of the path joining $(1,0)$ and

    $(2,1)$. (b) Evaluate the integral in (a).   Ans. (b) 5

INTEGRALS, CAUCHY'S THEOREM, CAUCHY'S INTEGRAL FORMULAS

79. Evaluate $\int_{1-2i}^{3+i} (2z + 3)\, dz$:

(a) along the path $x = 2t + 1$, $y = 4t^2 - t - 2$ where $0 \le t \le 1$.

(b) along the straight line joining $1 - 2i$ and $3 + i$.

(c) along straight lines from $1 - 2i$ to $1 + i$ and then to $3 + i$.

Ans. $17 + 19i$ in all cases

80. Evaluate $\int_C (z^2 - z + 2)\, dz$, where C is the upper half of the circle $|z| = 1$ traversed in the positive sense. *Ans.* $-14/3$

81. Evaluate $\oint_C \dfrac{z\, dz}{2z - 5}$, where C is the circle (a) $|z| = 2$, (b) $|z - 3| = 2$. *Ans.* (a) 0, (b) $5\pi i/2$

82. Evaluate $\oint_C \dfrac{z^2}{(z + 2)(z - 1)}\, dz$, where C is: (a) a square with vertices at $-1 - i$, $-1 + i$, $-3 + i$, $-3 - i$; (b) the circle $|z + i| = 3$; (c) the circle $|z| = \sqrt{2}$.   *Ans.* (a) $-8\pi i/3$ (b) $-2\pi i$ (c) $2\pi i/3$

83. Evaluate (a) $\oint_C \dfrac{\cos \pi z}{z - 1}\, dz$, (b) $\oint_C \dfrac{e^z + z}{(z - 1)^4}\, dz$ where C is any simple closed curve enclosing $z = 1$. *Ans.* (a) $-2\pi i$ (b) $\pi i e/3$

84. Prove Cauchy's integral formulas.

[*Hint.* Use the definition of derivative and then apply mathematical induction.]

SERIES AND SINGULARITIES

85. For what values of z does each series converge?

(a) $\displaystyle\sum_{n=1}^{\infty} \frac{(z + 2)^n}{n!}$,   (b) $\displaystyle\sum_{n=1}^{\infty} \frac{n(z - i)^n}{n + 1}$,   (c) $\displaystyle\sum_{n=1}^{\infty} (-1)^n n!\, (z^2 + 2z + 2)^{2n}$

Ans. (a) all z (b) $|z - i| < 1$ (c) $z = -1 \pm i$

86. Prove that the series $\displaystyle\sum_{n=1}^{\infty} \frac{z^n}{n(n + 1)}$ is (a) absolutely convergent, (b) uniformly convergent for $|z| \le 1$.

87. Prove that the series $\displaystyle\sum_{n=0}^{\infty} \frac{(z + i)^n}{2^n}$ converges uniformly within any circle of radius R such that $|z + i| < R < 2$.

88. Locate in the finite z plane all the singularities, if any, of each function and name them:

(a) $\dfrac{z - 2}{(2z + 1)^4}$,   (b) $\dfrac{z}{(z - 1)(z + 2)^2}$,   (c) $\dfrac{z^2 + 1}{z^2 + 2z + 2}$,   (d) $\cos \dfrac{1}{z}$,   (e) $\dfrac{\sin(z - \pi/3)}{3z - \pi}$,   (f) $\dfrac{\cos z}{(z^2 + 4)^2}$.

Ans.   (a) $z = -\frac{1}{2}$, pole of order 4   (d) $z = 0$, essential singularity

(b) $z = 1$, simple pole; $z = -2$, double pole   (e) $z = \pi/3$, removable singularity

(c) Simple poles $z = -1 \pm i$ (f) $z = \pm 2i$, double poles

89. Find Laurent series about the indicated singularity for each of the following functions, naming the singularity in each case. Indicate the region of convergence of each series.

(a) $\dfrac{\cos z}{z - \pi}$; $z = \pi$ (b) $z^2 e^{-1/z}$; $z = 0$ (c) $\dfrac{z^2}{(z - 1)^2 (z + 3)}$; $z = 1$

Ans.   (a) $-\dfrac{1}{z - \pi} + \dfrac{z - \pi}{2!} - \dfrac{(z - \pi)^3}{4!} + \dfrac{(z - \pi)^5}{6!} - \cdots$, simple pole, all $z \ne \pi$

(b) $z^2 - z + \dfrac{1}{2!} - \dfrac{1}{3!\, z} + \dfrac{1}{4!\, z^2} - \dfrac{1}{5!\, z^3} + \cdots$, essential singularity, all $z \ne 0$

(c) $\dfrac{1}{4(z - 1)^2} + \dfrac{7}{16(z - 1)} + \dfrac{9}{64} - \dfrac{9(z - 1)}{256} + \cdots$, double pole, $0 < |z - 1| < 4$

RESIDUES AND THE RESIDUE THEOREM

90. Determine the residues of each function at its poles:

(a) $\dfrac{2z+3}{z^2-4}$,　(b) $\dfrac{z-3}{z^3+5z^2}$,　(c) $\dfrac{e^{zt}}{(z-2)^3}$,　(d) $\dfrac{z}{(z^2+1)^2}$.

Ans.　(a)　$z=2$; $7/4$,　　$z=-2$; $1/4$　　　　(c)　$z=2$; $\frac{1}{2}t^2\,e^{2t}$

　　　　(b)　$z=0$; $8/25$,　　$z=-5$; $-8/25$　　　(d)　$z=i$; 0,　　$z=-i$; 0

91. Find the residue of $e^{zt}\tan z$ at the simple pole $z=3\pi/2$.　　　Ans. $-e^{3\pi t/2}$

92. Evaluate $\displaystyle\oint_C \dfrac{z^2\,dz}{(z+1)(z+3)}$,　where C is a simple closed curve enclosing all the poles.　　　Ans. $-8\pi i$

93. If C is a simple closed curve enclosing $z=\pm i$, show that

$$\frac{1}{2\pi i}\oint_C \frac{ze^{zt}}{(z^2+1)^2}\,dz \;=\; \tfrac{1}{2}t\sin t$$

94. If $f(z)=P(z)/Q(z)$, where $P(z)$ and $Q(z)$ are polynomials such that the degree of $P(z)$ is at least two less than the degree of $Q(z)$, prove that $\displaystyle\oint_C f(z)\,dz = 0$,　where C encloses all the poles of $f(z)$.

EVALUATION OF DEFINITE INTEGRALS

Use contour integration to verify each of the following:

95. $\displaystyle\int_0^\infty \frac{x^2\,dx}{x^4+1} = \frac{\pi}{2\sqrt{2}}$

96. $\displaystyle\int_{-\infty}^\infty \frac{dx}{x^6+a^6} = \frac{2\pi}{3a^5}$,　$a>0$

97. $\displaystyle\int_0^\infty \frac{dx}{(x^2+4)^2} = \frac{\pi}{32}$

98. $\displaystyle\int_0^\infty \frac{\sqrt{x}}{x^3+1}\,dx = \frac{\pi}{3}$

99. $\displaystyle\int_0^\infty \frac{dx}{(x^4+a^4)^2} = \frac{3\pi}{8\sqrt{2}}\,a^{-7}$,　$a>0$

100. $\displaystyle\int_{-\infty}^\infty \frac{dx}{(x^2+1)^2\,(x^2+4)} = \frac{\pi}{9}$

101. $\displaystyle\int_0^{2\pi} \frac{d\theta}{2-\cos\theta} = \frac{2\pi}{\sqrt{3}}$

102. $\displaystyle\int_0^{2\pi} \frac{d\theta}{(2+\cos\theta)^2} = \frac{4\pi\sqrt{3}}{9}$

103. $\displaystyle\int_0^{\pi} \frac{\sin^2\theta}{5-4\cos\theta}\,d\theta = \frac{\pi}{8}$

104. $\displaystyle\int_0^{2\pi} \frac{d\theta}{(1+\sin^2\theta)^2} = \frac{3\pi}{2\sqrt{2}}$

105. $\displaystyle\int_0^{2\pi} \frac{\cos n\theta\,d\theta}{1-2a\cos\theta+a^2} = \frac{2\pi a^n}{1-a^2}$,　$n=0,1,2,3,\ldots,\;0<a<1$

106. $\displaystyle\int_0^{2\pi} \frac{d\theta}{(a+b\cos\theta)^3} = \frac{(2a^2+b^2)\pi}{(a^2-b^2)^{5/2}}$,　$a>|b|$

107. $\displaystyle\int_0^\infty \frac{x\sin 2x}{x^2+4}\,dx = \frac{\pi e^{-4}}{4}$

108. $\displaystyle\int_0^\infty \frac{\cos 2\pi x}{x^4+4}\,dx = \frac{\pi e^{-\pi}}{8}$

109. $\displaystyle\int_0^\infty \frac{x\sin \pi x}{(x^2+1)^2}\,dx = \frac{\pi^2 e^{-\pi}}{4}$

110. $\displaystyle\int_0^\infty \frac{\sin x}{x(x^2+1)^2}\,dx = \frac{\pi(2e-3)}{4e}$

111. $\displaystyle\int_0^\infty \frac{\sin^2 x}{x^2}\,dx = \frac{\pi}{2}$

112. $\displaystyle\int_0^\infty \frac{\sin^3 x}{x^3}\,dx = \frac{3\pi}{8}$

113. $\displaystyle\int_0^\infty \frac{\cos x}{\cosh x}\,dx = \frac{\pi}{2\cosh(\pi/2)}$.　$\left[\textit{Hint.}\text{ Consider }\oint_C \dfrac{e^{iz}}{\cosh z}\,dz,\text{ where }C\text{ is a rectangle with vertices}\right.$

at $(-R,0)$, $(R,0)$, (R,π), $(-R,\pi)$.　Then let $R\to\infty$.$\Big]$

MISCELLANEOUS PROBLEMS

114. If $z = re^{i\theta}$ and $f(z) = u(r, \theta) + i\,v(r, \theta)$, where r and θ are polar coordinates, show that the Cauchy-Riemann equations are

$$\frac{\partial u}{\partial r} = \frac{1}{r}\frac{\partial v}{\partial \theta}, \qquad \frac{\partial v}{\partial r} = -\frac{1}{r}\frac{\partial u}{\partial \theta}$$

115. If $w = f(z)$, where $f(z)$ is analytic, defines a transformation from the z plane to the w plane where $z = x + iy$ and $w = u + iv$, prove that the Jacobian of the transformation is given by

$$\frac{\partial(u, v)}{\partial(x, y)} = |f'(z)|^2$$

116. Let $F(x, y)$ be transformed to $G(u, v)$ by the transformation $w = f(z)$. Show that if $\dfrac{\partial^2 F}{\partial x^2} + \dfrac{\partial^2 F}{\partial y^2} = 0$, then at all points where $f'(z) \neq 0$, $\dfrac{\partial^2 G}{\partial u^2} + \dfrac{\partial^2 G}{\partial v^2} = 0$.

117. Show that by the *bilinear transformation* $w = \dfrac{az + b}{cz + d}$, where $ad - bc \neq 0$, circles in the z plane are transformed into circles of the w plane.

118. If $f(z)$ is analytic inside and on the circle $|z - a| = R$, prove *Cauchy's inequality*, namely,

$$|f^{(n)}(a)| \;\leq\; \frac{n!\, M}{R^n}$$

where $|f(z)| \leq M$ on the circle.   [*Hint.* Use Cauchy's integral formulas.]

119. Let C_1 and C_2 be concentric circles having center a and radii r_1 and r_2 respectively, where $r_1 < r_2$. If $a + h$ is any point in the annular region bounded by C_1 and C_2, and $f(z)$ is analytic in this region, prove *Laurent's theorem* that

$$f(a + h) = \sum_{-\infty}^{\infty} a_n h^n$$

where

$$a_n = \frac{1}{2\pi i} \oint_C \frac{f(z)\, dz}{(z - a)^{n+1}}$$

C being any closed curve in the angular region surrounding C_1.

$$\left[\textit{Hint.} \quad \text{Write} \quad f(a + h) = \frac{1}{2\pi i} \oint_{C_2} \frac{f(z)\, dz}{z - (a + h)} - \frac{1}{2\pi i} \oint_{C_1} \frac{f(z)\, dz}{z - (a + h)} \quad \text{and expand} \quad \frac{1}{z - a - h} \text{ in} \right.$$
$$\left. \text{two different ways.} \right]$$

120. Find a Laurent series expansion for the function $f(z) = \dfrac{z}{(z + 1)(z + 2)}$ which converges for $1 < |z| < 2$ and diverges elsewhere.

$$\left[\textit{Hint.} \quad \text{Write} \quad \frac{z}{(z + 1)(z + 2)} = \frac{-1}{z + 1} + \frac{2}{z + 2} = \frac{-1}{z(1 + 1/z)} + \frac{1}{1 + z/2} \cdot \right]$$

Ans. $\quad \cdots - \dfrac{1}{z^5} + \dfrac{1}{z^4} - \dfrac{1}{z^3} + \dfrac{1}{z^2} - \dfrac{1}{z} + 1 - \dfrac{z}{2} + \dfrac{z^2}{4} - \dfrac{z^3}{8} + \cdots$

Chapter 6

Fourier Series And Integrals

FOURIER SERIES

Let $F(x)$ satisfy the following conditions:

  1. $F(x)$ is defined in the interval $c < x < c + 2l$.

  2. $F(x)$ and $F'(x)$ are sectionally continuous in $c < x < c + 2l$.

  3. $F(x + 2l) = F(x)$, i.e. $F(x)$ is periodic with period $2l$.

Then at every point of continuity, we have

$$F(x) \;=\; \frac{a_0}{2} \;+\; \sum_{n=1}^{\infty}\left(a_n \cos\frac{n\pi x}{l} \;+\; b_n \sin\frac{n\pi x}{l}\right) \tag{1}$$

where

$$\left. \begin{array}{rcl} a_n &=& \dfrac{1}{l}\displaystyle\int_{c}^{c+2l} F(x)\cos\dfrac{n\pi x}{l}\,dx \\[4mm] b_n &=& \dfrac{1}{l}\displaystyle\int_{c}^{c+2l} F(x)\sin\dfrac{n\pi x}{l}\,dx \end{array}\right\} \tag{2}$$

At a point of discontinuity, the left side of (1) is replaced by $\frac{1}{2}\{F(x+0) + F(x-0)\}$, i.e. the mean value at the discontinuity.

The series (1) with coefficients (2) is called the *Fourier series* of $F(x)$. For many problems, $c = 0$ or $-l$. In case $l = \pi$, $F(x)$ has period 2π and (1) and (2) are simplified.

The above conditions are often called *Dirichlet conditions* and are sufficient (but not necessary) conditions for convergence of Fourier series.

ODD AND EVEN FUNCTIONS

A function $F(x)$ is called *odd* if $F(-x) = -F(x)$. Thus x^3, $x^5 - 3x^3 + 2x$, $\sin x$, $\tan 3x$ are odd functions.

A function $F(x)$ is called *even* if $F(-x) = F(x)$. Thus x^4, $2x^6 - 4x^2 + 5$, $\cos x$, $e^x + e^{-x}$ are even functions.

The functions portrayed graphically in Figures 6-1 and 6-2 below are odd and even respectively, but that of Fig. 6-3 below is neither odd nor even.

In the Fourier series corresponding to an odd function, only sine terms can be present. In the Fourier series corresponding to an even function, only cosine terms (and possibly a constant which we shall consider a cosine term) can be present.

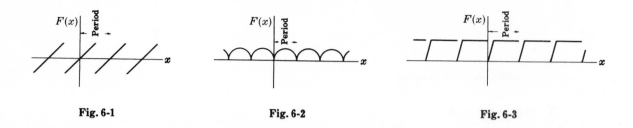

Fig. 6-1   Fig. 6-2   Fig. 6-3

HALF RANGE FOURIER SINE AND COSINE SERIES

A half range Fourier sine or cosine series is a series in which only sine terms or only cosine terms are present respectively. When a half range series corresponding to a given function is desired, the function is generally defined in the interval $(0, l)$ [which is half of the interval $(-l, l)$, thus accounting for the name *half range*] and then the function is specified as odd or even, so that it is clearly defined in the other half of the interval, namely $(-l, 0)$. In such case, we have

$$a_n = 0, \quad b_n = \frac{2}{l} \int_0^l F(x) \sin \frac{n\pi x}{l}\, dx \quad \text{for } \textit{half range sine series}$$

$$b_n = 0, \quad a_n = \frac{2}{l} \int_0^l F(x) \cos \frac{n\pi x}{l}\, dx \quad \text{for } \textit{half range cosine series}$$

$$(3)$$

COMPLEX FORM OF FOURIER SERIES

In complex notation, the Fourier series (*1*) and coefficients (*2*) can be written as

$$F(x) = \sum_{n=-\infty}^{\infty} c_n\, e^{in\pi x/l} \tag{4}$$

where, taking $c = -l$,

$$c_n = \frac{1}{2l} \int_{-l}^{l} F(x)\, e^{-in\pi x/l}\, dx \tag{5}$$

See Problem 74.

PARSEVAL'S IDENTITY FOR FOURIER SERIES

Parseval's identity states that

$$\frac{1}{l} \int_{-l}^{l} \{F(x)\}^2\, dx = \frac{a_0^2}{2} + \sum_{n=1}^{\infty} (a_n^2 + b_n^2) \tag{6}$$

where a_n and b_n are given by (*2*).

An important consequence is that

$$\lim_{n \to \infty} \int_{-l}^{l} F(x) \sin \frac{n\pi x}{l}\, dx = 0$$

$$\lim_{n \to \infty} \int_{-l}^{l} F(x) \cos \frac{n\pi x}{l}\, dx = 0$$

$$(7)$$

This is called *Riemann's theorem*.

FINITE FOURIER TRANSFORMS

The *finite Fourier sine transform* of $F(x)$, $0 < x < l$, is defined as

$$f_s(n) \; = \; \int_0^l F(x) \sin \frac{n\pi x}{l} \, dx \tag{8}$$

where n is an integer. The function $F(x)$ is then called the *inverse finite Fourier sine transform* of $f_s(n)$ and is given by

$$F(x) \; = \; \frac{2}{l} \sum_{n=1}^{\infty} f_s(n) \sin \frac{n\pi x}{l} \tag{9}$$

The *finite Fourier cosine transform* of $F(x)$, $0 < x < l$, is defined as

$$f_c(n) \; = \; \int_0^l F(x) \cos \frac{n\pi x}{l} \, dx \tag{10}$$

where n is an integer. The function $F(x)$ is then called the *inverse finite Fourier cosine transform* of $f_c(n)$ and is given by

$$F(x) \; = \; \frac{1}{l} f_c(0) \; + \; \frac{2}{l} \sum_{n=1}^{\infty} f_c(n) \cos \frac{n\pi x}{l} \tag{11}$$

See Problems 9-11.

Finite Fourier transforms can be useful in solving differential equations [see Prob. 32].

THE FOURIER INTEGRAL

Let $F(x)$ satisfy the following conditions:

1. $F(x)$ satisfies the Dirichlet conditions in every finite interval $-l \le x \le l$.

2. $\int_{-\infty}^{\infty} |F(x)| \, dx$ converges, i.e. $F(x)$ is absolutely integrable in $-\infty < x < \infty$.

Then *Fourier's integral theorem* states that

$$F(x) \; = \; \int_0^{\infty} \{A(\lambda) \cos \lambda x \; + \; B(\lambda) \sin \lambda x\} \, d\lambda \tag{12}$$

where

$$\left. \begin{array}{l} A(\lambda) \; = \; \dfrac{1}{\pi} \displaystyle\int_{-\infty}^{\infty} F(x) \cos \lambda x \, dx \\[2.5ex] B(\lambda) \; = \; \dfrac{1}{\pi} \displaystyle\int_{-\infty}^{\infty} F(x) \sin \lambda x \, dx \end{array} \right\} \tag{13}$$

This can be written equivalently as

$$F(x) \; = \; \frac{1}{2\pi} \int_{\lambda=-\infty}^{\infty} \int_{u=-\infty}^{\infty} F(u) \cos \lambda(x-u) \, du \, d\lambda \tag{14}$$

The result (*12*) holds if x is a point of continuity of $F(x)$. If x is a point of discontinuity, we must replace $F(x)$ by $\frac{1}{2}\{F(x+0) + F(x-0)\}$ as in the case of Fourier series. As for Fourier series, the above conditions are sufficient but not necessary.

The similarity of (*12*) and (*13*) with corresponding results (*1*) and (*2*) for Fourier series is apparent. The right side of (*12*) is sometimes called the *Fourier integral expansion* of $F(x)$, or briefly *Fourier integral*.

COMPLEX FORM OF FOURIER INTEGRALS

In complex notation, the Fourier integral (*12*) with coefficients (*13*) can be written as

$$F(x) \;=\; \frac{1}{2\pi} \int_{-\infty}^{\infty} e^{i\lambda x}\, d\lambda \int_{-\infty}^{\infty} F(u)\, e^{-i\lambda u}\, du \tag{15}$$

$$=\; \frac{1}{2\pi} \int_{-\infty}^{\infty} \int_{-\infty}^{\infty} F(u)\, e^{i\lambda(x-u)}\, du\, d\lambda$$

See Problem 77.

FOURIER TRANSFORMS

From (*15*) it follows that if

$$f(\lambda) \;=\; \int_{-\infty}^{\infty} e^{-i\lambda u}\, F(u)\, du \tag{16}$$

then

$$F(u) \;=\; \frac{1}{2\pi} \int_{-\infty}^{\infty} e^{i\lambda u}\, f(\lambda)\, d\lambda \tag{17}$$

which gives $F(x)$ on replacing u by x.

The function $f(\lambda)$ is called the *Fourier transform* of $F(x)$ and is sometimes written $f(\lambda) = \mathcal{F}\,\{F(x)\}$. The function $F(x)$ is the *inverse Fourier transform* of $f(\lambda)$ and is written $F(x) = \mathcal{F}^{-1}\,\{f(\lambda)\}$. We also call (*17*) an *inversion formula* corresponding to (*16*).

Note that the constants preceding the integral signs can be any constants whose product is $1/2\pi$. If they are each taken as $1/\sqrt{2\pi}$ we obtain the so-called *symmetric form*.

FOURIER SINE AND COSINE TRANSFORMS

The (*infinite*) *Fourier sine transform* of $F(x)$, $0 < x < \infty$, is defined as

$$f_S(\lambda) \;=\; \int_0^{\infty} F(u) \sin \lambda u\, du \tag{18}$$

The function $F(x)$ is then called the *inverse Fourier sine transform* of $f_S(\lambda)$ and is given by

$$F(x) \;=\; \frac{2}{\pi} \int_0^{\infty} f_S(\lambda) \sin \lambda x\, d\lambda \tag{19}$$

The (*infinite*) *Fourier cosine transform* of $F(x)$, $0 < x < \infty$, is defined as

$$f_C(\lambda) \;=\; \int_0^{\infty} F(u) \cos \lambda u\, du \tag{20}$$

The function $F(x)$ is then called the *inverse Fourier cosine transform* of $f_C(\lambda)$ and is given by

$$F(x) \;=\; \frac{2}{\pi} \int_0^\infty f_C(\lambda) \cos \lambda x \, d\lambda \tag{21}$$

See Problems 18-20.

Fourier transforms can be used in solving differential equations [see Problem 33].

THE CONVOLUTION THEOREM

The *convolution* of two functions $F(x)$ and $G(x)$, where $-\infty < x < \infty$, is defined as

$$F * G \;=\; \int_{-\infty}^\infty F(u) \, G(x-u) \, du \;=\; H(x) \tag{22}$$

An important result, known as the *convolution theorem for Fourier transforms*, is the following.

Theorem.   If $H(x)$ is the convolution of $F(x)$ and $G(x)$, then

$$\int_{-\infty}^\infty H(x) \, e^{-i\lambda x} \, dx \;=\; \left\{ \int_{-\infty}^\infty F(x) \, e^{-i\lambda x} \, dx \right\} \left\{ \int_{-\infty}^\infty G(x) \, e^{-i\lambda x} \, dx \right\} \tag{23}$$

or

$$\mathcal{F}\{F * G\} \;=\; \mathcal{F}\{F\} \, \mathcal{F}\{G\} \tag{24}$$

i.e. the Fourier transform of the convolution of F and G is the product of the Fourier transforms of F and G.

PARSEVAL'S IDENTITY FOR FOURIER INTEGRALS

If the Fourier transform of $F(x)$ is $f(\lambda)$, then

$$\int_{-\infty}^\infty |F(x)|^2 \, dx \;=\; \frac{1}{2\pi} \int_{-\infty}^\infty |f(\lambda)|^2 \, d\lambda \tag{25}$$

This is called *Parseval's identity for Fourier integrals*.   Generalizations of this are possible (see Problem 80).

RELATIONSHIP OF FOURIER AND LAPLACE TRANSFORMS

Consider the function

$$F(t) \;=\; \begin{cases} e^{-xt} \, \Phi(t) & t > 0 \\ 0 & t < 0 \end{cases} \tag{26}$$

Then from (16), Page 176, with λ replaced by y, we see that the Fourier transform of $F(t)$ is

$$\mathcal{F}\{F(t)\} \;=\; \int_0^\infty e^{-(x+iy)t} \, \Phi(t) \, dt \;=\; \int_0^\infty e^{-st} \, \Phi(t) \, dt \tag{27}$$

where we have written $s = x + iy$.   The right side of (27) is the Laplace transform of $\Phi(t)$ and the result indicates a relationship of Fourier and Laplace transforms.   It also indicates a need for considering s as a complex variable $x + iy$.

To indicate the relationship even further, note that if $F(t)$ and $G(t)$ are zero for $t < 0$, the convolution of F and G given by (22) can be written

$$F * G \;=\; \int_0^t F(u)\, G(t-u)\, du \tag{28}$$

and (24) corresponds to

$$\mathcal{L}\{F * G\} \;=\; \mathcal{L}\{F\}\, \mathcal{L}\{G\} \tag{29}$$

in agreement with (11) on Page 45.

In view of the fact that there is an inversion formula (17) corresponding to (16) for Fourier transforms, one would feel that there ought to be a corresponding inversion formula for Laplace transforms. Such an inversion formula is obtained in Chapter 7.

Solved Problems

FOURIER SERIES

1. Prove $\displaystyle \int_{-l}^{l} \sin \frac{k\pi x}{l}\, dx \;=\; \int_{-l}^{l} \cos \frac{k\pi x}{l}\, dx \;=\; 0 \quad$ if $k = 1, 2, 3, \ldots$.

$$\int_{-l}^{l} \sin \frac{k\pi x}{l}\, dx \;=\; -\frac{l}{k\pi} \cos \frac{k\pi x}{l}\Big|_{-l}^{l} \;=\; -\frac{l}{k\pi} \cos k\pi \,+\, \frac{l}{k\pi} \cos(-k\pi) \;=\; 0$$

$$\int_{-l}^{l} \cos \frac{k\pi x}{l}\, dx \;=\; \frac{l}{k\pi} \sin \frac{k\pi x}{l}\Big|_{-l}^{l} \;=\; \frac{l}{k\pi} \sin k\pi \,-\, \frac{l}{k\pi} \sin(-k\pi) \;=\; 0$$

2. Prove $\quad (a)\ \displaystyle \int_{-l}^{l} \cos \frac{m\pi x}{l} \cos \frac{n\pi x}{l}\, dx \;=\; \int_{-l}^{l} \sin \frac{m\pi x}{l} \sin \frac{n\pi x}{l}\, dx \;=\; \begin{cases} 0 & m \neq n \\ l & m = n \end{cases}$

$\qquad\qquad (b)\ \displaystyle \int_{-l}^{l} \sin \frac{m\pi x}{l} \cos \frac{n\pi x}{l}\, dx \;=\; 0$

where m and n can assume any of the values $1, 2, 3, \ldots$.

(a) From trigonometry: $\cos A \cos B = \tfrac{1}{2}\{\cos(A-B) + \cos(A+B)\}$, $\quad \sin A \sin B = \tfrac{1}{2}\{\cos(A-B) - \cos(A+B)\}$.

Then, if $m \neq n$, by Problem 1,

$$\int_{-l}^{l} \cos \frac{m\pi x}{l} \cos \frac{n\pi x}{l}\, dx \;=\; \frac{1}{2} \int_{-l}^{l} \left\{ \cos \frac{(m-n)\pi x}{l} \,+\, \cos \frac{(m+n)\pi x}{l} \right\} dx \;=\; 0$$

Similarly if $m \neq n$,

$$\int_{-l}^{l} \sin \frac{m\pi x}{l} \sin \frac{n\pi x}{l}\, dx \;=\; \frac{1}{2} \int_{-l}^{l} \left\{ \cos \frac{(m-n)\pi x}{l} \,-\, \cos \frac{(m+n)\pi x}{l} \right\} dx \;=\; 0$$

If $m = n$, we have

$$\int_{-l}^{l} \cos\frac{m\pi x}{l} \cos\frac{n\pi x}{l} \, dx \;\; = \;\; \frac{1}{2}\int_{-l}^{l}\left(1 + \cos\frac{2n\pi x}{l}\right) dx \;\; = \;\; l$$

$$\int_{-l}^{l} \sin\frac{m\pi x}{l} \sin\frac{n\pi x}{l} \, dx \;\; = \;\; \frac{1}{2}\int_{-l}^{l}\left(1 - \cos\frac{2n\pi x}{l}\right) dx \;\; = \;\; l$$

Note that if $m = n = 0$ these integrals are equal to $2l$ and 0 respectively.

(b) We have $\sin A \cos B = \frac{1}{2}\{\sin(A-B) + \sin(A+B)\}$. Then by Problem 1, if $m \neq n$,

$$\int_{-l}^{l} \sin\frac{m\pi x}{l} \cos\frac{n\pi x}{l} \, dx \;\; = \;\; \frac{1}{2}\int_{-l}^{l}\left\{\sin\frac{(m-n)\pi x}{l} + \sin\frac{(m+n)\pi x}{l}\right\} dx \;\; = \;\; 0$$

If $m = n$,

$$\int_{-l}^{l} \sin\frac{m\pi x}{l} \cos\frac{n\pi x}{l} \, dx \;\; = \;\; \frac{1}{2}\int_{-l}^{l} \sin\frac{2n\pi x}{l} \, dx \;\; = \;\; 0$$

The results of parts (a) and (b) remain valid even when the limits of integration $-l, l$ are replaced by $c, c + 2l$ respectively.

3. If the series $\;A + \sum_{n=1}^{\infty}\left(a_n \cos\frac{n\pi x}{l} + b_n \sin\frac{n\pi x}{l}\right)\;$ converges uniformly to $f(x)$ in $(-l, l)$, show that for $\;n = 1, 2, 3, \ldots,$

(a) $a_n = \dfrac{1}{l}\displaystyle\int_{-l}^{l} F(x)\cos\frac{n\pi x}{l}\,dx$, (b) $b_n = \dfrac{1}{l}\displaystyle\int_{-l}^{l} F(x)\sin\frac{n\pi x}{l}\,dx$, (c) $A = \dfrac{a_0}{2}$.

(a) Multiplying

$$F(x) \;\; = \;\; A + \sum_{n=1}^{\infty}\left(a_n \cos\frac{n\pi x}{l} + b_n \sin\frac{n\pi x}{l}\right) \tag{1}$$

by $\cos\dfrac{m\pi x}{l}$ and integrating from $-l$ to l, using Problem 2, we have

$$\int_{-l}^{l} F(x)\cos\frac{m\pi x}{l}\,dx \;\; = \;\; A\int_{-l}^{l}\cos\frac{m\pi x}{l}\,dx \tag{2}$$

$$+ \sum_{n=1}^{\infty}\left\{a_n\int_{-l}^{l}\cos\frac{m\pi x}{l}\cos\frac{n\pi x}{l}\,dx + b_n\int_{-l}^{l}\cos\frac{m\pi x}{l}\sin\frac{n\pi x}{l}\,dx\right\}$$

$$= \;\; a_m l \qquad \text{if } m \neq 0$$

Thus $\qquad\quad a_m \;\; = \;\; \dfrac{1}{l}\displaystyle\int_{-l}^{l} F(x)\cos\frac{m\pi x}{l}\,dx \qquad \text{if } m = 1, 2, 3, \ldots$

(b) Multiplying (1) by $\sin\dfrac{m\pi x}{l}$ and integrating from $-l$ to l, using Problem 2, we have

$$\int_{-l}^{l} F(x)\sin\frac{m\pi x}{l}\,dx \;\; = \;\; A\int_{-l}^{l}\sin\frac{m\pi x}{l}\,dx \tag{3}$$

$$+ \sum_{n=1}^{\infty}\left\{a_n\int_{-l}^{l}\sin\frac{m\pi x}{l}\cos\frac{n\pi x}{l}\,dx + b_n\int_{-l}^{l}\sin\frac{m\pi x}{l}\sin\frac{n\pi x}{l}\,dx\right\}$$

$$= \;\; b_m l$$

Thus $\qquad\quad b_m \;\; = \;\; \dfrac{1}{l}\displaystyle\int_{-l}^{l} F(x)\sin\frac{m\pi x}{l}\,dx \qquad \text{if } m = 1, 2, 3, \ldots$

(c) Integration of (1) from $-l$ to l, using Problem 1, gives

$$\int_{-l}^{l} F(x)\,dx \;=\; 2Al \quad\text{or}\quad A \;=\; \frac{1}{2l}\int_{-l}^{l} F(x)\,dx$$

Putting $m=0$ in the result of part (a), we find $\quad a_0 = \frac{1}{l}\int_{-l}^{l} F(x)\,dx \quad$ and so $\quad A = \frac{a_0}{2}$.

The above results also hold when the integration limits $-l, l$ are replaced by $c, c+2l$.

Note that in all parts above, interchange of summation and integration is valid because the series is *assumed* to converge uniformly to $F(x)$ in $(-l, l)$. Even when this assumption is not warranted, the coefficients a_m and b_m as obtained above are called *Fourier coefficients* corresponding to $F(x)$, and the corresponding series with these values of a_m and b_m is called the *Fourier series* corresponding to $F(x)$. An important problem in this case is to investigate conditions under which this series actually converges to $F(x)$. Sufficient conditions for this convergence are the *Dirichlet conditions* established below [see Problems 12-17].

4.   (a) Find the Fourier coefficients corresponding to the function

$$F(x) \;=\; \begin{cases} 0 & -5 < x < 0 \\ 3 & 0 < x < 5 \end{cases} \qquad \text{Period} = 10$$

(b) Write the corresponding Fourier series.

(c) How should $F(x)$ be defined at $x = -5$, $x = 0$ and $x = 5$ in order that the Fourier series will converge to $F(x)$ for $-5 \le x \le 5$?

The graph of $F(x)$ is shown in Fig. 6-4 below.

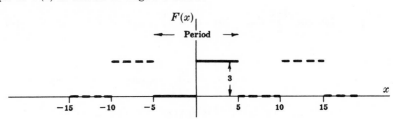

Fig. 6-4

(a) Period $= 2l = 10$ and $l = 5$. Choose the interval c to $c + 2l$ as -5 to 5, so that $c = -5$. Then

$$
\begin{aligned}
a_n &= \frac{1}{l}\int_{c}^{c+2l} F(x)\cos\frac{n\pi x}{l}\,dx \;=\; \frac{1}{5}\int_{-5}^{5} F(x)\cos\frac{n\pi x}{5}\,dx \\
&= \frac{1}{5}\left\{ \int_{-5}^{0}(0)\cos\frac{n\pi x}{5}\,dx + \int_{0}^{5}(3)\cos\frac{n\pi x}{5}\,dx \right\} \;=\; \frac{3}{5}\int_{0}^{5}\cos\frac{n\pi x}{5}\,dx \\
&= \frac{3}{5}\left(\frac{5}{n\pi}\sin\frac{n\pi x}{5}\right)\Big|_{0}^{5} \;=\; 0 \qquad \text{if } n \ne 0
\end{aligned}
$$

If $n = 0$, $\quad a_n = a_0 = \dfrac{3}{5}\displaystyle\int_{0}^{5}\cos\frac{0\pi x}{5}\,dx = \frac{3}{5}\int_{0}^{5}dx = 3.$

$$
\begin{aligned}
b_n &= \frac{1}{l}\int_{c}^{c+2l} F(x)\sin\frac{n\pi x}{l}\,dx \;=\; \frac{1}{5}\int_{-5}^{5} F(x)\sin\frac{n\pi x}{5}\,dx \\
&= \frac{1}{5}\left\{ \int_{-5}^{0}(0)\sin\frac{n\pi x}{5}\,dx + \int_{0}^{5}(3)\sin\frac{n\pi x}{5}\,dx \right\} \;=\; \frac{3}{5}\int_{0}^{5}\sin\frac{n\pi x}{5}\,dx \\
&= \frac{3}{5}\left(-\frac{5}{n\pi}\cos\frac{n\pi x}{5}\right)\Big|_{0}^{5} \;=\; \frac{3(1-\cos n\pi)}{n\pi}
\end{aligned}
$$

(b) The corresponding Fourier series is

$$\frac{a_0}{2} + \sum_{n=1}^{\infty}\left(a_n \cos\frac{n\pi x}{l} + b_n \sin\frac{n\pi x}{l}\right) = \frac{3}{2} + \sum_{n=1}^{\infty}\frac{3(1 - \cos n\pi)}{n\pi}\sin\frac{n\pi x}{5}$$

$$= \frac{3}{2} + \frac{6}{\pi}\left(\sin\frac{\pi x}{5} + \frac{1}{3}\sin\frac{3\pi x}{5} + \frac{1}{5}\sin\frac{5\pi x}{5} + \cdots\right)$$

(c) Since $F(x)$ satisfies the Dirichlet conditions, we can say that the series converges to $F(x)$ at all points of continuity and to $\dfrac{F(x+0) + F(x-0)}{2}$ at points of discontinuity. At $x = -5$, 0 and 5, which are points of discontinuity, the series converges to $(3+0)/2 = 3/2$ as seen from the graph. If we redefine $F(x)$ as follows,

$$F(x) = \begin{cases} 3/2 & x = -5 \\ 0 & -5 < x < 0 \\ 3/2 & x = 0 \\ 3 & 0 < x < 5 \\ 3/2 & x = 5 \end{cases} \qquad \text{Period} = 10$$

then the series will converge to $F(x)$ for $-5 \leqq x \leqq 5$.

5. Expand $F(x) = x^2$, $0 < x < 2\pi$ in a Fourier series if (a) the period is 2π, (b) the period is not specified.

(a) The graph of $F(x)$ with period 2π is shown in Fig. 6-5 below.

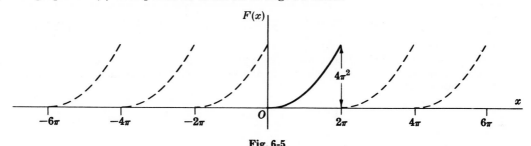

Fig. 6-5

Period $= 2l = 2\pi$ and $l = \pi$. Choosing $c = 0$, we have

$$a_n = \frac{1}{l}\int_{c}^{c+2l} F(x)\cos\frac{n\pi x}{l}\,dx = \frac{1}{\pi}\int_{0}^{2\pi} x^2 \cos nx\,dx$$

$$= \frac{1}{\pi}\left\{(x^2)\left(\frac{\sin nx}{n}\right) - (2x)\left(\frac{-\cos nx}{n^2}\right) + 2\left(\frac{-\sin nx}{n^3}\right)\right\}\Bigg|_{0}^{2\pi} = \frac{4}{n^2}, \qquad n \neq 0$$

If $n = 0$, $\quad a_0 = \dfrac{1}{\pi}\displaystyle\int_{0}^{2\pi} x^2\,dx = \dfrac{8\pi^2}{3}$.

$$b_n = \frac{1}{l}\int_{c}^{c+2l} F(x)\sin\frac{n\pi x}{l}\,dx = \frac{1}{\pi}\int_{0}^{2\pi} x^2 \sin nx\,dx$$

$$= \frac{1}{\pi}\left\{(x^2)\left(-\frac{\cos nx}{n}\right) - (2x)\left(-\frac{\sin nx}{n^2}\right) + (2)\left(\frac{\cos nx}{n^3}\right)\right\}\Bigg|_{0}^{2\pi} = \frac{-4\pi}{n}$$

Then $\quad F(x) = x^2 = \dfrac{4\pi^2}{3} + \displaystyle\sum_{n=1}^{\infty}\left(\frac{4}{n^2}\cos nx - \frac{4\pi}{n}\sin nx\right)$.

This is valid for $0 < x < 2\pi$. At $x = 0$ and $x = 2\pi$ the series converges to $2\pi^2$.

(b) If the period is not specified, the Fourier series cannot be determined uniquely in general.

ODD AND EVEN FUNCTIONS. HALF RANGE FOURIER SINE AND COSINE SERIES

6. If $F(x)$ is even, show that   (a) $a_n = \dfrac{2}{l} \displaystyle\int_0^l F(x) \cos\dfrac{n\pi x}{l}\, dx$,   (b) $b_n = 0$.

(a) $a_n = \dfrac{1}{l} \displaystyle\int_{-l}^l F(x) \cos\dfrac{n\pi x}{l}\, dx = \dfrac{1}{l} \int_{-l}^0 F(x) \cos\dfrac{n\pi x}{l}\, dx + \dfrac{1}{l} \int_0^l F(x) \cos\dfrac{n\pi x}{l}\, dx$

Letting $x = -u$,

$$\frac{1}{l} \int_{-l}^0 F(x) \cos\frac{n\pi x}{l}\, dx = \frac{1}{l} \int_0^l F(-u) \cos\left(\frac{-n\pi u}{l}\right) du = \frac{1}{l} \int_0^l F(u) \cos\frac{n\pi u}{l}\, du$$

since by definition of an even function $f(-u) = f(u)$.   Then

$$a_n = \frac{1}{l} \int_0^l F(u) \cos\frac{n\pi u}{l}\, du + \frac{1}{l} \int_0^l F(x) \cos\frac{n\pi x}{l}\, dx = \frac{2}{l} \int_0^l F(x) \cos\frac{n\pi x}{l}\, dx$$

(b) $b_n = \dfrac{1}{l} \displaystyle\int_{-l}^l F(x) \sin\dfrac{n\pi x}{l}\, dx = \dfrac{1}{l} \int_{-l}^0 F(x) \sin\dfrac{n\pi x}{l}\, dx + \dfrac{1}{l} \int_0^l F(x) \sin\dfrac{n\pi x}{l}\, dx$ (1)

If we make the transformation $x = -u$ in the first integral on the right of (1), we obtain

$$\frac{1}{l} \int_{-l}^0 F(x) \sin\frac{n\pi x}{l}\, dx = \frac{1}{l} \int_0^l F(-u) \sin\left(-\frac{n\pi u}{l}\right) du = -\frac{1}{l} \int_0^l F(-u) \sin\frac{n\pi u}{l}\, du \quad (2)$$

$$= -\frac{1}{l} \int_0^l F(u) \sin\frac{n\pi u}{l}\, du = -\frac{1}{l} \int_0^l F(x) \sin\frac{n\pi x}{l}\, dx$$

where we have used the fact that for an even function $F(-u) = F(u)$ and in the last step that the dummy variable of integration u can be replaced by any other symbol, in particular x. Thus from (1), using (2), we have

$$b_n = -\frac{1}{l} \int_0^l F(x) \sin\frac{n\pi x}{l}\, dx + \frac{1}{l} \int_0^l F(x) \sin\frac{n\pi x}{l}\, dx = 0$$

7. Expand $F(x) = x$, $0 < x < 2$,   in a half range (a) sine series, (b) cosine series.

(a) Extend the definition of the given function to that of the odd function of period 4 shown in Fig. 6-6 below. This is sometimes called the *odd extension* of $F(x)$. Then $2l = 4$, $l = 2$.

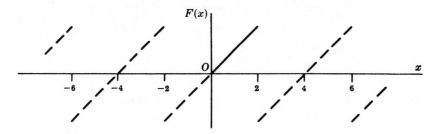

Fig. 6-6

Thus $a_n = 0$ and

$$b_n = \frac{2}{l} \int_0^l F(x) \sin\frac{n\pi x}{l}\, dx = \frac{2}{2} \int_0^2 x \sin\frac{n\pi x}{2}\, dx$$

$$= \left\{ (x)\left(\frac{-2}{n\pi} \cos\frac{n\pi x}{2}\right) - (1)\left(\frac{-4}{n^2\pi^2} \sin\frac{n\pi x}{2}\right) \right\}\Bigg|_0^2 = \frac{-4}{n\pi} \cos n\pi$$

Then $\qquad F(x) \quad = \quad \sum_{n=1}^{\infty} \dfrac{-4}{n\pi} \cos n\pi \, \sin \dfrac{n\pi x}{2}$

$$= \quad \frac{4}{\pi} \left(\sin \frac{\pi x}{2} - \frac{1}{2} \sin \frac{2\pi x}{2} + \frac{1}{3} \sin \frac{3\pi x}{2} - \cdots \right)$$

(*b*) Extend the definition of $F(x)$ to that of the even function of period 4 shown in Fig. 6-7 below. This is the *even extension* of $F(x)$. Then $2l = 4$, $l = 2$.

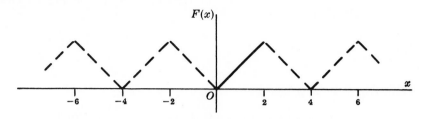

Fig. 6-7

Thus $b_n = 0$,

$$a_n \quad = \quad \frac{2}{l} \int_0^l F(x) \cos \frac{n\pi x}{l} \, dx \quad = \quad \frac{2}{2} \int_0^2 x \cos \frac{n\pi x}{2} \, dx$$

$$= \quad \left\{ (x) \left(\frac{2}{n\pi} \sin \frac{n\pi x}{2} \right) - (1) \left(\frac{-4}{n^2\pi^2} \cos \frac{n\pi x}{2} \right) \right\} \Big|_0^2$$

$$= \quad \frac{4}{n^2\pi^2} (\cos n\pi - 1) \qquad \text{if } n \neq 0$$

If $n = 0$, $a_0 = \int_0^2 x \, dx = 2.$

Then $\qquad F(x) \quad = \quad 1 + \sum_{n=1}^{\infty} \dfrac{4}{n^2\pi^2} (\cos n\pi - 1) \cos \dfrac{n\pi x}{2}$

$$= \quad 1 - \frac{8}{\pi^2} \left(\cos \frac{\pi x}{2} + \frac{1}{3^2} \cos \frac{3\pi x}{2} + \frac{1}{5^2} \cos \frac{5\pi x}{2} + \cdots \right)$$

It should be noted that the given function $F(x) = x$, $0 < x < 2$, is represented *equally well* by the two *different* series in (*a*) and (*b*).

PARSEVAL'S IDENTITY FOR FOURIER SERIES

8. Assuming that the Fourier series corresponding to $F(x)$ converges uniformly to $f(x)$ in $(-l, l)$, prove Parseval's identity

$$\frac{1}{l} \int_{-l}^{l} \{F(x)\}^2 \, dx \quad = \quad \frac{a_0^2}{2} + \sum (a_n^2 + b_n^2)$$

where the integral is assumed to exist.

If $F(x) = \dfrac{a_0}{2} + \sum_{n=1}^{\infty} \left(a_n \cos \dfrac{n\pi x}{l} + b_n \sin \dfrac{n\pi x}{l} \right)$, then multiplying by $F(x)$ and integrating term by term from $-l$ to l (which is justified since the series is uniformly convergent) we obtain

$$\int_{-l}^{l} \{F(x)\}^2 \, dx \quad = \quad \frac{a_0}{2} \int_{-l}^{l} F(x) \, dx + \sum_{n=1}^{\infty} \left\{ a_n \int_{-l}^{l} F(x) \cos \frac{n\pi x}{l} \, dx + b_n \int_{-l}^{l} F(x) \sin \frac{n\pi x}{l} \, dx \right\}$$

$$= \quad \frac{a_0^2}{2} l + l \sum_{n=1}^{\infty} (a_n^2 + b_n^2) \qquad\qquad\qquad (1)$$

where we have used the results

$$\int_{-l}^{l} F(x) \cos \frac{n\pi x}{l} dx = la_n, \qquad \int_{-l}^{l} F(x) \sin \frac{n\pi x}{l} dx = lb_n, \qquad \int_{-l}^{l} F(x) dx = la_0 \qquad (2)$$

obtained from the Fourier coefficients.

The required result follows on dividing both sides of (1) by l. Parseval's identity is valid under less restrictive conditions than that imposed here.

FINITE FOURIER TRANSFORMS

9. Establish (a) equation (9) and (b) equation (11) on Page 175.

(a) If $F(x)$ is an odd function in $(-l, l)$, then

$$F(x) = \sum_{n=1}^{\infty} b_n \sin \frac{n\pi x}{l} \qquad (1)$$

where

$$b_n = \frac{2}{l} \int_0^l F(x) \sin \frac{n\pi x}{l} dx \qquad (2)$$

Thus if we write

$$\int_0^l F(x) \sin \frac{n\pi x}{l} dx = f_s(n)$$

then $b_n = \frac{2}{l} f_s(n)$ and (1) can be written, as required,

$$F(x) = \frac{2}{l} \sum_{n=1}^{\infty} f_s(n) \sin \frac{n\pi x}{l} \qquad (3)$$

We can also write $F(x) = \mathcal{F}_s^{-1}\{f_s(n)\}$.

(b) If $F(x)$ is an even function in $(-l, l)$, then

$$F(x) = \frac{a_0}{2} + \sum_{n=1}^{\infty} a_n \cos \frac{n\pi x}{l} \qquad (4)$$

where

$$a_n = \frac{2}{l} \int_0^l F(x) \cos \frac{n\pi x}{l} dx \qquad (5)$$

Thus if we write

$$\int_0^l F(x) \cos \frac{n\pi x}{l} dx = f_c(n)$$

then $a_0 = \frac{2}{l} f_c(0)$ and (4) can be written, as required,

$$F(x) = \frac{1}{l} f_c(0) + \frac{2}{l} \sum_{n=1}^{\infty} f_c(n) \cos \frac{n\pi x}{l} \qquad (6)$$

We can also write $F(x) = \mathcal{F}_c^{-1}\{f_c(n)\}$.

10. Find the (a) finite Fourier sine transform and (b) finite Fourier cosine transform of the function $F(x) = 2x$, $0 < x < 4$.

(a) Since $l = 4$, we have

$$f_s(n) = \int_0^l F(x) \sin \frac{n\pi x}{l}\, dx = \int_0^4 2x \sin \frac{n\pi x}{4}\, dx$$

$$= \left\{ (2x)\left(\frac{-\cos n\pi x/4}{n\pi/4} \right) - (2)\left(\frac{-\sin n\pi x/4}{n^2\pi^2/16} \right) \right\}\Big|_0^4 = -\frac{32}{n\pi}\cos n\pi$$

(b) If $n > 0$, $\quad f_c(n) = \int_0^l F(x) \cos \frac{n\pi x}{l}\, dx = \int_0^4 2x \cos \frac{n\pi x}{4}\, dx$

$$= \left\{ (2x)\left(\frac{\sin n\pi x/4}{n\pi/4} \right) - (2)\left(\frac{-\cos n\pi x/4}{n^2\pi^2/16} \right) \right\}\Big|_0^4 = 32\left(\frac{\cos n\pi - 1}{n^2\pi^2} \right)$$

If $n = 0$, $\qquad f_c(n) = f_c(0) = \int_0^4 2x\, dx = 16$

11. Find $F(x)$ if: (a) $\mathcal{F}_s\{F(x)\} = 16(-1)^{n-1}/n^3$, $n = 1, 2, 3, \ldots$, where $0 < x < 8$; (b) $\mathcal{F}_c\{F(x)\} = \sin(n\pi/2)/2n$, $n = 1, 2, 3, \ldots$ and $\pi/4$ if $n = 0$, where $0 < x < 2\pi$.

(a) From equation (3) of Problem 9(a) with $l = 8$, we have

$$F(x) = \mathcal{F}_s^{-1}\left\{ \frac{16(-1)^{n-1}}{n^3} \right\}$$

$$= \frac{2}{8} \sum_{n=1}^{\infty} \frac{16(-1)^{n-1}}{n^3} \sin \frac{n\pi x}{8} = 4 \sum_{n=1}^{\infty} \frac{(-1)^{n-1}}{n^3} \sin \frac{n\pi x}{8}$$

(b) From equation (6) of Problem 9(b) with $l = 2\pi$, we have

$$F(x) = \mathcal{F}_c^{-1}\left\{ \frac{\sin(n\pi/2)}{2n} \right\}$$

$$= \frac{1}{\pi}\cdot\frac{\pi}{4} + \frac{2}{2\pi} \sum_{n=1}^{\infty} \frac{\sin(n\pi/2)}{2n} = \frac{1}{4} + \frac{1}{2\pi} \sum_{n=1}^{\infty} \frac{\sin(n\pi/2)}{n}$$

CONVERGENCE OF FOURIER SERIES

12. Prove that (a) $\dfrac{1}{2} + \cos t + \cos 2t + \cdots + \cos Mt = \dfrac{\sin(M + \frac{1}{2})t}{2\sin\frac{1}{2}t}$

(b) $\dfrac{1}{\pi} \displaystyle\int_0^{\pi} \dfrac{\sin(M + \frac{1}{2})t}{2\sin\frac{1}{2}t}\, dt = \dfrac{1}{2}$, $\quad \dfrac{1}{\pi} \displaystyle\int_{-\pi}^0 \dfrac{\sin(M + \frac{1}{2})t}{2\sin\frac{1}{2}t}\, dt = \dfrac{1}{2}$.

(a) We have $\cos nt \sin\frac{1}{2}t = \frac{1}{2}\{\sin(n+\frac{1}{2})t - \sin(n-\frac{1}{2})t\}$.

Then summing from $n = 1$ to M,

$$\sin\tfrac{1}{2}t\{\cos t + \cos 2t + \cdots + \cos Mt\} = (\sin\tfrac{3}{2}t - \sin\tfrac{1}{2}t) + (\sin\tfrac{5}{2}t - \sin\tfrac{3}{2}t)$$

$$+ \cdots + \{\sin(M+\tfrac{1}{2})t - \sin(M-\tfrac{1}{2})t\}$$

$$= \tfrac{1}{2}\{\sin(M+\tfrac{1}{2})t - \sin\tfrac{1}{2}t\}$$

On dividing by $\sin\frac{1}{2}t$ and adding $\frac{1}{2}$, the required result follows.

(b) Integrate the result in (a) from $-\pi$ to 0 and 0 to π respectively. This gives the required results, since the integrals of all the cosine terms are zero.

13. Prove that $\lim\limits_{n\to\infty} \int_{-\pi}^{\pi} F(x) \sin nx\, dx \;=\; \lim\limits_{n\to\infty} \int_{-\pi}^{\pi} F(x) \cos nx\, dx \;=\; 0$ if $F(x)$ is sectionally continuous.

This follows at once from Problem 8 with $l=\pi$, since if the series $\dfrac{a_0^2}{2} + \sum\limits_{n=1}^{\infty} (a_n^2 + b_n^2)$ is convergent, $\lim\limits_{n\to\infty} a_n = \lim\limits_{n\to\infty} b_n = 0$.

The result is sometimes called *Riemann's theorem*.

14. Prove that $\lim\limits_{M\to\infty} \int_{-\pi}^{\pi} F(x) \sin(M+\tfrac{1}{2})x\, dx \;=\; 0$ if $F(x)$ is sectionally continuous.

We have

$$\int_{-\pi}^{\pi} F(x) \sin(M+\tfrac{1}{2})x\, dx \;=\; \int_{-\pi}^{\pi} \{F(x) \sin\tfrac{1}{2}x\} \cos Mx\, dx \;+\; \int_{-\pi}^{\pi} \{F(x) \cos\tfrac{1}{2}x\} \sin Mx\, dx$$

Then the required result follows at once by using the result of Problem 13, with $F(x)$ replaced by $F(x) \sin\tfrac{1}{2}x$ and $F(x) \cos\tfrac{1}{2}x$ respectively which are sectionally continuous if $F(x)$ is.

The result can also be proved when the integration limits are a and b instead of $-\pi$ and π.

15. Assuming that $l=\pi$, i.e. that the Fourier series corresponding to $F(x)$ has period $2l=2\pi$, show that

$$S_M(x) \;=\; \frac{a_0}{2} + \sum_{n=1}^{M} (a_n \cos nx + b_n \sin nx) \;=\; \frac{1}{\pi} \int_{-\pi}^{\pi} F(t+x) \frac{\sin(M+\tfrac{1}{2})t}{2 \sin\tfrac{1}{2}t}\, dt$$

Using the formulas for the Fourier coefficients with $l=\pi$, we have

$$a_n \cos nx + b_n \sin nx \;=\; \left(\frac{1}{\pi} \int_{-\pi}^{\pi} F(u) \cos nu\, du\right) \cos nx \;+\; \left(\frac{1}{\pi} \int_{-\pi}^{\pi} F(u) \sin nu\, du\right) \sin nx$$

$$=\; \frac{1}{\pi} \int_{-\pi}^{\pi} F(u) (\cos nu \cos nx + \sin nu \sin nx)\, du$$

$$=\; \frac{1}{\pi} \int_{-\pi}^{\pi} F(u) \cos n(u-x)\, du$$

Also,
$$\frac{a_0}{2} \;=\; \frac{1}{2\pi} \int_{-\pi}^{\pi} F(u)\, du$$

Then
$$S_M(x) \;=\; \frac{a_0}{2} + \sum_{n=1}^{M} (a_n \cos nx + b_n \sin nx)$$

$$=\; \frac{1}{2\pi} \int_{-\pi}^{\pi} F(u)\, du \;+\; \frac{1}{\pi} \sum_{n=1}^{M} \int_{-\pi}^{\pi} F(u) \cos n(u-x)\, du$$

$$=\; \frac{1}{\pi} \int_{-\pi}^{\pi} F(u) \left\{ \frac{1}{2} \;+\; \sum_{n=1}^{M} \cos n(u-x) \right\} du$$

$$=\; \frac{1}{\pi} \int_{-\pi}^{\pi} F(u) \frac{\sin(M+\tfrac{1}{2})(u-x)}{2 \sin\tfrac{1}{2}(u-x)}\, du$$

using Problem 12. Letting $u-x=t$, we have

$$S_M(x) \;=\; \frac{1}{\pi} \int_{-\pi-x}^{\pi-x} F(t+x) \frac{\sin(M+\tfrac{1}{2})t}{2 \sin\tfrac{1}{2}t}\, dt$$

Since the integrand has period 2π, we can replace the interval $-\pi-x,\; \pi-x$ by any other interval of length 2π, in particular $-\pi, \pi$. Thus we obtain the required result.

16. Prove that

$$S_M(x) - \left(\frac{F(x+0) + F(x-0)}{2}\right) = \frac{1}{\pi} \int_{-\pi}^{0} \left(\frac{F(t+x) - F(x-0)}{2 \sin \frac{1}{2}t}\right) \sin (M + \tfrac{1}{2})t \, dt$$

$$+ \frac{1}{\pi} \int_{0}^{\pi} \left(\frac{F(t+x) - F(x+0)}{2 \sin \frac{1}{2}t}\right) \sin (M + \tfrac{1}{2})t \, dt$$

From Problem 12,

$$S_M(x) = \frac{1}{\pi} \int_{-\pi}^{0} F(t+x) \frac{\sin (M + \frac{1}{2})t}{2 \sin \frac{1}{2}t} \, dt + \frac{1}{\pi} \int_{0}^{\pi} F(t+x) \frac{\sin (M + \frac{1}{2})t}{2 \sin \frac{1}{2}t} \, dt \qquad (1)$$

Multiplying the integrals of Problem 12(b) by $F(x-0)$ and $F(x+0)$ respectively,

$$\frac{F(x+0) + F(x-0)}{2} = \frac{1}{\pi} \int_{-\pi}^{0} F(x-0) \frac{\sin (M + \frac{1}{2})t}{2 \sin \frac{1}{2}t} \, dt + \frac{1}{\pi} \int_{0}^{\pi} F(x+0) \frac{\sin (M + \frac{1}{2})t}{2 \sin \frac{1}{2}t} \, dt \qquad (2)$$

Subtracting (2) from (1) yields the required result.

17. If $F(x)$ and $F'(x)$ are sectionally continuous in $(-\pi, \pi)$, prove that

$$\lim_{M \to \infty} S_M(x) = \frac{F(x+0) + F(x-0)}{2}$$

The function $\dfrac{F(t+x) - F(x+0)}{2 \sin \frac{1}{2}t}$ is sectionally continuous in $0 < t \leqq \pi$ because $F(x)$ is sectionally continuous.

Also,

$$\lim_{t \to 0+} \frac{F(t+x) - F(x+0)}{2 \sin \frac{1}{2}t} = \lim_{t \to 0+} \frac{F(t+x) - F(x+0)}{t} \cdot \frac{t}{2 \sin \frac{1}{2}t} = \lim_{t \to 0+} \frac{F(t+x) - F(x+0)}{t}$$

exists, since by hypothesis $F'(x)$ is sectionally continuous so that the right hand derivative of $F(x)$ at each x exists.

Thus $\dfrac{F(t+x) - F(x+0)}{2 \sin \frac{1}{2}t}$ is sectionally continuous in $0 \leqq t \leqq \pi$.

Similarly, $\dfrac{F(t+x) - F(x+0)}{2 \sin \frac{1}{2}t}$ is sectionally continuous in $-\pi \leqq t \leqq 0$.

Then from Problems 14 and 16, we have

$$\lim_{M \to \infty} S_M(x) - \left\{\frac{F(x+0) + F(x-0)}{2}\right\} = 0 \qquad \text{or} \qquad \lim_{M \to \infty} S_M(x) = \frac{F(x+0) + F(x-0)}{2}$$

THE FOURIER INTEGRAL AND FOURIER TRANSFORMS

18. (a) Find the Fourier transform of $F(x) = \begin{cases} 1 & |x| < a \\ 0 & |x| > a \end{cases}$.

(b) Graph $F(x)$ and its Fourier transform for $a = 1$.

(a) The Fourier transform of $F(x)$ is

$$f(\lambda) = \int_{-\infty}^{\infty} F(u) \, e^{-i\lambda u} \, du = \int_{-a}^{a} (1) \, e^{-i\lambda u} \, du = \frac{e^{-i\lambda u}}{-i\lambda}\Big|_{-a}^{a}$$

$$= \left(\frac{e^{i\lambda a} - e^{-i\lambda a}}{i\lambda}\right) = 2\frac{\sin \lambda a}{\lambda}, \qquad \lambda \neq 0$$

For $\lambda = 0$, we obtain $f(\lambda) = 2a$.

(b) The graphs of $F(x)$ and $f(\lambda)$ for $a = 1$ are shown in Figures 6-8 and 6-9 respectively.

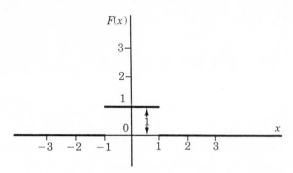

Fig. 6-8

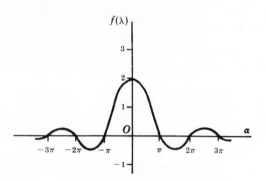

Fig. 6-9

19. (a) Use the result of Problem 18 to evaluate $\displaystyle\int_{-\infty}^{\infty} \frac{\sin \lambda a \cos \lambda x}{\lambda}\, d\lambda.$

(b) Deduce the value of $\displaystyle\int_{0}^{\infty} \frac{\sin u}{u}\, du.$

(a) From Fourier's integral theorem, if

$$f(\lambda) = \int_{-\infty}^{\infty} F(u)\, e^{-i\lambda u}\, du \qquad \text{then} \qquad F(x) = \frac{1}{2\pi} \int_{-\infty}^{\infty} f(\lambda)\, e^{i\lambda x}\, d\lambda$$

Then from Problem 18,

$$\frac{1}{2\pi} \int_{-\infty}^{\infty} 2\frac{\sin \lambda a}{\lambda}\, e^{i\lambda x}\, d\alpha = \begin{cases} 1 & |x| < a \\ 1/2 & |x| = a \\ 0 & |x| > a \end{cases} \tag{1}$$

The left side of (1) is equal to

$$\frac{1}{\pi} \int_{-\infty}^{\infty} \frac{\sin \lambda a \cos \lambda x}{\lambda}\, d\alpha \;+\; \frac{i}{\pi} \int_{-\infty}^{\infty} \frac{\sin \lambda a \sin \lambda x}{\lambda}\, d\lambda \tag{2}$$

The integrand in the second integral of (2) is odd and so the integral is zero. Then from (1) and (2), we have

$$\int_{-\infty}^{\infty} \frac{\sin \lambda a \cos \lambda x}{\lambda}\, d\lambda = \begin{cases} \pi & |x| < a \\ \pi/2 & |x| = a \\ 0 & |x| > a \end{cases} \tag{3}$$

(b) If $x = 0$ and $a = 1$ in the result of (a), we have

$$\int_{-\infty}^{\infty} \frac{\sin \lambda}{\lambda}\, d\lambda = \pi \qquad \text{or} \qquad \int_{0}^{\infty} \frac{\sin \lambda}{\lambda}\, d\lambda = \frac{\pi}{2}$$

since the integrand is even.

20. If $F(x)$ is an even function show that:

(a) $f(\lambda) = 2 \displaystyle\int_{0}^{\infty} F(u) \cos \lambda u\, du,$ (b) $F(x) = \dfrac{1}{\pi} \displaystyle\int_{0}^{\infty} f(\lambda) \cos \lambda x\, d\lambda.$

We have

$$f(\lambda) = \int_{-\infty}^{\infty} F(u)\, e^{-i\lambda u}\, du = \int_{-\infty}^{\infty} F(u) \cos \lambda u\, du - i \int_{-\infty}^{\infty} F(u) \sin \lambda u\, du \tag{1}$$

(a) If $F(u)$ is even, $F(u) \cos \lambda u$ is even and $F(u) \sin \lambda u$ is odd. Then the second integral on the right of (1) is zero and the result can be written

$$f(\lambda) = 2 \int_0^\infty F(u) \cos \lambda u \, du$$

(b) From (a), $f(-\lambda) = f(\lambda)$ so that $f(\lambda)$ is an even function. Then by using a proof exactly analogous to that in (a), the required result follows.

A similar result holds for odd functions and can be obtained by replacing the cosine by the sine.

PARSEVAL'S IDENTITY FOR FOURIER INTEGRALS

21. Verify Parseval's identity for Fourier integrals for the Fourier transforms of Prob. 18.

We must show that

$$\int_{-\infty}^\infty \{F(x)\}^2 \, dx = \frac{1}{2\pi} \int_{-\infty}^\infty \{f(\lambda)\}^2 \, d\lambda$$

where $F(x) = \begin{cases} 1 & |x| < a \\ 0 & |x| > a \end{cases}$ and $f(\lambda) = 2 \dfrac{\sin \lambda a}{\lambda}$.

This is equivalent to

$$\int_{-a}^a (1)^2 \, dx = \frac{1}{2\pi} \int_{-\infty}^\infty \frac{4 \sin^2 \lambda a}{\lambda^2} \, d\lambda$$

or

$$\int_{-\infty}^\infty \frac{\sin^2 \lambda a}{\lambda^2} \, d\lambda = 2 \int_0^\infty \frac{\sin^2 \lambda a}{\lambda^2} \, d\lambda = \pi a$$

i.e.,

$$\int_0^\infty \frac{\sin^2 \lambda a}{\lambda^2} \, d\alpha = \frac{\pi a}{2}$$

By letting $\lambda a = u$ and using Problem 111, Page 171, it is seen that this is correct. The method can also be used to find $\int_0^\infty \dfrac{\sin^2 u}{u^2} \, du$ directly.

PROOF OF THE FOURIER INTEGRAL THEOREM

22. Present a heuristic demonstration of Fourier's integral theorem by use of a limiting form of Fourier series.

Let

$$F(x) = \frac{a_0}{2} + \sum_{n=1}^\infty \left(a_n \cos \frac{n\pi x}{l} + b_n \sin \frac{n\pi x}{l} \right) \tag{1}$$

where $a_n = \dfrac{1}{l} \int_{-l}^l F(u) \cos \dfrac{n\pi u}{l} \, du$ and $b_n = \dfrac{1}{l} \int_{-l}^l F(u) \sin \dfrac{n\pi u}{l} \, du$.

Then by substitution (see Problem 15),

$$F(x) = \frac{1}{2l} \int_{-l}^l F(u) \, du + \frac{1}{l} \sum_{n=1}^\infty \int_{-l}^l F(u) \cos \frac{n\pi}{l} (u - x) \, du \tag{2}$$

If we assume that $\int_{-\infty}^\infty |F(u)| \, du$ converges, the first term on the right of (2) approaches zero as $l \to \infty$, while the remaining part appears to approach

$$\lim_{l \to \infty} \frac{1}{l} \sum_{n=1}^\infty \int_{-\infty}^\infty F(u) \cos \frac{n\pi}{l} (u - x) \, du \tag{3}$$

This last step is not rigorous and makes the demonstration heuristic.

Calling $\Delta\lambda = \pi/l$, (3) can be written

$$F(x) \;=\; \lim_{\Delta\lambda \to 0} \sum_{n=1}^{\infty} \Delta\lambda \; f(n\,\Delta\lambda) \tag{4}$$

where we have written

$$f(\lambda) \;=\; \frac{1}{\pi} \int_{-\infty}^{\infty} F(u) \cos\lambda(u-x)\,du \tag{5}$$

But the limit (4) is equal to

$$F(x) \;=\; \int_0^{\infty} f(\lambda)\,d\lambda \;=\; \frac{1}{\pi}\int_0^{\infty} d\lambda \int_{-\infty}^{\infty} F(u)\cos\lambda(u-x)\,du$$

which is Fourier's integral formula.

This demonstration serves only to provide a possible result. To be rigorous, we start with the integral

$$\frac{1}{\pi}\int_0^{\infty} d\lambda \int_{-\infty}^{\infty} F(u)\cos\lambda(u-x)\,dx$$

and examine the convergence. This method is considered in Problems 23-26.

23. Prove that: (a) $\displaystyle\lim_{\lambda\to\infty}\int_0^l \frac{\sin\lambda v}{v}\,dv = \frac{\pi}{2}$, (b) $\displaystyle\lim_{\lambda\to\infty}\int_{-l}^0 \frac{\sin\lambda v}{v}\,dv = \frac{\pi}{2}$.

(a) Let $\lambda v = y$. Then $\displaystyle\lim_{\lambda\to\infty}\int_0^l \frac{\sin\lambda v}{v}\,dv = \lim_{\lambda\to\infty}\int_0^{\lambda l}\frac{\sin y}{y}\,dy = \int_0^{\infty}\frac{\sin y}{y}\,dy = \frac{\pi}{2}$ by Problem 43, Page 164.

(b) Let $\lambda v = -y$. Then $\displaystyle\lim_{\lambda\to\infty}\int_{-l}^0 \frac{\sin\lambda v}{v}\,dv = \lim_{\lambda\to\infty}\int_0^{\lambda l}\frac{\sin y}{y}\,dy = \frac{\pi}{2}$.

24. Riemann's theorem states that if $G(x)$ is sectionally continuous in (a,b), then

$$\lim_{\lambda\to\infty}\int_a^b G(x)\sin\lambda x\,dx \;=\; 0$$

with a similar result for the cosine (see Problem 81). Use this to prove that

$$(a)\quad \lim_{\lambda\to\infty}\int_0^l F(x+v)\frac{\sin\lambda v}{v}\,dv \;=\; \frac{\pi}{2}F(x+0)$$

$$(b)\quad \lim_{\lambda\to\infty}\int_{-l}^0 F(x+v)\frac{\sin\lambda v}{v}\,dv \;=\; \frac{\pi}{2}F(x-0)$$

where $F(x)$ and $F'(x)$ are assumed sectionally continuous in $(0,l)$ and $(-l,0)$ respectively.

(a) Using Problem 23(a), it is seen that a proof of the given result amounts to proving that

$$\lim_{\lambda\to\infty}\int_0^l \{F(x+v) - F(x+0)\}\frac{\sin\lambda v}{v}\,dv \;=\; 0$$

This follows at once from Riemann's theorem, because $G(v) = \dfrac{F(x+v) - F(x+0)}{v}$ is sectionally continuous in $(0,l)$ since $\displaystyle\lim_{v\to 0+} F(v)$ exists and $f(x)$ is sectionally continuous.

(b) A proof of this is analogous to that in part (a) if we make use of Problem 23(b).

25. If $F(x)$ satisfies the additional condition that $\displaystyle\int_{-\infty}^{\infty} |F(x)|\, dx$ converges, prove that

$(a)\ \displaystyle\lim_{\alpha \to \infty} \int_0^{\infty} F(x+v)\frac{\sin \lambda v}{v}\, dv \;=\; \frac{\pi}{2}F(x+0),\ (b)\ \lim_{\alpha \to \infty} \int_{-\infty}^{0} F(x+v)\frac{\sin \lambda v}{v}\, dv \;=\; \frac{\pi}{2}F(x-0).$

We have

$$\int_0^{\infty} F(x+v)\,\frac{\sin \lambda v}{v}\, dv \;=\; \int_0^{l} F(x+v)\,\frac{\sin \lambda v}{v}\, dv \;+\; \int_l^{\infty} F(x+v)\,\frac{\sin \lambda v}{v}\, dv \qquad (1)$$

$$\int_0^{\infty} F(x+0)\,\frac{\sin \lambda v}{v}\, dv \;=\; \int_0^{l} F(x+0)\,\frac{\sin \lambda v}{v}\, dv \;+\; \int_l^{\infty} F(x+0)\,\frac{\sin \lambda v}{v}\, dv \qquad (2)$$

Subtracting,

$$\int_0^{\infty} \{F(x+v) - F(x+0)\}\frac{\sin \lambda v}{v}\, dv \qquad (3)$$

$$=\; \int_0^{l} \{F(x+v) - f(x+0)\}\frac{\sin \lambda v}{v}\, dv \;+\; \int_l^{\infty} F(x+v)\frac{\sin \lambda v}{v}\, dv \;-\; \int_l^{\infty} F(x+0)\frac{\sin \lambda v}{v}\, dv$$

Denoting the integrals in (3) by I, I_1, I_2 and I_3 respectively, we have $I = I_1 + I_2 + I_3$ so that

$$|I| \;\leqq\; |I_1| \;+\; |I_2| \;+\; |I_3| \qquad (4)$$

Now $$|I_2| \;\leqq\; \int_l^{\infty} \left| F(x+v)\frac{\sin \lambda v}{v}\right|\, dv \;\leqq\; \frac{1}{l}\int_l^{\infty} |F(x+v)|\, dv$$

Also $$|I_3| \;\leqq\; |F(x+0)| \left| \int_l^{\infty} \frac{\sin \lambda v}{v}\, dv\right|$$

Since $\displaystyle\int_0^{\infty} |F(x)|\, dx$ and $\displaystyle\int_0^{\infty} \frac{\sin \lambda v}{v}\, dv$ both converge, we can choose l so large that $|I_2| \leqq \epsilon/3$, $|I_3| \leqq \epsilon/3$. Also, we can choose λ so large that $|I_1| \leqq \epsilon/3$. Then from (4) we have $|I| < \epsilon$ for λ and l sufficiently large, so that the required result follows.

This result follows by reasoning exactly analogous to that in part (a).

26. Prove Fourier's integral formula where $F(x)$ satisfies the conditions stated on Page 175.

We must prove that $\displaystyle\lim_{l \to \infty} \frac{1}{\pi} \int_{\lambda=0}^{l} \int_{u=-\infty}^{\infty} F(u)\cos \lambda(x-u)\, du\, d\lambda \;=\; \frac{F(x+0) + F(x-0)}{2}$

Since $\displaystyle\left| \int_{-\infty}^{\infty} F(u)\cos \lambda(x-u)\, du \right| \leqq \int_{-\infty}^{\infty} |F(u)|\, du$ which converges, it follows by the Weierstrass test for integrals that $\displaystyle\int_{-\infty}^{\infty} F(u)\cos \lambda(x-u)\, du$ converges absolutely and uniformly for all λ. Thus we can reverse the order of integration to obtain

$$\frac{1}{\pi} \int_{\lambda=0}^{l} d\lambda \int_{u=-\infty}^{\infty} F(u)\cos \lambda(x-u)\, du \;=\; \frac{1}{\pi} \int_{u=-\infty}^{\infty} F(u)\, du \int_{\lambda=0}^{l} \cos \lambda(x-u)\, du$$

$$=\; \frac{1}{\pi} \int_{u=-\infty}^{\infty} F(u)\frac{\sin l(u-x)}{u-x}\, du$$

$$=\; \frac{1}{\pi} \int_{v=-\infty}^{\infty} F(x+v)\frac{\sin lv}{v}\, dv$$

$$=\; \frac{1}{\pi} \int_{-\infty}^{0} F(x+v)\frac{\sin lv}{v}\, dv \;+\; \frac{1}{\pi} \int_0^{\infty} F(x+v)\frac{\sin lv}{v}\, dv$$

where we have let $u = x + v$.

Letting $l \to \infty$, we see by Problem 24 that the given integral converges to $\dfrac{F(x+0) + F(x-0)}{2}$ as required.

MISCELLANEOUS PROBLEMS

27. Expand $F(x) = \sin x$, $0 < x < \pi$, in a Fourier cosine series.

A Fourier series consisting of cosine terms alone is obtained only for an even function. Hence we extend the definition of $F(x)$ so that it becomes even (dashed part of Fig. 6-10 below). With this extension, $F(x)$ is then defined in an interval of length 2π. Taking the period as 2π, we have $2l = 2\pi$ so that $l = \pi$.

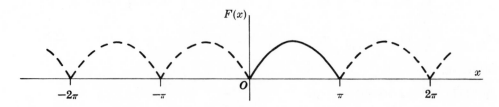

$$F(x)$$

$$-2\pi \qquad -\pi \qquad O \qquad \pi \qquad 2\pi \qquad x$$

Fig. 6-10

By Problem 6, $b_n = 0$ and

$$a_n = \frac{2}{l}\int_0^l F(x)\cos\frac{n\pi x}{l}\,dx = \frac{2}{\pi}\int_0^\pi \sin x \cos nx\,dx$$

$$= \frac{1}{\pi}\int_0^\pi \{\sin(x+nx) + \sin(x-nx)\}\,dx = \frac{1}{\pi}\left\{-\frac{\cos(n+1)x}{n+1} + \frac{\cos(n-1)x}{n-1}\right\}\Big|_0^\pi$$

$$= \frac{1}{\pi}\left\{\frac{1-\cos(n+1)\pi}{n+1} + \frac{\cos(n-1)\pi-1}{n-1}\right\} = \frac{1}{\pi}\left\{\frac{1+\cos n\pi}{n+1} - \frac{1+\cos n\pi}{n-1}\right\}$$

$$= \frac{-2(1+\cos n\pi)}{\pi(n^2-1)} \qquad \text{if } n \neq 1.$$

For $n = 1$, $\quad a_1 = \frac{2}{\pi}\int_0^\pi \sin x \cos x\,dx = \frac{2}{\pi}\frac{\sin^2 x}{2}\Big|_0^\pi = 0.$

For $n = 0$, $\quad a_0 = \frac{2}{\pi}\int_0^\pi \sin x\,dx = \frac{2}{\pi}(-\cos x)\Big|_0^\pi = \frac{4}{\pi}.$

Then $\quad\quad F(x) = \frac{2}{\pi} - \frac{2}{\pi}\sum_{n=2}^\infty \frac{(1+\cos n\pi)}{n^2-1}\cos nx$

$$= \frac{2}{\pi} - \frac{4}{\pi}\left(\frac{\cos 2x}{2^2-1} + \frac{\cos 4x}{4^2-1} + \frac{\cos 6x}{6^2-1} + \cdots\right)$$

28. Show that $\displaystyle\int_0^\infty \frac{\cos\lambda x}{\lambda^2+1}\,d\lambda = \frac{\pi}{2}e^{-x}$, $x \geqq 0$.

Let $F(x) = e^{-x}$ in the Fourier integral theorem

$$F(x) = \frac{2}{\pi}\int_0^\infty \cos\lambda x\,d\lambda \int_0^\infty F(u)\cos\lambda u\,du$$

Then $\quad\quad \frac{2}{\pi}\int_0^\infty \cos\lambda x\,d\lambda \int_0^\infty e^{-u}\cos\lambda u\,du = e^{-x}$

Since $\quad\displaystyle\int_0^\infty e^{-u}\cos\lambda u\,du = \frac{1}{\lambda^2+1}$, we have

$$\frac{2}{\pi}\int_0^\infty \frac{\cos\lambda x}{\lambda^2+1}\,d\lambda = e^{-x} \qquad \text{or} \qquad \int_0^\infty \frac{\cos\lambda x}{\lambda^2+1}\,d\lambda = \frac{\pi}{2}e^{-x}$$

29. Solve the integral equation $\displaystyle\int_0^\infty F(x)\cos\lambda x\,dx = \begin{cases} 1-\lambda & 0 \le \lambda \le 1 \\ 0 & \lambda > 1 \end{cases}$.

Let $\displaystyle\int_0^\infty F(x)\cos\lambda x\,dx = f(\lambda)$ and choose $f(\lambda) = \begin{cases} 1-\lambda & 0 \le \lambda \le 1 \\ 0 & \lambda > 1 \end{cases}$. Then by Fourier's integral theorem,

$$F(x) = \frac{2}{\pi}\int_0^\infty f(\lambda)\cos\lambda x\,d\lambda = \frac{2}{\pi}\int_0^1 (1-\lambda)\cos\lambda x\,d\lambda = \frac{2(1-\cos x)}{\pi x^2}$$

30. Find (a) the finite Fourier sine transform and (b) the finite Fourier cosine transform of $\partial U/\partial x$ where U is a function of x and t for $0 < x < l, \ t > 0$.

(a) By definition the finite Fourier sine transform of $\partial U/\partial x$ is, on integrating by parts,

$$\int_0^l \frac{\partial U}{\partial x}\sin\frac{n\pi x}{l}\,dx = \left. U(x,t)\sin\frac{n\pi x}{l}\right|_0^l - \frac{n\pi}{l}\int_0^l U(x,t)\cos\frac{n\pi x}{l}\,dx$$

or

$$\mathcal{F}_s\left\{\frac{\partial U}{\partial x}\right\} = -\frac{n\pi}{l}\,\mathcal{F}_c\{U\}$$

(b) The finite Fourier cosine transform is

$$\int_0^l \frac{\partial U}{\partial x}\cos\frac{n\pi x}{l}\,dx = \left. U(x,t)\cos\frac{n\pi x}{l}\right|_0^l + \frac{n\pi}{l}\int_0^l U(x,t)\sin\frac{n\pi x}{l}\,dx$$

or

$$\mathcal{F}_c\left\{\frac{\partial U}{\partial x}\right\} = \frac{n\pi}{l}\,\mathcal{F}_s\{U\} - \{U(0,t) - U(l,t)\cos n\pi\}$$

31. Work Problem 30(a) and (b) for the function $\partial^2 U/\partial x^2$.

Replacing U by $\partial U/\partial x$ in the results of Problem 30, we find

(a)
$$\mathcal{F}_s\left\{\frac{\partial^2 U}{\partial x^2}\right\} = -\frac{n\pi}{l}\,\mathcal{F}_c\left\{\frac{\partial U}{\partial x}\right\}$$

$$= -\frac{n^2\pi^2}{l^2}\,\mathcal{F}_s\{U\} + \frac{n\pi}{l}\{U(0,t) - U(l,t)\cos n\pi\}$$

(b)
$$\mathcal{F}_c\left\{\frac{\partial^2 U}{\partial x^2}\right\} = -\frac{n\pi}{l}\,\mathcal{F}_s\left\{\frac{\partial U}{\partial x}\right\} - \{U_x(0,t) - U_x(l,t)\cos n\pi\}$$

$$= -\frac{n^2\pi^2}{l^2}\,\mathcal{F}_c\{U\} - \{U_x(0,t) - U_x(l,t)\cos n\pi\}$$

where U_x denotes the partial derivative with respect to x.

32. Use finite Fourier transforms to solve

$$\frac{\partial U}{\partial t} = \frac{\partial^2 U}{\partial x^2}, \quad U(0,t)=0, \ U(4,t)=0, \ U(x,0)=2x$$

where $0 < x < 4, \ t > 0$.

Take the finite Fourier sine transform (with $l = 4$) of both sides of the partial differential equation to obtain

$$\int_0^4 \frac{\partial U}{\partial t} \sin \frac{n\pi x}{4} \, dx \;\; = \;\; \int_0^4 \frac{\partial^2 U}{\partial x^2} \sin \frac{n\pi x}{4} \, dx$$

Writing $u = \mathcal{F}_s\{U\}$ and using Problem 31(a) with the conditions $U(0, t) = 0$, $U(4, t) = 0$, we find

$$\frac{du}{dt} \;\; = \;\; -\frac{n^2\pi^2}{16} u \tag{1}$$

where $u = u(n, t)$.

Taking the finite Fourier sine transform of the condition $U(x, 0) = 2x$, we have as in Prob. 10(a)

$$u(n, 0) \;\; = \;\; \mathcal{F}_s\{2x\} \;\; = \;\; \frac{32(1 - \cos n\pi)}{n\pi} \tag{2}$$

Solving the differential equation (1), we find if c is an arbitrary constant

$$u \;\; = \;\; u(n, t) \;\; = \;\; c \, e^{-n^2\pi^2 t/16} \tag{3}$$

Since $c = u(n, 0)$, we have from (2) and (3)

$$u \;\; = \;\; \frac{32(1 - \cos n\pi)}{n\pi} \, e^{-n^2\pi^2 t/16}$$

Thus from Problem 9(a), the inverse Fourier sine transform is

$$U(x, t) \;\; = \;\; \frac{2}{4} \sum_{n=1}^{\infty} \frac{32(1 - \cos n\pi)}{n\pi} \, e^{-n^2\pi^2 t/16}$$

$$= \;\; \frac{16}{\pi} \sum_{n=1}^{\infty} \left(\frac{1 - \cos n\pi}{n} \right) e^{-n^2\pi^2 t/16}$$

Physically, $U(x, t)$ represents the temperature at any point x at any time t in a solid bounded by the planes $x = 0$ and $x = 4$. The conditions $U(0, t) = 0$ and $U(4, t) = 0$ express the fact that the ends are kept at temperature zero, while $U(x, 0) = 2x$ expresses the initial temperature as a function of x. Equivalently, the solid can be replaced by a bar on the x axis with endpoints at $x = 0$ and $x = 4$ whose surface is insulated.

33. Solve $\dfrac{\partial U}{\partial t} = \dfrac{\partial^2 U}{\partial x^2}$, $x > 0$, $t > 0$, subject to the conditions

$$U(0, t) = 0, \qquad U(x, 0) = \begin{cases} 1 & 0 < x < 1 \\ 0 & x \geqq 1 \end{cases}, \qquad U(x, t) \text{ is bounded}$$

Taking the Fourier sine transform of both sides of the given partial differential equation, we find

$$\int_0^{\infty} \frac{\partial U}{\partial t} \sin \lambda x \, dx \;\; = \;\; \int_0^{\infty} \frac{\partial^2 U}{\partial x^2} \sin \lambda x \, dx \tag{1}$$

Then if

$$u \;\; = \;\; u(\lambda, t) \;\; = \;\; \int_0^{\infty} U(x, t) \sin \lambda x \, dx$$

this becomes

$$\frac{du}{dt} \;\; = \;\; \left\{ \frac{\partial U}{\partial x} \sin \lambda x \; - \; \lambda U \cos \lambda x \right\} \Big|_0^{\infty} \; - \; \lambda^2 \int_0^{\infty} U \sin \lambda x \, dx$$

$$= \;\; \lambda \, U(0, t) \; - \; \lambda^2 u \tag{2}$$

on integrating the right hand side of (1) by parts and assuming that U and $\partial U/\partial x$ approach zero as $x \to \infty$.

From the condition for $U(x, 0)$, we have on taking the Fourier sine transform

$$u(\lambda, 0) \;=\; \int_0^\infty U(x, 0) \sin \lambda x \; dx$$

$$=\; \int_0^1 \sin \lambda x \; dx \;=\; \frac{1 - \cos \lambda}{\lambda} \tag{3}$$

Solving (2) subject to the condition (3) and $U(0, t) = 0$, we find

$$u(\lambda, t) \;=\; \frac{1 - \cos \lambda}{\lambda} \, e^{-\lambda^2 t}$$

Then taking the inverse Fourier sine transform, we find the required solution

$$U(x, t) \;=\; \frac{2}{\pi} \int_0^\infty \frac{1 - \cos \lambda}{\lambda} \, e^{-\lambda^2 t} \sin \lambda x \; d\lambda$$

Physically, this can represent the temperature in a solid $x > 0$ [see Problem 32].

Supplementary Problems

FOURIER SERIES, ODD AND EVEN FUNCTIONS, FOURIER SINE AND COSINE SERIES

34. Graph each of the following functions and find their corresponding Fourier series using properties of even and odd functions wherever applicable.

(a) $F(x) = \begin{cases} 8 & 0 < x < 2 \\ -8 & 2 < x < 4 \end{cases}$ Period 4   (c) $F(x) = 4x, \; 0 < x < 10, \quad$ Period 10

(b) $F(x) = \begin{cases} -x & -4 \leqq x \leqq 0 \\ x & 0 \leqq x \leqq 4 \end{cases}$ Period 8   (d) $F(x) = \begin{cases} 2x & 0 \leqq x < 3 \\ 0 & -3 < x < 0 \end{cases}$ Period 6

Ans.   (a) $\dfrac{16}{\pi} \displaystyle\sum_{n=1}^{\infty} \dfrac{(1 - \cos n\pi)}{n} \sin \dfrac{n\pi x}{2}$ (c) $20 - \dfrac{40}{\pi} \displaystyle\sum_{n=1}^{\infty} \dfrac{1}{n} \sin \dfrac{n\pi x}{5}$

(b) $2 - \dfrac{8}{\pi^2} \displaystyle\sum_{n=1}^{\infty} \dfrac{(1 - \cos n\pi)}{n^2} \cos \dfrac{n\pi x}{4}$ (d) $\dfrac{3}{2} + \displaystyle\sum_{n=1}^{\infty} \left\{ \dfrac{6(\cos n\pi - 1)}{n^2 \pi^2} \cos \dfrac{n\pi x}{3} - \dfrac{6 \cos n\pi}{n\pi} \sin \dfrac{n\pi x}{3} \right\}$

35. In each part of Problem 34, tell where the discontinuities of $F(x)$ are located and to what value the series converges at these discontinuities.

Ans.   (a) $x = 0, \pm 2, \pm 4, \ldots ; \; 0$ (c) $x = 0, \pm 10, \pm 20, \ldots ; \; 20$

(b) no discontinuities   (d) $x = \pm 3, \pm 9, \pm 15, \ldots ; \; 3$

36. Expand $F(x) = \begin{cases} 2 - x & 0 < x < 4 \\ x - 6 & 4 < x < 8 \end{cases}$ in a Fourier series of period 8.

Ans. $\dfrac{16}{\pi^2} \left\{ \cos \dfrac{\pi x}{4} + \dfrac{1}{3^2} \cos \dfrac{3\pi x}{4} + \dfrac{1}{5^2} \cos \dfrac{5\pi x}{4} + \cdots \right\}$

37. (a) Expand $F(x) = \cos x, \; 0 < x < \pi$, in a Fourier sine series.

(b) How should $F(x)$ be defined at $x = 0$ and $x = \pi$ so that the series will converge to $F(x)$ for $0 \leqq x \leqq \pi$?

Ans.   (a) $\dfrac{8}{\pi} \displaystyle\sum_{n=1}^{\infty} \dfrac{n \sin 2nx}{4n^2 - 1}$ (b) $F(0) = F(\pi) = 0$

38. (a) Expand in a Fourier series $F(x) = \cos x$, $0 < x < \pi$ if the period is π; and (b) compare with the result of Problem 37, explaining the similarities and differences if any.

　　　Ans. Answer is the same as in Problem 37.

39. Expand $F(x) = \begin{cases} x & 0 < x < 4 \\ 8 - x & 4 < x < 8 \end{cases}$ in a series of (a) sines, (b) cosines.

　　　Ans. (a) $\dfrac{32}{\pi^2} \displaystyle\sum_{n=1}^{\infty} \dfrac{1}{n^2} \sin\dfrac{n\pi}{2} \sin\dfrac{n\pi x}{8}$ 　　(b) $\dfrac{16}{\pi^2} \displaystyle\sum_{n=1}^{\infty} \left(\dfrac{2 \cos n\pi/2 - \cos n\pi - 1}{n^2} \right) \cos\dfrac{n\pi x}{8}$

40. Prove that for $0 \leqq x \leqq \pi$,

　　(a)　$x(\pi - x) = \dfrac{\pi^2}{6} - \left(\dfrac{\cos 2x}{1^2} + \dfrac{\cos 4x}{2^2} + \dfrac{\cos 6x}{3^2} + \cdots \right)$

　　(b)　$x(\pi - x) = \dfrac{8}{\pi} \left(\dfrac{\sin x}{1^3} + \dfrac{\sin 3x}{3^3} + \dfrac{\sin 5x}{5^3} + \cdots \right)$

41. Use Problem 40 to show that

　　(a) $\displaystyle\sum_{n=1}^{\infty} \dfrac{1}{n^2} = \dfrac{\pi^2}{6}$,　　(b) $\displaystyle\sum_{n=1}^{\infty} \dfrac{(-1)^{n-1}}{n^2} = \dfrac{\pi^2}{12}$,　　(c) $\displaystyle\sum_{n=1}^{\infty} \dfrac{(-1)^{n-1}}{(2n-1)^3} = \dfrac{\pi^3}{32}$.

42. Show that $\dfrac{1}{1^3} + \dfrac{1}{3^3} - \dfrac{1}{5^3} - \dfrac{1}{7^3} + \dfrac{1}{9^3} + \dfrac{1}{11^3} - \cdots = \dfrac{3\pi^2\sqrt{2}}{16}$.

PARSEVAL'S IDENTITY FOR FOURIER SERIES

43. By using Problem 40 and Parseval's identity, show that　(a) $\displaystyle\sum_{n=1}^{\infty} \dfrac{1}{n^4} = \dfrac{\pi^4}{90}$,　(b) $\displaystyle\sum_{n=1}^{\infty} \dfrac{1}{n^6} = \dfrac{\pi^6}{945}$.

44. Show that $\dfrac{1}{1^2 \cdot 3^2} + \dfrac{1}{3^2 \cdot 5^2} + \dfrac{1}{5^2 \cdot 7^2} + \cdots = \dfrac{\pi^2 - 8}{16}$.　[*Hint.* Use Problem 27.]

45. Show that　(a) $\displaystyle\sum_{n=1}^{\infty} \dfrac{1}{(2n-1)^4} = \dfrac{\pi^4}{96}$,　(b) $\displaystyle\sum_{n=1}^{\infty} \dfrac{1}{(2n-1)^6} = \dfrac{\pi^6}{960}$.

46. Show that $\dfrac{1}{1^2 \cdot 2^2 \cdot 3^2} + \dfrac{1}{2^2 \cdot 3^2 \cdot 4^2} + \dfrac{1}{3^2 \cdot 4^2 \cdot 5^2} + \cdots = \dfrac{4\pi^2 - 39}{16}$.

FINITE FOURIER TRANSFORMS

47. Find the (a) finite Fourier sine transform and (b) finite Fourier cosine transform of $F(x) = 1$ where $0 < x < l$.　　*Ans.* (a) $l(1 - \cos n\pi)/n\pi$　　(b) 0 if $n = 1, 2, 3, \ldots$; l if $n = 0$

48. Find the (a) finite Fourier sine transform and (b) finite Fourier cosine transform of $F(x) = x^2$ where $0 < x < l$.

　　　Ans. (a) $\dfrac{2l^3}{n^3\pi^3}(\cos n\pi - 1) - \dfrac{l^3}{n\pi}\cos n\pi$ if $n = 1, 2, 3, \ldots$; $\dfrac{l^3}{3}$ if $n = 0$　　(b) $\dfrac{2l^3}{n^2\pi^2}(\cos n\pi - 1)$

49. If $\mathscr{F}_s\{F(x)\} = \dfrac{1 - \cos n\pi}{n^2\pi^2}$ where $0 < x < \pi$, find $F(x)$.　　　*Ans.* $\dfrac{2}{\pi^3} \displaystyle\sum_{n=1}^{\infty} \left(\dfrac{1 - \cos n\pi}{n^2} \right) \sin nx$

50. If $\mathcal{F}_c\{F(x)\} = \dfrac{6(\sin n\pi/2 - \cos n\pi)}{(2n+1)\pi}$ for $n = 1, 2, 3, \ldots$ and $2/\pi$ for $n = 0$ where $0 < x < 4$,

find $F(x)$.   *Ans.* $\dfrac{1}{2\pi} + \dfrac{3}{\pi} \displaystyle\sum_{n=1}^{\infty} \left(\dfrac{\sin n\pi/2 - \cos n\pi}{2n+1} \right) \cos \dfrac{n\pi}{4}$

51. If $f(n) = \dfrac{\cos(2n\pi/3)}{(2n+1)^2}$, find (*a*) $\mathcal{F}_s^{-1}\{f(n)\}$ and (*b*) $\mathcal{F}_c^{-1}\{f(n)\}$ if $0 < x < 1$.

Ans.   (*a*) $2 \displaystyle\sum_{n=1}^{\infty} \dfrac{\cos(2n\pi/3)}{(2n+1)^2} \sin n\pi x$ (*b*) $1 + 2 \displaystyle\sum_{n=1}^{\infty} \dfrac{\cos(2n\pi/3)}{(2n+1)^2} \cos n\pi x$

THE FOURIER INTEGRAL AND FOURIER TRANSFORMS

52. (*a*) Find the Fourier transform of $F(x) = \begin{cases} 1/2\epsilon & |x| \leq \epsilon \\ 0 & |x| > \epsilon \end{cases}$.

(*b*) Determine the limit of this transform as $\epsilon \to 0+$ and discuss the result.

Ans. (*a*) $\dfrac{\sin \lambda\epsilon}{\lambda\epsilon}$, (*b*) 1

53. (*a*) Find the Fourier transform of $F(x) = \begin{cases} 1 - x^2 & |x| < 1 \\ 0 & |x| > 1 \end{cases}$.

(*b*) Evaluate $\displaystyle\int_0^{\infty} \left(\dfrac{x \cos x - \sin x}{x^3} \right) \cos \dfrac{x}{2}\, dx$.

Ans. (*a*) $-4 \left(\dfrac{\lambda \cos \lambda - \sin \lambda}{\lambda^3} \right)$, (*b*) $-\dfrac{3\pi}{16}$

54. If $F(x) = \begin{cases} 1 & 0 \leq x < 1 \\ 0 & x \geq 1 \end{cases}$ find the (*a*) Fourier sine transform, (*b*) Fourier cosine transform of $F(x)$.

In each case obtain the graph of $F(x)$ and its transform.   *Ans.* (*a*) $\dfrac{1 - \cos \lambda}{\lambda}$, (*b*) $\dfrac{\sin \lambda}{\lambda}$

55. (*a*) Find the Fourier sine transform of e^{-x}, $x \geq 0$.

(*b*) Show that $\displaystyle\int_0^{\infty} \dfrac{x \sin mx}{x^2+1}\, dx = \dfrac{\pi}{2} e^{-m}$, $m > 0$ by using the result in (*a*).

(*c*) Explain from the viewpoint of Fourier's integral theorem why the result in (*b*) does not hold for $m = 0$.

Ans. (*a*) $\lambda/(1 + \lambda^2)$

56. Solve for $Y(x)$ the integral equation

$$\int_0^{\infty} Y(x) \sin xt\, dx = \begin{cases} 1 & 0 \leq t < 1 \\ 2 & 1 \leq t < 2 \\ 0 & t \geq 2 \end{cases}$$

and verify the solution by direct substitution.   *Ans.* $Y(x) = (2 + 2\cos x - 4\cos 2x)/\pi x$

PARSEVAL'S IDENTITY FOR FOURIER INTEGRALS

57. Evaluate   (*a*) $\displaystyle\int_0^{\infty} \dfrac{dx}{(x^2+1)^2}$, (*b*) $\displaystyle\int_0^{\infty} \dfrac{x^2\, dx}{(x^2+1)^2}$ by use of Parseval's identity.

[*Hint.* Use the Fourier sine and cosine transforms of e^{-x}, $x > 0$.]   *Ans.* (*a*) $\pi/4$, (*b*) $\pi/4$

58. Use Problem 54 to show that   (*a*) $\displaystyle\int_0^{\infty} \left(\dfrac{1 - \cos x}{x} \right)^2 dx = \dfrac{\pi}{2}$, (*b*) $\displaystyle\int_0^{\infty} \dfrac{\sin^4 x}{x^2}\, dx = \dfrac{\pi}{2}$.

59. Show that $\displaystyle\int_0^{\infty} \dfrac{(x \cos x - \sin x)^2}{x^6}\, dx = \dfrac{\pi}{15}$.

MISCELLANEOUS PROBLEMS

60. If $-\pi < x < \pi$ and $\alpha \neq 0, \pm 1, \pm 2, \ldots,$ prove that

$$\frac{\pi}{2} \frac{\sin \alpha x}{\sin \alpha \pi} = \frac{\sin x}{1^2 - \alpha^2} - \frac{2 \sin 2x}{2^2 - \alpha^2} + \frac{3 \sin 3x}{3^2 - \alpha^2} - \cdots$$

61. If $-\pi < x < \pi$, prove that

(a)
$$\frac{\pi}{2} \frac{\sinh \alpha x}{\sinh \alpha \pi} = \frac{\sin x}{\alpha^2 + 1^2} - \frac{2 \sin 2x}{\alpha^2 + 2^2} + \frac{3 \sin 3x}{\alpha^2 + 3^2} - \cdots$$

(b)
$$\frac{\pi}{2} \frac{\cosh \alpha x}{\sinh \alpha \pi} = \frac{1}{2\alpha} - \frac{\alpha \cos x}{\alpha^2 + 1^2} + \frac{\alpha \cos 2x}{\alpha^2 + 2^2} - \cdots$$

62. (a) Prove that if $\alpha \neq 0, \pm 1, \pm 2, \ldots,$ then

$$\frac{\pi}{\sin \alpha \pi} = \frac{1}{\alpha} - \frac{2\alpha}{\alpha^2 - 1^2} + \frac{2\alpha}{\alpha^2 - 2^2} - \frac{2\alpha}{\alpha^2 - 3^2} + \cdots$$

(b) Prove that if $0 < \alpha < 1$, then

$$\int_0^\infty \frac{x^{\alpha-1}}{1+x} dx = \int_0^1 \frac{x^{\alpha-1} - x^{-\alpha}}{1+x} dx = \frac{1}{\alpha} - \frac{2\alpha}{\alpha^2 - 1^2} + \frac{2\alpha}{\alpha^2 - 2^2} - \frac{2\alpha}{\alpha^2 - 3^2} + \cdots$$

(c) Use (a) and (b) to prove that $\qquad \Gamma(\alpha)\, \Gamma(1-\alpha) = \dfrac{\pi}{\sin \alpha \pi}$

[*Hint.* For (a) expand $F(x) = \cos \alpha x,\ -\pi \leq x \leq \pi$ in a Fourier series. For (b) write the given integral as the sum of integrals from 0 to 1 and 1 to ∞, and let $x = 1/y$ in the last integral. Then use the fact that $\dfrac{1}{1+x} = 1 - x + x^2 - x^3 + \cdots.$]

63. If $0 < x < \pi$ prove that $\mathcal{F}_s^{-1}\left\{ \dfrac{1 - \cos n\pi}{n^3} \right\} = \tfrac{1}{2}x(\pi - x).$

64. Find (a) $\mathcal{F}_s\{\partial^3 U/\partial x^3\}$ and (b) $\mathcal{F}_c\{\partial^3 U/\partial x^3\}$.

65. Show that

(a)
$$\mathcal{F}_s\{Y^{(\mathrm{iv})}(x)\} = \frac{n^4 \pi^4}{l^4} \mathcal{F}_s\{Y(x)\} - \frac{n^3 \pi^3}{l^3}\{Y(0) + (-1)^{n+1} Y(l)\} + \frac{n\pi}{l}\{Y''(0) + (-1)^{n+1} Y''(l)\}$$

(b)
$$\mathcal{F}_c\{Y^{(\mathrm{iv})}(x)\} = \frac{n^4 \pi^4}{l^4} \mathcal{F}_c\{Y(x)\} + \frac{n^2 \pi^2}{l^2}\{Y'(0) + (-1)^{n+1} Y'(l)\} - \{Y'''(0) + (-1)^{n+1} Y'''(l)\}.$$

66. (a) Use finite Fourier transforms to solve

$$\frac{\partial U}{\partial t} = 2 \frac{\partial^2 U}{\partial x^2} \qquad 0 < x < 4,\ t > 0$$

$$U(0, t) = 0, \quad U(4, t) = 0, \quad U(x, 0) = 3 \sin \pi x - 2 \sin 5\pi x$$

(b) Give a possible physical interpretation of the problem and solution.

Ans. (a) $U(x, t) = 3e^{-2\pi^2 t} \sin \pi x - 2e^{-50\pi^2 t} \sin 5\pi x$

67. Solve $\dfrac{\partial U}{\partial t} = \dfrac{\partial^2 U}{\partial x^2},\ 0 < x < 6,\ t > 0,$ subject to the conditions

$$U(0, t) = 0, \qquad U(6, t) = 0, \qquad U(x, 0) = \begin{cases} 1 & 0 < x < 3 \\ 0 & 3 < x < 6 \end{cases}$$

and interpret physically.

Ans. $U(x, t) = \displaystyle\sum_{n=1}^\infty 2\left\{ \frac{1 - \cos(n\pi/2)}{n\pi} \right\} e^{-n^2\pi^2 t/36} \sin \frac{n\pi x}{6}$

68. (a) In solving the problem

$$\frac{\partial U}{\partial t} = \frac{\partial^2 U}{\partial x^2} \qquad 0 < x < 6, \ t > 0$$

$$U_x(0, t) = 0, \qquad U_x(6, t) = 0, \qquad U(x, 0) = 2x$$

which transform [sine or cosine] would you expect to be more useful? Explain.

(b) Find the solution to the problem in (a).

Ans. (b) $6 + \dfrac{24}{\pi^2} \displaystyle\sum_{n=1}^{\infty} \left(\dfrac{\cos n\pi - 1}{n^2} \right) e^{-n^2\pi^2 t/36} \cos \dfrac{n\pi x}{6}$

69. A flexible string of length π is tightly stretched between points $x = 0$ and $x = \pi$ on the x axis, its ends fixed at these points. When set into small transverse vibration the displacement $Y(x, t)$ from the x axis of any point x at time t is given by $\dfrac{\partial^2 Y}{\partial t^2} = a^2 \dfrac{\partial^2 Y}{\partial x^2}$ where $a^2 = T/\rho$, $T = $ tension, $\rho = $ mass per unit length.

(a) Using finite Fourier transforms, find a solution of this equation (sometimes called the *wave equation*) with $a^2 = 4$ which satisfies the conditions $Y(0, t) = 0$, $Y(\pi, t) = 0$, $Y(x, 0) = 0.1 \sin x + 0.01 \sin 4x$, $Y_t(x, 0) = 0$ for $0 < x < \pi$, $t > 0$.

(b) Interpret physically the boundary conditions in (a) and the solution.

Ans. (a) $Y(x, t) = 0.1 \sin x \cos 2t + 0.01 \sin 4x \cos 8t$

70. (a) Solve the boundary-value problem $\dfrac{\partial^2 Y}{\partial t^2} = 9 \dfrac{\partial^2 Y}{\partial x^2}$ subject to the conditions $Y(0, t) = 0$, $Y(2, t) = 0$, $Y(x, 0) = 0.05x(2 - x)$, $Y_t(x, 0) = 0$, where $0 < x < 2$, $t > 0$. (b) Interpret physically.

Ans. (a) $Y(x, t) = \dfrac{1.6}{\pi^3} \displaystyle\sum_{n=1}^{\infty} \dfrac{1}{(2n-1)^3} \sin \dfrac{(2n-1)\pi x}{2} \cos \dfrac{3(2n-1)\pi t}{2}$

71. Solve the boundary-value problem $\dfrac{\partial U}{\partial t} = \dfrac{\partial^2 U}{\partial x^2}$, $U(0, t) = 1$, $U(\pi, t) = 3$, $U(x, 0) = 2$, where $0 < x < \pi$, $t > 0$.

Ans. $U(x, t) = 1 + \dfrac{2x}{\pi} + \displaystyle\sum_{n=1}^{\infty} \dfrac{4 \cos n\pi}{n\pi} e^{-n^2 t} \sin nx$

72. Give a physical interpretation to Problem 71.

73. Solve Problem 70 with the boundary conditions for $Y(x, 0)$ and $Y_t(x, 0)$ interchanged, i.e. $Y(x, 0) = 0$, $Y_t(x, 0) = 0.05x(2 - x)$, and give a physical interpretation.

Ans. $Y(x, t) = \dfrac{3.2}{3\pi^4} \displaystyle\sum_{n=1}^{\infty} \dfrac{1}{(2n-1)^4} \sin \dfrac{(2n-1)\pi x}{2} \sin \dfrac{3(2n-1)\pi t}{2}$

74. Prove the results (4) and (5) on Page 174.

75. Verify the convolution theorem for the functions $F(x) = G(x) = \begin{cases} 1 & |x| < 1 \\ 0 & |x| > 1 \end{cases}$.

76. Write Parseval's identity in complex form using the results (4) and (5) on Page 174.

77. Prove the result (15) on Page 176.

78. Prove the results (19) and (21) on Pages 176 and 177 respectively.

79. Prove the results *(23)* or *(24)* on **Page 177.**

$$\left[Hint.\ \ If\ \ f(\lambda)\ =\ \int_{-\infty}^{\infty} e^{-i\lambda u}\, F(u)\, du\ \ \ and\ \ \ g(\lambda)\ =\ \int_{-\infty}^{\infty} e^{-i\lambda v}\, G(v)\, dv,\ \ \ then \right.$$

$$f(\lambda)\, g(\lambda)\ =\ \int_{-\infty}^{\infty} \int_{-\infty}^{\infty} e^{-i\lambda(u+v)}\, F(u)\, G(v)\, du\, dv$$

$$\left. Now\ make\ the\ transformation\ \ u+v=x. \right]$$

80. If $f(\lambda)$ and $g(\lambda)$ are the Fourier transforms of $F(x)$ and $G(x)$ respectively, prove that

$$\int_{-\infty}^{\infty} F(x)\, \overline{G(x)}\, dx\ \ =\ \ \frac{1}{2\pi} \int_{-\infty}^{\infty} f(\lambda)\, \overline{g(\lambda)}\, d\alpha$$

where the bar signifies the complex conjugate.

81. Prove Riemann's theorem (see Problem 24).

82. *(a)* Show how to use Fourier transforms to solve

$$\frac{\partial U}{\partial t}\ =\ 2\, \frac{\partial^2 U}{\partial x^2}, \qquad x > 0$$

      if $U(0, t) = 0,\ \ U(x, 0) = e^{-x},$ and $U(x, t)$ is bounded.

 (b) Give a physical interpretation.

 Ans. $U(x, t)\ =\ \dfrac{2}{\pi} \displaystyle\int_0^{\infty} \frac{\lambda e^{-2\lambda^2 t}\, \sin \lambda x}{\lambda^2 + 1}\, d\lambda$

83. *(a)* Solve $\dfrac{\partial U}{\partial t} = 2\, \dfrac{\partial^2 U}{\partial x^2},\ \ U(0, t) = 0,\ \ U(x, 0) = e^{-x},\ x > 0,\ \ U(x, t)$ is bounded where $x > 0,\ t > 0.$

 (b) Give a physical interpretation.

 Ans. $U(x, t)\ =\ \dfrac{2}{\pi} \displaystyle\int_0^{\infty} \frac{\lambda e^{-2\lambda^2 t}\, \sin \lambda x}{\lambda^2 + 1}\, d\lambda$

84. Solve $\dfrac{\partial U}{\partial t} = \dfrac{\partial^2 U}{\partial x^2},\ \ U_x(0, t) = 0,\ \ U(x, 0) = \begin{cases} x & 0 \leqq x \leqq 1 \\ 0 & x > 1 \end{cases},$ $U(x, t)$ is bounded where $x > 0,\ t > 0.$

 Ans. $U(x, t)\ =\ \dfrac{2}{\pi} \displaystyle\int_0^{\infty} \left(\frac{\sin \lambda}{\lambda} + \frac{\cos \lambda - 1}{\lambda^2} \right) e^{-\lambda^2 t}\, \cos \lambda x\, d\lambda$

85. *(a)* Show that the solution to Problem 33 can be written

$$U(x, t)\ =\ \frac{2}{\sqrt{\pi}} \int_0^{x/2\sqrt{t}} e^{-v^2}\, dv\ -\ \frac{1}{\sqrt{\pi}} \int_{(1-x)/2\sqrt{t}}^{(1+x)/2\sqrt{t}} e^{-v^2}\, dv$$

 (b) Prove directly that the function in *(a)* satisfies $\dfrac{\partial U}{\partial t} = \dfrac{\partial^2 U}{\partial x^2}$ and the conditions of **Problem 33.**

Chapter 7

The Complex Inversion Formula

THE COMPLEX INVERSION FORMULA

If $f(s) = \mathcal{L}\{F(t)\}$, then $\mathcal{L}^{-1}\{f(s)\}$ is given by

$$F(t) = \frac{1}{2\pi i} \int_{\gamma-i\infty}^{\gamma+i\infty} e^{st} f(s) \, ds, \qquad t > 0 \tag{1}$$

and $F(t) = 0$ for $t < 0$. This result is called the *complex inversion integral* or *formula*. It is also known as *Bromwich's integral formula*. The result provides a direct means for obtaining the inverse Laplace transform of a given function $f(s)$.

The integration in (1) is to be performed along a line $s = \gamma$ in the complex plane where $s = x + iy$. The real number γ is chosen so that $s = \gamma$ lies to the right of all the singularities (poles, branch points or essential singularities) but is otherwise arbitrary.

THE BROMWICH CONTOUR

In practice, the integral in (1) is evaluated by considering the contour integral

$$\frac{1}{2\pi i} \oint_C e^{st} f(s) \, ds \tag{2}$$

where C is the contour of Fig. 7-1. This contour, sometimes called the *Bromwich contour*, is composed of line AB and the arc $BJKLA$ of a circle of radius R with center at the origin O.

If we represent arc $BJKLA$ by Γ, it follows from (1) that since $T = \sqrt{R^2 - \gamma^2}$,

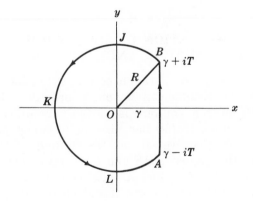

Fig. 7-1

$$F(t) = \lim_{R \to \infty} \frac{1}{2\pi i} \int_{\gamma-iT}^{\gamma+iT} e^{st} f(s) \, ds \tag{3}$$

$$= \lim_{R \to \infty} \left\{ \frac{1}{2\pi i} \oint_C e^{st} f(s) \, ds - \frac{1}{2\pi i} \int_\Gamma e^{st} f(s) \, ds \right\}$$

USE OF RESIDUE THEOREM IN FINDING INVERSE LAPLACE TRANSFORMS

Suppose that the only singularities of $f(s)$ are poles all of which lie to the left of the line $s = \gamma$ for some real constant γ. Suppose further that the integral around Γ in (3) approaches zero as $R \to \infty$. Then by the residue theorem we can write (3) as

$$F(t) \quad = \quad \text{sum of residues of } e^{st} f(s) \text{ at poles of } f(s) \tag{4}$$

$$= \quad \sum \text{ residues of } e^{st} f(s) \text{ at poles of } f(s)$$

A SUFFICIENT CONDITION FOR THE INTEGRAL AROUND Γ TO APPROACH ZERO

The validity of the result (4) hinges on the assumption that the integral around Γ in (3) approaches zero as $R \to \infty$. A sufficient condition under which this assumption is correct is supplied in the following

Theorem 7-1. If we can find constants $M > 0$, $k > 0$ such that on Γ (where $s = Re^{i\theta}$),

$$|f(s)| \quad < \quad \frac{M}{R^k} \tag{5}$$

then the integral around Γ of $e^{st} f(s)$ approaches zero as $R \to \infty$, i.e.,

$$\lim_{R \to \infty} \int_\Gamma e^{st} f(s) \, ds \quad = \quad 0 \tag{6}$$

The condition (5) always holds if $f(s) = P(s)/Q(s)$ where $P(s)$ and $Q(s)$ are polynomials and the degree of $P(s)$ is less than the degree of $Q(s)$. See Problem 15.

The result is valid even if $f(s)$ has other singularities besides poles.

MODIFICATION OF BROMWICH CONTOUR IN CASE OF BRANCH POINTS

If $f(s)$ has branch points, extensions of the above results can be made provided that the Bromwich contour is suitably modified. For example, if $f(s)$ has only one branch point at $s = 0$, then we can use the contour of Fig. 7-2. In this figure, *BDE* and *LNA* represent arcs of a circle of radius R with center at origin O, while *HJK* is the arc of a circle of radius ϵ with center at O. For details of evaluating inverse Laplace transforms in such cases see Prob. 9.

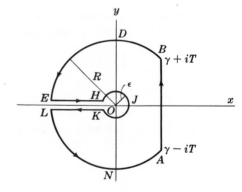

Fig. 7-2

CASE OF INFINITELY MANY SINGULARITIES

If we wish to find the inverse Laplace transform of functions which have infinitely many isolated singularities, the above methods can be applied. In such case the curved portion of the Bromwich contour is chosen to be of such radius R_m so as to enclose only a finite number of the singularities and so as not to pass through any singularity. The required inverse Laplace transform is then found by taking an appropriate limit as $m \to \infty$. See Problems 13 and 14.

Solved Problems

THE COMPLEX INVERSION FORMULA

1. Establish the validity of the complex inversion formula.

We have, by definition, $f(s) = \int_0^\infty e^{-su} F(u)\, du.$ Then

$$\lim_{T \to \infty} \frac{1}{2\pi i} \int_{\gamma - iT}^{\gamma + iT} e^{st} f(s)\, ds \;=\; \lim_{T \to \infty} \frac{1}{2\pi i} \int_{\gamma - iT}^{\gamma + iT} \int_0^\infty e^{st - su} F(u)\, du\, ds$$

Letting $s = \gamma + iy, \; ds = i\,dy,$ this becomes

$$\lim_{T \to \infty} \frac{1}{2\pi} e^{\gamma t} \int_{-T}^{T} e^{iyt}\, dy \int_0^\infty e^{-iyu} \left[e^{-\gamma u} F(u) \right] du \;=\; \frac{1}{2\pi} e^{\gamma t} \begin{cases} 2\pi e^{-\gamma t} F(t) & t > 0 \\ 0 & t < 0 \end{cases}$$

$$=\; \begin{cases} F(t) & t > 0 \\ 0 & t < 0 \end{cases}$$

by Fourier's integral theorem [see Chapter 6]. Thus we find

$$F(t) \;=\; \frac{1}{2\pi i} \int_{\gamma - i\infty}^{\gamma + i\infty} e^{st} f(s)\, ds \qquad t > 0$$

as required.

In the above proof, we assume that $e^{-\gamma u} F(u)$ is absolutely integrable in $(0, \infty)$, i.e.
$\int_0^\infty e^{-\gamma u} |F(u)|\, du$ converges, so that Fourier's integral theorem can be applied. To insure this
condition it is sufficient that $F(t)$ be of exponential order γ where the real number γ is chosen so that
the line $s = \gamma$ in the complex plane lies to the right of all the singularities of $f(s)$. Except for this
condition, γ is otherwise arbitrary.

2. Let Γ denote the curved portion $BJPKQLA$
of the Bromwich contour [Fig. 7-3] with
equation $s = Re^{i\theta},\; \theta_0 \leqq \theta \leqq 2\pi - \theta_0,$ i.e. Γ is
the arc of a circle of radius R with center
at O. Suppose that on Γ we have

$$|f(s)| \;<\; \frac{M}{R^k}$$

where $k > 0$ and M are constants. Show
that

$$\lim_{R \to \infty} \int_{\Gamma} e^{st} f(s)\, ds \;=\; 0$$

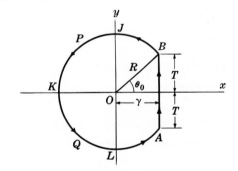

Fig. 7-3

If $\Gamma_1, \Gamma_2, \Gamma_3$ and Γ_4 represent arcs $BJ, JPK,$
KQL and LA respectively, we have

$$\int_{\Gamma} e^{st} f(s)\, ds \;=\; \int_{\Gamma_1} e^{st} f(s)\, ds \;+\; \int_{\Gamma_2} e^{st} f(s)\, ds \;+\; \int_{\Gamma_3} e^{st} f(s)\, ds \;+\; \int_{\Gamma_4} e^{st} f(s)\, ds$$

Then if we can show that each of the integrals on the right approach zero as $R \to \infty$ we will have
proved the required result. To do this we consider these four integrals.

Case 1.   Integral over Γ_1 or BJ.

Along Γ_1 we have, since $s = Re^{i\theta},\; \theta_0 \leqq \theta \leqq \pi/2,$

$$I_1 \;=\; \int_{\Gamma_1} e^{st} f(s)\, ds \;=\; \int_{\theta_0}^{\pi/2} e^{Re^{i\theta} t} f(Re^{i\theta})\, iRe^{i\theta}\, d\theta$$

Then $\qquad |I_1| \quad \leqq \quad \displaystyle\int_{\theta_0}^{\pi/2} |e^{(R\cos\theta)t}| \; |e^{i(R\sin\theta)t}| \; |f(Re^{i\theta})| \; |iRe^{i\theta}| \; d\theta$

$$\leqq \quad \int_{\theta_0}^{\pi/2} e^{(R\cos\theta)t} \; |f(Re^{i\theta})| \; R \; d\theta$$

$$\leqq \quad \frac{M}{R^{k-1}} \int_{\theta_0}^{\pi/2} e^{(R\cos\theta)t} \; d\theta \quad = \quad \frac{M}{R^{k-1}} \int_0^{\phi_0} e^{(R\sin\phi)t} \; d\phi$$

where we have used the given condition $|f(s)| \leqq M/R^k$ on Γ_1 and the transformation $\theta = \pi/2 - \phi$ where $\phi_0 = \pi/2 - \theta_0 = \sin^{-1}(\gamma/R)$.

Since $\sin\phi \leqq \sin\phi_0 \leqq \cos\theta_0 = \gamma/R$, this last integral is less than or equal to

$$\frac{M}{R^{k-1}} \int_0^{\phi_0} e^{\gamma t} \; d\phi \quad = \quad \frac{M \, e^{\gamma t} \, \phi_0}{R^{k-1}} \quad = \quad \frac{M \, e^{\gamma t}}{R^{k-1}} \sin^{-1}\frac{\gamma}{R}$$

But as $R \to \infty$, this last quantity approaches zero [as can be seen by noting, for example, that $\sin^{-1}(\gamma/R) \approx \gamma/R$ for large R]. Thus $\displaystyle\lim_{R\to\infty} I_1 = 0$.

Case 2. Integral over Γ_2 or JPK.

Along Γ_2 we have, since $s = Re^{i\theta}$, $\pi/2 \leqq \theta \leqq \pi$,

$$I_2 \quad = \quad \int_{\Gamma_2} e^{st} f(s) \; ds \quad = \quad \int_{\pi/2}^{\pi} e^{Re^{i\theta}t} f(Re^{i\theta}) \; iRe^{i\theta} \; d\theta$$

Then, as in Case 1, we have

$$|I_2| \quad \leqq \quad \frac{M}{R^{k-1}} \int_{\pi/2}^{\pi} e^{(R\cos\theta)t} \; d\theta \quad \leqq \quad \frac{M}{R^{k-1}} \int_0^{\pi/2} e^{-(R\sin\phi)t} \; d\phi$$

upon letting $\theta = \pi/2 + \phi$.

Now $\sin\phi \geqq 2\phi/\pi$ for $0 \leqq \phi \leqq \pi/2$ [see Problem 3], so that the last integral is less than or equal to

$$\frac{M}{R^{k-1}} \int_0^{\pi/2} e^{-2R\phi t/\pi} \; d\phi \quad = \quad \frac{\pi M}{2tR^k} (1 - e^{-Rt})$$

which approaches zero as $R \to \infty$. Thus $\displaystyle\lim_{R\to\infty} I_2 = 0$.

Case 3. Integral over Γ_3 or KQL.

This case can be treated in a manner similar to Case 2 [see Problem 58(a)].

Case 4. Integral over Γ_4 or LA.

This case can be treated in a manner similar to Case 1 [see Problem 58(b)].

3. Show that $\sin\phi \geqq 2\phi/\pi$ for $0 \leqq \phi \leqq \pi/2$.

Method 1. **Geometrical proof.**

From Fig. 7-4, in which curve OPQ represents an arc of the sine curve $y = \sin\phi$ and $y = 2\phi/\pi$ represents line OP, it is geometrically evident that $\sin\phi \geqq 2\phi/\pi$ for $0 \leqq \phi \leqq \pi/2$.

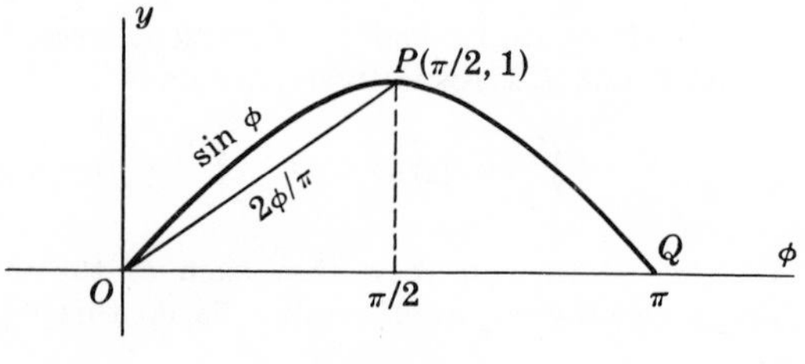

Method 2. **Analytical proof.**

Consider $F(\phi) = \dfrac{\sin\phi}{\phi}$. We have

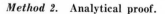

Fig. 7-4

$$\frac{dF}{d\phi} \quad = \quad F'(\phi) \quad = \quad \frac{\phi\cos\phi - \sin\phi}{\phi^2} \tag{1}$$

If $G(\phi) = \phi \cos \phi - \sin \phi$,   then

$$\frac{dG}{d\phi} = G'(\phi) = -\phi \sin \phi \tag{2}$$

Thus for $0 \leqq \phi < \pi/2$, $G'(\phi) \leqq 0$ and $G(\phi)$ is a decreasing function. Since $G(0) = 0$, it follows that $G(\phi) \leqq 0$.   Then from (1) we see that $F'(\phi) \leqq 0$, or $F(\phi)$ is a decreasing function.   Defining $F(0) = \lim\limits_{\phi \to 0} F(\phi) = 1$,   we see that $F(\phi)$ decreases from 1 to $2/\pi$ as ϕ goes from 0 to $\pi/2$. Thus

$$1 \geqq \frac{\sin \phi}{\phi} \geqq \frac{2}{\pi}$$

from which the required result follows.

USE OF RESIDUE THEOREM IN FINDING INVERSE LAPLACE TRANSFORMS

4.   Suppose that the only singularities of $f(s)$ are poles which all lie to the left of the line $s = \gamma$ for some real constant γ.   Suppose further that $f(s)$ satisfies the condition given in Problem 2.   Prove that the inverse Laplace transform of $f(s)$ is given by

$$F(t) = \text{sum of residues of } e^{st} f(s) \text{ at all the poles of } f(s)$$

We have $\dfrac{1}{2\pi i} \oint_C e^{st} f(s)\, ds = \dfrac{1}{2\pi i} \int_{\gamma - iT}^{\gamma + iT} e^{st} f(s)\, ds + \dfrac{1}{2\pi i} \int_\Gamma e^{st} f(s)\, ds$

where C is the Bromwich contour of Problem 2 and Γ is the circular arc $BJPKQLA$ of Fig. 7-3. By the residue theorem,

$$\frac{1}{2\pi i} \oint_C e^{st} f(s)\, ds = \text{sum of residues of } e^{st} f(s) \text{ at all poles of } f(s) \text{ inside } C$$

$$= \sum \text{ residues inside } C$$

Thus $\dfrac{1}{2\pi i} \displaystyle\int_{\gamma - iT}^{\gamma + iT} e^{st} f(s)\, ds = \sum \text{ residues inside } C - \dfrac{1}{2\pi i} \int_\Gamma e^{st} f(s)\, ds$

Taking the limit as $R \to \infty$, we find by Problem 2,

$$F(t) = \text{sum of residues of } e^{st} f(s) \text{ at all the poles of } f(s)$$

5.   (a) Show that $f(s) = \dfrac{1}{s - 2}$ satisfies the condition in Problem 2.

(b) Find the residue of $\dfrac{e^{st}}{s - 2}$ at the pole $s = 2$.

(c) Evaluate $\mathcal{L}^{-1}\left\{\dfrac{1}{s - 2}\right\}$ by using the complex inversion formula.

(a) For $s = Re^{i\theta}$, we have

$$\left|\frac{1}{s - 2}\right| = \left|\frac{1}{Re^{i\theta} - 2}\right| \leqq \frac{1}{|Re^{i\theta}| - 2} = \frac{1}{R - 2} < \frac{2}{R}$$

for large enough R (e.g. $R > 4$). Thus the condition in Problem 2 is satisfied when $k = 1$, $M = 2$. Note that in establishing the above we have used the result $|z_1 - z_2| \geqq |z_1| - |z_2|$ [see Problem 49(c), Page 167].

(b) The residue at the simple pole $s = 2$ is

$$\lim_{s \to 2} (s - 2) \left(\frac{e^{st}}{s - 2} \right) = e^{2t}$$

(c) By Problem 4 and the results of parts (a) and (b), we see that

$$\mathcal{L}^{-1} \left\{ \frac{1}{s - 2} \right\} = \text{ sum of residues of } e^{st} f(s) = e^{2t}$$

Note that the Bromwich contour in this case is chosen so that γ is any real number greater than 2 and the contour encloses the pole $s = 2$.

6. Evaluate $\mathcal{L}^{-1} \left\{ \dfrac{1}{(s + 1)(s - 2)^2} \right\}$ by using the method of residues.

Since the function whose Laplace inverse is sought satisfies condition (5) of the theorem on Page 202 [this can be established directly as in Problem 5 or by using Problem 15, Page 212], we have

$$\mathcal{L}^{-1} \left\{ \frac{1}{(s + 1)(s - 2)^2} \right\} = \frac{1}{2\pi i} \int_{\gamma - i\infty}^{\gamma + i\infty} \frac{e^{st} \, ds}{(s + 1)(s - 2)^2}$$

$$= \frac{1}{2\pi i} \oint_C \frac{e^{st} \, ds}{(s + 1)(s - 2)^2}$$

$$= \sum \text{ residues of } \frac{e^{st}}{(s + 1)(s - 2)^2} \text{ at poles } s = -1 \text{ and } s = 2$$

Now, residue at simple pole $s = -1$ is

$$\lim_{s \to -1} (s + 1) \left\{ \frac{e^{st}}{(s + 1)(s - 2)^2} \right\} = \frac{1}{9} e^{-t}$$

and residue at double pole $s = 2$ is

$$\lim_{s \to 2} \frac{1}{1!} \frac{d}{ds} \left[(s - 2)^2 \left\{ \frac{e^{st}}{(s + 1)(s - 2)^2} \right\} \right] = \lim_{s \to 2} \frac{d}{ds} \left[\frac{e^{st}}{s + 1} \right]$$

$$= \lim_{s \to 2} \frac{(s + 1)t e^{st} - e^{st}}{(s + 1)^2} = \frac{1}{3} t e^{2t} - \frac{1}{9} e^{2t}$$

Then

$$\mathcal{L}^{-1} \left\{ \frac{1}{(s + 1)(s - 2)^2} \right\} = \sum \text{ residues } = \frac{1}{9} e^{-t} + \frac{1}{3} t e^{2t} - \frac{1}{9} e^{2t}$$

7. Evaluate $\mathcal{L}^{-1} \left\{ \dfrac{s}{(s + 1)^3 (s - 1)^2} \right\}$.

As in Problem 6, the required inverse is the sum of the residues of

$$\frac{s e^{st}}{(s + 1)^3 (s - 1)^2}$$

at the poles $s = -1$ and $s = 1$ which are of orders three and two respectively.

Now, residue at $s = -1$ is

$$\lim_{s \to -1} \frac{1}{2!} \frac{d^2}{ds^2}\left[(s+1)^3 \frac{se^{st}}{(s+1)^3 (s-1)^2}\right] = \lim_{s \to -1} \frac{1}{2} \frac{d^2}{ds^2}\left[\frac{se^{st}}{(s-1)^2}\right] = \frac{1}{16} e^{-t}(1-2t^2)$$

and residue at $s = 1$ is

$$\lim_{s \to 1} \frac{1}{1!} \frac{d}{ds}\left[(s-1)^2 \frac{se^{st}}{(s+1)^3 (s-1)^2}\right] = \lim_{s \to 1} \frac{d}{ds}\left[\frac{se^{st}}{(s-1)^2}\right] = \frac{1}{16} e^{t}(2t-1)$$

Then $\quad \mathcal{L}^{-1}\left\{\dfrac{s}{(s+1)^3 (s-1)^2}\right\} = \sum \text{ residues } = \dfrac{1}{16} e^{-t}(1-2t^2) + \dfrac{1}{16} e^{t}(2t-1)$

8. Evaluate $\quad \mathcal{L}^{-1}\left\{\dfrac{1}{(s^2+1)^2}\right\}$.

We have $\qquad \dfrac{1}{(s^2+1)^2} = \dfrac{1}{[(s+i)(s-i)]^2} = \dfrac{1}{(s+i)^2 (s-i)^2}$

The required inverse is the sum of the residues of

$$\frac{e^{st}}{(s+i)^2 (s-i)^2}$$

at the poles $s = i$ and $s = -i$ which are of order two each.

Now, residue at $s = i$ is

$$\lim_{s \to i} \frac{d}{ds}\left[(s-i)^2 \frac{e^{st}}{(s+i)^2 (s-i)^2}\right] = -\frac{1}{4} te^{it} - \frac{1}{4} ie^{it}$$

and residue at $s = -i$ is

$$\lim_{s \to -i} \frac{d}{ds}\left[(s+i)^2 \frac{e^{st}}{(s+i)^2 (s-i)^2}\right] = -\frac{1}{4} te^{-it} + \frac{1}{4} ie^{-it}$$

which can also be obtained from the residue at $s = i$ by replacing i by $-i$. Then

$$\sum \text{ residues } = -\frac{1}{4} t(e^{it} + e^{-it}) - \frac{1}{4} i(e^{it} - e^{-it})$$

$$= -\frac{1}{2} t \cos t + \frac{1}{2} \sin t = \frac{1}{2}(\sin t - t \cos t)$$

Compare with Problem 18, Page 54.

INVERSE LAPLACE TRANSFORMS OF FUNCTIONS WITH BRANCH POINTS

9. Find $\quad \mathcal{L}^{-1}\left\{\dfrac{e^{-a\sqrt{s}}}{s}\right\}$ by use of the complex inversion formula.

By the complex inversion formula, the required inverse Laplace transform is given by

$$F(t) = \frac{1}{2\pi i} \int_{\gamma - i\infty}^{\gamma + i\infty} \frac{e^{st - a\sqrt{s}}}{s} ds \qquad (1)$$

Since $s = 0$ is a branch point of the integrand, we consider

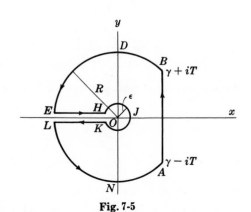

Fig. 7-5

$$\frac{1}{2\pi i} \oint_C \frac{e^{st-a\sqrt{s}}}{s}\, ds \;=\; \frac{1}{2\pi i} \int_{AB} \frac{e^{st-a\sqrt{s}}}{s}\, ds \;+\; \frac{1}{2\pi i} \int_{BDE} \frac{e^{st-a\sqrt{s}}}{s}\, ds$$

$$+\; \frac{1}{2\pi i} \int_{EH} \frac{e^{st-a\sqrt{s}}}{s}\, ds \;+\; \frac{1}{2\pi i} \int_{HJK} \frac{e^{st-a\sqrt{s}}}{s}\, ds$$

$$+\; \frac{1}{2\pi i} \int_{KL} \frac{e^{st-a\sqrt{s}}}{s}\, ds \;+\; \frac{1}{2\pi i} \int_{LNA} \frac{e^{st-a\sqrt{s}}}{s}\, ds$$

where C is the contour of Fig. 7-5 consisting of the line AB ($s=\gamma$), the arcs BDE and LNA of a circle of radius R and center at origin O, and the arc HJK of a circle of radius ϵ with center at O.

Since the only singularity $s=0$ of the integrand is not inside C, the integral on the left is zero by Cauchy's theorem. Also, the integrand satisfies the condition of Problem 2 [see Problem 61] so that on taking the limit as $R \to \infty$ the integrals along BDE and LNA approach zero. It follows that

$$F(t) \;=\; \lim_{\substack{R \to \infty \\ \epsilon \to 0}} \frac{1}{2\pi i} \int_{AB} \frac{e^{st-a\sqrt{s}}}{s}\, ds \;=\; \frac{1}{2\pi i} \int_{\gamma-i\infty}^{\gamma+i\infty} \frac{e^{st-a\sqrt{s}}}{s}\, ds$$

$$=\; -\lim_{\substack{R \to \infty \\ \epsilon \to 0}} \frac{1}{2\pi i} \left\{ \int_{EH} \frac{e^{st-a\sqrt{s}}}{s}\, ds \;+\; \int_{HJK} \frac{e^{st-a\sqrt{s}}}{s}\, ds \;+\; \int_{KL} \frac{e^{st-a\sqrt{s}}}{s}\, ds \right\} \qquad (2)$$

Along EH, $s = xe^{\pi i}$, $\sqrt{s} = \sqrt{x}\, e^{\pi i/2} = i\sqrt{x}$ and as s goes from $-R$ to $-\epsilon$, x goes from R to ϵ. Hence we have

$$\int_{EH} \frac{e^{st-a\sqrt{s}}}{s}\, ds \;=\; \int_{-R}^{-\epsilon} \frac{e^{st-a\sqrt{s}}}{s}\, ds \;=\; \int_{R}^{\epsilon} \frac{e^{-xt-ai\sqrt{x}}}{x}\, dx$$

Similarly, along KL, $s = xe^{-\pi i}$, $\sqrt{s} = \sqrt{x}\, e^{-\pi i/2} = -i\sqrt{x}$ and as s goes from $-\epsilon$ to $-R$, x goes from ϵ to R. Then

$$\int_{KL} \frac{e^{st-a\sqrt{s}}}{s}\, ds \;=\; \int_{-\epsilon}^{-R} \frac{e^{st-a\sqrt{s}}}{s}\, ds \;=\; \int_{\epsilon}^{R} \frac{e^{-xt+ai\sqrt{x}}}{x}\, dx$$

Along HJK, $s = \epsilon e^{i\theta}$ and we have

$$\int_{HJK} \frac{e^{st-a\sqrt{s}}}{s}\, ds \;=\; \int_{\pi}^{-\pi} \frac{e^{\epsilon e^{i\theta}t\, -\, a\sqrt{\epsilon}\, e^{i\theta/2}}}{\epsilon e^{i\theta}}\, i\epsilon e^{i\theta}\, d\theta$$

$$=\; i \int_{\pi}^{-\pi} e^{\epsilon e^{i\theta}t\, -\, a\sqrt{\epsilon}\, e^{i\theta/2}}\, d\theta$$

Thus (2) becomes

$$F(t) \;=\; -\lim_{\substack{R \to \infty \\ \epsilon \to 0}} \frac{1}{2\pi i} \left\{ \int_{R}^{\epsilon} \frac{e^{-xt-ai\sqrt{x}}}{x}\, dx \;+\; \int_{\epsilon}^{R} \frac{e^{-xt+ai\sqrt{x}}}{x}\, dx \;+\; i \int_{\pi}^{-\pi} e^{\epsilon e^{i\theta}t\, -\, a\sqrt{\epsilon}\, e^{i\theta/2}}\, d\theta \right\}$$

$$=\; -\lim_{\substack{R \to \infty \\ \epsilon \to 0}} \frac{1}{2\pi i} \left\{ \int_{\epsilon}^{R} \frac{e^{-xt}(e^{ai\sqrt{x}} - e^{-ai\sqrt{x}})}{x}\, dx \;+\; i \int_{\pi}^{-\pi} e^{\epsilon e^{i\theta}t\, -\, a\sqrt{\epsilon}\, e^{i\theta/2}}\, d\theta \right\}$$

$$=\; -\lim_{\substack{R \to \infty \\ \epsilon \to 0}} \frac{1}{2\pi i} \left\{ 2i \int_{\epsilon}^{R} \frac{e^{-xt} \sin a\sqrt{x}}{x}\, dx \;+\; i \int_{\pi}^{-\pi} e^{\epsilon e^{i\theta}t\, -\, a\sqrt{\epsilon}\, e^{i\theta/2}}\, d\theta \right\}$$

Since the limit can be taken underneath the integral sign, we have

$$\lim_{\epsilon \to 0} \int_{\pi}^{-\pi} e^{\epsilon e^{i\theta}t\, -\, a\sqrt{\epsilon}\, e^{i\theta/2}}\, d\theta \;=\; \int_{\pi}^{-\pi} 1\, d\theta \;=\; -2\pi$$

and so we find

$$F(t) \;=\; 1 - \frac{1}{\pi} \int_{0}^{\infty} \frac{e^{-xt} \sin a\sqrt{x}}{x}\, dx \qquad (3)$$

This can be written (see Problem 10) as

$$F(t) \;=\; 1 - \operatorname{erf}\,(a/2\sqrt{t}) \;=\; \operatorname{erfc}\,(a/2\sqrt{t}) \qquad (4)$$

10. Prove that $\dfrac{1}{\pi}\displaystyle\int_0^\infty \dfrac{e^{-xt}\sin a\sqrt{x}}{x}\,dx \;=\; \mathrm{erf}\,(a/2\sqrt{t})$ and thus establish the final result (4) of Problem 9.

Letting $x = u^2$, the required integral becomes

$$I \;=\; \frac{2}{\pi}\int_0^\infty \frac{e^{-u^2 t}\sin au}{u}\,du$$

Then differentiating with respect to a and using Problem 183, Page 41,

$$\frac{\partial I}{\partial a} \;=\; \frac{2}{\pi}\int_0^\infty e^{-u^2 t}\cos au\,du \;=\; \frac{2}{\pi}\left(\frac{\sqrt{\pi}}{2\sqrt{t}}\,e^{-a^2/4t}\right) \;=\; \frac{1}{\sqrt{\pi t}}\,e^{-a^2/4t}$$

Hence, using the fact that $I = 0$ when $a = 0$,

$$I \;=\; \int_0^a \frac{1}{\sqrt{\pi t}}\,e^{-p^2/4t}\,dp \;=\; \frac{2}{\sqrt{\pi}}\int_0^{a/2\sqrt{t}} e^{-u^2}\,du \;=\; \mathrm{erf}\,(a/2\sqrt{t})$$

and the required result is established.

11. Find $\mathcal{L}^{-1}\{e^{-a\sqrt{s}}\}$.

If $\mathcal{L}\{F(t)\} = f(s)$, then we have $\mathcal{L}\{F'(t)\} = s\,f(s) - F(0) = s\,f(s)$ if $F(0) = 0$. Thus if $\mathcal{L}^{-1}\{f(s)\} = F(t)$ and $F(0) = 0$, then $\mathcal{L}^{-1}\{s\,f(s)\} = F'(t)$.

By Problems 9 and 10, we have

$$F(t) \;=\; \mathrm{erfc}\,(a/2\sqrt{t}) \;=\; 1 - \frac{2}{\sqrt{\pi}}\int_0^{a/2\sqrt{t}} e^{-u^2}\,du$$

so that $F(0) = 0$ and

$$f(s) \;=\; \mathcal{L}\{F(t)\} \;=\; \frac{e^{-a\sqrt{s}}}{s}$$

Then it follows that

$$\mathcal{L}^{-1}\{e^{-a\sqrt{s}}\} \;=\; F'(t) \;=\; \frac{d}{dt}\left\{1 - \frac{2}{\sqrt{\pi}}\int_0^{a/2\sqrt{t}} e^{-u^2}\,du\right\}$$

$$=\; \frac{a}{2\sqrt{\pi}}\,t^{-3/2}\,e^{-a^2/4t}$$

INVERSE LAPLACE TRANSFORMS OF FUNCTIONS WITH INFINITELY MANY SINGULARITIES

12. Find all the singularities of $f(s) = \dfrac{\cosh x\sqrt{s}}{s\cosh\sqrt{s}}$ where $0 < x < 1$.

Because of the presence of $\sqrt{s}$, it would appear that $s = 0$ is a branch point. That this is not so, however, can be seen by noting that

$$f(s) \;=\; \frac{\cosh x\sqrt{s}}{s\cosh\sqrt{s}} \;=\; \frac{1 + (x\sqrt{s})^2/2! + (x\sqrt{s})^4/4! + \cdots}{s\{1 + (\sqrt{s})^2/2! + (\sqrt{s})^4/4! + \cdots\}}$$

$$=\; \frac{1 + x^2 s/2! + x^4 s^2/4! + \cdots}{s\{1 + s/2! + s^2/4! + \cdots\}}$$

from which it is evident that there is no branch point at $s = 0$. However, there is a simple pole at $s = 0$.

The function $f(s)$ also has infinitely many poles given by the roots of the equation

$$\cosh\sqrt{s} \;=\; \frac{e^{\sqrt{s}} + e^{-\sqrt{s}}}{2} \;=\; 0$$

These occur where $\qquad e^{2\sqrt{s}} = -1 = e^{\pi i + 2k\pi i} \qquad k = 0, \pm 1, \pm 2, \ldots$

from which $\qquad\qquad \sqrt{s} = (k + \tfrac{1}{2})\pi i \quad$ or $\quad s = -(k + \tfrac{1}{2})^2\pi^2$

These are simple poles [see Problem 56].

Thus $f(s)$ has simple poles at

$$s = 0 \ \text{ and } \ s = s_n \quad \text{where} \quad s_n = -(n - \tfrac{1}{2})^2\pi^2, \ n = 1, 2, 3, \ldots$$

13. Find $\quad \mathcal{L}^{-1}\left\{\dfrac{\cosh x\sqrt{s}}{s \cosh \sqrt{s}}\right\} \quad$ where $\ 0 < x < 1.$

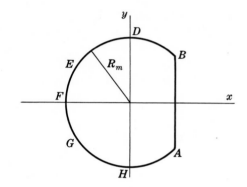

Fig. 7-6

The required inverse can be found by using the Bromwich contour of Fig. 7-6. The line AB is chosen so as to lie to the right of all the poles which, as seen in Problem 12, are given by

$$s = 0 \ \text{ and } \ s = s_n = -(n - \tfrac{1}{2})^2\pi^2, \ n = 1, 2, 3, \ldots$$

We choose the Bromwich contour so that the curved portion $BDEFGHA$ is an arc of a circle Γ_m with center at the origin and radius

$$R_m = m^2\pi^2$$

where m is a positive integer. This choice insures that the contour does not pass through any of the poles.

We now find the residues of

$$\frac{e^{st} \cosh x\sqrt{s}}{s \cosh \sqrt{s}}$$

at the poles. We have:

Residue at $s = 0$ is $\qquad \lim\limits_{s \to 0} (s - 0)\left\{\dfrac{e^{st} \cosh x\sqrt{s}}{s \cosh \sqrt{s}}\right\} = 1$

Residue at $\quad s = -(n - \tfrac{1}{2})^2\pi^2, \ n = 1, 2, 3, \ldots \quad$ is

$$\lim_{s \to s_n} (s - s_n)\left\{\frac{e^{st} \cosh x\sqrt{s}}{s \cosh \sqrt{s}}\right\} = \lim_{s \to s_n}\left\{\frac{s - s_n}{\cosh \sqrt{s}}\right\} \lim_{s \to s_n}\left\{\frac{e^{st} \cosh x\sqrt{s}}{s}\right\}$$

$$= \lim_{s \to s_n}\left\{\frac{1}{(\sinh \sqrt{s})(1/2\sqrt{s})}\right\} \lim_{s \to s_n}\left\{\frac{e^{st} \cosh x\sqrt{s}}{s}\right\}$$

$$= \frac{4(-1)^n}{\pi(2n - 1)}\, e^{-(n - 1/2)^2\pi^2 t}\, \cos (n - \tfrac{1}{2})\pi x$$

If C_m is the contour of Fig. 7-6, then

$$\frac{1}{2\pi i} \oint_{C_m} \frac{e^{st} \cosh x\sqrt{s}}{s \cosh \sqrt{s}}\, ds = 1 + \frac{4}{\pi} \sum_{n=1}^{m} \frac{(-1)^n}{2n - 1}\, e^{-(n - 1/2)^2\pi^2 t}\, \cos (n - \tfrac{1}{2})\pi x$$

Taking the limit as $m \to \infty$ and noting that the integral around Γ_m approaches zero [see Problem 54], we find

$$\mathcal{L}^{-1}\left\{\frac{\cosh x\sqrt{s}}{s \cosh \sqrt{s}}\right\} = 1 + \frac{4}{\pi} \sum_{n=1}^{\infty} \frac{(-1)^n}{2n - 1}\, e^{-(n - 1/2)^2\pi^2 t}\, \cos (n - \tfrac{1}{2})\pi x$$

$$= 1 + \frac{4}{\pi} \sum_{n=1}^{\infty} \frac{(-1)^n}{2n - 1}\, e^{-(2n - 1)^2\pi^2 t/4}\, \cos \frac{(2n - 1)\pi x}{2}$$

14. Find $\mathcal{L}^{-1}\left\{\dfrac{\sinh sx}{s^2 \cosh sa}\right\}$ **where** $0 < x < a$.

The function $f(s) = \dfrac{\sinh sx}{s^2 \cosh sa}$ has poles at $s = 0$ and at values of s for which $\cosh sa = 0$, i.e.,

$$s \;=\; s_k \;=\; (k + \tfrac{1}{2})\pi i/a \qquad k \;=\; 0, \pm 1, \pm 2, \ldots$$

Because of the presence of s^2, it would appear that $s = 0$ is a pole of order two. However, by observing that near $s = 0$,

$$\frac{\sinh sx}{s^2 \cosh sa} \;=\; \frac{sx + (sx)^3/3! + (sx)^5/5! + \cdots}{s^2\{1 + (sa)^2/2! + (sa)^4/4! + \cdots\}}$$

$$=\; \frac{x + s^2 x^3/3! + s^4 x^5/5!}{s\{1 + s^2 a^2/2! + s^4 a^4/4! + \cdots\}}$$

we see that $s = 0$ is a pole of order one, i.e. a simple pole. The poles s_k are also simple poles [see Problem 56].

Proceeding as in Problem 13, we obtain the residues of $e^{st} f(s)$ at these poles.

Residue at $s = 0$ is

$$\lim_{s \to 0}\, (s - 0)\left\{\frac{e^{st}\sinh sx}{s^2 \cosh sa}\right\} \;=\; \left\{\lim_{s \to 0}\frac{\sinh sx}{s}\right\}\left\{\lim_{s \to 0}\frac{e^{st}}{\cosh sa}\right\} \;=\; x$$

using L'Hospital's rule.

Residue at $s = s_k$ is

$$\lim_{s \to s_k}\, (s - s_k)\left\{\frac{e^{st}\sinh sx}{s^2 \cosh sa}\right\}$$

$$=\; \left\{\lim_{s \to s_k}\frac{s - s_k}{\cosh sa}\right\}\left\{\lim_{s \to s_k}\frac{e^{st}\sinh sx}{s^2}\right\}$$

$$=\; \left\{\lim_{s \to s_k}\frac{1}{a\sinh sa}\right\}\left\{\lim_{s \to s_k}\frac{e^{st}\sinh sx}{s^2}\right\}$$

$$=\; \frac{1}{ai\sin (k + \tfrac{1}{2})\pi} \cdot \frac{e^{(k + \frac{1}{2})\pi it/a}\, i\, \sin (k + \tfrac{1}{2})\pi x/a}{-\,(k + \tfrac{1}{2})^2 \pi^2/a^2}$$

$$=\; -\,\frac{a(-1)^k\, e^{(k + \frac{1}{2})\pi it/a}\, \sin (k + \tfrac{1}{2})\pi x/a}{\pi^2 (k + \tfrac{1}{2})^2}$$

By an appropriate limiting procedure similar to that used in Problem 13, we find on taking the sum of the residues the required result,

$$\mathcal{L}^{-1}\left\{\frac{\sinh sx}{s^2 \cosh sa}\right\} \;=\; x \;-\; \frac{a}{\pi^2}\sum_{k=-\infty}^{\infty}\frac{(-1)^k\, e^{(k + \frac{1}{2})\pi it/a}\, \sin (k + \tfrac{1}{2})\pi x/a}{(k + \tfrac{1}{2})^2}$$

$$=\; x \;+\; \frac{2a}{\pi^2}\sum_{n=1}^{\infty}\frac{(-1)^n \cos (n - \tfrac{1}{2})\pi t/a\, \sin (n - \tfrac{1}{2})\pi x/a}{(n - \tfrac{1}{2})^2}$$

$$=\; x \;+\; \frac{8a}{\pi^2}\sum_{n=1}^{\infty}\frac{(-1)^n}{(2n - 1)^2}\sin\frac{(2n - 1)\pi x}{2a}\cos\frac{(2n - 1)\pi t}{2a}$$

MISCELLANEOUS PROBLEMS

15. Let $f(s) = P(s)/Q(s)$ where $P(s)$ and $Q(s)$ are polynomials such that the degree of $P(s)$ is less than the degree of $Q(s)$. Prove that $f(s)$ satisfies the condition in Problem 2.

Let
$$P(s) = a_0 s^m + a_1 s^{m-1} + \cdots + a_m$$
$$Q(s) = b_0 s^n + b_1 s^{n-1} + \cdots + b_n$$

where $a_0 \neq 0$, $b_0 \neq 0$ and $0 \leqq m < n$. Then if $s = Re^{i\theta}$, we have

$$|f(s)| = \left| \frac{P(s)}{Q(s)} \right| = \left| \frac{a_0 s^m + a_1 s^{m-1} + \cdots + a_m}{b_0 s^n + b_1 s^{n-1} + \cdots + b_n} \right|$$

$$= \left| \frac{a_0 R^m e^{mi\theta} + a_1 R^{m-1} e^{(m-1)i\theta} + \cdots + a_m}{b_0 R^n e^{ni\theta} + b_1 R^{n-1} e^{(n-1)i\theta} + \cdots + a_n} \right|$$

$$= \left| \frac{a_0}{b_0} \right| \frac{1}{R^{n-m}} \left| \frac{1 + (a_1/a_0 R)e^{-i\theta} + (a_2/a_0 R^2)e^{-2i\theta} + \cdots + (a_m/a_0 R^m)e^{-ni\theta}}{1 + (b_1/b_0 R)e^{-i\theta} + (b_2/b_0 R^2)e^{-2i\theta} + \cdots + (b_n/b_0 R^n)e^{-ni\theta}} \right|$$

Let A denote the maximum of $|a_1/a_0|$, $|a_2/a_0|$, ..., $|a_m/a_0|$.

Let B denote the maximum of $|b_1/b_0|$, $|b_2/b_0|$, ..., $|b_n/b_0|$.

Then

$$\left| 1 + \frac{a_1}{a_0 R} e^{-i\theta} + \frac{a_2}{a_0 R^2} e^{-2i\theta} + \cdots + \frac{a_m}{a_0 R^m} e^{-mi\theta} \right| \leqq 1 + \frac{A}{R} + \frac{A}{R^2} + \cdots + \frac{A}{R^m}$$

$$\leqq 1 + \frac{A}{R}\left(1 + \frac{1}{R} + \frac{1}{R^2} + \cdots \right)$$

$$\leqq 1 + \frac{A}{R-1} < 2$$

for $R > A + 1$.

Also,
$$\left| 1 + \frac{b_1}{b_0 R} e^{-i\theta} + \frac{b_2}{b_0 R^2} e^{-2i\theta} + \cdots + \frac{b_n}{b_0 R^n} e^{-ni\theta} \right|$$

$$\geqq 1 - \left| \frac{b_1}{b_0 R} e^{-i\theta} + \frac{b_2}{b_0 R^2} e^{-2i\theta} + \cdots + \frac{b_n}{b_0 R^n} e^{-ni\theta} \right|$$

$$\geqq 1 - \left(\frac{B}{R} + \frac{B}{R^2} + \cdots + \frac{B}{R^n} \right)$$

$$\geqq 1 - \frac{B}{R}\left(1 + \frac{1}{R^2} + \frac{1}{R^2} + \cdots \right)$$

$$\geqq 1 - \frac{B}{R-1} \geqq \frac{1}{2}$$

for $R > 2B + 1$.

Thus for R larger than either $A + 1$ or $2B + 1$, we have

$$|f(s)| \leqq \left| \frac{a_0}{b_0} \right| \cdot \frac{1}{R^{n-m}} \cdot \frac{1}{1/2} \leqq \frac{M}{R^k}$$

where M is any constant greater than $2|a_0/b_0|$ and $k = n - m \geqq 1$. This proves the required result.

16. Find $\mathcal{L}^{-1}\left\{ \dfrac{\cosh x\sqrt{s}}{s \cosh a\sqrt{s}} \right\}$ where $0 < x < a$.

(a) *Method 1.* From Problem 13, we have

$$\mathcal{L}^{-1}\left\{ \frac{\cosh x\sqrt{s}}{s \cosh \sqrt{s}} \right\} = 1 + \frac{4}{\pi} \sum_{n=1}^{\infty} \frac{(-1)^n}{2n-1} e^{-(2n-1)^2 \pi^2 t/4} \cos \frac{(2n-1)\pi x}{2}$$

Replacing s by ks, we find by the change of scale property, Page 44,

$$\mathcal{L}^{-1}\left\{\frac{\cosh x\sqrt{ks}}{ks\cosh\sqrt{ks}}\right\} \;=\; \frac{1}{k}\left\{1 \;+\; \frac{4}{\pi}\sum_{n=1}^{\infty}\frac{(-1)^n}{2n-1}\,e^{-(2n-1)^2\pi^2 t/4k}\cos\frac{(2n-1)\pi x}{2}\right\}$$

Then multiplying both sides by k, replacing k by a^2 and x by x/a, we find the required result

$$\mathcal{L}^{-1}\left\{\frac{\cosh x\sqrt{s}}{s\cosh a\sqrt{s}}\right\} \;=\; 1 \;+\; \frac{4}{\pi}\sum_{n=1}^{\infty}\frac{(-1)^n}{2n-1}\,e^{-(2n-1)^2\pi^2 t/4a^2}\cos\frac{(2n-1)\pi x}{2a}$$

Method 2.   We can also use the inversion formula directly as in Problem 13.

17. Find $\mathcal{L}^{-1}\left\{\dfrac{\cosh sx}{s^3\cosh sb}\right\}$ where $0 < x < b$.

Let $f(s) = \dfrac{\cosh sx}{s^3\cosh sb}$.   Then $s=0$ is a pole of order 3, while $s = s_k = (2k+1)\pi i/2b$, $k = 0$, $\pm 1, \pm 2, \ldots$ [which are roots of $\cosh sb = 0$], are simple poles. Proceeding as in Problem 13, we have: Residue of $e^{st} f(s)$ at $s = s_k$ is

$$\lim_{s\to s_k}(s - s_k)\left\{\frac{e^{st}\cosh sx}{s^3\cosh sb}\right\}$$

$$=\; \left\{\lim_{s\to s_k}\frac{s - s_k}{\cosh sb}\right\}\left\{\lim_{s\to s_k}\frac{e^{st}\cosh sx}{s^3}\right\}$$

$$=\; \frac{1}{b\sinh(2k+1)\pi i/2}\cdot\frac{e^{(2k+1)\pi it/2b}\cosh(2k+1)\pi ix/2b}{\{(2k+1)\pi i/2b\}^3}$$

$$=\; \frac{(-1)^k\,8b^2\,e^{(2k+1)\pi it/2b}}{(2k+1)\pi^3}\cos\frac{(2k+1)\pi x}{2b}$$

To find the residue at $s = 0$, we write

$$\frac{e^{st}\cosh sx}{s^3\cosh sb} \;=\; \frac{1}{s^3}\left(1 + st + \frac{s^2t^2}{2!} + \cdots\right)\left\{\frac{1 + s^2x^2/2! + s^4x^4/4! + \cdots}{1 + s^2b^2/2! + s^4b^4/4! + \cdots}\right\}$$

$$=\; \frac{1}{s^3}\left(1 + st + \frac{s^2t^2}{2!} + \cdots\right)\left(1 + \frac{s^2x^2}{2!} + \frac{s^4x^4}{4!} + \cdots\right)\left(1 - \frac{s^2b^2}{2} + \frac{5s^4b^4}{24} - \cdots\right)$$

$$=\; \frac{1}{s^3}\left\{1 + st + \frac{s^2t^2}{2} + \frac{s^2x^2}{2} - \frac{s^2b^2}{2} + \cdots\right\}$$

Thus the residue [which is the coefficient of $1/s$ in this series] is $\frac{1}{2}(t^2 + x^2 - b^2)$.

The residue at $s = 0$ can also be obtained by evaluating

$$\lim_{s\to 0}\frac{1}{2!}\frac{d^3}{ds^3}\left\{(s-0)^3\frac{e^{st}\cosh sx}{s^3\cosh sb}\right\}$$

The required inverse Laplace transform is the sum of the above residues and is

$$\frac{1}{2}(t^2 + x^2 - b^2) \;+\; \frac{8b^2}{\pi^3}\sum_{k=-\infty}^{\infty}\frac{(-1)^k\,e^{(2k+1)\pi it/2b}}{(2k+1)^3}\cos\frac{(2k+1)\pi x}{2b}$$

$$=\; \frac{1}{2}(t^2 + x^2 - b^2) \;-\; \frac{16b^2}{\pi^3}\sum_{n=1}^{\infty}\frac{(-1)^n}{(2n-1)^3}\cos\frac{(2n-1)\pi t}{2b}\cos\frac{(2n-1)\pi x}{2b}$$

which is entry 123 in the Table on Page 252.

18. A periodic voltage $E(t)$ in the form of a "square wave" as shown in Fig. 7-7 is applied to the electric circuit of Fig. 7-8. Assuming that the current is zero at time $t = 0$, find it at any later time.

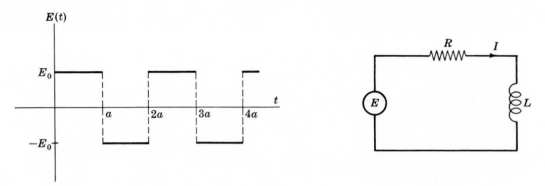

Fig. 7-7   **Fig. 7-8**

The differential equation for the current $I(t)$ in the circuit is

$$L\frac{dI}{dt} + RI = E(t) \qquad \text{where} \quad I(0) = 0 \tag{1}$$

Taking Laplace transforms, using entry 135 in the Table on Page 253, we find

$$Ls\,\tilde{I} + R\tilde{I} = \frac{E_0}{s}\tanh\frac{as}{2} \qquad \text{or} \qquad \tilde{I}(s) = \frac{E_0}{s(Ls+R)}\tanh\frac{as}{2}$$

where $\tilde{I}(s) = \mathcal{L}\{I(t)\}$. Thus

$$I(t) = \frac{E_0}{L}\mathcal{L}^{-1}\left\{\frac{1}{s(s+R/L)}\tanh\frac{as}{2}\right\} \tag{2}$$

The function $f(s) = \dfrac{1}{s(s+R/L)}\tanh\dfrac{as}{2}$ has a simple pole at $s = -R/L$ and simple poles at $s = s_k = (2k+1)\pi i/a$, $k = 0, \pm 1, \ldots$ where $\cosh(as/2) = 0$ [compare Problem 17]. The value $s = 0$ is not a pole since $\displaystyle\lim_{s\to 0}\frac{\tanh(as/2)}{s} = \frac{a}{2}$ is finite. Thus $s = 0$ is a removable singularity.

Proceeding as in Problems 13 and 17, we obtain the residues of $e^{st}f(s)$ at the poles. We find:

Residue at $s = -R/L$ is

$$\lim_{s\to -R/L}(s+R/L)\left\{\frac{e^{st}}{s(s+R/L)}\tanh\frac{as}{2}\right\} = \frac{L}{R}e^{-Rt/L}\tanh\frac{aR}{2L}$$

Residue at $s = s_k = (2k+1)\pi i/a$ is

$$\lim_{s\to s_k}(s-s_k)\left\{\frac{e^{st}}{s(s+R/L)}\tanh\frac{as}{2}\right\}$$

$$= \left\{\lim_{s\to s_k}\frac{s-s_k}{\cosh(as/2)}\right\}\left\{\lim_{s\to s_k}\frac{e^{st}\sinh(as/2)}{s(s+R/L)}\right\}$$

$$= \left\{\frac{1}{(a/2)\sinh(as_k/2)}\right\}\left\{\frac{e^{s_k t}\sinh(as_k/2)}{s_k(s_k+R/L)}\right\}$$

$$= \frac{2e^{(2k+1)\pi it/a}}{(2k+1)\pi i\{(2k+1)\pi i/a+R/L\}}$$

Then the sum of the residues is

$$\frac{L}{R}\,e^{-Rt/L}\,\tanh\frac{aR}{2L} \;+\; \sum_{k=-\infty}^{\infty}\frac{2e^{(2k+1)\pi it/a}}{(2k+1)\pi i\,\{(2k+1)\pi i/a + R/L\}}$$

$$=\;\frac{L}{R}\,e^{-Rt/L}\,\tanh\frac{aR}{2L} \;+\; \frac{4aL}{\pi}\sum_{n=1}^{\infty}\frac{aR\sin(2n-1)\pi t/a \;-\;(2n-1)\pi L\cos(2n-1)\pi t/a}{(2n-1)\{a^2R^2 + (2n-1)^2\pi^2L^2\}}$$

Thus from (2) we have the required result

$$I(t)\;=\;\frac{E_0}{R}\,e^{-Rt/L}\,\tanh\frac{aR}{2L} \;+\; \frac{4aE_0}{\pi}\sum_{n=1}^{\infty}\frac{aR\sin(2n-1)\pi t/a \;-\;(2n-1)\pi L\cos(2n-1)\pi t/a}{(2n-1)\{a^2R^2 + (2n-1)^2\pi^2L^2\}}$$

This can also be written in the form

$$I(t)\;=\;\frac{E_0}{R}\,e^{-Rt/L}\,\tanh\frac{aR}{2L} \;+\; \frac{4aE_0}{\pi}\sum_{n=1}^{\infty}\frac{\sin\{(2n-1)\pi t/a \;-\;\phi_n\}}{(2n-1)\{a^2R^2 + (2n-1)^2\pi^2L^2\}^{1/2}}$$

where $\phi_n = \tan^{-1}\{(2n-1)\pi L/aR\}$.

Supplementary Problems

THE COMPLEX INVERSION FORMULA AND USE OF RESIDUE THEOREM

19. Use the complex inversion formula to evaluate

(a) $\mathcal{L}^{-1}\left\{\dfrac{s}{s^2+a^2}\right\}$ (b) $\mathcal{L}^{-1}\left\{\dfrac{1}{s^2+a^2}\right\}$ (c) $\mathcal{L}^{-1}\left\{\dfrac{1}{(s+1)(s^2+1)}\right\}$

Ans. (a) $\cos at$,   (b) $(\sin at)/a$,   (c) $\frac{1}{2}(\sin t - \cos t + e^{-t})$

20. Find the inverse Laplace transform of each of the following using the complex inversion formula:

(a) $1/(s+1)^2$,   (b) $1/s^3(s^2+1)$.

Ans. (a) te^{-t},   (b) $\frac{1}{2}t^2 + \cos t - 1$

21. (a) Show that $f(s) = \dfrac{1}{s^2-3s+2}$ satisfies the conditions of the inversion formula.   (b) Find $\mathcal{L}^{-1}\{f(s)\}$.
   Ans. (b) $e^{2t} - e^t$

22. Evaluate $\mathcal{L}^{-1}\left\{\dfrac{s^2}{(s^2+4)^2}\right\}$ justifying all steps.

   Ans. $\frac{1}{4}\sin 2t + \frac{1}{2}t\cos 2t$

23. (a) Evaluate $\mathcal{L}^{-1}\left\{\dfrac{s}{(s^2+1)^3}\right\}$ justifying all steps and

   (b) check your answer.

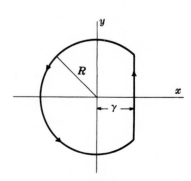

24. (a) Evaluate $\dfrac{1}{2\pi i}\displaystyle\oint_C\frac{se^{st}}{(s^2-1)^2}\,ds$ around the contour C
shown in the adjoining figure where $R \geqq 3$ and $\gamma > 1$.

   (b) Give an interpretation of your answer as far as Laplace transform theory is concerned.

Fig. 7-9

25. Use the inversion formula to evaluate $\mathcal{L}^{-1}\left\{\dfrac{s}{(s+a)(s-b)^2}\right\}$ where a and b are any positive constants.

26. Use the inversion formula to work: (a) Problem 13, Page 53; (b) Problem 25, Page 58; (c) Problem 28, Page 60; (d) Problem 110, Page 74.

INVERSE LAPLACE TRANSFORMS OF FUNCTIONS WITH BRANCH POINTS

27. Find $\mathcal{L}^{-1}\{e^{-\sqrt{s}}\}$ using the complex inversion formula.

28. Find $\mathcal{L}^{-1}\left\{\dfrac{1}{\sqrt{s}}\right\}$ by the inversion formula.

29. Show that $\mathcal{L}^{-1}\left\{\dfrac{1}{s\sqrt{s+1}}\right\} = \operatorname{erf}\sqrt{t}$ by using the inversion formula.

30. Find $\mathcal{L}^{-1}\left\{\dfrac{\sqrt{s}}{s-1}\right\}$ by using the complex inversion formula.

31. (a) Use the complex inversion formula to evaluate $\mathcal{L}^{-1}\{s^{-1/3}\}$ and (b) check your result by another method.

32. Evaluate $\mathcal{L}^{-1}\{\ln(1+1/s)\}$ by using the inversion formula.   Ans. $(1-e^{-t})/t$

33. Evaluate $\mathcal{L}^{-1}\{\ln(1+1/s^2)\}$ by the inversion formula.   Ans. $2(1-\cos t)/t$

INVERSE LAPLACE TRANSFORMS OF FUNCTIONS WITH INFINITELY MANY SINGULARITIES

34. Find $\mathcal{L}^{-1}\left\{\dfrac{1}{s(e^s+1)}\right\}$ using the complex inversion formula.

35. Prove that $\mathcal{L}^{-1}\left\{\dfrac{1}{s\cosh s}\right\} = 1 - \dfrac{4}{\pi}\left\{\cos\dfrac{\pi t}{2} - \dfrac{1}{3}\cos\dfrac{3\pi t}{2} + \dfrac{1}{5}\cos\dfrac{5\pi t}{2} - \cdots\right\}.$

36. Find $\mathcal{L}^{-1}\left\{\dfrac{1}{s^2\sinh s}\right\}.$ Ans. $\dfrac{1}{2}t^2 + \dfrac{2}{\pi^2}\sum_{n=1}^{\infty}\dfrac{(-1)^n}{n^2}(1-\cos n\pi t)$

37. By using the complex inversion formula, prove that
$$\mathcal{L}^{-1}\left\{\dfrac{1}{s^3\sinh as}\right\} = \dfrac{t(t^2-a^2)}{6a} - \dfrac{2a^2}{\pi^3}\sum_{n=1}^{\infty}\dfrac{(-1)^n}{n^3}\sin\dfrac{n\pi t}{a}$$

38. Show that $\mathcal{L}^{-1}\left\{\dfrac{1}{(s^2+\omega^2)(1+e^{-2as})}\right\} = \dfrac{\sin\omega(t+a)}{2\omega} + \dfrac{1}{a}\sum_{n=1}^{\infty}\dfrac{\cos(2n-1)\pi t/2a}{\omega^2-(2n-1)^2\pi^2/4a^2}.$

MISCELLANEOUS PROBLEMS

39. Evaluate (a) $\mathcal{L}^{-1}\{1/(s-1)^4\}$, (b) $\mathcal{L}^{-1}\{e^{-2s}/(s-1)^4\}$, by using the complex inversion formula.

40. Find $\mathcal{L}^{-1}\left\{\dfrac{s^2-1}{(s^2+1)^2}\right\}$ by contour integration.   Ans. $t\cos t$

41. Evaluate $\mathcal{L}^{-1}\left\{\dfrac{s}{(s^2+1)^4}\right\}.$ Ans. $\dfrac{1}{48}\{3t^2\cos t + (t^3-3t)\sin t\}$

42. Find $\mathcal{L}^{-1}\left\{\dfrac{3s-1}{s(s-1)^2\,(s+1)}\right\}$ by the complex inversion formula and check your result by another method.

43. (a) Prove that the function $f(s)=\dfrac{1}{s^2\cosh s}$ satisfies the conditions of *Theorem 7-1*, Page 202.

(b) Prove that $\mathcal{L}^{-1}\left\{\dfrac{1}{s^2\cosh s}\right\} = t + \dfrac{8}{\pi^2}\sum\limits_{n=1}^{\infty}\dfrac{(-1)^n}{(2n-1)^2}\sin\left(\dfrac{2n-1}{2}\right)\pi t.$

44. Discuss the relationship between the results of Problem 43(b) and Problem 35.

45. Evaluate $\mathcal{L}^{-1}\left\{\dfrac{1}{s^4+4}\right\}$ by the inversion formula, justifying all steps.

Ans. $\tfrac{1}{4}(\sin t\cosh t - \cos t\sinh t)$

46. (a) Prove that if $x>0$,

$$\mathcal{L}^{-1}\left\{\dfrac{se^{-x\sqrt{s}}}{s^2+\omega^2}\right\} = e^{-x\sqrt{\omega/2}}\cos(\omega t - x\sqrt{\omega/2}) - \dfrac{1}{\pi}\int_0^{\infty}\dfrac{ue^{-ut}\sin x\sqrt{u}}{u^2+\omega^2}\,du$$

(b) Prove that for large values of t the integral in part (a) can be neglected.

47. Prove that for $0<x<1$, $\dfrac{\sinh sx}{s^2\cosh s} = \dfrac{4}{\pi}\sum\limits_{n=1}^{\infty}\dfrac{(-1)^n}{2n-1}\dfrac{\cos(2n-1)\pi x/2}{s^2+(2n-1)\pi^2/4}.$

48. Find $\mathcal{L}^{-1}\left\{\dfrac{\operatorname{csch}^2 s}{s}\right\}.$

49. Prove that for $0<x<1$, $\dfrac{\sinh x\sqrt{s}}{\sqrt{s}\cosh\sqrt{s}} = 2\sum\limits_{n=1}^{\infty}\dfrac{(-1)^{n-1}\sin(2n-1)\pi x/2}{s+(2n-1)^2\pi^2/4}.$

50. Show that

$$\mathcal{L}^{-1}\left\{\dfrac{\ln(1+1/s^2)}{1+e^{-2as}}\right\} = \dfrac{1-\cos(t+a)}{t+a} + \dfrac{1}{a}\sum\limits_{n=1}^{\infty}\ln\left(1-\dfrac{4a^2}{(2n-1)^2\pi^2}\right)\cos\dfrac{(2n-1)\pi t}{2a}$$

51. Show that for $0<x<a$,

$$\mathcal{L}^{-1}\left\{\dfrac{\sinh\sqrt{s}\,(a-x)}{\sinh\sqrt{s}\,a}\right\} = \dfrac{a-x}{a} - \dfrac{2}{\pi}\sum\limits_{n=1}^{\infty}\dfrac{e^{-n^2\pi^2 t/a^2}}{n}\sin\dfrac{n\pi x}{a}$$

52. Use the inversion formula to work: (a) Problem 3(g), Page 48; (b) Problem 9(a), Page 51; (c) Problem 14, Page 53.

53. Using the inversion formula, solve $Y^{(iv)}(t) - a^4 Y(t) = \sin at + e^{-at}$ subject to the conditions $Y(0)=2,\ Y'(0)=0,\ Y''(0)=-1,\ Y'''(0)=0.$

54. Prove that the integral around Γ in Problem 13 goes to zero as $R\to\infty$.

55. By use of the complex inversion formula, prove: (a) *Theorem 2-3*, Page 43; (b) *Theorem 2-5*, Page 44; (c) *Theorem 2-10*, Page 45.

56. Prove that the poles found in (a) Problem 12 and (b) Problem 14 are simple poles. [*Hint.* Use the fact that if $s = a$ is a double root of $g(s) = 0$, then $s = a$ must be a simple root of $g'(s) = 0$.]

57. Evaluate $\dfrac{1}{2\pi i} \displaystyle\int_{\gamma - i\infty}^{\gamma + i\infty} \dfrac{e^{st}}{\sqrt{s+1}}\, ds$ where $\gamma > 0$.   (b) How can you check your answer?

Ans. $t^{-1/2}\, e^{-t}/\sqrt{\pi}$ if $t > 0$; 0 if $t < 0$

58. Complete the proofs of (a) Case 3 and (b) Case 4 of Problem 2.

59. A periodic voltage $E(t)$ in the form of a half-wave rectified sine curve as indicated in Fig. 7-10 is applied to the electric circuit of Fig. 7-11. Assuming that the charge on the capacitor and current are zero at $t = 0$, show that the charge on the capacitor at any later time t is given by

$$Q(t) \;=\; \frac{\pi E_0}{LT^2 \alpha^2 \omega^2} \;+\; \frac{\pi E_0}{2LT}\left\{ \frac{\sin \omega t - \sin \omega(t+T)}{\omega(\alpha^2 - \omega^2)(1 - \cos \omega T)} \;+\; \frac{\sin \alpha t - \sin \alpha(t+T)}{\alpha(\omega^2 - \alpha^2)(1 - \cos \alpha T)} \right\}$$

$$+\; \frac{2\pi E_0}{LT^2} \sum_{n=1}^{\infty} \frac{\cos 2\pi n t/T}{(\omega^2 - 4\pi^2 n^2/T^2)(\alpha^2 - 4\pi^2 n^2/T^2)}$$

where $\omega^2 = 1/LC$, $\alpha^2 = \pi^2/T^2$ and $\omega \neq \alpha$.

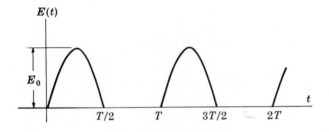

Fig. 7-10

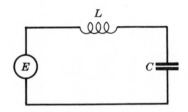

Fig. 7-11

60. Work Problem 59 in case $\alpha = \omega$ and discuss the physical significance of your results.

61. Verify *Theorem 7-1*, Page 202, for the function $e^{-a\sqrt{s}}/s$, $a > 0$ [see Problem 9].

62. Find $\mathcal{L}^{-1}\left\{ \dfrac{1}{s^2(1 - e^{-as})} \right\}$ where $a > 0$, by use of the inversion formula and check by another method.

63. Prove that $\mathcal{L}^{-1}\{e^{-s^{1/3}}\} \;=\; \dfrac{3}{\pi} \displaystyle\int_{0}^{\infty} v^2\, e^{-tv^3 - v/2} \sin \dfrac{\sqrt{3}\, v}{2}\, dv$.

64. Generalize the result of Problem 63.

65. A spring of stiffness k and of negligible mass is suspended vertically from a fixed point and carries a mass m at its lowest point. The mass m is set into vibration by pulling it down a distance x_0 and releasing it. At each time that the mass is at its lowest position, starting at $t = 0$, a unit impulse is applied. Find the position of the mass at any time $t > 0$ and discuss physically.

Chapter 8

Applications To Boundary-Value Problems

BOUNDARY-VALUE PROBLEMS INVOLVING PARTIAL DIFFERENTIAL EQUATIONS

Various problems in science and engineering, when formulated mathematically, lead to partial differential equations involving one or more unknown functions together with certain prescribed conditions on the functions which arise from the physical situation.

The conditions are called *boundary conditions*. The problem of finding solutions to the equations which satisfy the boundary conditions is called a *boundary-value problem*.

SOME IMPORTANT PARTIAL DIFFERENTIAL EQUATIONS

1. One dimensional heat conduction equation

$$\frac{\partial U}{\partial t} = k \frac{\partial^2 U}{\partial x^2}$$

Here $U(x, t)$ is the temperature in a solid at position x at time t. The constant k, called the *diffusivity*, is equal to $K/c\rho$ where the *thermal conductivity* K, the *specific heat* c and the *density* (mass per unit volume) ρ are assumed constant. The amount of heat per unit area per unit time conducted across a plane is given by $-K U_x(x, t)$.

2. One dimensional wave equation

$$\frac{\partial^2 Y}{\partial t^2} = a^2 \frac{\partial^2 Y}{\partial x^2}$$

This is applicable to the small transverse vibrations of a taut, flexible string initially located on the x axis and set into motion [see Fig. 8-1]. The variable $Y(x, t)$ is the displacement of any point x of the string at time t. The constant $a^2 = T/\rho$, where T is the (constant) tension in the string and ρ is the (constant) mass per unit length of the string.

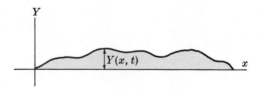

Fig. 8-1

3. Longitudinal vibrations of a beam

$$\frac{\partial^2 Y}{\partial t^2} = c^2 \frac{\partial^2 Y}{\partial x^2}$$

This equation describes the motion of a beam (Fig. 8-2) which can vibrate longitudinally (i.e. in the x direction). The variable $Y(x, t)$ is the longitudinal displacement from the equilibrium position of the cross section at x. The constant $c^2 = gE/\rho$ where g is the

Fig. 8-2

acceleration due to gravity, E is the *modulus of elasticity* (stress divided by strain) and depends on the properties of the beam, ρ is the density (mass per unit volume) of the beam.

Note that this equation is the same as that for a vibrating string.

4. Transverse vibrations of a beam

$$\frac{\partial^2 Y}{\partial t^2} + b^2\frac{\partial^4 Y}{\partial x^4} = 0$$

This equation describes the motion of a beam (initially located on the x axis, see Fig. 8-3) which is vibrating transversely (i.e. perpendicular to the x direction). In this case $Y(x,t)$ is the transverse displacement or deflection at any time t of any point x. The constant $b^2 = EIg/\rho$ where E is the modulus of elasticity, I is the moment of inertia of any cross section about the x axis, g is the acceleration due to gravity and ρ is the mass per unit length. In case an external transverse force $F(x,t)$ is applied, the right hand side of the equation is replaced by $b^2 F(x,t)/EI$.

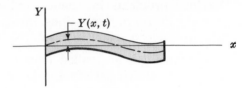

Fig. 8-3

5. Heat conduction in a cylinder

$$\frac{\partial U}{\partial t} = k\left(\frac{\partial^2 U}{\partial r^2} + \frac{1}{r}\frac{\partial U}{\partial r}\right)$$

Here $U(r,t)$ is the temperature at any time t at a distance r from the axis of a cylindrical solid. It is assumed that heat flow can take place only in the radial direction.

6. Transmission lines

$$\frac{\partial E}{\partial x} = -RI - L\frac{\partial I}{\partial t}$$

$$\frac{\partial I}{\partial x} = -GE - C\frac{\partial E}{\partial t}$$

These are simultaneous equations for the current I and voltage E in a transmission line [Fig. 8-4] at any position x and at any time t. The constants R, L, G and C are respectively the resistance, inductance, conductance and capacitance per unit length. The end $x = 0$ is called the *sending end*. Any other value of x can be considered as the *receiving end*.

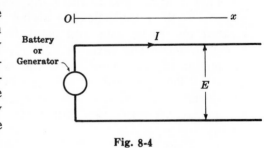

Fig. 8-4

TWO AND THREE DIMENSIONAL PROBLEMS

Many of the above partial differential equations can be generalized to apply to problems in two and three dimensions. For example, if $Z(x,y,t)$ is the transverse displacement of any point (x,y) of a membrane in the xy plane at any time t, then the vibrations of this membrane, assumed small, are governed by the equation

$$\frac{\partial^2 Z}{\partial t^2} = a^2\left(\frac{\partial^2 Z}{\partial x^2} + \frac{\partial^2 Z}{\partial y^2}\right) \tag{1}$$

Similarly,

$$\frac{\partial^2 \Phi}{\partial t^2} \;=\; a^2 \left(\frac{\partial^2 \Phi}{\partial x^2} + \frac{\partial^2 \Phi}{\partial y^2} + \frac{\partial^2 \Phi}{\partial z^2} \right) \;=\; a^2 \nabla^2 \phi \qquad (2)$$

where $\nabla^2 \phi$ is called the *Laplacian* of $\Phi(x, y, z, t)$, is the equation for the transverse vibrations of a pulsating membrane in three dimensions.

The general equation for heat conduction in a three dimensional solid is, assuming constant thermal conductivity, specific heat and density,

$$\frac{\partial U}{\partial t} \;=\; k\left(\frac{\partial^2 U}{\partial x^2} + \frac{\partial^2 U}{\partial y^2} + \frac{\partial^2 U}{\partial z^2} \right) \;=\; k\nabla^2 U \qquad (3)$$

The equation for steady-state temperature [where U is independent of time so that $\partial U/\partial t = 0$] is

$$\frac{\partial^2 U}{\partial x^2} + \frac{\partial^2 U}{\partial y^2} + \frac{\partial^2 U}{\partial z^2} \;=\; \nabla^2 U \;=\; 0 \qquad (4)$$

which is called *Laplace's equation*. This is also the equation for the electric (or gravitational) potential due to a charge (or mass) distribution at points where there is no charge (or mass).

SOLUTION OF BOUNDARY-VALUE PROBLEMS BY LAPLACE TRANSFORMS

By use of the Laplace transformation (with respect to t or x) in a one-dimensional boundary-value problem, the partial differential equation (or equations) can be transformed into an ordinary differential equation. The required solution can then be obtained by solving this equation and inverting by use of the inversion formula or any other methods already considered.

For two-dimensional problems, it is sometimes useful to apply the Laplace transform twice [for example, with respect to t and then with respect to x] and arrive at ordinary differential equation. In such case the required solution is obtained by a *double inversion*. The process is sometimes referred to as *iterated Laplace transformation*. A similar technique can be applied to three (or higher) dimensional problems. Boundary-value problems can sometimes also be solved by using both Fourier and Laplace transforms [see Prob. 14].

Solved Problems

HEAT CONDUCTION

1. A semi-infinite solid $x > 0$ [see Fig. 8-5] is initially at temperature zero. At time $t = 0$, a constant temperature $U_0 > 0$ is applied and maintained at the face $x = 0$. Find the temperature at any point of the solid at any later time $t > 0$.

   The boundary-value problem for the determination of the temperature $U(x, t)$ at any point x and any time t is

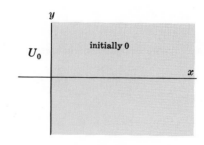

Fig. 8-5

$$\frac{\partial U}{\partial t} \;=\; k\frac{\partial^2 U}{\partial x^2} \qquad x>0,\; t>0$$

$$U(x,0) \;=\; 0, \qquad U(0,t) \;=\; U_0, \qquad |U(x,t)| \;<\; M$$

where the last condition expresses the requirement that the temperature is bounded for all x and t.

Taking Laplace transforms, we find

$$su - U(x,0) \;=\; k\frac{d^2u}{dx^2} \qquad \text{or} \qquad \frac{d^2u}{dx^2} - \frac{s}{k}u \;=\; 0 \tag{1}$$

where

$$u(0,s) \;=\; \mathcal{L}\{U(0,t)\} \;=\; \frac{U_0}{s} \tag{2}$$

and $u = u(x,s)$ is required to be bounded.

Solving (1), we find

$$u(x,s) \;=\; c_1\,e^{\sqrt{s/k}\,x} \;+\; c_2\,e^{-\sqrt{s/k}\,x}$$

Then we choose $c_1 = 0$ so that u is bounded as $x \to \infty$, and we have

$$u(x,s) \;=\; c_2\,e^{-\sqrt{s/k}\,x} \tag{3}$$

From (2) we have $c_2 = U_0/s$, so that

$$u(x,s) \;=\; \frac{U_0}{s}\,e^{-\sqrt{s/k}\,x}$$

Hence by Problem 9, Page 207, and Problem 10, Page 209, we find

$$U(x,t) \;=\; U_0\,\mathrm{erfc}\,(x/2\sqrt{kt}) \;=\; U_0\left\{1 - \frac{2}{\sqrt{\pi}}\int_0^{x/2\sqrt{kt}} e^{-u^2}\,du\right\}$$

2. Work Problem 1 if at $t=0$ the temperature applied is given by $G(t)$, $t>0$.

The boundary-value problem in this case is the same as in the preceding problem except that the boundary condition $U(0,t) = U_0$ is replaced by $U(0,t) = G(t)$. Then if the Laplace transform of $G(t)$ is $g(s)$, we find from (3) of Problem 1 that $c_2 = g(s)$ and so

$$u(x,s) \;=\; g(s)\,e^{-\sqrt{s/k}\,x}$$

Now by Problem 11, Page 209,

$$\mathcal{L}^{-1}\{e^{-\sqrt{s/k}\,x}\} \;=\; \frac{x}{2\sqrt{\pi k}}\,t^{-3/2}\,e^{-x^2/4kt}$$

Hence by the convolution theorem,

$$U(x,t) \;=\; \int_0^t \frac{x}{2\sqrt{\pi k}}\,u^{-3/2}\,e^{-x^2/4ku}\,G(t-u)\,du$$

$$=\; \frac{2}{\sqrt{\pi}}\int_{x/2\sqrt{kt}}^{\infty} e^{-v^2}\,G\left(t - \frac{x^2}{4kv^2}\right)dv$$

on letting $v = x^2/4ku$.

3. A bar of length l [see Fig. 8-6] is at constant temperature U_0. At $t = 0$ the end $x = l$ is suddenly given the constant temperature U_1 and the end $x = 0$ is insulated. Assuming that the surface of the bar is insulated, find the temperature at any point x of the bar at any time $t > 0$.

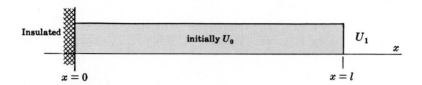

Fig. 8-6

The boundary-value problem is

$$\frac{\partial U}{\partial t} \;=\; k\,\frac{\partial^2 U}{\partial x^2} \qquad 0 < x < l,\; t > 0$$

$$U(x, 0) \;=\; U_0, \qquad U_x(0, t) \;=\; 0, \qquad U(l, t) \;=\; U_1$$

Taking Laplace transforms, we find

$$su - U(x, 0) \;=\; k\frac{d^2u}{dx^2} \qquad \text{or} \qquad \frac{d^2u}{dx^2} - \frac{su}{k} \;=\; -\frac{U_0}{k} \tag{1}$$

$$u_x(0, s) \;=\; 0, \qquad u(l, s) \;=\; \frac{U_1}{s} \tag{2}$$

The general solution of (1) is

$$u \;=\; c_1 \cosh \sqrt{s/k}\,x \;+\; c_2 \sinh \sqrt{s/k}\,x \;+\; \frac{U_0}{s}$$

From the first condition of (2) we find $c_2 = 0$ and so

$$u \;=\; c_1 \cosh \sqrt{s/k}\,x \;+\; \frac{U_0}{s}$$

From the second condition of (2) we find

$$c_1 \cosh \sqrt{s/k}\,l \;+\; \frac{U_0}{s} \;=\; \frac{U_1}{s} \qquad \text{or} \qquad c_1 \;=\; \frac{U_1 - U_0}{s \cosh \sqrt{s/k}\,l}$$

Thus

$$u(x, s) \;=\; \frac{U_0}{s} \;+\; (U_1 - U_0)\frac{\cosh \sqrt{s/k}\,x}{s \cosh \sqrt{s/k}\,l}$$

The inverse of the first term is U_0. By the complex inversion formula, the inverse of the second term is, apart from the constant factor $U_1 - U_0$, given by

$$\frac{1}{2\pi i} \int_{\gamma - i\infty}^{\gamma + i\infty} e^{st}\, \frac{\cosh \sqrt{s/k}\,x}{s \cosh \sqrt{s/k}\,l}\, ds$$

As in Problem 13, Page 210, this is easily shown to be equal to the sum of all the residues of the integrand at the poles which are all simple poles and occur at

$$s = 0, \qquad \sqrt{s/k}\,l \;=\; (n - \tfrac{1}{2})\pi i \qquad n \;=\; 0, \pm 1, \pm 2, \ldots$$

or

$$s = 0, \qquad s \;=\; -\frac{(2n-1)^2\pi^2 k}{4l^2} \qquad n \;=\; 1, 2, 3, \ldots$$

Now:

Residue at $s = 0$ is $\qquad \lim\limits_{s \to 0} (s) \left(\dfrac{e^{st} \cosh \sqrt{s/k}\, x}{s \cosh \sqrt{s/k}\, l} \right) = 1$

Residue at $s = -\dfrac{(2n-1)^2 \pi^2 k}{4l^2} = s_n$ is

$$\lim_{s \to s_n} (s - s_n) \left(\frac{e^{st} \cosh \sqrt{s/k}\, x}{s \cosh \sqrt{s/k}\, l} \right)$$

$$= \left\{ \lim_{s \to s_n} \frac{s - s_n}{\cosh \sqrt{s/k}\, l} \right\} \left\{ \lim_{s \to s_n} \frac{e^{st} \cosh \sqrt{s/k}\, x}{s} \right\}$$

$$= \left\{ \lim_{s \to s_n} \frac{1}{(\sinh \sqrt{s/k}\, l)(l/2\sqrt{ks}\,)} \right\} \left\{ \lim_{s \to s_n} \frac{e^{st} \cosh \sqrt{s/k}\, x}{s} \right\}$$

$$= \frac{4(-1)^n}{(2n-1)\pi} e^{-(2n-1)^2 \pi^2 kt/4l^2} \cos \frac{(2n-1)\pi x}{2l}$$

using L'Hospital's rule. Thus we obtain

$$U(x, t) = U_1 + \frac{4(U_1 - U_0)}{\pi} \sum_{n=1}^{\infty} \frac{(-1)^n}{2n-1} e^{-(2n-1)^2 \pi^2 kt/4l^2} \cos \frac{(2n-1)\pi x}{2l}$$

THE VIBRATING STRING

4. An infinitely long string having one end at $x = 0$ is initially at rest on the x axis. The end $x = 0$ undergoes a periodic transverse displacement given by $A_0 \sin \omega t$, $t > 0$. Find the displacement of any point on the string at any time.

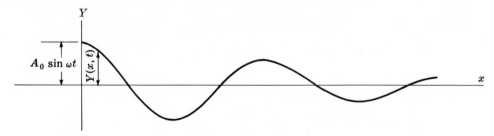

Fig. 8-7

If $Y(x, t)$ is the transverse displacement of the string at any point x at any time t, then the boundary-value problem is

$$\frac{\partial^2 Y}{\partial t^2} = a^2 \frac{\partial^2 Y}{\partial x^2} \qquad x > 0, \ t > 0 \tag{1}$$

$$Y(x, 0) = 0, \qquad Y_t(x, 0) = 0, \qquad Y(0, t) = A_0 \sin \omega t, \qquad |Y(x, t)| < M \tag{2}$$

where the last condition specifies that the displacement is bounded.

Taking Laplace transforms, we find, if $y(x, s) = \mathcal{L}\{Y(x, t)\}$,

$$s^2 y - s\, Y(x, 0) - Y_t(x, 0) = a^2 \frac{d^2 y}{dx^2} \qquad \text{or} \qquad \frac{d^2 y}{dx^2} - \frac{s^2}{a^2} y = 0 \tag{3}$$

$$y(0, t) = \frac{A_0 \omega}{s^2 + \omega^2}, \qquad y(x, s) \text{ is bounded} \tag{4}$$

The general solution of the differential equation is

$$y(x, s) \;=\; c_1\, e^{sx/a} \;+\; c_2\, e^{-sx/a}$$

From the condition on boundedness, we must have $c_1 = 0$.   Then

$$y(x, s) \;=\; c_2 e^{-sx/a}$$

From the first condition in (4), $c_2 = A_0\omega/(s^2 + \omega^2)$.   Then

$$y(x, s) \;=\; \frac{A_0\omega}{s^2 + \omega^2}\, e^{-sx/a}$$

and so
$$Y(x, t) \;=\; \begin{cases} A_0 \sin \omega(t - x/a) & t > x/a \\ 0 & t < x/a \end{cases}$$

This means physically that a point x of the string stays at rest until the time $t = x/a$.   Thereafter it undergoes motion identical with that of the end $x = 0$ but lags behind it in time by the amount x/a. The constant a is the speed with which the wave travels.

5. A tightly stretched flexible string has its ends fixed at $x = 0$ and $x = l$.   At time $t = 0$ the string is given a shape defined by $F(x) = \mu x(l - x)$, where μ is a constant, and then released.   Find the displacement of any point x of the string at any time $t > 0$.

The boundary-value problem is

$$\frac{\partial^2 Y}{\partial t^2} \;=\; a^2 \frac{\partial^2 Y}{\partial x^2} \qquad 0 < x < l,\; t > 0$$

$$Y(0, t) \;=\; 0, \qquad Y(l, t) \;=\; 0, \qquad Y(x, 0) \;=\; \mu x(l - x), \qquad Y_t(x, 0) \;=\; 0$$

Taking Laplace transforms, we find, if $y(x, s) = \mathcal{L}\{Y(x, t)\}$,

$$s^2 y \;-\; s\, Y(x, 0) \;-\; Y_t(x, 0) \;=\; a^2 \frac{d^2 y}{dx^2}$$

or
$$\frac{d^2 y}{dx^2} \;-\; \frac{s^2}{a^2} y \;=\; -\frac{\mu s x(l - x)}{a^2} \tag{1}$$

where
$$y(0, s) \;=\; 0, \qquad y(l, s) \;=\; 0 \tag{2}$$

The general solution of (1) is

$$y \;=\; c_1 \cosh \frac{sx}{a} \;+\; c_2 \sinh \frac{sx}{a} \;+\; \frac{\mu x(l - x)}{s} \;-\; \frac{2a^2 \mu}{s^3} \tag{3}$$

Then from conditions (2) we find

$$c_1 \;=\; \frac{2a^2\mu}{s^3}, \qquad c_2 \;=\; \frac{2a^2\mu}{s^3}\!\left(\frac{1 - \cosh sl/a}{\sinh sl/a}\right) \;=\; -\frac{2a^2\mu}{s^3} \tanh sl/2a \tag{4}$$

so that (3) becomes
$$y \;=\; \frac{2a^2\mu}{s^3} \frac{\cosh s(2x - l)/2a}{\cosh sl/2a} \;+\; \frac{\mu x(l - x)}{s} \;-\; \frac{2a^2\mu}{s^3}$$

By using residues [see Problem 17, Page 213] we find

$$Y(x, t) \;=\; a^2\mu\left\{ t^2 + \left(\frac{2x - l}{2a}\right)^2 - \left(\frac{l}{2a}\right)^2 \right\}$$

$$-\; \frac{32a^2\mu}{\pi^3}\left(\frac{l}{2a}\right)^2 \sum_{n=1}^{\infty} \frac{(-1)^n}{(2n-1)^3} \cos \frac{(2n-1)\pi(2x - l)}{2l} \cos \frac{(2n-1)\pi a t}{l}$$

$$+\; \mu x(l - x) \;-\; a^2\mu t^2$$

or
$$Y(x, t) \;=\; \frac{8\mu l^2}{\pi^3} \sum_{n=1}^{\infty} \frac{1}{(2n-1)^3} \sin \frac{(2n-1)\pi x}{l} \cos \frac{(2n-1)\pi a t}{l}$$

VIBRATIONS OF BEAMS

6. A beam of length l which has its end $x = 0$ fixed, as shown in Fig. 8-8, is initially at rest. A constant force F_0 per unit area is applied longitudinally at the free end. Find the longitudinal displacement of any point x of the beam at any time $t > 0$.

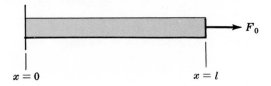

Fig. 8-8

If $Y(x, t)$ is the longitudinal displacement of any point x of the beam at time t, the boundary-value problem is

$$\frac{\partial^2 Y}{\partial t^2} = c^2 \frac{\partial^2 Y}{\partial x^2} \qquad 0 < x < l, \ t > 0$$

$$Y(x, 0) = 0, \qquad Y_t(x, 0) = 0, \qquad Y(0, t) = 0, \qquad Y_x(l, t) = F_0/E$$

where E is Young's modulus.

Taking Laplace transforms, we have, if $y(x, s) = \mathcal{L}\{Y(x, t)\}$,

$$s^2 y(x, s) - s\, Y(x, 0) - Y_t(x, 0) = c^2 \frac{d^2 y}{dx^2} \qquad \text{or} \qquad \frac{d^2 y}{dx^2} - \frac{s^2}{c^2} y = 0$$

$$y(0, s) = 0, \qquad y_x(l, s) = F_0/Es \tag{1}$$

Solving the differential equation, we find

$$y(x, s) = c_1 \cosh(sx/c) + c_2 \sinh(sx/c)$$

From the first condition in (1), $c_1 = 0$ and so

$$y(x, s) = c_2 \sinh(sx/c)$$

$$y_x(x, s) = c_2 (s/c) \cosh(sx/c)$$

From the second condition in (1), we have

$$c_2 (s/c) \cosh(sl/c) = F_0/Es \qquad \text{or} \qquad c_2 = \frac{cF_0}{Es^2 \cosh(sl/c)}$$

Then

$$y(x, s) = \frac{cF_0}{E} \cdot \frac{\sinh(sx/c)}{s^2 \cosh(sl/c)} \tag{2}$$

Hence by Problem 14, Page 211,

$$Y(x, t) = \frac{F_0}{E}\left[x + \frac{8l}{\pi^2} \sum_{n=1}^{\infty} \frac{(-1)^n}{(2n-1)^2} \sin\frac{(2n-1)\pi x}{2l} \cos\frac{(2n-1)\pi ct}{2l} \right] \tag{3}$$

7. In the beam of the preceding problem, determine the motion of the free end $x = l$ as a function of time t.

For $x = l$ we obtain from (2) of Problem 6,

$$y(x, s) = \frac{cF_0}{E} \frac{\sinh(sl/c)}{s^2 \cosh(sl/c)}$$

But from Problem 92, Page 34 or entry 134, Page 253, this is the Laplace transform of the triangular wave of Fig. 8-9 below which describes the motion of end $x = l$ as a function of t.

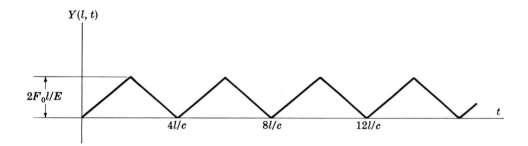

Fig. 8-9

8. A semi-infinite beam which is initially at rest on the x axis is at time $t = 0$ given a transverse displacement h at its end $x = 0$. Determine the transverse displacement $Y(x, t)$ at any position $x > 0$ and at any time $t > 0$.

The boundary-value problem is

$$\frac{\partial^2 Y}{\partial t^2} + b^2 \frac{\partial^4 Y}{\partial x^4} = 0 \qquad x > 0, \ t > 0 \tag{1}$$

$$Y(x, 0) = 0, \quad Y_t(x, 0) = 0, \quad Y(0, t) = h, \quad Y_{xx}(0, t) = 0, \quad |Y(x, t)| < M \tag{2}$$

Taking Laplace transforms, we find

$$s^2 y(x, s) - s\,Y(x, 0) - Y_t(x, 0) + b^2 \frac{d^4 y}{dx^4} = 0 \qquad \text{or} \qquad \frac{d^4 y}{dx^4} + \frac{s^2}{b^2} y = 0$$

$$y(0, s) = h/s, \qquad y_{xx}(0, s) = 0, \qquad y(x, s) \ \text{is bounded} \tag{3}$$

The general solution of the differential equation is

$$y(x, s) = e^{\sqrt{s/2b}\,x}(c_1 \cos \sqrt{s/2b}\,x + c_2 \sin \sqrt{s/2b}\,x) + e^{-\sqrt{s/2b}\,x}(c_3 \cos \sqrt{s/2b}\,x + c_4 \sin \sqrt{s/2b}\,x)$$

From the boundedness condition we require $c_1 = c_2 = 0$ so that

$$y(x, s) = e^{-\sqrt{s/2b}\,x}(c_3 \cos \sqrt{s/2b}\,x + c_4 \sin \sqrt{s/2b}\,x)$$

From the first and second boundary condition in (3), we find $c_4 = 0$ and $c_3 = h/s$ so that

$$y(x, s) = \frac{h}{s} e^{-\sqrt{s/2b}\,x} \cos \sqrt{s/2b}\,x$$

The inverse Laplace transform is, by the complex inversion formula,

$$Y(x, t) = \frac{1}{2\pi i} \int_{\gamma - i\infty}^{\gamma + i\infty} \frac{h e^{st - \sqrt{s/2b}\,x} \cos \sqrt{s/2b}\,x}{s} \, ds$$

To evaluate this we use the contour of Fig. 8-10 since $s = 0$ is a branch point. Proceeding as in Problem 9, Page 207, we find, omitting the integrand for the sake of brevity, that

$$Y(x, t) = -\lim_{\substack{R \to \infty \\ \epsilon \to 0}} \frac{1}{2\pi i} \left\{ \int_{EH} + \int_{HJK} + \int_{KL} \right\} \tag{4}$$

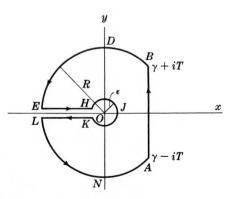

Fig. 8-10

Along EH, $s = ue^{\pi i}$, $\sqrt{s} = i\sqrt{u}$ and we find

$$\int_{EH} = \int_R^\epsilon \frac{he^{-ut - i\sqrt{u/2b}\,x}\cosh\sqrt{u/2b}\,x}{u}\,du$$

Along KL, $s = ue^{-\pi i}$, $\sqrt{s} = -i\sqrt{u}$ and we find

$$\int_{KL} = \int_\epsilon^R \frac{he^{-ut + i\sqrt{u/2b}\,x}\cosh\sqrt{u/2b}\,x}{u}\,du$$

Along HJK, $s = \epsilon e^{i\theta}$ and we find

$$\int_{HJK} = \int_\pi^{-\pi} h\,e^{\epsilon e^{i\theta}t - \sqrt{\epsilon e^{i\theta}/2b}\,x}\cos\sqrt{\epsilon e^{i\theta}/2b}\,x\,d\theta$$

Then (4) becomes

$$Y(x,t) = h\left\{1 - \frac{1}{\pi}\int_0^\infty \frac{e^{-ut}\sin\sqrt{u/2b}\,x\,\cosh\sqrt{u/2b}\,x}{u}\,du\right\}$$

Letting $u/2b = v^2$, this can be written

$$Y(x,t) = h\left\{1 - \frac{2}{\pi}\int_0^\infty \frac{e^{-2bv^2t}\sin vx\,\cosh vx}{v}\,dv\right\}$$

The result can also be written in terms of *Fresnel integrals* as [see Problem 66 and entries 10 and 11, Page 255]

$$Y(x,t) = h\left\{1 - \sqrt{\frac{2}{\pi}}\int_0^{x/\sqrt{bt}}(\cos w^2 + \sin w^2)\,dw\right\}$$

TRANSMISSION LINES

9. A semi-infinite transmission line of negligible inductance and conductance per unit length has a voltage applied to it at the sending end, $x = 0$, given by

$$E(0,t) = \begin{cases} E_0 & 0 < t < T \\ 0 & t > T \end{cases}$$

Find the voltage $E(x,t)$ and current $I(x,t)$ at any point $x > 0$ at any time $t > 0$.

If we take $L = 0$ and $G = 0$, the transmission line equations are given by

$$\frac{\partial E}{\partial x} = -RI, \quad \frac{\partial I}{\partial x} = -C\frac{\partial E}{\partial t} \tag{1}$$

The boundary conditions are

$$E(x,0) = 0, \quad I(x,0) = 0, \quad E(0,t) = \begin{cases} E_0 & 0 < t < T \\ 0 & t > T \end{cases}, \quad |E(x,t)| < M$$

Taking Laplace transforms using the notations $\mathcal{L}\{E(x,t)\} = \widetilde{E}(x,s)$, $\mathcal{L}\{I(x,t)\} = \widetilde{I}(x,s)$, we have

$$\frac{d\widetilde{E}}{dx} = -R\widetilde{I}, \quad \frac{d\widetilde{I}}{dx} = -C\{s\widetilde{E} - E(x,0)\}$$

i.e.,

$$\frac{d\widetilde{E}}{dx} = -R\widetilde{I}, \quad \frac{d\widetilde{I}}{dx} = -Cs\widetilde{E} \tag{2}$$

Eliminating $\widetilde{I}$ by differentiating the first of equations (2) with respect to x, we find

$$\frac{d^2\widetilde{E}}{dx^2} = -R\frac{d\widetilde{I}}{dx} = RCs\widetilde{E} \quad \text{or} \quad \frac{d^2\widetilde{E}}{dx^2} - RCs\widetilde{E} = 0 \tag{3}$$

The general solution of (3) is

$$\widetilde{E}(x, s) \;=\; c_1\, e^{\sqrt{RCs}\,x} \;+\; c_2\, e^{-\sqrt{RCs}\,x}$$

and from the boundedness condition we must have $c_1 = 0$.   Then

$$\widetilde{E}(x, s) \;=\; c_2\, e^{-\sqrt{RCs}\,x} \tag{4}$$

Let us write $E(0, t) = G(t)$ and $\mathcal{L}\{E(0, t)\} = \widetilde{E}(0, s) = g(s)$.   Then from (4) we find $c_2 = g(s)$, and so

$$\widetilde{E}(x, s) \;=\; g(s)\, e^{-\sqrt{RCs}\,x} \tag{5}$$

Hence as in Problem 2 we find by the convolution theorem,

$$E(x, t) \;=\; \int_0^t \frac{x\sqrt{RC}}{2\sqrt{\pi}}\, u^{-3/2}\, e^{-RCx^2/4u}\, G(t - u)\, du$$

Now since

$$G(t - u) \;=\; \begin{cases} E_0 & 0 < t - u < T \ \text{or} \ t - T = u < t \\ 0 & t - u > T \qquad\ u < t - T \end{cases}$$

it follows that if $t > T$,

$$\begin{aligned}
E(x, t) \;&=\; \int_{t-T}^t \frac{x\sqrt{RC}}{2\sqrt{\pi}}\, u^{-3/2}\, e^{-RCx^2/4u}\, E_0\, du \\[2mm]
&=\; \frac{2E_0}{\sqrt{\pi}} \int_{x\sqrt{RC}/2\sqrt{t}}^{x\sqrt{RC}/2\sqrt{t-T}} e^{-v^2}\, dv \qquad (\text{letting } RCx^2/4u = v^2) \\[2mm]
&=\; E_0 \left\{ \frac{2}{\sqrt{\pi}} \int_0^{x\sqrt{RC}/2\sqrt{t-T}} e^{-v^2}\, dv \;-\; \frac{2}{\sqrt{\pi}} \int_0^{x\sqrt{RC}/2\sqrt{t}} e^{-v^2}\, dv \right\} \\[2mm]
&=\; E_0 \left\{ \operatorname{erf}\left(\frac{x\sqrt{RC}}{2\sqrt{t-T}} \right) \;-\; \operatorname{erf}\left(\frac{x\sqrt{RC}}{2\sqrt{t}} \right) \right\}
\end{aligned}$$

while if $0 < t < T$,

$$\begin{aligned}
E(x, t) \;&=\; \int_0^t \frac{x\sqrt{RC}}{2\sqrt{\pi}}\, u^{-3/2}\, e^{-RCx^2/4u}\, E_0\, du \;=\; \frac{2E_0}{\sqrt{\pi}} \int_{x\sqrt{RC}/2\sqrt{t}}^{\infty} e^{-v^2}\, dv \\[2mm]
&=\; E_0 \{ 1 - \operatorname{erf}(x\sqrt{RC}/2\sqrt{t}) \} \\[2mm]
&=\; E_0\, \operatorname{erfc}(x\sqrt{RC}/2\sqrt{t})
\end{aligned}$$

Since $I = -\dfrac{1}{R}\dfrac{\partial E}{\partial x}$,   we obtain by differentiation

$$I(x, t) \;=\; \begin{cases} \dfrac{E_0 x}{2\sqrt{\pi}} \sqrt{\dfrac{C}{R}}\, t^{-3/2}\, e^{-RCx^2/4t} & 0 < t < T \\[5mm] \dfrac{E_0 x}{2\sqrt{\pi}} \sqrt{\dfrac{C}{R}} \left[t^{-3/2}\, e^{-RCx^2/4t} \;-\; (t-T)^{-1/2}\, e^{-RCx^2/4(t-T)} \right] & t > T \end{cases}$$

MISCELLANEOUS PROBLEMS

10. (a) Solve the boundary-value problem

$$\frac{\partial U}{\partial t} \;=\; k\, \frac{\partial^2 U}{\partial x^2} \qquad x > 0, \ t > 0$$

$$U(x, 0) \;=\; U_0, \qquad U_x(0, t) \;=\; -\alpha U(0, t), \qquad |U(x, t)| < M$$

(b) Give a heat flow interpretation of the problem.

The problem arises in considering a semi-infinite conducting solid whose initial temperature is U_0 in which radiation into a medium $x < 0$ at temperature zero can take place. This radiation is assumed to be such that the flux at the face $x = 0$ is proportional to the difference in temperatures of the face $x = 0$ and the medium $x < 0$, i.e.,

$$U_x(0, t) = -\alpha[U(0, t) - 0] = -\alpha U(0, t)$$

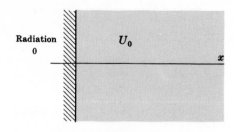

Fig. 8-11

To obtain the solution, we take Laplace transforms and find

$$su - U_0 = k\frac{d^2u}{dx^2} \quad \text{or} \quad \frac{d^2u}{dx^2} - \frac{su}{k} = -\frac{U_0}{k} \tag{1}$$

$$u_x(0, s) = -\alpha u(0, s), \qquad u(x, s) \text{ is bounded} \tag{2}$$

The general solution of the differential equation is

$$u(x, s) = c_1 e^{\sqrt{s/k}\,x} + c_2 e^{-\sqrt{s/k}\,x} + \frac{U_0}{s}$$

From the boundedness condition, $c_1 = 0$. Then

$$u(x, s) = c_2 e^{-\sqrt{s/k}\,x} + \frac{U_0}{s}$$

From the first condition of (2), we find $c_2 = \dfrac{\alpha U_0}{s(\sqrt{s} - \alpha)}$ so that

$$u(x, s) = \frac{\alpha U_0}{s(\sqrt{s} - \alpha)} e^{-\sqrt{s/k}\,x} + \frac{U_0}{s}$$

Then using the complex inversion formula,

$$U(x, t) = U_0 + \alpha U_0 \mathcal{L}^{-1}\left\{\frac{e^{-\sqrt{s/k}\,x}}{s(\sqrt{s} - \alpha)}\right\}$$

$$= U_0 + \frac{\alpha U_0}{2\pi i}\int_{\gamma - i\infty}^{\gamma + i\infty} \frac{e^{st - \sqrt{s/k}\,x}}{s(\sqrt{s} - \alpha)}\, ds$$

As in Problem 8 we have, omitting the integrand,

$$\frac{1}{2\pi i}\int_{\gamma - i\infty}^{\gamma + i\infty} \frac{e^{st - \sqrt{s/k}\,x}}{s(\sqrt{s} - \alpha)}\, ds = -\lim_{\substack{R \to \infty \\ \epsilon \to 0}} \frac{1}{2\pi i}\left\{\int_{EH} + \int_{HJK} + \int_{KL}\right\} \tag{3}$$

Along EH, $s = ue^{\pi i}$, $\sqrt{s} = i\sqrt{u}$ and we find

$$\int_{EH} = \int_R^\epsilon \frac{e^{-ut - i\sqrt{s/k}\,x}}{u(i\sqrt{u} - \alpha)}\, du$$

Along KL, $s = ue^{-\pi i}$, $\sqrt{s} = -i\sqrt{u}$ and we find

$$\int_{KL} = \int_\epsilon^R \frac{e^{-ut + i\sqrt{s/k}\,x}}{u(-i\sqrt{u} - \alpha)}\, du$$

Along HJK, $s = \epsilon e^{i\theta}$ and we find

$$\int_{HJK} = \int_\pi^{-\pi} \frac{e^{\epsilon e^{i\theta} t - \sqrt{\epsilon e^{i\theta}/k}\,x}}{\sqrt{\epsilon}\, e^{i\theta/2} - \alpha}\, i\, d\theta$$

Using these results in (3), we see that

$$\frac{1}{2\pi i}\int_{\gamma - i\infty}^{\gamma + i\infty} \frac{e^{st - \sqrt{s/k}\,x}}{s(\sqrt{s} - \alpha)}\, ds = -\frac{1}{\alpha} + \frac{1}{\pi}\int_0^\infty \frac{e^{-ut}}{u}\left[\frac{\sqrt{u}\cos x\sqrt{u} - \alpha \sin x\sqrt{u}}{u + \alpha^2}\right] du$$

Hence
$$U(x, t) = \frac{\alpha U_0}{\pi} \int_0^\infty \frac{e^{-ut}}{u} \left[\frac{\sqrt{u} \cos x\sqrt{u} - \alpha \sin x\sqrt{u}}{u + \alpha^2} \right] du$$

$$= \frac{2\alpha U_0}{\pi} \int_0^\infty \frac{e^{-v^2 t}}{v} \left[\frac{v \cos xv - \alpha \sin xv}{v^2 + \alpha^2} \right] dv$$

if $u = v^2$.

11. A taut, flexible string has its endpoints on the x axis at $x = 0$ and $x = 1$.   At time $t = 0$, the string is given a shape defined by $F(x)$, $0 < x < 1$, and released.   Find the displacement of any point x of the string at any time $t > 0$.

The boundary-value problem is

$$\frac{\partial^2 Y}{\partial t^2} = a^2 \frac{\partial^2 Y}{\partial x^2} \qquad 0 < x < 1, \ t > 0 \tag{1}$$

$$Y(0, t) = 0, \qquad Y(1, t) = 0, \qquad Y(x, 0) = F(x), \qquad Y_t(x, 0) = 0 \tag{2}$$

It is convenient to consider, instead of equation (1), the equation

$$\frac{\partial^2 Y}{\partial t^2} = \frac{\partial^2 Y}{\partial x^2}$$

and after the final solution is obtained to replace t by at [see Problem 49].

Taking Laplace transforms, we find

$$s^2 y - s Y(x, 0) - Y_t(x, 0) = \frac{d^2 y}{dx^2} \qquad \text{or} \qquad \frac{d^2 y}{dx^2} - s^2 y = -s F(x) \tag{3}$$

$$y(0, s) = 0, \qquad y(1, s) = 0 \tag{4}$$

The general solution of (3) is [see Problem 8, Page 85]

$$y(x, s) = c_1 \cosh sx + c_2 \sinh sx - \int_0^x F(u) \sinh s(x - u) \, du$$

From the first condition in (4) we find $c_1 = 0$, so that

$$y(x, s) = c_2 \sinh sx - \int_0^x F(u) \sinh s(x - u) \, du \tag{5}$$

From the second condition in (4) we find

$$0 = c_2 \sinh s - \int_0^1 F(u) \sinh s(1 - u) \, du$$

or

$$c_2 = \int_0^1 F(u) \frac{\sinh s(1 - u)}{\sinh s} \, du$$

Thus (5) becomes

$$y(x, s) = \int_0^1 F(u) \frac{\sinh s(1 - u) \sinh sx}{\sinh s} \, du - \int_0^x F(u) \sinh s(x - u) \, du$$

The first integral can be written as the sum of two integrals, one from 0 to x, the other from x to 1. Then

$$y(x, s) = \int_0^x F(u) \left\{ \frac{\sinh s(1 - u) \sinh sx}{\sinh s} - \sinh s(x - u) \right\} du + \int_x^1 F(u) \frac{\sinh s(1 - u) \sinh sx}{\sinh s} \, du$$

$$= \int_0^x F(u) \frac{\sinh s(1 - x) \sinh su}{\sinh s} \, du + \int_x^1 F(u) \frac{\sinh s(1 - u) \sinh sx}{\sinh s} \, du$$

We must now find the inverse Laplace transform. By the complex inversion formula, the inverse of the first term is

$$\frac{1}{2\pi i} \int_{\gamma-i\infty}^{\gamma+i\infty} e^{st} \left\{ \int_0^x F(u) \frac{\sinh s(1-x) \sinh su}{\sinh s} \, du \right\} ds$$

Since this is equal to the sum of the residues at the simple poles $s = n\pi i$, we find the required inverse

$$\sum_{n=+\infty}^{\infty} e^{n\pi it} \int_0^x F(u) \frac{\sin n\pi(1-x) \sin n\pi u}{-\cos n\pi} \, du \;\; = \;\; \sum_{n=1}^{\infty} \left\{ \int_0^x F(u) \sin n\pi u \, du \right\} \sin n\pi x \cos n\pi t$$

Similarly, the inverse of the second term is

$$\sum_{n=1}^{\infty} \left\{ \int_x^1 F(u) \sin n\pi u \, du \right\} \sin n\pi x \cos n\pi t$$

Adding these we find

$$Y(x,t) \;\; = \;\; \sum_{n=1}^{\infty} \left\{ \int_0^1 F(u) \sin n\pi u \, du \right\} \sin n\pi x \cos n\pi t$$

If now we replace t by at, we have

$$Y(x,t) \;\; = \;\; \sum_{n=1}^{\infty} \left\{ \int_0^1 F(u) \sin n\pi u \, du \right\} \sin n\pi x \cos n\pi at$$

12. An infinitely long circular cylinder of unit radius has a constant initial temperature T. At $t = 0$ a temperature of 0°C is applied to the surface and is maintained. Find the temperature at any point of the cylinder at any later time t.

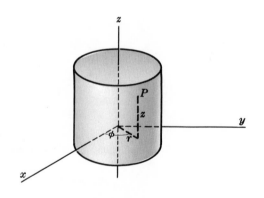

Fig. 8-12

If (r, ϕ, z) are cylindrical coordinates of any point of the cylinder and the cylinder has its axis coincident with the z axis [see Fig. 8-12], it is clear that the temperature is independent of ϕ and z and can thus be denoted by $U(r, t)$. The boundary-value problem is

$$\frac{\partial U}{\partial t} \;\; = \;\; k\left(\frac{\partial^2 U}{\partial r^2} + \frac{1}{r}\frac{\partial U}{\partial r}\right) \qquad 0 < r < 1 \qquad (1)$$

$$U(1,t) = 0, \quad U(r,0) = T, \quad |U(r,t)| < M \qquad (2)$$

It is convenient to consider instead of (1) the equation

$$\frac{\partial U}{\partial t} \;\; = \;\; \frac{\partial^2 U}{\partial r^2} + \frac{1}{r}\frac{\partial U}{\partial r}$$

and then to replace t by kt.

Taking Laplace transforms, we find

$$su - U(r,0) \;\; = \;\; \frac{d^2u}{dr^2} + \frac{1}{r}\frac{du}{dr} \qquad \text{or} \qquad \frac{d^2u}{dr^2} + \frac{1}{r}\frac{du}{dr} - su \;\; = \;\; -T$$

$$u(1,s) = 0, \qquad u(r,s) \text{ is bounded}$$

The general solution of this equation is given in terms of Bessel functions as

$$u(r,s) \;\; = \;\; c_1 J_0(i\sqrt{s}\,r) + c_2 Y_0(i\sqrt{s}\,r) + \frac{T}{s}$$

Since $Y_0(i\sqrt{s}\,r)$ is unbounded as $r \to 0$, we must choose $c_2 = 0$.

Then
$$u(r, s) \;=\; c_1 J_0(i\sqrt{s}\, r) \,+\, \frac{T}{s}$$

From $u(1, s) = 0$, we find
$$c_1 J_0(i\sqrt{s}) \,+\, \frac{T}{s} \;=\; 0 \qquad \text{or} \qquad c_1 \;=\; -\frac{T}{s\, J_0(i\sqrt{s})}$$

Thus
$$u(r, s) \;=\; \frac{T}{s} \,-\, \frac{T\, J_0(i\sqrt{s}\, r)}{s\, J_0(i\sqrt{s})}$$

By the inversion formula,
$$U(r, t) \;=\; T \,-\, \frac{T}{2\pi i} \int_{\gamma-i\infty}^{\gamma+i\infty} \frac{e^{st}\, J_0(i\sqrt{s}\, r)}{s\, J_0(i\sqrt{s})} \, ds$$

Now $J_0(i\sqrt{s})$ has simple zeros where $i\sqrt{s} = \lambda_1, \lambda_2, \ldots \lambda_n, \ldots$. Thus the integrand has simple poles at $s = -\lambda_n^2$, $n = 1, 2, 3, \ldots$ and also at $s = 0$. Furthermore it can be shown that the integrand satisfies the conditions of Problem 2, Page 203, so that the method of residues can be used.

We have:

Residue of integrand at $s = 0$ is
$$\lim_{s \to 0} s \, \frac{e^{st}\, J_0(i\sqrt{s}\, r)}{s\, J_0(i\sqrt{s})} \;=\; 1$$

Residue of integrand at $s = -\lambda_n^2$ is
$$\lim_{s \to -\lambda_n^2} (s + \lambda_n^2)\, \frac{e^{st}\, J_0(i\sqrt{s}\, r)}{s\, J_0(i\sqrt{s})} \;=\; \left\{ \lim_{s \to -\lambda_n^2} \frac{s + \lambda_n^2}{J_0(i\sqrt{s})} \right\} \left\{ \lim_{s \to -\lambda_n^2} \frac{e^{st}\, J_0(i\sqrt{s}\, r)}{s} \right\}$$

$$= \left\{ \lim_{s \to -\lambda_n^2} \frac{1}{J_0'(i\sqrt{s})\, i/2\sqrt{s}} \right\} \left\{ \frac{e^{-\lambda_n^2 t}\, J_0(\lambda_n r)}{-\lambda_n^2} \right\}$$

$$= -\frac{2 e^{-\lambda_n^2 t}\, J_0(\lambda_n r)}{\lambda_n\, J_1(\lambda_n)}$$

where we have used L'Hospital's rule in evaluating the limit and also the fact that $J_0'(u) = -J_1(u)$. Then
$$U(r, t) \;=\; T \,-\, T \left\{ 1 \,-\, \sum_{n=1}^{\infty} \frac{2 e^{-\lambda_n^2 t}\, J_0(\lambda_n r)}{\lambda_n\, J_1(\lambda_n)} \right\}$$

$$= 2T \sum_{n=1}^{\infty} \frac{e^{-\lambda_n^2 t}\, J_0(\lambda_n r)}{\lambda_n\, J_1(\lambda_n)}$$

Replacing t by kt, we obtain the required solution
$$U(r, t) \;=\; 2T \sum_{n=1}^{\infty} \frac{e^{-k\lambda_n^2 t}\, J_0(\lambda_n r)}{\lambda_n\, J_1(\lambda_n)}$$

13. A semi-infinite insulated bar which coincides with the x axis, $x > 0$, is initially at temperature zero. At $t = 0$, a quantity of heat is instantaneously generated at the point $x = a$ where $a > 0$. Find the temperature at any point of the bar at any time $t > 0$.

The equation for heat conduction in the bar is
$$\frac{\partial U}{\partial t} \;=\; k \frac{\partial^2 U}{\partial x^2} \qquad x > 0, \; t > 0 \tag{1}$$

The fact that a quantity of heat is instantaneously generated at the point $x = a$ can be represented by the boundary condition

$$U(a, t) = Q \, \delta(t) \tag{2}$$

where Q is a constant and $\delta(t)$ is the Dirac delta function. Also, since the initial temperature is zero and since the temperature must be bounded, we have

$$U(x, 0) = 0, \qquad |U(x, t)| < M \tag{3}$$

Taking Laplace transforms of (1) and (2), using the first of conditions (3), we find

$$su - U(x, 0) = k \frac{d^2 u}{dx^2} \quad \text{or} \quad \frac{d^2 u}{dx^2} - \frac{su}{k} = 0 \tag{4}$$

$$u(a, s) = Q \tag{5}$$

From (4), we have $u(x, s) = c_1 e^{\sqrt{s/k}\,x} + c_2 e^{-\sqrt{s/k}\,x}$

and from the boundedness condition, we require $c_1 = 0$ so that

$$u(x, s) = c_2 e^{-\sqrt{s/k}\,x} \tag{6}$$

Then from (5) $u(a, s) = c_2 e^{-\sqrt{s/k}\,a} = Q \quad \text{or} \quad c_2 = Q e^{\sqrt{s/k}\,a}$

so that $$u(x, s) = Q e^{-(x-a)\sqrt{s/k}} \tag{7}$$

Inverting, using Problem 11, Page 209, we find the required temperature

$$U(x, t) = \frac{Q}{2\sqrt{\pi kt}} e^{-(x-a)^2/4kt} \tag{8}$$

The point source $x = a$ is sometimes called a *heat source of strength Q*.

14. A semi-infinite plate having width π [see Fig. 8-13] has its faces insulated. The semi-infinite edges are maintained at 0°C, while the finite edge is maintained at 100°C. Assuming that the initial temperature is 0°C, find the temperature at any point at any time.

Assuming that the diffusivity is one, the boundary-value problem for the determination of the temperature $U(x, y, t)$ is

$$\frac{\partial U}{\partial t} = \frac{\partial^2 U}{\partial x^2} + \frac{\partial^2 U}{\partial y^2} \tag{1}$$

$$U(0, y, t) = 0 \tag{2}$$

$$U(\pi, y, t) = 0 \tag{3}$$

$$U(x, y, 0) = 0 \tag{4}$$

$$U(x, 0, t) = 100 \tag{5}$$

$$|U(x, y, t)| < M \tag{6}$$

where $0 < x < \pi$, $y > 0$, $t > 0$.

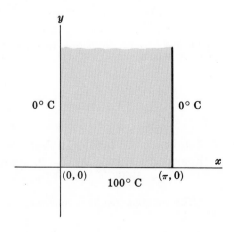

Fig. 8-13

Taking the Laplace transform of equation (1) and using condition (4), we find, if $u = u(x, y, s) = \mathcal{L}\{U(x, y, t)\}$,

$$\frac{\partial^2 u}{\partial x^2} + \frac{\partial^2 u}{\partial y^2} = su \qquad (7)$$

Multiplying (7) by $\sin nx$ and integrating from 0 to π [i.e. taking the sine transform; see Page 175], we find

$$\int_0^\pi \frac{\partial^2 u}{\partial x^2} \sin nx\ dx + \int_0^\pi \frac{\partial^2 u}{\partial y^2} \sin nx\ dx = \int_0^\pi su \sin nx\ dx$$

or, if $\tilde{u} = \int_0^\pi u \sin nx\ dx$,

$$-n^2 \tilde{u} + nu(\pi, y, s) \cos n\pi + nu(0, y, s) + \frac{d^2 \tilde{u}}{dy^2} = s\tilde{u} \qquad (8)$$

Since from the Laplace transforms of conditions (2) and (3) we have

$$u(0, y, s) = 0, \qquad u(\pi, y, s) = 0$$

(8) becomes

$$\frac{d^2 \tilde{u}}{dy^2} - (n^2 + s)\tilde{u} = 0$$

This has the solution

$$\tilde{u} = A e^{y\sqrt{n^2+s}} + B e^{-y\sqrt{n^2+s}}$$

From the boundedness of $\tilde{u}$ as $y \to \infty$, we require $A = 0$ so that

$$\tilde{u} = B e^{-y\sqrt{n^2+s}} \qquad (9)$$

From condition (5)

$$\tilde{u}(n, 0, s) = \int_0^\pi \frac{100}{s} \sin nx\ dx = \frac{100}{s}\left(\frac{1 - \cos n\pi}{n}\right)$$

Hence letting $y = 0$ in (9), we find

$$B = \frac{100}{s}\left(\frac{1 - \cos n\pi}{n}\right)$$

or

$$\tilde{u} = \frac{100}{s}\left(\frac{1 - \cos n\pi}{n}\right) e^{-y\sqrt{n^2+s}}$$

By the Fourier sine inversion formula [see Page 175], we have

$$u = \frac{2}{\pi} \sum_{n=1}^\infty \frac{100}{s}\left(\frac{1 - \cos n\pi}{n}\right) e^{-y\sqrt{n^2+s}} \sin nx \qquad (10)$$

We must now obtain the inverse Laplace transform of this. We know that

$$\mathcal{L}^{-1}\{e^{-y\sqrt{s}}\} = \frac{y}{2\sqrt{\pi t^3}} e^{-y^2/4t}$$

so that

$$\mathcal{L}^{-1}\{e^{-y\sqrt{s+n^2}}\} = \frac{y}{2\sqrt{\pi t^3}} e^{-y^2/4t} e^{-n^2 t}$$

Hence

$$\mathcal{L}^{-1}\left\{\frac{e^{-y\sqrt{s+n^2}}}{s}\right\} = \int_0^t \frac{y}{2\sqrt{\pi v^3}} e^{-y^2/4v} e^{-n^2 v}\ dv$$

$$= \frac{2}{\sqrt{\pi}} \int_{y/2\sqrt{t}}^\infty e^{-(p^2 + n^2 y^2/4p^2)}\ dp$$

on letting $y^2/4v = p^2$.

Then inverting term by term in (10) and using this result, we find

$$U(x, y, t) \;=\; \frac{400}{\pi^{3/2}} \sum_{n=1}^{\infty} \left(\frac{1 - \cos n\pi}{n} \right) \sin nx \int_{y/2\sqrt{t}}^{\infty} e^{-(p^2 + n^2 y^2/4 p^2)}\, dp$$

Supplementary Problems

HEAT CONDUCTION

15. A semi-infinite solid $x > 0$ has its initial temperature equal to zero. A constant heat flux A is applied at the face $x = 0$ so that $-K U_x (0, t) = A$. Show that the temperature at the face after time t is $\dfrac{2A}{K} \sqrt{\dfrac{kt}{\pi}}$.

16. Find the temperature at any point $x > 0$ of the solid in Problem 15.

$Ans.$ $\dfrac{2A}{K} \{ \sqrt{kt/\pi}\; e^{-x^2/4kt} - \tfrac{1}{2} x\; \text{erfc} \,(x/2\sqrt{kt}\,) \}$

17. A solid $0 \leqq x \leqq l$ is insulated at both ends $x = 0$ and $x = l$. If the initial temperature is equal to $ax(l - x)$ where a is a constant, find the temperature at any point x and at any time t.

$Ans.$ $\dfrac{al^2}{6} - \dfrac{al^2}{\pi^2} \sum_{n=1}^{\infty} \dfrac{e^{-4kn^2\pi^2 t/l^2}}{n^2} \cos \dfrac{2n\pi x}{l}$

18. (a) Use Laplace transforms to solve the boundary-value problem

$$\frac{\partial U}{\partial t} \;=\; .25 \frac{\partial^2 U}{\partial x^2} + 1 \qquad 0 < x < 10, \; t > 0$$

$$U(10, t) = 20, \qquad U_x (0, t) = 0, \qquad U(x, 0) = 50$$

(b) Give a heat flow interpretation to this problem.

$Ans.$ $\quad (a) \quad U(x, t) \;=\; 220 - 2x^2 + \dfrac{6400}{\pi^3} \sum_{n=1}^{\infty} \dfrac{(-1)^n}{(2n-1)^3}\; e^{-(2n-1)^2\pi^2 t/1600} \cos \dfrac{(2n-1)\pi x}{20}$

$$- \;\dfrac{120}{\pi} \sum_{n=1}^{\infty} \dfrac{(-1)^n}{2n-1}\; e^{-(2n-1)^2\pi^2 t/1600} \cos \dfrac{(2n-1)\pi x}{20}$$

19. (a) Solve $\qquad\qquad 2\dfrac{\partial U}{\partial t} \;=\; \dfrac{\partial^2 U}{\partial x^2} \qquad x > 0, \; t > 0$

$$U_x (0, t) = 0, \qquad U(x, 0) = e^{-x}, \qquad U(x, t) \text{ is bounded}$$

(b) Give a heat flow interpretation to this problem.

$Ans.$ $\quad U(x, t) \;=\; e^{t-x} - \dfrac{2e^t}{\sqrt{\pi}} \int_0^{\sqrt{t}} e^{-v^2 - x^2/4v^2}\, dv$

20. (a) A semi-infinite solid $x > 0$ has the face $x = 0$ kept at temperature $U_0 \cos \omega t, \; t > 0$. If the initial temperature is everywhere zero, show that the temperature at any point $x > 0$ at any time $t > 0$ is

$$U(x, t) \;=\; U_0\, e^{-\sqrt{\omega/2k}\, x} \cos (\omega t - \sqrt{\omega/2k}\, x) - \frac{U_0}{\pi} \int_0^{\infty} \frac{u e^{-ut} \sin x\sqrt{u/k}}{u^2 + \omega^2}\, du$$

(b) Show that for large t, the integral in the result of part (a) is negligible.

21. A semi-infinite solid $x \geqq 0$ is initially at temperature zero. At $t = 0$ the face $x = 0$ is suddenly raised to a constant temperature T_0 and kept at this temperature for a time t_0, after which the temperature is immediately reduced to zero. Show that after an additional time t_0 has elapsed, the temperature is a maximum at a distance given by $x = 2\sqrt{kt_0 \ln 2}$ where k is the diffusivity, assumed constant.

22. At $t = 0$, a semi-infinite solid $x > 0$ which is at temperature zero has a sinusoidal heat flux applied to the face $x = 0$ so that $-K U_x(0, t) = A + B \sin \omega t$, $t > 0$. Show that the temperature of the face at any later time is given by

$$\frac{2\sqrt{k}\, A}{K\sqrt{\pi}}\, t^{1/2} \;+\; \frac{2B\sqrt{k}\, \omega}{K}\left\{ \left(\int_0^{\sqrt{t}} \cos \omega v^2 \, dv \right) \sin \omega t \;-\; \left(\int_0^{\sqrt{t}} \sin \omega v^2 \, dv \right) \cos \omega t \right\}$$

23. Find the temperature of the solid in Problem 22 at any point $x > 0$.

THE VIBRATING STRING

24. (a) Solve the boundary-value problem

$$\frac{\partial^2 Y}{\partial t^2} \;=\; 4 \frac{\partial^2 Y}{\partial x^2} \qquad 0 < x < \pi, \; t > 0$$

$$Y_x(0, t) = 0, \quad Y(\pi, t) = h, \quad Y(x, 0) = 0, \quad Y_t(x, 0) = 0$$

(b) Give a physical interpretation of the problem in (a).

Ans. $\quad Y(x, t) \;=\; \dfrac{8h}{\pi} \displaystyle\sum_{n=1}^{\infty} \dfrac{(-1)^n}{2n-1} \sin\left(n - \tfrac{1}{2}\right)x \, \sin(2n-1)t$

25. Solve the boundary-value problem

$$Y_{tt} \;=\; Y_{xx} + g \qquad 0 < x < \pi, \; t > 0$$

$$Y(0, t) = 0, \quad Y(\pi, t) = 0, \quad Y(x, 0) = \mu\, x(\pi - x), \quad Y_t(x, 0) = 0$$

and interpret physically.

Ans. $\quad Y(x, t) \;=\; \tfrac{1}{2} g x(\pi - x) \;+\; \dfrac{4(2\mu x - g)}{\pi} \displaystyle\sum_{n=1}^{\infty} \dfrac{1}{(2n-1)^3} \sin(2n-1)x \, \cos(2n-1)t$

26. A tightly stretched flexible string has its ends fixed at $x = 0$ and $x = l$. At $t = 0$ its midpoint is displaced a distance h and released. Find the resulting displacement at any time $t > 0$.

Ans. $\quad Y(x, t) \;=\; \dfrac{8h}{\pi^2} \displaystyle\sum_{n=1}^{\infty} \dfrac{(-1)^{n-1}}{(2n-1)^2} \sin \dfrac{(2n-1)\pi x}{l} \, \cos \dfrac{(2n-1)\pi a t}{l}$

27. (a) Solve

$$\frac{\partial^2 Y}{\partial t^2} \;=\; a^2 \frac{\partial^2 Y}{\partial x^2} \qquad x > 0, \; t > 0$$

$$Y_x(0, t) = A \sin \omega t, \quad Y(x, 0) = 0, \quad Y_t(x, 0) = 0$$

(b) Give a physical interpretation to this problem.

Ans. (a) $\quad Y(x, t) \;=\; \dfrac{Aa}{\omega}\{1 - \cos \omega (t - x/a\} \quad$ if $\; t > x/a \;$ and 0 if $\; t \leqq x/a$

VIBRATIONS OF BEAMS

28. A beam of length l has the end $x = 0$ fixed and $x = l$ free. Its end $x = l$ is suddenly displaced longitudinally a distance α and then released. Show that the resulting displacement at any point x at time t is given by

$$Y(x, t) \;=\; \frac{\alpha x}{l} \;+\; \frac{2\alpha}{\pi} \sum_{n=1}^{\infty} \frac{(-1)^n}{n} \sin \frac{n\pi x}{l} \cos \frac{n\pi c t}{l}$$

29. A beam has its ends hinged at $x = 0$ and $x = l$. At $t = 0$ the beam is struck so as to give it a transverse velocity $V_0 \sin \pi x/l$. Find the transverse displacement of any point of the beam at any later time.

30. Work Problem 29 if the transverse velocity is $V_0 x(l - x)$.

31. A beam of length l has its ends hinged. Show that its natural frequencies of transverse oscillations are given by

$$f_n = \frac{n^2 \pi}{2l^2} \sqrt{\frac{EIg}{\rho}} \qquad n = 1, 2, 3, \ldots$$

32. A semi-infinite elastic beam is moving endwise with a velocity $-v_0$ when one end is suddenly brought to rest, the other end remaining free. (*a*) Explain with reference to this problem the significance of each of the following and (*b*) solve the resulting boundary-value problem.

$$Y_{tt}(x, t) = a^2 Y_{xx}(x, t) \qquad x > 0, \ t > 0$$

$$Y(x, 0) = 0, \qquad Y_t(x, 0) = -v_0, \qquad Y(0, t) = 0, \qquad \lim_{x \to \infty} Y_x(x, t) = 0$$

Ans. (*b*) $Y(x, t) = -v_0 x/a$ if $t > x/a$ and $-v_0 t$ if $t \leqq x/a$

TRANSMISSION LINES

33. A semi-infinite transmission line of negligible inductance and conductance per unit length has its voltage and current equal to zero. At $t = 0$, a constant voltage E_0 is applied at the sending end $x = 0$. (*a*) Show that the voltage at any point $x > 0$ at any time $t > 0$ is given by

$$E(x, t) = E_0 \operatorname{erfc}\left(x\sqrt{RC}/2\sqrt{t}\right)$$

and (*b*) that the corresponding current is

$$I(x, t) = E_0 \sqrt{\frac{C}{\pi R}} \, t^{-1/2} \, e^{-RCx^2/4t}$$

34. In Problem 33 show that the current at any specific time is a maximum at a position $\sqrt{2t/RC}$ from the receiving end.

35. A semi-infinite transmission line has negligible resistance and conductance per unit length and its initial voltage and current are zero. At $t = 0$ a voltage $E_0(t)$ is applied at the sending end $x = 0$. (*a*) Show that the voltage at any position $x > 0$ is

$$E(x, t) = \begin{cases} E_0(t - x\sqrt{LC}) & t > x\sqrt{LC} \\ 0 & t < x\sqrt{LC} \end{cases}$$

and (*b*) that the corresponding current is

$$I(x, t) = \begin{cases} \sqrt{C/L} \, E_0(t - x\sqrt{LC}) & t > x\sqrt{LC} \\ 0 & t < x\sqrt{LC} \end{cases}$$

36. Suppose that the transmission line of Problem 35 is such that $R/L = G/C$. Show that the voltage is given by

$$E(x, t) = \begin{cases} e^{-x\sqrt{RG}} \, E_0(t - x\sqrt{LC}) & t > x\sqrt{LC} \\ 0 & t < x\sqrt{LC} \end{cases}$$

and compare results with that of Problem 35. What is the current in this case?

37. (*a*) A transmission line of negligible resistance and capacitance has its sending end at $x = 0$ and its receiving end at $x = l$. A constant voltage E_0 is applied at the sending end while an open circuit is maintained at the receiving end so that the current there is zero. Assuming the initial voltage and current are zero, show that the voltage and current at any position x at any time $t > 0$ are given by

$$E(x, t) = \frac{E_0 \cosh \sqrt{L/C}\,(l - x)}{\cosh \sqrt{L/C}\, l}$$

$$I(x, t) = \frac{E_0 \sqrt{L/C} \sinh \sqrt{L/C}\,(l - x)}{\cosh \sqrt{L/C}}$$

(b) Discuss the significance of the fact that the voltage and current in (a) are independent of time.

38. (a) Work Problem 37 if the line has negligible resistance and conductance but not negligible inductance and capacitance, showing that in this case

$$E(x, t) = E_0 \left\{ 1 - \frac{4}{\pi} \sum_{n=1}^{\infty} \frac{1}{2n - 1} \cos \frac{(2n - 1)\pi x}{2l} \cos \frac{(2n - 1)\pi t}{2l\sqrt{LC}} \right\}$$

(b) What is the current in this case? Discuss the convergence of the series obtained and explain the significance.

MISCELLANEOUS PROBLEMS

39. (a) Solve the boundary-value problem

$$\frac{\partial U}{\partial t} = \frac{\partial^2 U}{\partial x^2} + 2x \qquad 0 < x < 1, \ t > 0$$

$$U(0, t) = 0, \qquad U(1, t) = 0, \qquad U(x, 0) = x - x^2$$

(b) Give a physical interpretation to the problem in part (a).

Ans. $U(x, t) = x(1 - x) - \dfrac{4}{\pi^3} \sum_{n=1}^{\infty} \left(\dfrac{1 - e^{-n^2\pi^2 t}}{n^3} \right) \sin n\pi x$ or $U(x, t) = \dfrac{4}{\pi^3} \sum_{n=1}^{\infty} \dfrac{e^{-n^2\pi^2 t}}{n^3} \sin n\pi x$

40. Work Problem 39 if the condition $U(0, t) = 0$ is replaced by $U_x(0, t) = 0$.

Ans. $U(x, t) = \dfrac{5}{3} - 2x^2 + \dfrac{1}{3} x^3 - \dfrac{8}{\pi^2} \sum_{n=1}^{\infty} \dfrac{e^{-(2n-1)^2\pi^2 t/4}}{(2n - 1)^2} \cos \dfrac{(2n - 1)\pi x}{2}$

$$- \frac{64}{\pi^4} \sum_{n=1}^{\infty} \frac{e^{-(2n-1)^2\pi^2 t/4}}{(2n - 1)^4} \cos \frac{(2n - 1)\pi x}{2}$$

41. A solid, $0 < x < l$, is initially at temperature zero. The face $x = 0$ is given a temperature $U(0, t) = G(t)$, $t > 0$, while the end $x = l$ is kept at 0°C. Show that the temperature at any point x at any time t is

$$U(x, t) = \frac{2\pi}{l^2} \sum_{n=1}^{\infty} \left\{ n \int_0^t e^{-n^2\pi^2 u/l^2} G(t - u)\, du \right\} \sin \frac{n\pi x}{l}$$

42. Work Problem 41 if the end $x = l$ is insulated.

43. Show that in solving a boundary-value problem involving the equation $\dfrac{\partial U}{\partial t} = k \dfrac{\partial^2 U}{\partial x^2}$ it is equivalent to solve the problem by replacing the equation by $\dfrac{\partial U}{\partial t} = \dfrac{\partial^2 U}{\partial x^2}$ and then replacing t by kt.

44. A solid, $0 < x < l$, has its end temperatures maintained at zero while the initial temperature is $F(x)$. Show that the temperature at any point x at any time t is

$$U(x, t) = \frac{2}{l} \sum_{n=1}^{\infty} e^{-kn^2\pi^2 t/l^2} \sin \frac{n\pi x}{l} \int_0^l F(u) \sin \frac{n\pi u}{l}\, du$$

45. Find a bounded solution of

$$x\frac{\partial \Phi}{\partial x} + \frac{\partial \Phi}{\partial y} = xe^{-y} \qquad 0 < x < 1, \ y > 0$$

which satisfies $\Phi(x, 0) = x$, $0 < x < 1$.   *Ans.* $\Phi(x, y) = xe^{-y}(1 + y)$

46. A string stretched between $x = 0$ and $x = l$ is plucked at its center a distance D and released. Find the resulting displacement of any point x from the equilibrium position at any time t.

Ans. $Y(x, t) = \dfrac{8D}{\pi^2} \displaystyle\sum_{n=1}^{\infty} \dfrac{1}{n^2} \sin \dfrac{n\pi}{2} \sin \dfrac{n\pi x}{l} \cos \dfrac{n\pi at}{l}$

47. Show that a transmission line problem in which inductance and conductance per unit length are negligible is equivalent to a problem in heat conduction.

48. Solve the boundary-value problem

$$\frac{\partial Y}{\partial t} + x \frac{\partial Y}{\partial x} + Y = x \qquad x > 0,\ t > 0$$

where $Y(0, t) = 0$, $Y(x, 0) = 0$.   *Ans.* $Y(x, t) = \frac{1}{2} x (1 - e^{-2t})$

49. Show that in solving a boundary-value problem involving the equation $\dfrac{\partial^2 Y}{\partial t^2} = a^2 \dfrac{\partial^2 Y}{\partial x^2}$, it is equivalent to solve the problem by replacing the equation by $\dfrac{\partial^2 Y}{\partial t^2} = \dfrac{\partial^2 Y}{\partial x^2}$ and then replace t by at.

50. Show that a transmission line problem in which resistance and conductance are negligible, is equivalent to a problem in the vibration of a string.

51. A string is stretched between $x = 0$ and $x = l$. The end $x = 0$ is given a transverse displacement according to $Y(0, t) = F(t)$ where $F(t)$ is a prescribed function of time, while the end $x = l$ remains fixed. Find the transverse displacement.

52. A semi-infinite plate having width π [see Fig. 8-14] has its faces insulated. The semi-infinite edges are maintained at $0°C$, while the finite edge is insulated. If the initial temperature is $100°C$, find the temperature at any point at any time.

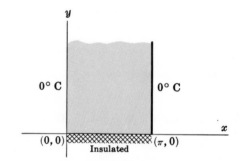

Fig. 8-14

53. A solid, $0 < x < l$, is initially at constant temperature U_0 while the ends $x = 0$ and $x = l$ are maintained at temperature zero. Show that the temperature at any position x at any time t is given by

$$U(x, t) = U_0 \operatorname{erf}\left(\frac{x}{2\sqrt{kt}}\right) + U_0 \sum_{n=1}^{\infty} (-1)^n \left\{ \operatorname{erf}\left(\frac{nl - x}{2\sqrt{kt}}\right) - \operatorname{erf}\left(\frac{nl + x}{2\sqrt{kt}}\right) \right\}$$

54. A beam has its ends hinged at $x = 0$ and $x = l$. At time $t = 0$, a concentrated transverse load of magnitude w is suddenly applied at the midpoint. Show that the resulting transverse displacement of any point x of the beam at any time $t > 0$ is

$$Y(x, t) = \frac{wx}{12EI}(\tfrac{3}{4}l^2 - x^2) - \frac{2wl^3}{\pi^4 EI}\left\{ \frac{\sin \pi x/l}{1^4} + \frac{\sin 3\pi x/l}{3^4} + \frac{\sin 5\pi x/l}{5^4} + \cdots \right\}$$

if $0 < x < l/2$, while the corresponding result for $l/2 < x < l$ is obtained by symmetry.

55. Show that the boundary-value problem

$$\frac{\partial U}{\partial t} = \frac{\partial^2 U}{\partial x^2} - \alpha^2 U \qquad 0 < x < l,\ t > 0$$

$$U(0, t) = U_1, \qquad U(l, t) = U_2, \qquad U(x, 0) = 0$$

has the solution

$$U(x, t) = \frac{U_1 \sinh \alpha(l - x) + U_2 \sinh \alpha x}{\sinh \alpha l} + \frac{2\pi}{l^2} e^{-\alpha^2 t} \sum_{n=1}^{\infty} \frac{n\, e^{-n^2\pi^2 t/l^2}\, (U_2 \cos n\pi - U_1)}{\alpha^2 + n^2\pi^2/l^2} \sin \frac{n\pi x}{l}$$

56. Show that Problem 55 can be interpreted as a heat flow problem in which a bar of length l can radiate heat into its surroundings.

57. A transverse force given by $F(x) = x(\pi - x)$ acts at each point x of a beam which is hinged at its ends $x = 0$ and $x = \pi$. If the initial transverse displacement and velocity are zero, find the transverse displacement at a later time t.

58. A semi-infinite transmission line of negligible inductance and conductance per unit length has a voltage applied to its sending end $x = 0$ given by $E(0, t) = E_0 \cos \omega t$, $t > 0$. Assuming the initial voltage and current to be zero, (a) show that after a long time the voltage at any point $x > 0$ is given by

$$E(x, t) = E_0 \, e^{-\sqrt{\omega RC/2}\, x} \cos (\omega t - \sqrt{\omega RC/2}\, x)$$

and (b) show that the corresponding current is given by

$$I(x, t) = E_0 \sqrt{\omega C/R} \, e^{-\sqrt{\omega RC/2}} \cos (\omega t - \sqrt{\omega RC/2}\, x - \pi/4)$$

59. A semi-infinite string is initially at rest on the x axis, and its end $x = 0$ is fixed. At $t = 0$ each point x of the string is given an initial velocity defined by $F(x)$, $x > 0$. Find the resulting displacement of each point x at time $t > 0$.

60. A concentrated transverse force $F = F_0 \sin \omega t$, $t > 0$, is applied at the midpoint of a beam hinged at its ends $x = 0$ and $x = l$. Show that the resulting transverse displacement is

$$Y(x, t) = \frac{bF_0 \sin \omega t}{4EI} \sqrt{\frac{b}{\omega}} \left\{ \frac{\sin x\sqrt{\omega/b}}{\cos l\sqrt{\omega}/2\sqrt{b}} - \frac{\sinh x\sqrt{\omega/b}}{\cosh l\sqrt{\omega}/2\sqrt{b}} \right\}$$

$$- \frac{2bF_0 l}{\pi^2 EI} \sum_{n=1}^{\infty} \frac{\sin n\pi/2}{n^2(\omega^2 - b^2 n^4 \pi^4/l^2)} \sin \frac{n\pi x}{l} \sin \frac{bn^2 \pi^2 t}{l^2}$$

if $0 < x < l/2$, with a result obtained by symmetry for $l/2 < x < l$. Discuss the physical significance of having $\omega = bn^2\pi^2/l^2$ for some $n = 1, 2, 3, \ldots$.

61. Find the steady-state temperature in the square indicated in Fig. 8-15 if the plane faces are insulated and the sides are maintained at the constant temperatures shown.

    Ans. $U(x, y) = \dfrac{4T}{\pi} \displaystyle\sum_{n=1}^{\infty} \dfrac{\sin (2n-1)\pi x \, \sinh (2n-1)\pi(1-y)}{(2n-1) \sinh (2n-1)\pi}$

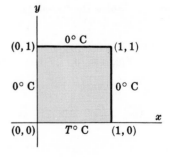

Fig. 8-15

62. Work Problem 62 if all four sides are kept at constant temperatures T_1, T_2, T_3, T_4.

63. Suppose that in Problem 62 the initial temperature is $0°C$. What would be the temperature at every point of the square at any time?

64. A beam of length l has its end $x = l$ fixed. At $t = 0$ the end $x = 0$ is given a longitudinal displacement D and released. Show that the resulting longitudinal displacement of any point x at any time $t > 0$ is given by

$$Y(x, t) = D \left\{ u(t - x/a) - u\left(t - \frac{2l - x}{a}\right) + u\left(t - \frac{2l + x}{a}\right) - \cdots \right\}$$

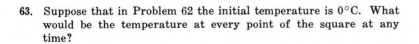

where u is Heaviside's unit step function. Discuss this solution graphically.

65. Two semi-infinite conducting solids, $x < 0$ and $x > 0$ [see Fig. 8-16], have constant thermal conductivities and diffusivities given by K_1, k_1 and K_2, k_2 respectively. The initial temperatures of these solids are constant and equal to U_1 and U_2 respectively. Show that the temperature at any point of the solid $x > 0$ at any time t is

$$U(x, t) \;=\; U_1 \;+\; \frac{U_2 - U_1}{1 + \alpha}\left\{1 \;+\; \alpha\,\mathrm{erf}\!\left(\frac{x}{2\sqrt{k_2 t}}\right)\right\}$$

where $\alpha = K_1\sqrt{k_2}/K_2\sqrt{k_1}$.

$\left[\,Hint.\right.$ The heat conduction equations are $\dfrac{\partial U}{\partial t} = k_1 \dfrac{\partial^2 U}{\partial x^2}$,

$x < 0$ and $\dfrac{\partial U}{\partial t} = k_2 \dfrac{\partial^2 U}{\partial x^2}$, $\;x > 0\;$ and we must have

$\displaystyle\lim_{x \to 0-} U(x, t) \;=\; \lim_{x \to 0+} U(x, t)$ and $\displaystyle\lim_{x \to 0-} K_1 U_x(x, t) \;=\;$

$\displaystyle\lim_{x \to 0+} K_2 U_x(x, t).\,\Big]$

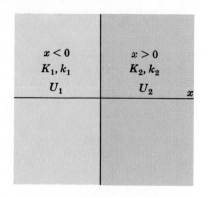

Fig. 8-16

66. Verify the result at the end of Problem 8, Page 228.

67. An infinite circular cylinder of unit radius has its initial temperature zero. A constant flux A is applied to the convex surface. Show that the temperature at points distant r from the axis at any time t is given by

$$U(r, t) \;=\; \frac{A}{4k}\{1 - 8kt - 2r^2\} \;+\; \frac{2A}{k}\sum_{n=1}^{\infty} e^{-k\lambda_n^2 t}\,\frac{J_0(\lambda_n r)}{\lambda_n^2 J_0(\lambda_n)}$$

where λ_n are the positive roots of $J_0(\lambda) = 0$.

68. A cylinder of unit radius and height has its circular ends maintained at temperature zero while its convex surface is maintained at constant temperature U_0. Assuming that the cylinder has its axis coincident with the z axis, show that the steady-state temperature at any distance r from the axis and z from one end is

$$U(r, z) \;=\; \frac{4U_0}{\pi}\sum_{n=1}^{\infty} \frac{\sin(2n-1)\pi z}{2n-1}\,\frac{I_0\{(2n-1)\pi r\}}{I_0\{(2n-1)\pi\}}$$

69. (a) Solve the boundary-value problem

$$\frac{\partial^2 Y}{\partial t^2} \;+\; b^2 \frac{\partial^4 Y}{\partial x^4} \;=\; 0 \qquad 0 < x < l,\; t > 0$$

$Y(0, t) = 0, \quad Y(l, t) = 0, \quad Y(x, 0) = 0, \quad Y_t(x, 0) = 0, \quad Y_{xx}(l, t) = 0, \quad EI\,Y_{xx}(0, t) = P_0 \sin \omega t$

(b) Interpret the problem in (a) physically.

Ans.   (a) $Y(x, t) \;=\; \dfrac{bP_0 \sin \omega t}{2EI\omega}\left\{\dfrac{\sinh(l-x)\sqrt{\omega/b}}{\sinh l\sqrt{\omega/b}} - \dfrac{\sin(l-x)\sqrt{\omega/b}}{\sin l\sqrt{\omega/b}}\right\}$

$$+\; \frac{2\omega P_0\, b}{\pi EI}\sum_{n=1}^{\infty} \frac{\sin n\pi x/l\;\sin bn^2\pi^2 t/l^2}{n(\omega^2 - b^2 n^4 \pi^4/l^4)}$$

70. A semi-infinite transmission line of negligible inductance has its initial voltage and current equal to zero. At $t = 0$ a constant voltage E_0 is applied at the sending end $x = 0$. Show that the voltage at any point $x > 0$ at any time $t > 0$ is

$$E(x, t) \;=\; \tfrac{1}{2}E_0\left\{e^{-x\sqrt{GR}}\,\mathrm{erf}\left(\sqrt{\frac{Gt}{C}} - \tfrac{1}{2}x\sqrt{\frac{RC}{t}}\right)\right.$$

$$\left. -\; e^{x\sqrt{GR}}\,\mathrm{erf}\left(\sqrt{\frac{Gt}{C}} + \tfrac{1}{2}x\sqrt{\frac{RC}{t}}\right)\right\} \;-\; E_0 \cosh x\sqrt{GR}$$

What is the corresponding current?

Appendix A

$$f(s) \; = \; \int_0^\infty e^{-st} F(t) \, dt$$

	$f(s)$	$F(t)$
1.	$a f_1(s) \, + \, b f_2(s)$	$a F_1(t) \, + \, b F_2(t)$
2.	$f(s/a)$	$a F(at)$
3.	$f(s - a)$	$e^{at} F(t)$
4.	$e^{-as} f(s)$	$F(t - a) \, \mathcal{U}(t - a) \; = \; \begin{cases} F(t-a) & t > a \\ 0 & t < a \end{cases}$
5.	$s f(s) \, - \, F(0)$	$F'(t)$
6.	$s^2 f(s) \, - \, s F(0) \, - \, F'(0)$	$F''(t)$
7.	$s^n f(s) - s^{n-1} F(0) - s^{n-2} F'(0) - \cdots - F^{(n-1)}(0)$	$F^{(n)}(t)$
8.	$f'(s)$	$-t F(t)$
9.	$f''(s)$	$t^2 F(t)$
10.	$f^{(n)}(s)$	$(-1)^n t^n F(t)$
11.	$\dfrac{f(s)}{s}$	$\displaystyle\int_0^t F(u) \, du$
12.	$\dfrac{f(s)}{s^n}$	$\displaystyle\int_0^t \cdots \int_0^t F(u) \, du^n \; = \; \int_0^t \frac{(t-u)^{n-1}}{(n-1)!} F(u) \, du$
13.	$f(s) \, g(s)$	$\displaystyle\int_0^t F(u) \, G(t-u) \, du$

	$f(s)$	$F(t)$
14.	$\displaystyle\int_s^\infty f(u)\,du$	$\dfrac{F(t)}{t}$
15.	$\dfrac{1}{1-e^{-sT}}\displaystyle\int_0^T e^{-su}\,F(u)\,du$	$F(t) = F(t+T)$
16.	$\dfrac{f(\sqrt{s}\,)}{\sqrt{s}}$	$\dfrac{1}{\sqrt{\pi t}}\displaystyle\int_0^\infty e^{-u^2/4t}\,F(u)\,du$
17.	$\dfrac{1}{s}\,f(1/s)$	$\displaystyle\int_0^\infty J_0(2\sqrt{ut}\,)\,F(u)\,du$
18.	$\dfrac{1}{s^{n+1}}\,f(1/s)$	$t^{n/2}\displaystyle\int_0^\infty u^{-n/2}\,J_n(2\sqrt{ut}\,)\,F(u)\,du$
19.	$\dfrac{f(s+1/s)}{s^2+1}$	$\displaystyle\int_0^t J_0(2\sqrt{u(t-u)}\,)\,F(u)\,du$
20.	$\dfrac{1}{2\sqrt{\pi}}\displaystyle\int_0^\infty u^{-3/2}\,e^{-s^2/4u}\,f(u)\,du$	$F(t^2)$
21.	$\dfrac{f(\ln s)}{s\ln s}$	$\displaystyle\int_0^\infty \dfrac{t^u\,F(u)}{\Gamma(u+1)}\,du$
22.	$\dfrac{P(s)}{Q(s)}$ $P(s) =$ polynomial of degree less than n, $Q(s) = (s-\alpha_1)(s-\alpha_2)\cdots(s-\alpha_n)$ where $\alpha_1, \alpha_2, \ldots, \alpha_n$ are all distinct.	$\displaystyle\sum_{k=1}^n \dfrac{P(\alpha_k)}{Q'(\alpha_k)}\,e^{\alpha_k t}$

Appendix B

	$f(s)$	$F(t)$
1.	$\dfrac{1}{s}$	1
2.	$\dfrac{1}{s^2}$	t
3.	$\dfrac{1}{s^n} \qquad n = 1, 2, 3, \ldots$	$\dfrac{t^{n-1}}{(n-1)!}, \quad 0! = 1$
4.	$\dfrac{1}{s^n} \qquad n > 0$	$\dfrac{t^{n-1}}{\Gamma(n)}$
5.	$\dfrac{1}{s-a}$	e^{at}
6.	$\dfrac{1}{(s-a)^n} \qquad n = 1, 2, 3, \ldots$	$\dfrac{t^{n-1}e^{at}}{(n-1)!}, \quad 0! = 1$
7.	$\dfrac{1}{(s-a)^n} \qquad n > 0$	$\dfrac{t^{n-1}e^{at}}{\Gamma(n)}$
8.	$\dfrac{1}{s^2+a^2}$	$\dfrac{\sin at}{a}$
9.	$\dfrac{s}{s^2+a^2}$	$\cos at$
10.	$\dfrac{1}{(s-b)^2+a^2}$	$\dfrac{e^{bt}\sin at}{a}$
11.	$\dfrac{s-b}{(s-b)^2+a^2}$	$e^{bt}\cos at$
12.	$\dfrac{1}{s^2-a^2}$	$\dfrac{\sinh at}{a}$
13.	$\dfrac{s}{s^2-a^2}$	$\cosh at$
14.	$\dfrac{1}{(s-b)^2-a^2}$	$\dfrac{e^{bt}\sinh at}{a}$

	$f(s)$	$F(t)$
15.	$\dfrac{s-b}{(s-b)^2-a^2}$	$e^{bt}\cosh at$
16.	$\dfrac{1}{(s-a)(s-b)}\qquad a\neq b$	$\dfrac{e^{bt}-e^{at}}{b-a}$
17.	$\dfrac{s}{(s-a)(s-b)}\qquad a\neq b$	$\dfrac{be^{bt}-ae^{at}}{b-a}$
18.	$\dfrac{1}{(s^2+a^2)^2}$	$\dfrac{\sin at-at\cos at}{2a^3}$
19.	$\dfrac{s}{(s^2+a^2)^2}$	$\dfrac{t\sin at}{2a}$
20.	$\dfrac{s^2}{(s^2+a^2)^2}$	$\dfrac{\sin at+at\cos at}{2a}$
21.	$\dfrac{s^3}{(s^2+a^2)^2}$	$\cos at-\tfrac{1}{2}at\sin at$
22.	$\dfrac{s^2-a^2}{(s^2+a^2)^2}$	$t\cos at$
23.	$\dfrac{1}{(s^2-a^2)^2}$	$\dfrac{at\cosh at-\sinh at}{2a^3}$
24.	$\dfrac{s}{(s^2-a^2)^2}$	$\dfrac{t\sinh at}{2a}$
25.	$\dfrac{s^2}{(s^2-a^2)^2}$	$\dfrac{\sinh at+at\cosh at}{2a}$
26.	$\dfrac{s^3}{(s^2-a^2)^2}$	$\cosh at+\tfrac{1}{2}at\sinh at$
27.	$\dfrac{s^2+a^2}{(s^2-a^2)^2}$	$t\cosh at$
28.	$\dfrac{1}{(s^2+a^2)^3}$	$\dfrac{(3-a^2t^2)\sin at-3at\cos at}{8a^5}$
29.	$\dfrac{s}{(s^2+a^2)^3}$	$\dfrac{t\sin at-at^2\cos at}{8a^3}$
30.	$\dfrac{s^2}{(s^2+a^2)^3}$	$\dfrac{(1+a^2t^2)\sin at-at\cos at}{8a^3}$
31.	$\dfrac{s^3}{(s^2+a^2)^3}$	$\dfrac{3t\sin at+at^2\cos at}{8a}$

	$f(s)$	$F(t)$
32.	$\dfrac{s^4}{(s^2 + a^2)^3}$	$\dfrac{(3 - a^2t^2)\sin at + 5at\cos at}{8a}$
33.	$\dfrac{s^5}{(s^2 + a^2)^3}$	$\dfrac{(8 - a^2t^2)\cos at - 7at\sin at}{8}$
34.	$\dfrac{3s^2 - a^2}{(s^2 + a^2)^3}$	$\dfrac{t^2 \sin at}{2a}$
35.	$\dfrac{s^3 - 3a^2s}{(s^2 + a^2)^3}$	$\tfrac{1}{2}t^2 \cos at$
36.	$\dfrac{s^4 - 6a^2s^2 + a^4}{(s^2 + a^2)^4}$	$\tfrac{1}{6}t^3 \cos at$
37.	$\dfrac{s^3 - a^2s}{(s^2 + a^2)^4}$	$\dfrac{t^3 \sin at}{24a}$
38.	$\dfrac{1}{(s^2 - a^2)^3}$	$\dfrac{(3 + a^2t^2)\sinh at - 3at\cosh at}{8a^5}$
39.	$\dfrac{s}{(s^2 - a^2)^3}$	$\dfrac{at^2 \cosh at - t\sinh at}{8a^3}$
40.	$\dfrac{s^2}{(s^2 - a^2)^3}$	$\dfrac{at \cosh at + (a^2t^2 - 1)\sinh at}{8a^3}$
41.	$\dfrac{s^3}{(s^2 - a^2)^3}$	$\dfrac{3t \sinh at + at^2\cosh at}{8a}$
42.	$\dfrac{s^4}{(s^2 - a^2)^3}$	$\dfrac{(3 + a^2t^2)\sinh at + 5at\cosh at}{8a}$
43.	$\dfrac{s^5}{(s^2 - a^2)^3}$	$\dfrac{(8 + a^2t^2)\cosh at + 7at\sinh at}{8}$
44.	$\dfrac{3s^2 + a^2}{(s^2 - a^2)^3}$	$\dfrac{t^2 \sinh at}{2a}$
45.	$\dfrac{s^3 + 3a^2s}{(s^2 - a^2)^3}$	$\tfrac{1}{2}t^2 \cosh at$
46.	$\dfrac{s^4 + 6a^2s^2 + a^4}{(s^2 - a^2)^4}$	$\tfrac{1}{6}t^3 \cosh at$
47.	$\dfrac{s^3 + a^2s}{(s^2 - a^2)^4}$	$\dfrac{t^3 \sinh at}{24a}$
48.	$\dfrac{1}{s^3 + a^3}$	$\dfrac{e^{at/2}}{3a^2}\left\{ \sqrt{3}\sin\dfrac{\sqrt{3}\,at}{2} - \cos\dfrac{\sqrt{3}\,at}{2} + e^{-3at/2}\right\}$

	$f(s)$	$F(t)$
49.	$\dfrac{s}{s^3 + a^3}$	$\dfrac{e^{at/2}}{3a}\left\{\cos\dfrac{\sqrt{3}\,at}{2} + \sqrt{3}\sin\dfrac{\sqrt{3}\,at}{2} - e^{-3at/2}\right\}$
50.	$\dfrac{s^2}{s^3 + a^3}$	$\dfrac{1}{3}\left(e^{-at} + 2e^{at/2}\cos\dfrac{\sqrt{3}\,at}{2}\right)$
51.	$\dfrac{1}{s^3 - a^3}$	$\dfrac{e^{-at/2}}{3a^2}\left\{e^{3at/2} - \cos\dfrac{\sqrt{3}\,at}{2} - \sqrt{3}\sin\dfrac{\sqrt{3}\,at}{2}\right\}$
52.	$\dfrac{s}{s^3 - a^3}$	$\dfrac{e^{-at/2}}{3a}\left\{\sqrt{3}\sin\dfrac{\sqrt{3}\,at}{2} - \cos\dfrac{\sqrt{3}\,at}{2} + e^{3at/2}\right\}$
53.	$\dfrac{s^2}{s^3 - a^3}$	$\dfrac{1}{3}\left(e^{at} + 2e^{-at/2}\cos\dfrac{\sqrt{3}\,at}{2}\right)$
54.	$\dfrac{1}{s^4 + 4a^4}$	$\dfrac{1}{4a^3}(\sin at \cosh at - \cos at \sinh at)$
55.	$\dfrac{s}{s^4 + 4a^4}$	$\dfrac{\sin at \sinh at}{2a^2}$
56.	$\dfrac{s^2}{s^4 + 4a^4}$	$\dfrac{1}{2a}(\sin at \cosh at + \cos at \sinh at)$
57.	$\dfrac{s^3}{s^4 + 4a^4}$	$\cos at \cosh at$
58.	$\dfrac{1}{s^4 - a^4}$	$\dfrac{1}{2a^3}(\sinh at - \sin at)$
59.	$\dfrac{s}{s^4 - a^4}$	$\dfrac{1}{2a^2}(\cosh at - \cos at)$
60.	$\dfrac{s^2}{s^4 - a^4}$	$\dfrac{1}{2a}(\sinh at + \sin at)$
61.	$\dfrac{s^3}{s^4 - a^4}$	$\tfrac{1}{2}(\cosh at + \cos at)$
62.	$\dfrac{1}{\sqrt{s+a} + \sqrt{s+b}}$	$\dfrac{e^{-bt} - e^{-at}}{2(b-a)\sqrt{\pi t^3}}$
63.	$\dfrac{1}{s\sqrt{s+a}}$	$\dfrac{\operatorname{erf}\sqrt{at}}{\sqrt{a}}$
64.	$\dfrac{1}{\sqrt{s}\,(s-a)}$	$\dfrac{e^{at}\operatorname{erf}\sqrt{at}}{\sqrt{a}}$
65.	$\dfrac{1}{\sqrt{s-a} + b}$	$e^{at}\left\{\dfrac{1}{\sqrt{\pi t}} - b\,e^{b^2 t}\operatorname{erfc}(b\sqrt{t})\right\}$

	$f(s)$	$F(t)$
66.	$\dfrac{1}{\sqrt{s^2 + a^2}}$	$J_0(at)$
67.	$\dfrac{1}{\sqrt{s^2 - a^2}}$	$I_0(at)$
68.	$\dfrac{(\sqrt{s^2 + a^2} - s)^n}{\sqrt{s^2 + a^2}} \quad n > -1$	$a^n J_n(at)$
69.	$\dfrac{(s - \sqrt{s^2 - a^2})^n}{\sqrt{s^2 - a^2}} \quad n > -1$	$a^n I_n(at)$
70.	$\dfrac{e^{b(s - \sqrt{s^2 + a^2})}}{\sqrt{s^2 + a^2}}$	$J_0(a\sqrt{t(t + 2b)})$
71.	$\dfrac{e^{-b\sqrt{s^2 + a^2}}}{\sqrt{s^2 + a^2}}$	$\begin{cases} J_0(a\sqrt{t^2 - b^2}) & t > b \\ 0 & t < b \end{cases}$
72.	$\dfrac{1}{(s^2 + a^2)^{3/2}}$	$\dfrac{t J_1(at)}{a}$
73.	$\dfrac{s}{(s^2 + a^2)^{3/2}}$	$t J_0(at)$
74.	$\dfrac{s^2}{(s^2 + a^2)^{3/2}}$	$J_0(at) - at J_1(at)$
75.	$\dfrac{1}{(s^2 - a^2)^{3/2}}$	$\dfrac{t I_1(at)}{a}$
76.	$\dfrac{s}{(s^2 - a^2)^{3/2}}$	$t I_0(at)$
77.	$\dfrac{s^2}{(s^2 - a^2)^{3/2}}$	$I_0(at) + at I_1(at)$
78.	$\dfrac{1}{s(e^s - 1)} = \dfrac{e^{-s}}{s(1 - e^{-s})}$ See also entry 141, Page 254.	$F(t) = n, \quad n \leqq t < n+1, \ n = 0, 1, 2, \ldots$
79.	$\dfrac{1}{s(e^s - r)} = \dfrac{e^{-s}}{s(1 - re^{-s})}$	$F(t) = \displaystyle\sum_{k=1}^{[t]} r^k$ where $[t] = $ greatest integer $\leqq t$
80.	$\dfrac{e^s - 1}{s(e^s - r)} = \dfrac{1 - e^{-s}}{s(1 - re^{-s})}$ See also entry 143, Page 254.	$F(t) = r^n, \quad n \leqq t < n+1, \ n = 0, 1, 2, \ldots$
81.	$\dfrac{e^{-a/s}}{\sqrt{s}}$	$\dfrac{\cos 2\sqrt{at}}{\sqrt{\pi t}}$

	$f(s)$	$F(t)$
82.	$\dfrac{e^{-a/s}}{s^{3/2}}$	$\dfrac{\sin 2\sqrt{at}}{\sqrt{\pi a}}$
83.	$\dfrac{e^{-a/s}}{s^{n+1}} \qquad n > -1$	$\left(\dfrac{t}{a}\right)^{n/2} J_n(2\sqrt{at})$
84.	$\dfrac{e^{-a\sqrt{s}}}{\sqrt{s}}$	$\dfrac{e^{-a^2/4t}}{\sqrt{\pi t}}$
85.	$e^{-a\sqrt{s}}$	$\dfrac{a}{2\sqrt{\pi t^3}} \, e^{-a^2/4t}$
86.	$\dfrac{1 - e^{-a\sqrt{s}}}{s}$	$\operatorname{erf}(a/2\sqrt{t})$
87.	$\dfrac{e^{-a\sqrt{s}}}{s}$	$\operatorname{erfc}(a/2\sqrt{t})$
88.	$\dfrac{e^{-a\sqrt{s}}}{\sqrt{s}\,(\sqrt{s} + b)}$	$e^{b(bt+a)} \operatorname{erfc}\left(b\sqrt{t} + \dfrac{a}{2\sqrt{t}}\right)$
89.	$\dfrac{e^{-a/\sqrt{s}}}{s^{n+1}} \qquad n > -1$	$\dfrac{1}{\sqrt{\pi t}\,a^{2n+1}} \displaystyle\int_0^\infty u^n \, e^{-u^2/4a^2 t} J_{2n}(2\sqrt{u})\,du$
90.	$\ln\left(\dfrac{s + a}{s + b}\right)$	$\dfrac{e^{-bt} - e^{-at}}{t}$
91.	$\dfrac{\ln\left[(s^2 + a^2)/a^2\right]}{2s}$	$\operatorname{Ci}(at)$
92.	$\dfrac{\ln\left[(s + a)/a\right]}{s}$	$\operatorname{Ei}(at)$
93.	$-\dfrac{(\gamma + \ln s)}{s}$ $\gamma = \text{Euler's constant} = .5772156\ldots$	$\ln t$
94.	$\ln\left(\dfrac{s^2 + a^2}{s^2 + b^2}\right)$	$\dfrac{2\,(\cos at - \cos bt)}{t}$
95.	$\dfrac{\pi^2}{6s} + \dfrac{(\gamma + \ln s)^2}{s}$ $\gamma = \text{Euler's constant} = .5772156\ldots$	$\ln^2 t$
96.	$\dfrac{\ln s}{s}$	$-(\ln t + \gamma)$ $\gamma = \text{Euler's constant} = .5772156\ldots$
97.	$\dfrac{\ln^2 s}{s}$	$(\ln t + \gamma)^2 - \frac{1}{6}\pi^2$ $\gamma = \text{Euler's constant} = .5772156\ldots$

	$f(s)$	$F(t)$
98.	$\dfrac{\Gamma'(n+1) - \Gamma(n+1)\ln s}{s^{n+1}} \qquad n > -1$	$t^n \ln t$
99.	$\tan^{-1}(a/s)$	$\dfrac{\sin at}{t}$
100.	$\dfrac{\tan^{-1}(a/s)}{s}$	$\mathrm{Si}\,(at)$
101.	$\dfrac{e^{a/s}}{\sqrt{s}}\,\mathrm{erfc}\,(\sqrt{a/s})$	$\dfrac{e^{-2\sqrt{at}}}{\sqrt{\pi t}}$
102.	$e^{s^2/4a^2}\,\mathrm{erfc}\,(s/2a)$	$\dfrac{2a}{\sqrt{\pi}}\,e^{-a^2 t^2}$
103.	$\dfrac{e^{s^2/4a^2}\,\mathrm{erfc}\,(s/2a)}{s}$	$\mathrm{erf}\,(at)$
104.	$\dfrac{e^{as}\,\mathrm{erfc}\,\sqrt{as}}{\sqrt{s}}$	$\dfrac{1}{\sqrt{\pi(t+a)}}$
105.	$e^{as}\,\mathrm{Ei}\,(as)$	$\dfrac{1}{t+a}$
106.	$\dfrac{1}{a}\left[\cos as\left\{\dfrac{\pi}{2} - \mathrm{Si}\,(as)\right\} - \sin as\,\mathrm{Ci}\,(as)\right]$	$\dfrac{1}{t^2+a^2}$
107.	$\sin as\left\{\dfrac{\pi}{2} - \mathrm{Si}\,(as)\right\} + \cos as\,\mathrm{Ci}\,(as)$	$\dfrac{t}{t^2+a^2}$
108.	$\dfrac{\cos as\left\{\dfrac{\pi}{2} - \mathrm{Si}\,(as)\right\} - \sin as\,\mathrm{Ci}\,(as)}{s}$	$\tan^{-1}(t/a)$
109.	$\dfrac{\sin as\left\{\dfrac{\pi}{2} - \mathrm{Si}\,(as)\right\} + \cos as\,\mathrm{Ci}\,(as)}{s}$	$\dfrac{1}{2}\ln\left(\dfrac{t^2+a^2}{a^2}\right)$
110.	$\left[\dfrac{\pi}{2} - \mathrm{Si}\,(as)\right]^2 + \mathrm{Ci}^2\,(as)$	$\dfrac{1}{t}\ln\left(\dfrac{t^2+a^2}{a^2}\right)$
111.	0	$\mathcal{N}(t)$
112.	1	$\delta(t)$
113.	e^{-as}	$\delta(t-a)$
114.	$\dfrac{e^{-as}}{s}$	$\mathcal{U}(t-a)$

See also entry 139, Page 254.

	$f(s)$	$F(t)$
115.	$\dfrac{\sinh sx}{s \sinh sa}$	$\dfrac{x}{a} + \dfrac{2}{\pi} \displaystyle\sum_{n=1}^{\infty} \dfrac{(-1)^n}{n} \sin \dfrac{n\pi x}{a} \cos \dfrac{n\pi t}{a}$
116.	$\dfrac{\sinh sx}{s \cosh sa}$	$\dfrac{4}{\pi} \displaystyle\sum_{n=1}^{\infty} \dfrac{(-1)^n}{2n-1} \sin \dfrac{(2n-1)\pi x}{2a} \sin \dfrac{(2n-1)\pi t}{2a}$
117.	$\dfrac{\cosh sx}{s \sinh sa}$	$\dfrac{t}{a} + \dfrac{2}{\pi} \displaystyle\sum_{n=1}^{\infty} \dfrac{(-1)^n}{n} \cos \dfrac{n\pi x}{a} \sin \dfrac{n\pi t}{a}$
118.	$\dfrac{\cosh sx}{s \cosh sa}$	$1 + \dfrac{4}{\pi} \displaystyle\sum_{n=1}^{\infty} \dfrac{(-1)^n}{2n-1} \cos \dfrac{(2n-1)\pi x}{2a} \cos \dfrac{(2n-1)\pi t}{2a}$
119.	$\dfrac{\sinh sx}{s^2 \sinh sa}$	$\dfrac{xt}{a} + \dfrac{2a}{\pi^2} \displaystyle\sum_{n=1}^{\infty} \dfrac{(-1)^n}{n^2} \sin \dfrac{n\pi x}{a} \sin \dfrac{n\pi t}{a}$
120.	$\dfrac{\sinh sx}{s^2 \cosh sa}$	$x + \dfrac{8a}{\pi^2} \displaystyle\sum_{n=1}^{\infty} \dfrac{(-1)^n}{(2n-1)^2} \sin \dfrac{(2n-1)\pi x}{2a} \cos \dfrac{(2n-1)\pi t}{2a}$
121.	$\dfrac{\cosh sx}{s^2 \sinh sa}$	$\dfrac{t^2}{2a} + \dfrac{2a}{\pi^2} \displaystyle\sum_{n=1}^{\infty} \dfrac{(-1)^n}{n^2} \cos \dfrac{n\pi x}{a} \left(1 - \cos \dfrac{n\pi t}{a}\right)$
122.	$\dfrac{\cosh sx}{s^2 \cosh sa}$	$t + \dfrac{8a}{\pi^2} \displaystyle\sum_{n=1}^{\infty} \dfrac{(-1)^n}{(2n-1)^2} \cos \dfrac{(2n-1)\pi x}{2a} \sin \dfrac{(2n-1)\pi t}{2a}$
123.	$\dfrac{\cosh sx}{s^3 \cosh sa}$	$\frac{1}{2}(t^2 + x^2 - a^2) - \dfrac{16a^2}{\pi^3} \displaystyle\sum_{n=1}^{\infty} \dfrac{(-1)^n}{(2n-1)^3} \cos \dfrac{(2n-1)\pi x}{2a} \cos \dfrac{(2n-1)\pi t}{2a}$
124.	$\dfrac{\sinh x\sqrt{s}}{\sinh a\sqrt{s}}$	$\dfrac{2\pi}{a^2} \displaystyle\sum_{n=1}^{\infty} (-1)^n\, n\, e^{-n^2\pi^2 t/a^2} \sin \dfrac{n\pi x}{a}$
125.	$\dfrac{\cosh x\sqrt{s}}{\cosh a\sqrt{s}}$	$\dfrac{\pi}{a^2} \displaystyle\sum_{n=1}^{\infty} (-1)^{n-1} (2n-1)\, e^{-(2n-1)^2\pi^2 t/4a^2} \cos \dfrac{(2n-1)\pi x}{2a}$
126.	$\dfrac{\sinh x\sqrt{s}}{\sqrt{s}\, \cosh a\sqrt{s}}$	$\dfrac{2}{a} \displaystyle\sum_{n=1}^{\infty} (-1)^{n-1} e^{-(2n-1)^2\pi^2 t/4a^2} \sin \dfrac{(2n-1)\pi x}{2a}$
127.	$\dfrac{\cosh x\sqrt{s}}{\sqrt{s}\, \sinh a\sqrt{s}}$	$\dfrac{1}{a} + \dfrac{2}{a} \displaystyle\sum_{n=1}^{\infty} (-1)^n e^{-n^2\pi^2 t/a^2} \cos \dfrac{n\pi x}{a}$
128.	$\dfrac{\sinh x\sqrt{s}}{s\, \sinh a\sqrt{s}}$	$\dfrac{x}{a} + \dfrac{2}{\pi} \displaystyle\sum_{n=1}^{\infty} \dfrac{(-1)^n}{n} e^{-n^2\pi^2 t/a^2} \sin \dfrac{n\pi x}{a}$
129.	$\dfrac{\cosh x\sqrt{s}}{s\, \cosh a\sqrt{s}}$	$1 + \dfrac{4}{\pi} \displaystyle\sum_{n=1}^{\infty} \dfrac{(-1)^n}{2n-1} e^{-(2n-1)^2\pi^2 t/4a^2} \cos \dfrac{(2n-1)\pi x}{2a}$
130.	$\dfrac{\sinh x\sqrt{s}}{s^2\, \sinh a\sqrt{s}}$	$\dfrac{xt}{a} + \dfrac{2a^2}{\pi^3} \displaystyle\sum_{n=1}^{\infty} \dfrac{(-1)^n}{n^3} (1 - e^{-n^2\pi^2 t/a^2}) \sin \dfrac{n\pi x}{a}$
131.	$\dfrac{\cosh x\sqrt{s}}{s^2\, \cosh a\sqrt{s}}$	$\frac{1}{2}(x^2 - a^2) + t - \dfrac{16a^2}{\pi^3} \displaystyle\sum_{n=1}^{\infty} \dfrac{(-1)^n}{(2n-1)^3} e^{-(2n-1)^2\pi^2 t/4a^2} \cos \dfrac{(2n-1)\pi x}{2a}$

	$f(s)$	$F(t)$
132.	$\dfrac{J_0(ix\sqrt{s})}{s\,J_0(ia\sqrt{s})}$	$1 \;-\; 2 \displaystyle\sum_{n=1}^{\infty} \dfrac{e^{-\lambda_n^2 t/a^2}\,J_0(\lambda_n x/a)}{\lambda_n\,J_1(\lambda_n)}$ where $\lambda_1, \lambda_2, \ldots$ are the positive roots of $J_0(\lambda)=0$
133.	$\dfrac{J_0(ix\sqrt{s})}{s^2\,J_0(ia\sqrt{s})}$	$\tfrac{1}{4}(x^2 - a^2) \;+\; t \;+\; 2a^2 \displaystyle\sum_{n=1}^{\infty} \dfrac{e^{-\lambda_n^2 t/a^2}\,J_0(\lambda_n x/a)}{\lambda_n^3\,J_1(\lambda_n)}$ where $\lambda_1, \lambda_2, \ldots$ are the positive roots of $J_0(\lambda)=0$
134.	$\dfrac{1}{as^2}\tanh\left(\dfrac{as}{2}\right)$	**Triangular wave function**
135.	$\dfrac{1}{s}\tanh\left(\dfrac{as}{2}\right)$	**Square wave function**
136.	$\dfrac{\pi a}{a^2 s^2 + \pi^2}\coth\left(\dfrac{as}{2}\right)$	**Rectified sine wave function**
137.	$\dfrac{\pi a}{(a^2 s^2 + \pi^2)(1 - e^{-as})}$	**Half rectified sine wave function**
138.	$\dfrac{1}{as^2} - \dfrac{e^{-as}}{s(1 - e^{-as})}$	**Saw tooth wave function**

$f(s)$	$F(t)$
139. $\dfrac{e^{-as}}{s}$ See also entry 114, Page 251.	**Heaviside's unit function** $\mathcal{U}(t-a)$
140. $\dfrac{e^{-as}(1-e^{-\epsilon s})}{s}$	**Pulse function**
141. $\dfrac{1}{s(1-e^{-as})}$ See also entry 78, Page 249.	**Step function**
142. $\dfrac{e^{-s}+e^{-2s}}{s(1-e^{-s})^2}$	$F(t) = n^2, \quad n \le t < n+1, \ n = 0,1,2,\ldots$
143. $\dfrac{1-e^{-s}}{s(1-re^{-s})}$ See also entry 80, Page 249.	$F(t) = r^n, \quad n \le t < n+1, \ n = 0,1,2,\ldots$
144. $\dfrac{\pi a(1+e^{-as})}{a^2 s^2 + \pi^2}$	$F(t) = \begin{cases} \sin(\pi t/a) & 0 \le t \le a \\ 0 & t > a \end{cases}$

Appendix C

TABLE OF SPECIAL FUNCTIONS

1. Gamma function

$$\Gamma(n) = \int_0^\infty u^{n-1} e^{-u}\, du, \qquad n > 0$$

2. Beta function

$$B(m,n) = \int_0^1 u^{m-1}(1-u)^{n-1}\, du = \frac{\Gamma(m)\,\Gamma(n)}{\Gamma(m+n)}, \qquad m, n > 0$$

3. Bessel function

$$J_n(x) = \frac{x^n}{2^n\,\Gamma(n+1)}\left\{1 - \frac{x^2}{2(2n+2)} + \frac{x^4}{2\cdot 4(2n+2)(2n+4)} - \cdots\right\}$$

4. Modified Bessel function

$$I_n(x) = i^{-n} J_n(ix) = \frac{x^n}{2^n\,\Gamma(n+1)}\left\{1 + \frac{x^2}{2(2n+2)} + \frac{x^4}{2\cdot 4(2n+2)(2n+4)} + \cdots\right\}$$

5. Error function

$$\operatorname{erf}(t) = \frac{2}{\sqrt{\pi}}\int_0^t e^{-u^2}\, du$$

6. Complementary error function

$$\operatorname{erfc}(t) = 1 - \operatorname{erf}(t) = \frac{2}{\sqrt{\pi}}\int_t^\infty e^{-u^2}\, du$$

7. Exponential integral

$$\operatorname{Ei}(t) = \int_t^\infty \frac{e^{-u}}{u}\, du$$

8. Sine integral

$$\operatorname{Si}(t) = \int_0^t \frac{\sin u}{u}\, du$$

9. Cosine integral

$$\operatorname{Ci}(t) = \int_t^\infty \frac{\cos u}{u}\, du$$

10. Fresnel sine integral

$$S(t) = \int_0^t \sin u^2\, du$$

11. Fresnel cosine integral

$$C(t) = \int_0^t \cos u^2\, du$$

12. Laguerre polynomials

$$L_n(t) = \frac{e^t}{n!}\frac{d^n}{dt^n}(t^n e^{-t}), \qquad n = 0, 1, 2, \ldots$$

INDEX

Schaum's Outlines
and the Power of Computers...
The Ultimate Solution!

Now Available! An electronic, interactive version of *Theory and Problems of Electric Circuits* from the **Schaum's Outline Series.**

MathSoft, Inc. has joined with McGraw-Hill to offer you an electronic version of the *Theory and Problems of Electric Circuits* from the **Schaum's Outline Series.** Designed for students, educators, and professionals, this resource provides comprehensive interactive on-screen access to the entire Table of Contents including over 390 solved problems using Mathcad technical calculation software for PC Windows and Macintosh.

When used with Mathcad, this "live" electronic book makes your problem solving easier with quick power to do a wide range of technical calculations. Enter your calculations, add graphs, math and explanatory text anywhere on the page and you're done – Mathcad does the calculating work for you. Print your results in presentation-quality output for truly informative documents, complete with equations in real math notation. As with all of Mathcad's Electronic Books, *Electric Circuits* will save you even more time by giving you hundreds of interactive formulas and explanations you can immediately use in your own work.

Topics in *Electric Circuits* cover all the material in the **Schaum's Outline** including circuit diagramming and analysis, current voltage and power relations with related solution techniques, and DC and AC circuit analysis, including transient analysis and Fourier Transforms. All topics are treated with "live" math, so you can experiment with all parameters and equations in the book or in your documents.

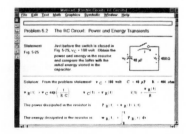

To obtain the latest prices and terms and to order Mathcad and the electronic version of *Theory and Problems of Electric Circuits* from the **Schaum's Outline Series**, call 1-800-628-4223 or 617-577-1017.

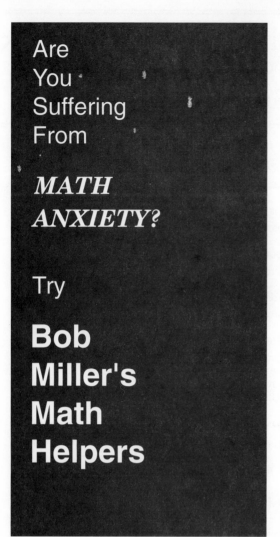

Are
You
Suffering
From

*MATH
ANXIETY?*

Try

**Bob
Miller's
Math
Helpers**

A unique new series of three class-tested books which will supplement your required texts. Bob Miller teaches Precalculus, Calculus I, and Calculus II in a friendly, personable way. You will learn through creative explanations of topics and multiple examples which are found throughout the text. Here are some comments from students who have used the CALC I HELPER:

*"Without this book I'm not so sure
I would have come close to passing.
With it I not only passed but received
an 'A'. I recommend this book highly
to anyone taking a calculus course."*

*"Your book is really excellent; you
explained every problem step by step.
This book makes every topic seem very
simple compared to other books."*

Bob Miller's **PRECALC HELPER**
Bob Miller's **CALC I HELPER**
Bob Miller's **CALC II HELPER**

Affordably priced for students at $8.95 each. *

Available at your local bookstore or use the order form below.

SCHAUM'S SOLVED PROBLEMS SERIES

- ■ **Learn the best strategies for solving tough problems in step-by-step detail**
- ■ **Prepare effectively for exams and save time in doing homework problems**
- ■ **Use the indexes to quickly locate the types of problems you need the most help solving**
- ■ **Save these books for reference in other courses and even for your professional library**

To order, please check the appropriate box(es) and complete the following coupon.

❑ **3000 SOLVED PROBLEMS IN BIOLOGY**
ORDER CODE 005022-8/**$16.95 406 pp.**

❑ **3000 SOLVED PROBLEMS IN CALCULUS**
ORDER CODE 041523-4/**$19.95 442 pp.**

❑ **3000 SOLVED PROBLEMS IN CHEMISTRY**
ORDER CODE 023684-4/**$20.95 624 pp.**

❑ **2500 SOLVED PROBLEMS IN COLLEGE ALGEBRA & TRIGONOMETRY**
ORDER CODE 055373-4/**$14.95 608 pp.**

❑ **2500 SOLVED PROBLEMS IN DIFFERENTIAL EQUATIONS**
ORDER CODE 007979-x/**$19.95 448 pp.**

❑ **2000 SOLVED PROBLEMS IN DISCRETE MATHEMATICS**
ORDER CODE 038031-7/**$16.95 412 pp.**

❑ **3000 SOLVED PROBLEMS IN ELECTRIC CIRCUITS**
ORDER CODE 045936-3/**$21.95 746 pp.**

❑ **2000 SOLVED PROBLEMS IN ELECTROMAGNETICS**
ORDER CODE 045902-9/**$18.95 480 pp.**

❑ **2000 SOLVED PROBLEMS IN ELECTRONICS**
ORDER CODE 010284-8/**$19.95 640 pp.**

❑ **2500 SOLVED PROBLEMS IN FLUID MECHANICS & HYDRAULICS**
ORDER CODE 019784-9/**$21.95 800 pp.**

❑ **1000 SOLVED PROBLEMS IN HEAT TRANSFER**
ORDER CODE 050204-8/**$19.95 750 pp.**

❑ **3000 SOLVED PROBLEMS IN LINEAR ALGEBRA**
ORDER CODE 038023-6/**$19.95 750 pp.**

❑ **2000 SOLVED PROBLEMS IN Mechanical Engineering THERMODYNAMICS**
ORDER CODE 037863-0/**$19.95 406 pp.**

❑ **2000 SOLVED PROBLEMS IN NUMERICAL ANALYSIS**
ORDER CODE 055233-9/**$20.95 704 pp.**

❑ **3000 SOLVED PROBLEMS IN ORGANIC CHEMISTRY**
ORDER CODE 056424-8/**$22.95 688 pp.**

❑ **2000 SOLVED PROBLEMS IN PHYSICAL CHEMISTRY**
ORDER CODE 041716-4/**$21.95 448 pp.**

❑ **3000 SOLVED PROBLEMS IN PHYSICS**
ORDER CODE 025734-5/**$20.95 752 pp.**

❑ **3000 SOLVED PROBLEMS IN PRECALCULUS**
ORDER CODE 055365-3/**$16.95 385 pp.**

❑ **800 SOLVED PROBLEMS IN VECTOR MECHANICS FOR ENGINEERS**
Vol I: STATICS
ORDER CODE 056582-1/**$20.95 800 pp.**

❑ **700 SOLVED PROBLEMS IN VECTOR MECHANICS FOR ENGINEERS**
Vol II: DYNAMICS
ORDER CODE 056687-9/**$20.95 672 pp.**

**ASK FOR THE *SCHAUM'S* SOLVED PROBLEMS SERIES AT YOUR LOCAL BOOKSTORE
OR CHECK THE APPROPRIATE BOX(ES) ON THE PRECEDING PAGE
AND MAIL WITH THIS COUPON TO:**

MCGRAW-HILL, INC.
ORDER PROCESSING S-1
PRINCETON ROAD
HIGHTSTOWN, NJ 08520

OR CALL
1-800-338-3987

NAME (PLEASE PRINT LEGIBLY OR TYPE)

ADDRESS (NO P.O. BOXES)

CITY   **STATE**   **ZIP**

ENCLOSED IS   ❑ A CHECK   ❑ MASTERCARD   ❑ VISA   ❑ AMEX   (✓ ONE)

ACCOUNT # _____   **EXP. DATE** _____

SIGNATURE _____

MAKE CHECKS PAYABLE TO MCGRAW-HILL, INC. <u>PLEASE INCLUDE LOCAL SALES TAX AND $1.25 SHIPPING/HANDLING</u>
PRICES SUBJECT TO CHANGE WITHOUT NOTICE AND MAY VARY OUTSIDE THE U.S.   FOR THIS
INFORMATION, WRITE TO THE ADDRESS ABOVE OR CALL THE 800 NUMBER.